Wars and Capital

Announcing early →
losing the baby

SEMIOTEXT(E) NATIVE AGENTS SERIES

Published by Semiotext(e)
PO BOX 629. South Pasadena, CA 91031
www.semiotexte.com

Special thanks to John Ebert and Robin Mackay.

Design by Hedi El Kholti
ISBN: 978-1-63590-004-0

Distributed by The MIT Press, Cambridge, Mass. and London, England
Printed in the United States of America

Éric Alliez

Maurizio Lazzarato

Wars and Capital

Translated by Ames Hodges

semiotext(e)

CONTENTS

TO OUR ENEMIES

1. We are living in the time of the subjectivation of civil wars. We did not leave the period of triumph of the market, automation of governmentality, and depoliticization of the economy of debt to go back to the era of "world pictures" and the conflicts between them. We have entered a time of constructing new war machines.

2. Capitalism and neoliberalism carry wars within them like clouds contain storms. While the financialization of the late 19th and early 20th centuries led to total war and the Russian Revolution, the 1929 crash and European civil wars, contemporary financialization is at the helm of global civil war and controls all its polarizations.

3. Since 2011, the multiple forms of subjectivation of civil wars have deeply altered both the semiology of capital and the pragmatics of the struggle to keep the manifold powers of war from being the perpetual framework of life. Among the experiments with anti-capitalist machines, Occupy Wall Street in the US, the *Indignados* in Spain, the student movements in Chile and Quebec, and Greece in 2015 all fought with unequal arms against the debt economy and austerity policies. The "Arab Spring," the major protests in Brazil, and the Gezi Park clashes in Turkey circulated the same watchwords of organization and disorder throughout the Global South. *Nuit Debout* in France is the latest development in a cycle of conflict and occupation that may have started with Tiananmen Square in 1989. On the side of power, neoliberalism promotes an authoritarian and policed post-democracy managed by market technicians to stoke the flames of its predatory economic policies, while the new right (or "hard right") declares war on foreigners, immigrants, Muslims, and the underclasses in the name of the "de-demonized" extreme right. This extreme right openly comes to occupy the terrain of civil wars, which it subjectivizes by rekindling *racial class warfare.* Neo-fascist hegemony over the processes of subjectivation is confirmed by the renewed war on the autonomy of women and the becoming-minor of sexuality (in France, "La Manif pour tous") as an *extension of the endocolonial domain of civil war.*

The era of limitless deterritorialization under Thatcher and Reagan is now followed by the racist, nationalist, sexist, and xenophobic reterritorialization of Trump, who has already become the leader of the new fascisms. The American Dream has been transformed into the nightmare of an insomniac planet.

4. There is a flagrant imbalance between the war machines of Capital and the new fascisms on the one hand and the multiform struggles against the world-system of new capitalism on the other. It is a political imbalance but also an *intellectual* one. This book focuses on a void, a blank, a theoretical and practical repressed which is, however, always at the heart of the power and powerlessness of revolutionary movements: the concept of "war" and "civil war."

5. "It's like being in a war," was heard in Athens during the weekend of July 11–12, 2015. And for good reason. The population

was faced with a large-scale strategy of continuing war by means of debt: it completed the destruction of Greece and, at the same time, triggered the self-destruction of the "construction of Europe." The goal of the European Commission, the ECB, and the IMF was never mediation or finding compromise but defeating the adversary on an open field.

The statement "It's like being in a war" should be immediately corrected: *it is a war*. The reversibility of war and economy is at the very basis of capitalism. And it has been a long time since Carl Schmitt revealed the "pacifist" hypocrisy of liberalism by reestablishing the continuity between economy and war: the economy pursues the objectives of war through other means ("blocking credit, embargo on raw materials, devaluation of foreign currency").

Two superior officers in the Chinese Air Force, Qiao Liang and Wang Xiangsui, define financial offensives as "bloodless wars"; a *cold* violence, just as cruel and effective as "bloody wars." With globalization, as they explain, "while constricting the battlespace in the narrow sense, at the same time we have turned the entire world into a battlefield in the broad sense." The expansion of war and the multiplication of its domain names has led to the establishment of a continuum between war, economy, and politics. Yet from the beginning, liberalism has been a *philosophy of total war*.

(Pope Francis seems to be preaching in the desert when he asserts, with a clarity that is lacking in politicians, experts of all stripes, and even the most hardened critics of capitalism: "Let's recognize it. *The world is in a state of war in bits and pieces.* [...] When I speak of war, I talk about real war. Not a war of religion. No. There is a war of interests. There is a war for money. There is a war for natural resources. There is a war for domination of peoples. This is the war.")

6. During that same year of 2015, a few months after the defeat of the Greek "radical left," the President of the French Republic announced on the evening of November 13 that France was "at war" and declared a state of emergency. The law authorizing him to do so and authorizing the suspension of "democratic freedoms" to grant "extraordinary" powers to the administration of public security had been passed in 1955 during the colonial war in Algeria. Implemented in New Caledonia in 1984 and during the "suburban riots" in 2005, the state of emergency brought colonial and postcolonial war back into the spotlight.

What happened in Paris on an awful night in November is what occurs daily in cities in the Middle East. This is the horror that the millions of refugees "pouring" into Europe are fleeing. They are visible evidence of the oldest colonialist technology to regulate migratory movement by its "apocalyptic" extension in the "infinite wars" started by Christian fundamentalist George Bush and his cabinet of neo-cons. Neo-colonial war is no longer taking place only in the "margins" of the world. In every way possible, it moves through the "center" by taking on the figure of the "internal Islamist enemy," immigrant populations, refugees, and migrants. The eternal outcasts are not left out: the poor and impoverished workers, those in unstable jobs and long term unemployment, and the "endocolonized" on both sides of the Atlantic...

7. The "stability pact" ("financial" state of emergency in Greece) and the "security pact" ("political" state of emergency in France) are two sides of the same coin. Constantly dismantling and restructuring the world-economy, the flows of credit and the flows of war are, with the States that *integrate* them, the condition of existence, production, and reproduction of contemporary capitalism.

Money and war are the global market's military police, which is still referred to as the "governance" of the world-economy. In Europe, it is incarnated in the financial state of emergency that shrinks workers' rights and social security rights (health, education, housing, etc.) to nothing while the anti-terrorist state of emergency suspends already emptied "democratic" rights.

8. Our first thesis is that war, money, and the State are constitutive or constituent forces, in other words the ontological forces of capitalism. The critique of political economy is insufficient to the extent that the economy does not replace war but continues it by other means, ones that go necessarily through the State: monetary regulation and the legitimate monopoly on force for internal and external wars. To produce the genealogy of capitalism and reconstruct its "development," we must always engage and articulate together the critique of political economy, critique of war, and critique of the State.

The accumulation of and monopoly on property titles by Capital, and the accumulation of and monopoly on force by the State feed off of each other. Without the external exercise of war, and without the exercise of civil war by the State inside its borders, it would never have been possible to amass capital. And inversely: without the capture and valorization of wealth carried out by capital, the State would never have been able to exercise its administrative, legal, and governmental functions or organize armies of ever growing power. The expropriation of the means of production and the appropriation of the means of exercising force are the conditions of the formation of Capital and the constitution of the State that develop in parallel. Military proletarization goes hand in hand with industrial proletarization.

9. But what "war" are we talking about? Does the concept of "global civil war," advanced at the same time (1961) by Carl Schmitt and Hannah Arendt, impose itself at the end of the Cold War as the most appropriate form? Do the categories of "infinite war," "just war," and "war on terrorism" correspond to the new conflicts of globalization?

And is it possible to use the syntagma of "the" war without immediately assuming the point of view of the State? The history of capitalism, since its origin, is crisscrossed and constituted by a multiplicity of wars: wars of class(es), race(s), sex(es),[1] wars of sub-jectivity(ies), wars of civilization (the singular gave its capital letter to History). "*Wars*" and not the *war* is our second thesis. "Wars" as the foundation of internal and external order, as organizing principle of society. Wars, not only wars of class, but also military, civil, sex, and race wars are integrated so constitutively in the definition of Capital that *Das Kapital* should be rewritten from start to finish to account for their dynamic in its most real functioning. At all of the major turning points in capitalism, we do not find the "creative destruction" of Schumpeter carried out by entrepreneurial innovation, but always the enterprise of civil wars.

10. Since 1492, Year One of Capital, the formation of capital has unfolded through this multiplicity of wars on both sides of the Atlantic. Internal colonization (Europe) and external colonization (Americas) are parallel, mutually reinforcing, and together define the world-economy. This dual colonization defines what Marx called primitive accumulation. Unlike, if not Marx, then at least a certain long-dominant Marxism, we do not restrict primitive accumulation to a mere phase in the development of capital destined to be surpassed in and through the "specific mode of production" of capital. We consider that it constitutes a condition of existence that constantly accompanies the development of capital, such that if primitive accumulation is pursued in all the forms of expropriation of a continued accumulation, then *the wars* of class, race, sex, and subjectivity are *endless*. The conjunction of these wars, and in particular the wars against the poor and women in the internal colonization of Europe, and the wars against the "first" peoples in external colonization, precede and make possible the "class struggles" of the 19th and 20th centuries by projecting them into a common war against *productive pacification*. Pacification obtained by any means ("bloody" and "not bloody") is the goal of the war of capital as "social relationship."

11. "By focusing exclusively on the relationship between capitalism and industrialism, in the end, Marx gives no attention to the close connection between these two phenomena and militarism." War and the arms race have been conditions for both economic development and technological and scientific innovation since the start of capitalism. Each stage in the development of capital invents its own "Keynesianism of war." The only fault in this thesis by Giovanni Arrighi is in limiting itself to "the" war between States and paying "no attention to the close connection" that Capital, technology, and science maintain with civil wars. A colonel in the French army sums up the directly economic functions of war as follows: "We are producers like any other." He reveals one of the most troubling aspects of the concept of production and work, an aspect that economists, unions, and Marxist recruits avoid thematizing.

12. Since primitive accumulation, the strategic force of destructuration/restructuration of the world-economy is Capital in its most deterritorialized form: financial Capital (which had to be

expressed as such before receiving its letters of credit from Balzac). Foucault critiques the Marxist conception of Capital because there will never be "the" capitalism but always a historically qualified "political-institutional ensemble" (an argument that received much attention).

Although Marx never in fact used the concept of capitalism, we must still maintain the distinction between it and "the" capital, because "its" logic, the logic of financial Capital (M–M'), is (still historically) the most operational one. What has been called the "financial crisis" shows it at work even in its most "innovative" post-critical performances. The multiplicity of State forms and transnational organizations of power, the plurality of political-institutional ensembles defining the variety of national "capitalisms" are violently centralized, subordinated, and commanded by globalized financial Capital in its aim of "growth." The multiplicity of power formations submits, more or less docilely (albeit more rather than less) to the logic of the most abstract property, that of the creditors. "The" Capital, with "its" logic (M–M') of planetary reconfiguration of space through the constant acceleration of time, is an historical category, a "real abstraction" as Marx would say, producing the most real effects of universal privatization of "human" and "non-human" Earth, and removal of the "commons" of the world. (Think here of the land grabbing which is both a direct consequence of the "food crisis" of 2007–2008 and one of the *exit strategies* from the "worst financial crisis in Global History.") We are using the "historical-transcendental" concept of Capital in this way by pulling it (and dropping the capitalization as often as possible) towards the systematic colonization of the world of which it is the long-distance agent.

13. Why doesn't the development of capitalism go through cities, which have long served as its vectors, but instead through the State? Because only the State, throughout the 16th, 17th, and 18th centuries was capable of achieving the expropriation/appropriation of the multiplicity of war machines of the feudal period (turned towards "private" wars) to centralize them and institutionalize them in a war machine transformed into an army with the legitimate monopoly on public force. The division of labor does not only take place in production, but also in the specialization of war and the professional soldier. While centralization and the exercise of force in a "regulated army" is the work of the State, it is also the condition for the accumulation of "wealth" by "civilized and opulent" nations at the expense of poor nations (Adam Smith)—which, in truth, are not nations at all but "waste lands" (*Locke in Wasteland*).

14. The constitution of the State as a "megamachine" of power thus relied on the capture, centralization, and institutionalization of the means of exercising force. Starting in the 1870s, however, and especially under the effect of the brutal acceleration imposed by "total war," Capital was no longer satisfied with maintaining a relationship of alliance with the State and its war machine. It started to appropriate it *directly* by integrating its instruments of polarization. The construction of this new capitalist war machine integrated the State, its sovereignty (political and military), and all its "administrative" functions by profoundly modifying them under the direction of financial capital. Starting with the First World War, the model of scientific organization of labor and the military model of organization and execution of war deeply penetrated the political functioning of the State by reconfiguring the liberal division of powers under the hegemony of the executive, while inversely the politics, not of the State but of Capital, were imposed on the organization, execution, and aims of war. With neoliberalism, this process of capture of the war machine and the State was fully realized in the axiomatics of Integrated Global Capitalism. In this way, we bring in Félix Guattari's IGC to serve our third thesis: Integrated Global Capitalism is the axiomatic of the war machine of Capital that was able to submit the military deterritorialization of the State to the superior deterritorialization of Capital. The machine of production is no longer distinguishable from the war machine integrating civilian and military, peace and war, in the single process of a continuum of isomorphic power in all its forms of valuation.

15. In the *longue durée* of the capital/war relationship, the outbreak of "economic war" between imperialisms at the end of the 19th century represented a turning point, a process of irreversible transformation of war and the economy, the State and society. *Financial capital transmits the unlimitedness (of its valuation) to war by making it into a power without limits (total war).* The conjunction of the unlimited flows of war and the unlimited flows of financial capital during the First World War pushed back the limits of both production and war by raising the terrifying specter of *unlimited production for unlimited war.* The two world wars are responsible for realizing, for the first time, "total" subordination (or "real subsumption") of society and its "productive forces" to the war economy through the organization and planning of production, labor and technology, science and consumption, at a hitherto unheard-of scale. Implicating the entire population in "production" was accompanied by the constitution of processes of mass subjectivation through the management of communications techniques and opinion creation. From the establishment of unprecedented research programs with the aim of "destruction" came scientific and technological discoveries that, transferred to the production of the means of production of "goods," would constitute the new generations of constant capital. This entire process was missed by Workerism (and Post-Workerism) in the short-circuit which made it situate the Great Bifurcation of Capital in the 1960s–1970s, combined in this way with the critical movement of self-affirmation of Workerism *in the factory* (it would take the arrival of post-Fordism to reach the "diffuse factory").

16. The origin of *welfare* cannot be found solely within a logic of insurance against the risks of "work" and the risks of "life" (the Foucauldian school under managerial influence), but first and foremost in the logic of war. *Warfare* largely anticipated and prepared *welfare*. Starting in the 1930s, the two became indistinguishable.

The enormous militarization of total war, which transformed internationalist workers into 60 million nationalist soldiers, was "democratically" reterritorialized by and in welfare. The conversion of the war economy into the liberal economy, the conversion of the science and technology of the instruments of death into the means of production of "goods," and the subjective conversion of the militarized population into "workers" took place thanks to the enormous apparatus of state intervention along with the active participation of "companies" (corporate capitalism). Warfare pursued its logic by other means in welfare. Keynes himself recognized that the policy of effective demand had no other model of realization than a regime of war.

17. Inserted in 1951 into his "Overcoming Metaphysics" (the overcoming in question was conceived during the Second World War), this passage by Heidegger defines exactly what the concepts of "war" and "peace" became at the end of the two total wars:

> Changed into their deformation of essence, "war" and "peace" are taken up into erring, and disappear into the mere course of the escalating manufacture of what can be manufactured, because they have become unrecognizable with regard to any distinction. The question of when and where there will be peace cannot be answered not because the duration of war is unfathomable, but rather because the question already asks about something which no longer exists, since war is no longer anything which could terminate in peace. War has become a distortion of the consumption of beings which is continued in peace. [...] This long war in its length slowly eventuated not in a peace of the traditional kind, but rather in a condition in which warlike characteristics are no longer as such at all and peaceful characteristics have become meaningless and without content.

This passage was later rewritten at the end of *A Thousand Plateaus* to indicate how technical-scientific "capitalization" (referring to what we call the "military-industrial, scientific-university complex") creates "a new conception of security as materialized war, as organized insecurity or molecularized, distributed, programmed catastrophe."

18. The Cold War is intensive socialization and capitalization of the real subsumption of society and populations in the war

economy of the first half of the 20th century. It constitutes a fundamental passage in the formation of the war machine of Capital, which does not appropriate the State and war without subordinating "knowledge" to its process. The Cold War stoked the hearth of technological and scientific production that had been lit by the total wars. Practically all contemporary technologies, and in particular cybernetics, computer and information technologies are, directly or indirectly, the fruits of total war re-totalized by the Cold War. What Marx called "General Intellect" was born of/in the "production for destruction" of total wars before being reorganized by the Operational Research (OR) of the Cold War into an instrument (R&D) of command and control of the world-economy. The war history of Capital constrains us to this other major displacement in relation to Workerism and post-Workerism. The order of labor (*"Arbeit macht frei"*) established by the total wars is transformed into a liberal-democratic order of full employment as an instrument of social regulation of the "mass-worker" *and of his or her entire domestic environment.*

19. '68 is situated under the sign of the political reemergence of wars of class, race, sex, and subjectivity that the "working class" could no longer subordinate to its "interests" and its forms of organization (Party-unions). While labor struggles "reached the highest absolute level of their development" in the United States ("Marx in Detroit"), they were also defeated there after the major post-war strikes. The destruction of the order of labor resulting from the total wars and continuing in and through the Cold War as "order of the wage system" was not only the objective of a new working class rediscovering its political autonomy, it is also the effect of the multiplicity of all these wars which, somewhat all at the same time, were inflamed by tracing back from the singular experiences of "group-subjects" that carried them towards their common conditions of subjective rupture. The wars of decolonization and of all the racial minorities, women, students, homosexuals, alternatives, anti-nuclear protesters, "*lumpen*," etc. thus define new modalities of struggle, organization, and especially the delegitimation of all "power-knowledge" throughout the 1960s and 1970s. We not only read the history of capital through war, but we also read war through '68, which is the only possible way to make the theoretical and political passage from "war" to "wars."

20. War and strategy occupy a central place in the revolutionary theory and practices of the 19th century and the first half of the 20th century. Lenin, Mao, and General Giap conscientiously annotated Clausewitz's *On War*. '68 thought (*la pensée 68*)* refrained from theorizing war, with the notable exception of Foucault and Deleuze-Guattari. They not only proposed a reversal of Clausewitz's celebrated formula ("war is the continuation of politics by other means") by analyzing the modalities through which "politics" can be seen as war continued by other means: *they especially and radically transformed the concepts of war and politics*. Their problematization of war is strictly dependent on the mutations of capitalism and the struggles against it in the so-called post-war period, before crystallizing in the strange revolution of 1968: the "microphysics" of power advanced by Foucault is a critical actualization of "generalized civil war"; the "micropolitics" of Deleuze and Guattari is inseparable from the concept of "war machine" (its construction relies on the activist history of one of the pair). If we isolate the analysis of power

---

* See note, p. 269.

relations from generalized civil war, like Foucauldian critique does, the theory of governmentality is nothing more than a variant of neoliberal "governance"; and if we cut micropolitics from the war machine, like Deleuzian critique does (it also undertakes an aestheticization of the war machine), only "minorities" remain that are powerless in the face of Capital, which keeps the initiative.

21. Siliconed by new technologies that they developed into a strike force, the military merged technological machines with war machines. The political consequences were formidable.

The USA planned and led the war in Afghanistan (2001) and in Iraq (2003) based on the principle "Clausewitz out, computer in" (the same operation is oddly enough used by the defenders of cognitive capitalism who dissolve the omni-reality of wars into computers and the "algorithms" that had served in the first place to wage them). Believing they could dissipate the "fog" and uncertainty of war by the nothing less than primitive accumulation of information, the strategists of hyper-technological, digital and "network-centered" war quickly changed their tune: the victory that was so rapidly attained turned into a political-military debacle that triggered the disaster in the Middle East *in situ*, without sparing the Free World that had brought its values like a remake of *Dr. Strangelove*. The technical machine explains nothing and can do little without mobilizing all the other "machines." Its efficacy and its very existence depend on the social machine and the war machine, which most often outline the technological avatar according to a model of society based on divisions, dominations, and exploitations (*Fast Cars, Clean Bodies*, to use the title of Kristin Ross' fine work).

22. If the fall of the Wall delivered the death certificate of a mummy whose communist pre-history we were made to forget by '68, and if it is to be considered a non-event (as the thesis of the End of History states in its melancholic way), the bloody fiasco of the first post-communist wars by the imperial war machine made history. In part because of the debate that it started *inside the military*, where a new paradigm of war appeared. An antithesis of the industrial wars of the 20th century, the new paradigm is defined as a "war amongst the people/population."* This concept, which inspired an improbable "military humanism," is one we make our own by returning its meaning to the source and real terrain of wars of capital, and by rewriting this "war amongst the population" in the plural of *our wars*. The population is the battlefield in which counter-insurrectional operations of all kinds are underway. At the same time, and indistinguishably, they are both military and non-military because they also carry the new identity of "bloody wars" and "bloodless wars."

Under Fordism, the State not only guaranteed State territorialization of Capital but also of war. As a result, globalization cannot not free capital from State control without also freeing war, which passes to the superior power of continuum by integrating the *plane of capital*. Deterritorialized war is no longer inter-State war at all, but an uninterrupted succession of multiple wars against populations, definitively sending "governmentality" to the side of governance in a common enterprise of denial of global civil wars. What is governed and what allows governing are the *divisions* that project wars into the heart of the population at the level of the real content of biopolitics. A biopolitical governmentality of war as differential distribution of instability and norm of "daily life."

---

* See Translator's note, p. 441.

The complete opposite of the Great Narrative of the liberal birth of biopolitics taking place in a famous course at the Collège de France in the break between the 1970s and 1980s.

23. Accentuating divisions, aggravating the polarization of every capitalist society, the debt economy transforms "global civil war" (Schmitt, Arendt) into interconnected civil wars: class wars, neo-colonialist wars on "minorities," wars on women, wars of subjectivity. The matrix of these civil wars is the colonial war. Colonial war was never a war between States but, in essence, a war *amongst and against* the population, where the distinctions between war and peace, between combatants and non-combatants, between economy, politics, and military were never used. Colonial war amongst and against populations is the model of the war that financial Capital unleashed starting in the 1970s in the name of a neoliberalism of combat. Its war is both fractal and transversal: fractal, because it indefinitely produces its invariance by constant changes of scale (its "irregularity" and the "cracks" it introduces operate at different scales of reality); and transversal, because it is simultaneously deployed at the macro political level (by playing on all of the major binary oppositions: social classes, whites and non-whites, men and women) and the micro political level (by molecular "engineering" privileging the highest interactions). It can also connect the civilian and military levels in the Global South and North, in the Souths and Norths *of everyone* (or almost everyone). Its first characteristic is therefore to be less *indiscriminate* war than *irregular* war.

The war machine of capital which, in the early 1970s, definitively integrated the State, war, science, and technology, clearly declares the strategy of contemporary globalization: to bring to an end the very short history of reforming capital—*Full*

Employment in a Free Society, according to the manifesto of Lord Beveridge published in 1944—by attacking everywhere and with all means available the conditions of reality of the power struggle that imposed it. An infernal creativity is deployed by the neoliberal political project in pretending to grant the "market" superhuman qualities of information processing: the market as the ultimate cyborg.

24. The newfound consistency of neofascisms starting with the financial "crisis" in 2008 represents a turning point in the waging of wars amongst the population. Their dimensions, both fractal and transversal, take on a new and formidable effectiveness in dividing and polarizing. The new fascisms challenge all of the resources of the "war machine," because if the "war machine" is not necessarily identified with the State, it can also escape the control of Capital. While the war machine of Capital governs through an "inclusive" differentiation of property and wealth, the new fascist war machines function through exclusion based on racial, sexual, and national identity. The two logics seem incompatible. In reality, they inevitably converge (see "national preference") as the state of economic and political emergency takes residence in the coercive time of *global flow*.

If the capitalist machine continues to be wary of the new fascisms, it is not because of its democratic principles (Capital is ontologically anti-democratic!) or the *rule of law*, but because, as it happened with Nazism, post-fascism can claim its "autonomy" from the war machine of Capital and escape its control. Isn't this exactly the same thing that has happened with Islamic fascisms? Trained, armed, and financed by the USA, they turned their weapons against the superpower and its allies who had instrumentalized them. From the West to the lands of the Caliphate *and back*, the neo-Nazis of all allegiances embody the suicidal subjectivation of the capitalist "mode of destruction." It is also the final scene of the return of the colonial repressed: the Jihadists of generation 2.0 haunt Western cities like their most internal enemy. Endocolonization also becomes the generalized conjugation of "topical" violence of the most intense domination of capitalism over populations. As for the process of convergence or divergence between the capitalist and neo-fascist *war machines*, it will depend on the evolution of the civil wars now underway and the risks that a future revolutionary process could run for private property, and more generally for the power of Capital.

25. Prohibiting the reduction of Capital and capitalism to a system or a structure, and of the economy to a history of self-enclosed cycles, wars of class, race, sex, and subjectivity also challenge every principle of autonomy in science and technology, every highway to "complexity" or emancipation forged by the progressive (and now accelerationist) idea of the movement of History.

Wars constantly inject the indeterminacy of conflict into open strategic relationships, making inoperable every mechanism of self-regulation (of the market) or every regulation by feedback ("man-machine systems" open their "complexity" to the future). The strategic "opening" of war is radically other than the systematic opening of cybernetics, which was not born in/of war for nothing. Capital is not structure or system; it is "machine" and war machine, of which the economy, politics, technology, the State, the media, etc. are only the articulations informed by strategic relations. In the Marxist/Marxian definition of *General Intellect*, the war machine integrating science, technology, and communication into its functioning is curiously neglected for the sake of a hardly credible "communism of capital."

26. Capital is not a mode of production without being at the same time a mode of destruction. The infinite accumulation that constantly moves its limits to recreate them again is at the same time unlimited, widespread destruction. The gains in productivity and gains of destructiveness progress in parallel. They manifest themselves in the generalized war that scientists prefer to call *Anthropocene* rather than *Capitalocene*, even if, in all evidence, the destruction of the environments in and through which we live does not begin with "humans" and their growing needs, but with Capital. The "ecological crisis" is not the result of a modernity and humanity blinded to the negative effects of technological development but the "fruit of the will" of some people to exercise absolute domination over other people through a global geopolitical strategy of unlimited exploitation of all human and non-human resources.

Capitalism is not only the deadliest civilization in the history of humanity, the one that introduced us to the "shame of being human"; it is also the civilization through which labor, science, and technology have created—another (absolute) privilege in the history of humanity—the possibility of (absolute) annihilation of all species and the planet that houses them. In the meantime, the "complexity" of (saving) "nature" still offers the prospect of healthy profits combining the *techno* utopia of *geo-engineering* and the reality of the new markets of "polluting rights." At the confluence of one and the other, the Capitalocene does not send capitalism to the Moon (it has been there and back), it completes the global merchandizing of the planet by asserting its rights to the well-named troposphere.

27. The logic of Capital is the logistics of an infinite valuation. It implies the accumulation of a power that is not merely economic for the simple reason that it is complicated by strategic power and knowledge of the *strength* and *weakness* of the classes struggling, to which it is applied and with which they are in constant explanation. Foucault tells us that the Marxists turned their attention to the concept of "class" to the detriment of the concept of "struggle." Knowledge of strategy is thus evacuated in favor of an alternative enterprise of pacification (Tronti offers the most *epic* version of this). Who is strong and who is weak? In what way did the strong become weak, and why did the weak become strong? How to strengthen oneself and weaken the other to dominate and exploit it? We propose to follow and reinvent the anti-capitalist path of French Nietzscheism.

28. Capital came out the victor in the total wars and in the confrontation with global revolution, for which the number for us is 1968. Since then, it has gone from victory to victory, perfecting its *self-cooled motor*. Where it verifies that the first function of power is to deny the existence of civil wars by erasing even the memory of them (pacification is a *scorched earth* policy). Walter Benjamin is there to remind us that reactivating the memory of the victories and defeats from which the victors take their domination can only come from the "defeated." Problem: the "defeated" of '68 threw out the bath water of civil wars with the old Leninist baby at the end of the "Hot Autumn" sealed by the failure of the dialectic of the "party of autonomy." Entry into the "winter years" on the edge of a second Cold War that ensures the triumph of the "people of capitalism" ("*People's Capitalism'—This IS America!*"), the End of History will take the relay without stopping at a Gulf War that "did not take place." Except there is a constellation of new wars, revolutionary machines, or mutant militants (Chiapas,

Birmingham, Seattle, Washington, Genoa...) and new defeats. The new writing generations describe "the missing people" dreaming of insomnia and processes of destitution unfortunately reserved *for their friends*.

29. We will cut it short, in addressing *our enemies*. Because this book has no other object, under the economy and its "democracy," behind the technological revolutions and "mass intellectuality" of the General Intellect, than to make heard the "rumble" of real wars now underway in all of their multiplicity. A multiplicity which is not to be made but *unmade and remade* to charge the "masses or flows," which are doubly *subjects*, with new possibilities. On the side of relations of power as subject *to* war or/and on the side of strategic relationships that are capable of projecting them to the rank of subjects *of wars*, with "their mutations, their quanta of deterritorialization, their connections, their precipitations." In short, it is a question of drawing the lessons from what seems to us like the failure of '68 thought which we have inherited, even in our inability to think and construct a collective war machine equal to the civil war unleashed in the name of neo-liberalism and the absolute primacy of the economy as exclusive policy of capital. Everything is taking place as if '68 was unable *to think all the way*, not its defeat (there are, since the New Philosophers, professionals in the matter), but the warring order of reasons that broke its insistence through a *continuous destruction*, placed in the present infinitive of the struggles of "resistance."

30. It is not a question, it is not at all a question of *stopping resistance*. It is a question of dropping a "theoricism" satisfied with a strategic discourse that is powerless in the face of what is happening. And what has happened to us. Because if the mechanisms of power are constitutive, to the detriment of strategic relationships and the wars taking place there, there can only be phenomena of "resistance" against them. With the success we all know. *Graecia docet.*

— July 30, 2016

Post-scriptum: This book is placed under the sign of an (impossible) "master of politics"—or, more precisely, the Althusserian adage forged in the corner of an historical materialism in which we recognize ourselves: "If you want to know a question, do the history of it." 1968, a major deviation from the laws of Althusserianism (and all that they represent), will be the flight diagram of a second volume, with the title *Wars and Revolution.* We propose to take up the study of the *strange revolution of '68* and of its consequences, where the train of "the" counter-revolution hides many others: a *multiplicity of counter-revolutions* in the form of *restorations.* They will be analyzed from the point of view of a theoretical practice politically "overdetermined" by the warring realities of the present. In this mindset, we will attempt a "symptomal reading" of the New Spirit of Capitalism (for which the windfalls come from the "artistic critique" made in '68), of Accelerationism (both the most up-to-date and the most regressive version of post-Workerism) and speculative Realism (we have therefore decided not to include it in our reading of the Anthropocene).

STATE, WAR MACHINE, MONEY

Marx describes Capital as the process that comes to "constantly revolutionize" the conditions of production to transform the limits of valuation (the capitalization of added value, or "surplus value") into conditions for a later development reproducing its internal limits on an ever-expanding scale. Closer to the *Grundrisse*, which begins with a chapter on money, than *Capital*, Deleuze and Guattari see this process as the introduction of the infinite into production through money as an exclusive form of the law of value. Money keeps and keeps up the entire system by constantly expanding the "circle" of credit and debt that determines, in an increasingly immanent way, the relationship of enslavement (*asservissement*) of (abstract) labor to (the becoming-concrete of) Capital.

As the most deterritorialized flow, the real abstraction of money functions both as the motor of the unlimited movement of capital and as the apparatus (*dispositif*) of strategic command in the hands of capitalists. From there, money keeps taking on functions other than those connected to its mercantile form of "general equivalent." And the very principle of deduction of the money-form from the simple necessities of the circulation of goods is undermined by contradicting the most *classic* formulation of the "critique of political economy." Against every tradition of political economy, Marx asserts that *Force is an economic agent* in his analysis of primitive accumulation (in other words, the "genesis" of capitalism), where he brings in war alongside "state power" and "public credit."

Our necessary point of departure for rethinking the entire history of capitalism—even in its most contemporary forms—is the close, constitutive, and ontological relationship between the most deterritorialized form of capital, money, and the most deterritorialized form of sovereignty, war. We will endeavor to rewrite this history, starting with, restarting with what we see as one of the theoretical-political gestures that *carries* "'68 thought" (*pensée 68*) the most, and that could even carry this thought beyond its own limits.

With Foucault, whose analysis was taken up soon after by Deleuze and Guattari in *Anti-Oedipus*, money, war, and the state are placed at the heart of the apparatus (*dispositif*)—and at the heart of the assemblage of apparatuses of power—allowing an *understanding of all history in light of the discontinuity of capitalism*. How in fact could the critical use of history not be genealogically directed towards capitalism by a prospective know-ledge that "gives equal weight to its own sight and to its objects"?[1]

The institution of money, as Foucault asserts in his first course at the Collège de France (1970–1971) focusing on its introduction in ancient Greece, cannot be explained for market, commercial, or mercantile reasons: while the use of money developed in the "exchange of products," its "historical root" is not found there. The institution of "Greek money" is first and above all connected to a displacement in the exercise of power, to a *new type of power* in which the sovereignty cannot be distinguished from the appropriation it makes to its advantage of the new war machine started by the "hoplitic revolution." This is a social revolution as much as a military one, since the war machine is no longer in the hands of the nobility (the warrior caste, the knight, or the chariot rider surrounded by servants faithful to the heroic ideal), but the small farmers who became indispensable to the defense of the growing city (hoplites). The collective strength and actions of the "people," who start to call themselves *demos*, are incarnated in the military formation open to the greatest number and for which the tactics are based on combat in phalanxes with a tight line of soldiers—"with lance and buckler, [...] man standing to man."[2] Yet the principle of the phalanx and its system of weaponry (the same for all)[3] implies a "reciprocity of service and help, the synchronization of movements, and the spontaneous regulation of the whole"[4] in a common order accepted by each and performed by all. So much so that the armed force of the hoplites was characterized by the rise of an *egalitarian demand* by citizen-soldiers, always threatening to turn against those who would use it to maintain "class power." This expression indicates how *contemporary* this question is when merged with the general history of revolution, starting with the struggle between the poor (*polloi*) and the rich (*ploutoi*), always at war in the city-*polis*. The response to this question, genealogically requalified as the "primitive scene" of politics, is what Foucault points to as a "new form of power" in his first return to the Greeks, one that is connected to "the institution of money."

Foucault therefore begins by studying the major political upheavals of the sixth and seventh centuries, paying particular attention to the "hoplitic strategy" leading to the eviction of the old aristocracies of lineal descendance.[5] This is the case of Corinth, where the polemarch Cypselus was brought to power by those who had been his soldiers in an army of hoplites. What interests Foucault the most, however, is the way Cypselus aimed to stay in power: by introducing the use of money in a (political) apparatus of (economic) integration of military power for which the key is to "limit social demands, [...] which the formation of hoplite armies make more dangerous"[6] in the context of agrarian crises worsening the debt of peasants. Knowing he has to maintain the regime of property and power held by the possessing class, what does the tyrant do? He implements only a partial redistribution to the soldier-peasants (without forgiving their debt), while imposing an income tax of 10 percent on the fortune of the "rich." One part is directly redistributed to the "poor," another finances "major work projects" and advance payments to craftspeople. The constitution of this complex system could not be paid "in kind." The economic cycle bringing the money distributed to the "poor" into the coffers of the "rich" (by indemnity for the redistributed land and "salaried" work), who could then pay the tax (in money), ensures—according to the demonstration by Édouard Will to which Foucault refers—"a circulation or rotation of money, and an equivalency with goods and services."[7] Money is confirmed as the standard of "exchange" and "equivalencies" which imply *a first political institution of the state in the order of the city* by expanding and intensifying the regime of debt: tax, deduction, concurrence, defining value, displacement of the commercial activity of agriculture towards commerce, and development of colonization create the formal conditions of a market and produce this market space as immediately controlled by the state apparatus.

Created "*ex nihilo*" or almost,[8] money appears as dependent on a new and "extraordinary" form of political power, that of a tyrant or legislator who intervenes "in the regime of property, in the play of debt and acquittal" and ensures the territorial institutionalization (reterritorialization) of the war machine. It is identified with the exercise of power in the sense that "[it is not] because one possesses money that one acquires and exercises power. Rather, it is because some took power that money was institutionalized."9

Money is therefore not a simple economic "capital," as seen in its market origins. In the hands of the "state," which institutes its use and that it contributes to instituting in turn, money has less a function of *redistribution* than of *expanded reproduction* of positions of power in society. Such that money is the continuation of civil war by other means, more *political* means, that inserts *for all* the "truth" of what one owes into the play of power, and what it is worth. On the one hand, it produces and reproduces while displacing them the divisions (aristocrat, warrior, craftsperson, "salaried worker") that feed the always present possibility of civil war as the social reality that politics must learn to *handle*. On the other, it is through an entire "interplay of new regulations" that aim to bring an end to the deregulated struggle of the poor and rich, that the institution of money ensures "the preservation of class domination,"10 for which the condition is the displacement of "social separation" and civil war (the "truly warlike war" that Plato preferred to call *dia-stasis*, the dis-cord of division in two, rather than *stasis*) on another terrain: that of the *reign of measure* as an ordering of the social responding to the hoplitic revolution from which would come, not *the* Greek city-state, but its first egalitarian *projection* (or the ideal schema of a republic of hoplites).

The economy becomes political for the first time there through the power that *combines war and money*. We can immediately see their critical purpose for Foucault, in relation to the Marxist economism that combines the functions of the state, power, and war in the final determination of the "economic infrastructure."

From the new alliance that money (*nomisma*) concluded by warding off civil war under a form that is still tyranny, the *nomos* (the "law" that all have to share) emerges as the juridical-political structure of the City-State (*polis*). Some twenty years later, in Athens, where the "poor are sent into slavery due to their debts," and property owners are "pursued by violence to the heart of their household," *nomos* and *eunomia* ("good government," good civic organization) assert themselves as the "good and regular distribution" of power in an opposite and complementary way to the operation of Cypselus. "The *eunomia* instituted by Solon was a way of substituting a distribution of political power for the distribution of wealth demanded (*isomoiria*): where land was demanded, power was given. Power as a substitute for wealth in the operation of *eunomia*. [...] Solon, on the other hand [unlike Cypselus], shared out power, up to a point, so as not to have to redistribute wealth."[11]

Yet as Foucault explains it, *the overall effect is the same* in what is less a shift than a continuation, revealing the complementarity between *nomisma* and *eunomia*: "where the rich have been forced to make an economic sacrifice, money comes to the fore, enabling the preservation of power through the intermediary of the tyrant; where the rich have been forced to make a political sacrifice, *eunomia* enables them to preserve economic privileges." What is "Solon's Reform" if not the distribution of political power in function of the economic distribution of wealth (the four poll tax classes), which is hidden by including all citizens, even the poorest, in the new system where power takes a *democratic* form? Power is "no longer what is held exclusively by the few" and "power is what is exercised permanently through all the citizens" in a permanent political warding-off of civil war taking the form of *power-sharing* instead of wealth-sharing. It is therefore necessary that they obey a different order and mechanisms, following a break such that "if one seizes too much power, one is punished by the city; if one seizes too much wealth, one must expect punishment from Zeus"[1] since it is "chance, luck, fate or the Gods" that determine the poverty and wealth of each in the limits of what would prevent their participation in the assembly of citizens. Under Solon's guidance, the democratic, "good legislation" of *eunomia* is able to substitute the abolition of debt slavery and the concurrent operation of adjusting the value of money in favor of debtors[13] for the total elimination of debts and the general redistribution of land (*isonomia*, the division in "equal parts") demanded by the *greatest number* (*polloi*). Money is deployed there as "the simulacrum of the power shared out among everyone, while it ensures, at the cost of a certain economic sacrifice, the preservation of power in the hands of some. In Athenian hands, the tetradrachma, stamped with the owl, made the mere simulacrum of power held elsewhere shine for a moment"[14]—which *by right* (that of the *nomos*), belongs *in common* to all. All being (un-)equally encouraged, for the sake of *eunomia* but at the rank occupied by each person, to develop craftwork, commerce turned towards exportation, and colonies.[15] This certainly alters the very conception of war, cutting it off from the hoplitic civic model while at the same time turning towards the sea (control of islands and maritime routes, priority given to the fleet financed by the state) and siege warfare (development of "poliorcetics," military techniques, and mercenaries). Starting with the Peloponnesian Wars, Athenian imperialism is accompanied by the professionalization of the army in a permanent war using every means available: "Battles became more costly, with the spirit of conflict yielding to the desire to annihilate, while 'hand-to-hand' war of 'commandos' and 'guerrillas' [...] started to compete with battles."[16] Yet internal war also returns constantly in the cycle of division of power and the distribution of goods with the monetary chrematistics denounced by Aristotle because it only seeks "the acquisition of money itself and consequently in unlimited quantities."[17] It explodes the principle of measure of "neither too much nor too little" (excess wealth and excess poverty) that held the Solonian split between politics and economy, which can be clearly seen as a fiction destined to displace an otherwise real rupture between rich and poor. Yet the function of warding-off the Solonian "neither too much nor too little" must also be measured in relation to a *capitalization* that threatens to provoke a manner of proto-capitalism (manufacturing, commercial, and military).

The monetarization of the economy that made it possible to ward-off civil war places the *polis* and its institutions under mortal danger, because the "unlimited" appropriation and accumulation that money contains and frees with its effects of immediate economic capture always risks intensifying "excess wealth and excess poverty." This power of money must be warded off through a set of codifications that impose political, religious, moral, and social limits on its power of deterritorialization.

Where it is verified that "if capitalism is the universal truth, it is so in the sense that makes capitalism *the negative* of all social formations"[18] that preceded it because they encountered decoded flows of money (which undoes institutions, laws, modalities of subjectivation) like a *real limit* signifying their death coming from the outside because it was rising from the inside (here, the disappearance of the Greek city-state). Capitalism is the only social formation that makes the unlimitedness of money its principle of organization. This opens the possibility of a retrospective rereading of all history in function of capitalism, of which one aspect is to make unlimited accumulation its internal drive. The infinite valorization as *norm of the excessiveness* of capital is affirmed there, leading the state to play an increasingly important role in monetary regulation by relaunching its becoming-immanent at the level of "contradictions" of accumulation.

This explains how the Foucauldian description of the institution of money can be taken up in a parallel made by Deleuze and Guattari with the policies of the New Deal. "As if the Greeks had discovered in their own way what the Americans rediscovered after the New Deal: that heavy taxes are good for business."[19] Because "taxation monetarizes the economy,"[20] by giving the state a power of abstraction and *penetration* that gives it the means of a both economic and political redistribution while preserving "class power." This is the issue of the New Deal, which had to breathe new life into the same operation in a critical situation where capitalism, in order to survive, had to contradict its tendency towards absolute deterritorialization of flows of exchange and production by inventing the unprecedented (and oh so temporary) figure of a *reformism of capital*.

We must also remember that the passage through Corinth was aimed more generally at establishing the relationship between economic cycle, war, and army: the appropriation of the war machine by the state consists less of its transformation into a professional army than in its integration into the circuit of production, taxation, technological innovation, science, and employment.

Army and war are integral parts of the political organization of power and the economic circuit of capital, and we will describe their different functions throughout this book. The economy as the *war policy* of capital.

Money and capital remain empty (economic) "abstractions" without the flow of power; war and civil war constitute the most deterritorialized modalities of this flow. The market economy is not autonomous, it has no possibility of independent existence outside the power of these flows. The "economic" functions of money (measure, accumulation, general equivalent, means of payment) depend on a flow of destruction/creation that refers to something completely other than the Irenic, Schumpeterian definition of the entrepreneur's activity. If money is not supported by a flow of strategic power that finds its absolute form in war, it *loses its value* as capital.

The expropriation of the means of production and the appropriation of the means of exercising force (the war machine) are the conditions of formation of capital and constitution of the state that develop in parallel. Capital's accumulation and monopoly on force and the state's accumulation and monopoly on force sustain each other reciprocally. Without war being waged externally (colonial and inter-state war) and without the state waging civil war and internal wars of subjectivities, capital would never have formed. And inversely: without capture and the valorization of wealth operated by capital, the state would never have been able to exercise its "sovereign" functions, all of which are based on the organization of an army.

The logic of Capital is a logic of infinite valorization that implies the accumulation of forces, and therefore a *continued* accumulation of a power that is not only economic but also strategic power over and knowledge of the strengths and weaknesses of the classes fighting.

PRIMITIVE ACCUMULATION CONTINUED

The different moments of primitive accumulation can be assigned in particular to Spain, Portugal, Holland, France and England, in more or less chronological order. These different moments are systematically combined together at the end of the seventeenth century in England; the combination embraces the colonies, the national debt, the modern tax system, and the system of protection. These methods depend in part on brute force, for instance the colonial system. But they all employ the power of the state, the concentrated and organized force of society, to hasten, as in a hothouse, the process of transformation of the feudal mode of production into the capitalist mode, and to shorten the transition. *Force is the midwife of every old society which is pregnant with a new one. It is itself an economic power.*

　　　　　　　　— Karl Marx, *Capital*, Book I, Section VIII

In the section of *Capital* dedicated to primitive accumulation, Marx perfectly describes the two powers of deterritorialization that gave rise to capitalism: on the one hand, wars of conquest, the violence of invasions and appropriations of the "virgin" lands of the New World; on the other, credit, public debt ("Public credit becomes the *credo* of Capital"[1]), supported, carried, and organized by European states. For Marx, they only constitute the preconditions of capital, destined to be surpassed and reconfigured by "industrial capital" in the development of productive forces that provides the *progressive* material basis for the technology of revolution. Against this dialectic founded in the idea of a "truly revolutionary" path of (national) transition to the capitalism of bourgeois "revolution," we offer this first and obvious fact: war and credit are the strategic weapons of capital throughout capitalism. As such, primitive accumulation and its telluric forces of deterritorialization are continuously repeated and differentiated, the better to advance by *accelerating* it as much as possible—the process of domination and commodification of all existence. To put it another way: *in the center as well as in the periphery*, primitive accumulation is the continued creation of capitalism itself.

Capitalism has been a global market from the beginning. For that reason, it can only be analyzed as a world-economy. What Marx called "primitive accumulation" (or "original accumulation": *ursprüngliche Akkumulation*) to express the *capital*[2] meaning of this first major deterritorialization initially produced by war, conquest, and invasions takes place *at the same time* in the "New World" that was just "discovered" (external colonization) and in Europe (internal colonization). "Primitive accumulation" does not create the economic conditions of capitalism and the international division of labor describing North-South geopolitical division of a world that we still call our own without establishing the hierarchies of sexes, races, ages, and civilizations on which strategies of division, differentiation, and inequality are based that span the class composition of the international proletariat.

As a result, by extension, and by *intension*, the *locus classicus* of the description of *wars of accumulation* must be reworked starting with the moment, between the fifteenth and sixteenth centuries, when landed gentry and the nascent bourgeoisie launched a civil war in England against peasant farmers, artisans, and day laborers for the privatization of common lands. The destruction of the community structure of villages and centers of domestic production, the abandon of subsistence crops and the expropriation of farms, reducing populations to misery, forcing a growing number of *uprooted* into mendicancy and vagrancy, and leaving them no other choice than between extermination and the forced march of disciplinarization towards wage labor. Simultaneously, *enclosures*, the concentration of land and merging of tenures throughout Europe—a Europe submitted to the "bloody legislation" that Marx analyzed at length and that brought back slavery[3] before generalizing the practice of internment as a structure of forced labor—was combined with the appropriation of the "masterless lands" of the "Americas."

Conquest, or the pillaging of natural and mineral wealth combined with agricultural exploitation of "fallow lands," led to a veritable genocide of indigenous populations. Their "void"[4] would be filled by the slave trade due to "the turning of Africa into a warren for the commercial hunting of black-skins" signaling "the dawn of the era of capitalist production." "These idyllic proceedings are the chief moments of primitive accumulation,"[5] *and they perpetuate it*: "Direct slavery is as much the pivot upon which our present-day industrialism turns as are machinery, credit, etc.," wrote Marx in a letter from 1846.[6] Primitive accumulation merges with the capitalistic conjunction of all of these processes that would never have come together without the illimitation of violence brought from the interior to the exterior in a manner of *anthropological war* that would quickly be called *pacification*.[7]

Flows of credit, public debt (operating "as one of the most energetic agents of primitive accumulation"), and wars of conquest maintain and support each other mutually in a process of immediately global deterritorialization. "The system of public credit, i.e. of public debts," definitively invades Europe while the "colonial system, with its maritime trade and commercial wars, served as a forcing-house." The tight relationship between war and credit, and the birth of the latter from the financial necessities of the former in its power of projection in *Guns and Sails*[8] determine the global structure of the process of accumulation that started its ascent in 1492. (Before the discovery of America, J. M. Blaut insists, "Europeans indeed had no superiority over non-Europeans at any time prior to 1492."[9]) Whatever the mercantile and usurious precedents, the origin of finance takes a new turn here, an *unspeakable* turn, one which makes all the difference. "Along with the national debt there arose an international credit system, which often conceals one of the sources of primitive accumulation in this or that people. [...] A great deal of capital, which appears today in the United States without any birth-certificate, was yesterday, in England, the capitalized blood of children."[10]

And inversely, more primitively, when African blood cemented the bricks of the factories and banks of Liverpool and Manchester. Behind the extreme mathematical sophistication of finance, there is always the "brood of bankocrats, financiers, *rentiers*, brokers, stock-jobbers, etc." described by Marx.

2.1 The War against Women

Systematizing the Italian and American work that has been developed since the 1970s in the context of the International

Feminist Collective, Silvia Federici does not hesitate to connect the destiny of women in Europe to that of the people colonized by Europe in a book that takes on the form of a manifesto, with a title inspired by Shakespeare's *The Tempest* and the anti-colonialist recuperation of the character of Caliban: *Caliban and the Witch*.[11] The birth of capitalism, she explains there, is not only synonymous with a war against the poor, it was "coeval with a war against women"[12] to subject them to the social division of labor at the *enclosure* of all forms of human relations—each of which passes through a new sexual order which *accumulates divisions in the production and reproduction of the labor force*. The debasement and demonization of women ("married to the devil"), the destruction of the knowledge they bore, the criminalization of contraception and "magical" practices of care took away control from women over their own bodies, which became the property of men, guaranteed by the state, while participating in putting the population to work.[13] The conditions for assigning women to the labor of biological, economic, and "affective" reproduction of the labor force were thus defined.

"Unproductive work," as the classical economists and a good number of Marxists sagely explain, since it is situated before the valorization of capital and, therefore, non-payable work on the level of a *natural resource* and a *common good*, but regulated in the framework of natal and familial (bio-)politics fiercely promoted by mercantilism. With Maria Mies, Silvia Federici can therefore risk a parallel between the unpaid work of reproduction performed by women (paired with the appropriation of their profits by male workers) and the forced labor of slaves; and she studies the way in which the "war against women" aimed at disciplining them is part of the framework of a new type of patriarchy, the salaried patriarchy.[14]

With its hundreds of thousands of executions, the "witch hunts" were the bloodiest episode of this war against the relative autonomy and freedom of women waged since the end of the Middle Ages.[15] "Witch hunts" are not the infamous mark of a God of the Middle Ages as described by a "history of mentalities" but the *Sabbath of Capital.*

In the most common functioning of an "art of government" which is "neither sovereignty nor the pastorate"[16] military campaigns of "evangelization" allowed witch hunts to be exported to the New World, while the resistance of the "Indians" contributed to bringing the myth of the Good Savage to an end[17] and to declaring that women, who were very involved in indigenous revolts, were essentially a danger to the colonial order. (And yet it is Caliban and not his mother Sicorax, the "sorceress" whose powers and influence over her son are not at all hidden by Shakespeare, who becomes the hero of Latin American revolutionaries....) Conversely, and at the risk of throwing off even the most well-established chronologies, the political strategy of extermination of the Savages could have influenced the massacre of Protestants while inspiring the long-term witch hunts (sodomites and cannibals) in our old Europe threatened by the *turba damnationis* of the poor.[18] More generally, Michel Foucault was able to show the action, starting at the end of the sixteenth century, of this "sort of boomerang effect colonial practice can have on the juridico-political structures of the West." And he explains:

> It should never be forgotten that while colonization, with its techniques and its political and juridical weapons, obviously transported European models to other continents, it also had a considerable boomerang effect on the mechanisms of power in the West, and on the apparatuses, institutions, and

techniques of power. A whole series of colonial models was brought back to the West, and the result was that the West could practice something resembling colonization, or an internal colonialism, on itself.[19]

Such that the turns, detours, and boomerang effects of the *cycle of historical reciprocity of nationalism, racism, and sexism* are in every sense constitutive of the ecumenical power of capitalistic enveloping of the world in the permanent war that serves as vector and tensor. This *ecumene* cannot be imagined without the "technologies" of biopower and a biopolitics that is contemporary with the emergence of capitalism, of which the colonies are also the laboratory, and it throws a rather harsh light on the supposedly "progessist" reality of the transition, which could more appropriately be called a *continued break*.

2.2 Wars of Subjectivity and the Majoritarian Model

In his course at the Collège de France under the title *Security, Territory, Population*, Foucault undertakes to expand the meaning of war and the typology of wars that took place during the first period of primitive accumulation. To do so, he draws our attention to a generally overlooked aspect of the "major social struggles" that marked the transition from feudalism to capitalism, and of which the "Peasants' War" (1524–1526) is one of the most striking aspects.

Foucault observes that this "transition" was the theater of a specific type of war where the stakes were modes of subjectivation and behavior. The Christian "pastorate," which exercised a subjective power of control over individual behavior ("One must become subject to become an individual"—and *subject* in every sense of the word), entered into crisis under "the assault of counter-behavior," of these "behavioral insurrections," which he calls "pastoral revolts," against the new economic conditions and government of behavior. The passage from "governing souls" to "political governing of people" did not consist in a simple transfer of pastoral functions from the Church to the State. It was much more both the intensification of the spiritual forms of control of individual behavior (both the Reform and Counter-Reform exercised "a much greater hold on the spiritual life of individuals than in the past"[20]) and the extension of their temporal efficacity, redirected by these mechanisms of "governmentalization of the *res publica*"[21] that put the new theological ethics of labor and wealth at the service of the disciplinarization and forced labor of the population.

The cardinal sin is no longer avarice but sloth, the fruit of "weakening discipline" and "loosening of morals" that must be *reduced* in the passage from disorder to order. Which also explains, as Foucault emphasizes in *Madness and Civilization* that "the relationship between the practice of confinement and the insistence on work is not fully defined by economic conditions,"[22] because the imperative to work is all the more *indissociably economic and moral* in that it encounters innumerable forms of resistance requiring a combination of civil law and moral obligation.

The importance and radicalness of the wars of subjectivity in Europe and in the New World are made manifest in the destruction carried out by primitive accumulation not only on the level of the material conditions of life, but also in terms of existential territories, universes of values, cosmology, and the mythologies at the foundation of the "subjective life" of the colonized people and the poor of the so-called "civilized world." Deterritorialization deprives the colonized, women, and the proletariat of their "an-organic" life, to use one of Deleuze and Guattari's expressions that should be redirected towards Foucault's analysis. In fact, biopower can only invest life as administration of the "biological" conditions of the species through the state (fecundity, mortality, health, etc.) because primitive accumulation was previously the agent of destruction of this "subjective" dimension. The wars of subjectivity are therefore not a "supplement" to Capital in its "subjective" face, they constitute the most "objective" specificity of the wars against women, the mentally ill, the poor, criminals, day-laborers, workers, and more. They are not content with "overcoming" the adversary (to negotiate a better peace treaty, according to the classical idea of inter-state warfare) since their aim is precisely the "conversion" of subjectivity, the conformance of behavior and practices to the logic of the accumulation and reproduction of capital.

In this sense, the production of subjectivity is both the first of the capitalist productions and a major *object* of war and civil war. The formatting of subjectivity is their *strategic concern*, and it is found throughout the history of capitalism. For Félix Guattari, from whom we are borrowing the term, the "wars of subjectivity" are political wars of "formatting" and "steering" of the subjectivity needed for the production, consumption, and the reproduction of Capital. They are not foreign to the intense struggles waged inside insurrectional and protest movements to define the forms of organization and subjectivation of the revolutionary war machine (militancy, modes of action, strategy, tactics, etc.). For Michel Foucault, they form the web of resistance and invention of an "other" subjectivation that is found not only in every experience of revolutionary rupture,[23] but also in the last displacement that he was able to consider, since the passage to the ethics of a "militant life" through *parrêsia* is itself a "war against the other."[24]

The violent processes of deterritorialization that are at the heart of primitive accumulation (understood in the narrowest sense of the term, even in the witch hunt[25]) and of the globalization that accompanies it are therefore always inseparable from wars of subjectivity. Construction of the "majoritarian model" of Man as male, white, and adult transforming women into a minority gender and the colonized into a minority race is a strategic mechanism that *necessarily* takes place simultaneously in the colonies of the New World and in Europe, where it was well known that "diversities provide Satan with marvelous commodities."[26] Such that the first *European construction* becomes that of a "Little Big Man" emerging from this space of terror benefitting all of the strategic "exchanges" in favor of the continued formation of a *global proletariat*.

The power relations and divisions established by the majoritarian model became deeply linked to organizing relationships of exploitation both in the homeland and in its peripheries. Because it is *with* primitive accumulation and *as* the continued accumulation of capitalism that the model majority (men)/minorities (women) functions within European wage labor by being combined with class exploitation.

The war against women produces a differentiation and a sexual division of labor that is revealed to be strategic for the history of the accumulation of capital and the struggles that oppose it. In a society in the process of being monetized, women only have access to money indirectly, through the wages of the male worker to whom the women find themselves in a situation of dependence and inferiority. Dominated according to class logic, male wage laborers became dominant in the logic of the majority/

minority model. Wages and their modalities of distribution are synonymous with a form of domination of women and forced promotion of the "bourgeois" nuclear family in the labor world, which repeats the refrain even in its most revolutionary movements. "Proletarian antifeminism" (to use Thönnessen's expression) and workers' defense of women's rights reduced to the condition of mother and homemaker go hand in hand. As Maria Mies observes: "Proletarianization of men is based on the housewifization of women. Thus, the Little White Man also got his 'colony,' namely, the family and a domesticated housewife."[27]

Despite some feminist critiques, the Foucauldian microphysics of power reveals itself here to be a vital instrument in accounting for the way power also passes through the dominated, such that "micropolitics" becomes the privileged terrain of the dynamics of division, differentiation, and antagonism. In fact, the entire "class composition" of the proletariat is traversed with lines of fracture that at the origin are veritable molecular "civil wars" that cannot be reduced to any type of ideological conflict.

Ashis Nandy has remarkably described how, in India, construction of the majoritarian model by the British colonizers still passes, essentially, through the same stages since the establishment of a new "colonial hierarchy of sexual identities," according to which "the masculine is superior to the feminine and the feminine is in turn superior to femininity in men" through a devalorization of Indian androgynous cosmology.[28] Normality is identified with the adult *homo europeaus*, at one and the same time virile, competitive, full of a warrior spirit, rejecting the impotence of the effeminate, while children like the colonized are relegated to the "primitive" world, synonymous with a situation of inferiority that only "development" (the process of civilization) can correct.

The mechanism of majority/minority power energizes the war of subjectivities of internal colonization and external colonization by establishing hierarchies of race and sex, but also civilization. The latter is perfectly "performed" by the Schmittian assertion according to which Indians "lacked the scientific power of Christian-European rationality. [...] The intellectual advantage was entirely on the European side."[29] Which also explains how the discovery of the New World could appear as an "authentic epistemological event" compensating for Galilean decentering with a "terrestrial-imperialist recentering of Europe."[30]

"Primitive accumulation" would therefore have to be called *first accumulation* (*initiale* in the French translation by Jean-Pierre Lefebvre, or *originelle* (original): *ursprünglich*) from which an international division of labor can already be traced with the hierarchies that are only of "class" because they are also of gender, race, and civilization. In other words, an *accumulation of potential and power* (*puissance et pouvoir*) that prevents simplifying the world-economy in its process of emerging by opposing the class struggle in the homeland and the race struggle in the colonies when the majority/minority mechanism is operational, under different modalities, on both sides of the Atlantic. There is an identity of nature and differences of regimes with multiple intersections.

2.3 Liberalism and Colonization: The Case of Locke

The intellectual biography and doctrinal apparatus of John Locke have long been studied to ascertain whether he was the founding father of political liberalism, at the origin of the entire American tradition, and the "elder statesman of modern political economy" (Marx). Despite there being a sizable amount of Anglo-Saxon literature on Locke, most of which is unknown in

France, little of it has been focused on his long colonial career and the repercussions it had on his philosophy as a whole—a philosophy in which the concept of "America" is omnipresent. The study of Locke's liberalism—and liberalism *itself*—would be singularly enriched by it and reinserted in the history (or counter-history) that we are retracing here in broad strokes.

Locke was in fact a secretary of the Lords Proprietors of the Province of Carolina (1668), where he held land under the constitutional rules to which he contributed and according to which "every freeman of Carolina shall have absolute Power and Authority over his negro slaves."[31] Starting in 1673, he became secretary and treasurer on the Council of Trade and Foreign Plantations (1673) but also a stockholder in different companies, including the Royal African Company, which managed the slave trade and held a monopoly over it in West Africa.

The English "agricultural" model of colonization, of which Locke was an ardent defender, relied on this very lucrative trade. The fact that there is an immediate contradiction with the opening lines of the first of the two *Treatises on Government* ("Slavery is so vile and miserable..."[32]), which condemn slavery and contributed to establishing his position as a liberal philosopher, is evidence that cannot be resolved by subtle distinctions between "contradictions in practice" and "contradictions in principle" or between "strong racism" and "weak racism." It is in fact the *contradictory reality* of the liberal model's universalism that is established here in the usage and in the name on an "Englishman," including the racism "of civilization" in his colonial/colonialist constitution, at a time when the modern concept of race was not yet biologically—or "scientifically"—defined, and where the legal system of plantation slavery was negotiated under pressure from a circle of "Royal Adventurers" to which Locke fully belonged. Which also explains how the English philosopher can, *without contradiction* from *his* liberal perspective, stigmatize the *political* "slavery" that absolute monarchy would like to introduce *in Europe* by subjecting all nations to a permanent state of war dominated by the arbitrary against all. The description given of it (the king has "degenerated into a wild beast") is reminiscent of the Black Legend of the "Spanish technique" of colonization by systematic "rapin and plunder" deftly maintained in the context of "mercantilist" rivalries between the major European powers. That is the charge leveled against absolute monarchy: *confusing Europe with the worst of the colonies*, at the risk of maintaining "eternal seditions" and giving rise to principles capable of encouraging "popular uprisings" by threatening the very principle of government. In the foreword to the French translation by David Mazel, published in Paris in Year III of the Republic (1795), Locke's political project is presented in a formula full of Solonian classicism: "finding a midpoint between these extremes."[33]

Because a man "*cannot*, by compact, or his own consent, *enslave himself* to any one, nor put himself under the absolute, arbitrary power of another,"[34] it is up to the "people," by "consent" to be the source of *political power* and *civil society*—"of political or civil society," to use the title of the central chapter of the *Second Treatise of Civil Government*. Its members place their "natural power" into the hands of the "community" which is asserted as a *commonwealth* by the power of "preservation of property" (VII, 85) without resorting to war, which is also for Locke, as a good European, the only true condition of *slavery* as it is "the state of war continued, between a lawful conqueror and a captive" (IV, 24). Since "that absolute monarchy [...] is indeed inconsistent with civil society" (VII, 90) because it is a *continuation*

of war by other means directed against its people, it is no less evi-
dent that civil society will be the affair of a *people of property
owners* for whom the political problem—with which liberalism
identifies through the intermediary of Locke—is that of a *return
(of the repressed) of enslavement* of the "negroes" of America on
European soil and in England, of which he ensures the "prosperity"
by means of war that are the means of *colonial difference*. How, in
fact, could the *razzia* of slaves and the slave trade fall under the
laws of "just war" in the European theater? Yet isn't this colonial
difference completely relative given the conditions of the *poor* in
this same theater of operations?

It falls to a people of property owners to *express* nascent
capitalism and its concepts of labor, private property, and
money, concepts which are lacking in the colonized, even in the
state of nature of which they transgress the laws. Land is left
fallow and spaces left vacant (*vacuis locis*) because "the wild Indian,
who knows no enclosure" (V, 26) does not subject them to
"human industry" and the work of *making value* (mise en valeur)
which is supposed to be at the *natural* foundation of "property."
Nomads living off hunting and gathering do not "work" to *give
each thing its proper value* and to exempt themselves from the
divine injunction to make the earth fruitful: "God gave the world
[…] to the use of the industrious and rational, (and *labour* was
to be his *title* to it)" (V, 34). It is a first breach of natural law, of
individual property, of the *exclusive private property* (*proprietas*)
of land that a person *encloses* by labor and separates from what
is common in the ("very modest") limits of the use he or she
will make of it. It is also, at least indirectly, a first justification
of the colonial appropriation of these shared and *waste* lands of
the Americas by the enactment of a politics of enclosure that
can only mean *expropriation without consent* of its inhabitants

without law, even natural law (it does not occur to Locke that here, in this act of war and in this reason that could be authorized by Grotius,[35] there is the principle of explanation of these *vacant places, vacant habitations* after two centuries of European colonization...).

The difference in civilization is revealed to be so absolute ("the morals of these people [...], what strangers they are to humane feelings"[36]) that the place of the savages that are said to live "in harmony with nature" is far from assured in a state of nature of which the trait is to make "private possessions" (V, 35[37]) compatible with a "state also of equality, wherein all the power and jurisdiction is reciprocal." It is such an improbable historical state that "the promises and bargains for truck" *require* people to have relationships of truth and respect for giving one's word that they could take place between "a Swiss and an Indian, in the woods of America" (II, 4 and 14) ... The European in America would thus come to incarnate the law of nature, which is nothing other than a pure *self-interested calculation* shared by those who make their own laws! Returning to the work that would give the earth its value, the demonstration finally shows its anachronism in full by making itself accountable to the present: in America, "a king of a large and fruitful territory there feeds, lodges, and is clad worse than a daylabourer in England" (V, 41) because of the difference in revenue between an "acre of land" cultivated here (for which Locke deems the profits to be very precisely 5£) and there: "if all the profit an Indian received from it were to be valued, and sold here; at least, I may truly say, not one thousandth." (V, 43). There is no passage between here and there for Indians who have not been able to reach the final stage of the state of nature which is the invention of money: in its use "by consent," it transforms the land into *capital* aimed at producing goods for commerce. Announcing the end of equality and the *natural limits* linked with the satisfaction of needs, money opens the way to the unlimited appropriation of land *and labor*, and to a first form of government (or governmentality) between individuals who have become unequal by "larger possessions and a right to them" (V, 36). Here a first form of development is reached, both monetary and proto-legal (in this order), of a *Far West* that is decomposed into a *war on waste*.[38] For Locke, however, it is a *good* that must be sought by society because it increases its overall wealth and benefits even the poorest day-laborers... A *fairytale*, duly retold by Adam Smith in *The Wealth of Nations*, in the name of a "*previous accumulation*" dismantled by Marx (*the wealth of the nation* ensures *the poverty of the people*).

It is hard to disagree with MacPherson when he asserts that the institution of civil government that arose from this monetized state of nature to safeguard the "property of each person" means making the market economy and its class divisions the permanent foundation of civilized society.[39] Thus Locke inscribes the development of colonialism in America in the global economy of nascent capitalism as a step in civilizing *a single world*: "for I ask, what would a man value ten thousand, or an hundred thousand acres of excellent *land*, ready cultivated and well stocked too with cattle, in the middle of the inland parts of *America*, where he had no hopes of commerce with other parts of the world, to draw *money* to him by the sale of the product? It would not be worth the enclosing" (V, 50).

The full capitalist rationality deployed here in a colonial geopolitics of the state of nature obeys the historical logic of accumulation by the "commerce" of appropriation of the world. It allows the philosopher to replay, reconstruct, and displace onto the American stage in a veritable order of reasons the expropriation without consent of the English peasants, which does not appear as such in the two *Treatises*—except in its supposedly most *natural* result: the people no longer owning land would have the capability of acquiring through their labor the *monetary* means to subsist by *transferring the gain in recompense for the labor into the pocket of another*[40]... If the politics of enclosure were for Locke the "touchstone of the English path to colonizing America,"[41] it is the fate of the "poor," who must at all cost be put to work by submitting them to the regime of *workhouses* and "industry schools" for the children, by forcing them to enlist in the navy, or by deporting them to plantations,[42] evocative of slavery in their *indentured servitude* in a world that commerce has made more "prosperous" than ever. Proof if needed that "the growth of the poor must therefore have some other cause, and it can be nothing else but the relaxation of discipline and corruption of manners; virtue and industry being as constant companions on the one side as vice and idleness are on the other."[43]

The limits of the civilizing function of labor are immediately measured after the introduction of money which founds the principle of rationality of unlimited accumulation by disassociating appropriation (of land) and labor (of landless men), *which can be appropriated* by following a law of nature *and of reason*. The full development of rationality coinciding with the flourishing of the *persona œconomica* is then more an affair of appropriation and expropriation than of labor, and the "industrious man" is no longer the "rational man." He is the poor, laborious man submitted to the authority of the state which administers and disciplines its labor force by maintaining it in the shortest circuit of subsistence "from hand to mouth," and the least capable of "elevating its thoughts beyond the immediate problems of existence" on a daily basis. The laborious class, which is as limited in its possibilities of acquiring knowledge as it is of wealth,[44] could not be granted the right to revolt, since exercising insurgence depends, as a right, on a choice of reason and constitutes in fact *the only criteria of citizenship*[45]—in its difference with subjection to an arbitrary and absolute power against which the "people" is right to revolt against to maintain its own safety and the security of its goods, "the reason why men enter into society" (XIX, 222). We find "freedom against slavery" by inclusive exclusion of the new proletariat, whose condition is considered so harshly by English economists after 1660 that there is no other "modern parallel except in the behavior of the least reputable of White colonists towards colored labor."[46] White or Black, the labor force, which represents "the most essential, fundamental, and precious commodity"[47] is definitively not the "political" people where each person leads his or her understanding enough by reason to give themselves by mutual consent a "civil government" to be constituted into a "civil society" of which the *legislative* is "the soul that gives [it] form, life, and unity" (XIX, 212).

This liberal idea of a contract-consent founding legislation on the legitimacy of the people included in it imposes on Locke a *continuist* perspective on servitude and a *differential* perspective on reason,[48] according to which beings incapable of governing themselves, both inside (children, women, "madmen," "idiots," and the poor: *laboring poor* and *idle poor*) and outside (primitives/savages), should, in one way or another, be governed without consent.

It is based on a (geo-)politics of the understanding connecting in a new way internal and external colonization in the "identity of consciousness" of a new *subject of governance of the self and of others* which is established in this history of the state of nature where each "man has a property in his own person" (V, 27). Since

Locke, who forges in his *An Essay Concerning Human Understanding* the nominal expression *the Self*, subjection (*subjectio*) to work is connected with the *propriation* and the appropriation of a "Self" in the construction of the *possessive subject* as it combines, at the junction of psychology, epistemology, law, politics, and economics, with the European invention of the liberal consciousness.

"The Dominion of Man, in this little World of his own Understanding, being much the same, as it is in the great World of visible things."[49] Critical of the universality of "innate ideas" imprinted in the soul by divine insemination, Locke's empiricism endeavors to define the real "operations" of the mind that affirm by "reflection" the identity of thought and knowing for a consciousness whose self-consciousness is the promise of a conquering the process of totalization of knowledge and condition of reality of the responsibility of the person. Thought is no longer a metaphysical "substance" (Descartes), it becomes the object of work and an *appropriation* (it is *appropriated*) that makes me *accountable as a* (moral and legal) *Person* "capable of Law" and "responsible for his actions" by this "self-consciousness." A *con-science* to use the neologism proposed by Pierre Coste in his translation done in close consultation with Locke to account for what the philosopher was the first to call "self-consciousness,"[50] without which the White Man, launched into the "discovery of the material world,"[51] placed at the intersection of empiricism and Empire in the strictest correlation between economic power, cognitive power, and normative power, would not know how to guide his understanding—or launch his ship—on the "great ocean of knowledge," like England was able to "make trade work" with the other nations of the world. All of this movement of "reflection" that is implied in the *Western identification* of the identity of the same and the identity of the self, of the "proper" and "propriety"—in such a way that it is on this personal identity which means "the sameness of a rational Being" that should be "founded all the right and justice of reward and punishment; happiness and misery being that for which every one is concerned for *himself*."[52]

Yet this personal identity must of course be built on a *self-discipline* conceived of as an apprenticeship of authority and power over oneself and others, the keys to which are education ("suited to our English gentry") and submission to the hierarchical matrix of the patriarchal family. The fact that *Some Thoughts Concerning Education* (published by Locke in 1693) was a bestseller throughout the eighteenth century is a clear indication, fully resonating with the puritan and accountable ethics of capitalism,[53] and the system of *habits* that it endeavored to promote.[54] More than a simple *instruction*, it is "a regulation of the whole of conduct which, penetrating to all departments of private and public life, was infinitely burdensome and earnestly enforced"[55] that is at the heart of this capitalist *civilization* (to use another of Max Weber's words) and of the wars of subjectivity it promotes in the name of a proprietary universality that "teaches" *others* about their inclusive exclusion/exclusive inclusion in the majority model of the wars of the *Self*. Because it goes without saying that all people will be members of "political and civil society" when it is a question of being governed, albeit with different status. The "Self-service" of liberalism.

2.4 Foucault and Primitive Accumulation

Various authors in the nebula of postcolonial studies have criticized Foucault for largely overlooking the colonial genealogy of biopower, except in his 1976 course at the Collège de France, where the passage we cited above appears to be a hapax.[56] Others, this time in the field of feminist studies, like Silvia Federici, reproach the French philosopher for his silence concerning "witch hunts," and more generally his lack of interest in the question of "reproduction" and the disciplinarization of women in the *longue durée* of the techniques of power and phenomena of resistance that he studies. They all agree on emphasizing the discursive abstraction of Foucault's analysis of power, functioning as a Prime Mover of History.

Yet we also understand that if the genealogy of the techniques of discipline and biopower was traced back to the "launch" of primitive accumulation, then the history, functioning, and successive transformations of these power apparatuses (*dispositifs*) cannot be separated from war in all its forms that in large part created them. In the different modalities that they take on starting at the end of the seventeenth century, these apparatuses (*dispositifs*) are the privileged way to express the continuation of war by other means and make it appear as an *analyzer of power relationships*. This logic is at play in the 1976 course, when the philosopher *does not reverse* Clausewitz's formula (as it is all too often said[57]) but postulates on the contrary that it was Clausewitz who *inverted* "a principle that existed long before [...], a sort of thesis that had been in circulation since the seventeenth and eighteenth centuries and which was both diffuse and specific."[58] This led him to study the appearance and the spread of discourse that for the first time conceived of politics as the continuation of war.

It cannot be said therefore that Foucault was not interested in the period corresponding to primitive accumulation. Nevertheless, it is true that he analyzes it from the perspective of the "epochal" constitution of states in early capitalism (the "govern-mentalization of the state") and from the perspective of the wars of subjectivity that characterized the transition from feudalism to capitalism. Here we reach the sticking point where the irre-placeable work of Michel Foucault suffers from a major limitation. His Eurocentric point of view (and even largely "British-centric" in relation to the genealogy of "race wars" con-nected—in a somewhat rash way—to the effects of the conquest in England in the 1976 course) is in itself problematic and reduces the scope of the analysis of the constitution of the power relations of emerging capitalism which were being woven trans-versally on both sides of the Atlantic. The three aspects that stand out (state accumulation, crisis of the priesthood on the horizon of a "governmentality" defined in terms of strategies and tactics, possible feedback effects of the relationship disciplines/colonized on the mechanisms of power in the West) should therefore be taken up again and extended beyond the limits that characterize them, since they contribute strongly to problematizing the question of war as "numeral" (*chiffre*) or number numbering the social relationship of capital, by imposing the analysis of political power as *disciplinarization of war*.

The wars of conquest and predation of the New World over-saw the *expanded self-manifestation* of another institution that was indispensable to the birth and rise of capitalism. Primitive accumulation is in fact also, and maybe first of all, accumulation of state power and wealth. Michel Foucault is probably the one who describes it most pertinently while neglecting the *constitu-tive globalization* of capitalism, which must be reinserted between the threads of his analysis.

At the end of the Thirty Years' War, in the mid-seventeenth century, he explains, "a new historical perspective opens up of indefinite governmentality and the permanence of states" that "requires us to accept acts of violence as the purest form of reason, and of raison d'État."[59] Resulting from the institutionalization of war machines in the feudal period, the diplomatic-military system constituted the "first technological ensemble" characteristic of the new art of governing, of which the goal is the power and wealth of states. It protects a balance of forces ensuring the "empowerment" of states. The second "technological ensemble," which had the same goal, consisted of the "police" and its government of society and the population.

We must return here to the essential analysis of Carl Schmitt when he reminds us that one of the conditions, and not the least among them, for the institution of the *Jus publicum* in Europe was the separation between the continental space, where a "balance of forces" was established to limit the power of states, and the "free lands" of the New World, where the same states could partake in unlimited competition and rivalry. While on the continent, and in the perspective of a certain equilibrium between states, war is *de facto* a continuation of politics by other means (such that, for Foucault, Clausewitz's theory is a systematization, two centuries later, of this relationship of forces between states); in the rest of the world, where war did not stop being conquest, pillage, limitless violence against people, goods, and land, Clausewitz's formula was always already reversed into the most brutal expression of "race war" fed by the extra-European war of states carving out their colonial empires.

The scope and signification of mercantilism are also truncated by the focus of Foucault's methodology on Europe, forcing him to articulate an unlimited power over the population internally (the police state) and a limited power externally by a *raison d'État* limiting itself in its own objectives given the "European balance" of nations.[60] The contrast could not be greater with the classic work of Eric Williams on the relationship between slavery and capitalism, who proposed the equation mercantilism = slavery ("the essence of mercantilism is slavery"[61]), by opening a completely different perspective, one much *further from the European balance* of the diplomatic-military make-up of states, on the "phase" that preceded and stimulated the Industrial Revolution. The fact that the power and wealth of states came in large part from the exploitation of colonies and the slave trade ("Europe's biggest single external contribution to its own economic growth"[62]) is so obvious that its imprint is even found in John Stuart Mill, at the heart of the liberal recourse to mercantilism and slavery, when he states in his *Principles of Political Economy* (1848) that "trade with the West Indies is therefore hardly to be considered as external trade, but more resembles the traffic between town and country."[63] With the relative adaptation between forced labor in the colonies and "free wage labor" in Europe,[64] which also made the disciplinarization of the poor pass through the enslavement of Blacks, the capitalist mode of production of the new international division of labor confirmed that, no matter what side of the question capitalism is approached from, it is impossible to ignore the geopolitical dimension outside Europe. For the simple reason that it is *one* with the upswing of Europe, and that it was responsible for starting the cycle of *mass* production-consumption by developing military-commercial enterprises whose success relied in the end on the establishment of an economy of discipline, the *seriatim* organization of labor, time, and space on a large scale that pushed the sugar cane plantations to the rank of capitalistic laboratories for the factory regime. We can thus confirm that if the colonial regime was a "foreign God" who, according to Marx, cast out the "old idols of Europe," it could only do so by proclaiming and opening by *Force* the path of "surplus-value making (*Plusmacherei*) as the sole end and aim of humanity."[65]

2.5 Colonial Genealogy of the Disciplines of Biopolitics

Without needing to share them fully here, the critiques expressed by postcolonial authors are useful in problematizing Foucault's approach and its lapses. Returning to the two poles of development in the exercise of power over people since the break with the feudal rituals of sovereign power, disciplinary power focused on the body as *machine integrated* "into systems of efficient and economic controls" and biopower, which "formed somewhat later" as a *biopolitics of the population*,[66] date, respectively, from the middle or end of the seventeenth century and the eighteenth century. In our view, their differentiated rise only represents a second stage in the construction of the power apparatuses (*dispositifs*) of capitalism, which becomes more significant if it is considered both in its rupture and its continuity with the first two centuries of "primitive accumulation."

A few traces of this relationship of rupture and continuity are found in the 1973–1974 course, *Psychiatric Power*, where Foucault expands the space of construction of apparatuses (*dispositifs*) of knowledge and power to the world-economy by establishing a parallel between homeland and colonies. In these pages, the "internal colonization" of vagabonds, nomads, delinquents, and prostitutes is mirrored by the "external colonization" of colonized peoples on which the same disciplinary apparatuses (*dispositifs*) as those used in Europe are exercised and tested. "How disciplinary schemas were both applied and refined in the colonial populations should be examined in some detail. It seems that disciplinarization took place fairly unobtrusively and marginally to start with, and, interestingly, as a counterpoint to slavery."[67]

The world-economy couples its apparatuses (*dispositifs*) of power with knowledge and a new concept of "truth" adequate for the functions of control and government of the populations, according to a "procedure of continuous control" ("It is a seizure of the body and not of the product; it is a seizure of time in its totality, and not of the time of service") for which the model is provided by the disciplinary system of the army.[68] This model spread to the entire surface of the globe. Its planetary extension was combined with a "double movement of colonization" that was mutually reinforcing: "colonization in depth, which fed on the actions, bodies, and thoughts of individuals, and then colonization at the level of territories and surfaces."[69] We are here—a *here* that transports us to the quasi-panoptical disciplinary microcosms of production and surveillance that are the Jesuit establishments in Paraguay[70]—at the heart of the "generalized investigation of the entire surface of the earth" producing knowledge on human behavior, the way they live, think, make love. "That is to say, at any time, at any place, and with regard to anything in the world, the question of truth can and must be posed. Truth is everywhere and awaits us everywhere."[71] According to the modalities that Locke helped us to discover, this *universal production of truth* requires forms of thought and "technologies" allowing access to it *by producing the subject of its utterance and its reception*. Indeed, there must be "a universal subject of this universal truth, but it will be an abstract subject because, concretely, the universal subject able to grasp this truth is rare, since it must be a subject qualified by procedures of pedagogy and selection."[72] It will be a subject educated by the knowledge of accumulation of capital, a subject equipped for power over the accumulation of people and their *systematic colonization*. It is decidedly unfortunate that the "disciplinary" experiment carried out by the Jesuits on the Guarani communities of Paraguay was not pursued in Foucault's later work, as this opening towards the global bio-geopolitics of capitalism was quickly closed.

Understanding the articulation of the concepts of biopower and disciplinary power in a genealogy that includes primitive accumulation as its origin would allow us to grasp the way they continue war by other means, in particular in relation to the "war against women." The definition of biopower as apparatuses (*dispositifs*) of production and control of processes "such as the ratio of births to deaths, the rate of reproduction, the fertility of the population" and as management of the "reproduction" of the population by the state[73] would benefit greatly from being considered a successor to the policies of expropriation and appropriation of the "bodies" of women that engage their power over "reproduction" of the labor force and an entire *biopolitics of the body*.[74] It would be found that the power of "regularization" of a biopolitics characterized by taking charge of the life of populations depends on "a whole disciplinary series that proliferates under mechanisms of security and is necessary to make them function."[75] It would also give an entirely different scope to the analysis of economic liberalism, *in every point* connected to disciplinary techniques, to the extent that the disciplinarization of life appears as the *biopolitical matrix* of economic-political control of production. It seems in any case necessary to interpret in this sense the formula of Bentham-Foucault: "the Panopticon is the very formula of liberal government."[76]

2.6 Racism and Race War

The thorniest question concerns the Foucaldian genealogy of "state racism." In the final lecture of "*Society Must Be Defended*," Michel Foucault urges us to understand the concept of biopower as a "biological relationship" and "not military, warlike or political." This assertion deserves problematization in light of the processes of reduction of women and the colonized to a biological existence that could only be realized and pursued through race war and the war against women: in fact, if primitive accumulation shows the strict implication between biopower and war, and the impossibility of distinguishing between them, then the "Foucaldian" apparatuses constitute the continuation of wars of primitive accumulation by other means. While recognizing that racism developed "first with colonization, or in other words, with colonizing genocide,"[77] Foucault remained strongly focused on Europe. His problematization of war as figure of social relations and his genealogy of state racism are considerably weakened by it. For him, "it is indeed the emergence of this biopower that inscribes [racism] in the mechanisms of the state," which he traces symptomatically *back* to the nineteenth century.[78]

While biopower is a power that "takes charge of life," that "protects, guarantees, and cultivates [it] in biological terms,"[79] while biopower, unlike sovereign power ("make die and let live"), is exercised through a new right ("make live and let die"), how is the specific function of war, the right to mete out death, ensured? Through racism, responds Foucault! "Racism makes it possible to establish a relationship between my life and the death of the other that is not a military or warlike relationship of confrontation but a biological relationship" allowing both a "biological extrapolation from the theme of the political enemy" and the inscription of "the death-function in the economy of biopower" which thus enacts a "break" in the biological *continuum* and thereby recovers "the old sovereign right to kill."[80] In these pages, the rise of racism at the end of the nineteenth century seems to have no connection to the evolution of the world-economy or with imperialism, which brought colonial conquest to its climax and raced towards the First World War. Here again, the Eurocentric framing of the analysis limits the explication (which regresses towards *the characteristic proper to the power of sovereignty* by leading Foucault towards a curious chiasmus effect),[81] since the first manifestations of the policies of "state racism" do not concern Europe but the colonies and slavery.

The origins of slavery are surely not to be found in "race" policies. It is first of all an economic problem ensuing from, on the one hand, the policy of extermination and, on the other, the "weakness" of the Indians and "hired" Whites who were unable to carry out forced labor in the mines and plantations of the New World. "Slavery was not born of racism: rather, racism was the consequence of slavery."[82] Yet maintaining and stabilizing slavery policies required the establishment of racial policies. Early on in the Spanish colonies, during the 1540s, "'race' was established as a key factor in the transmission of property, and a racial hierarchy was put in place to separate indigenous, *mestizos*, and *mulatos* from each other and from the white population."[83] The French state for its part gave a "legal" framework to race wars with the *Code noir* (1685) and the *Code de l'indigénat* (1881).

State racism was therefore not born at the end of the nineteenth century in Europe as a consequence of the deployment of biopower in a "society of normalization" and by the adaptation of the scientific themes of evolutionism. It is constitutive of the construction of the state function that projected a *disciplinary biopower* onto the world-economy. And while it is true that state racism of the late nineteenth century is undoubtedly different, its novelty resides in the importation and transformation of racial policies that were inseparable from the techniques of "government" of colonized populations used for centuries. Throughout the nineteenth century, and particularly in France, civil war techniques were imported from the colonies to demolish worker insurrections; and as for the wars of the twentieth century, according to Paul Virilio, total war "was already closer to the colonial enterprise than traditional war in Europe."[84]

Nazism, the climax and *final solution* of state racism, in which Foucault sees the absolute coincidence of a total disciplinary state, of a generalized biopower, and the diffusion of the "old sovereign right to kill" throughout the social body, was not only the suicidal result of the European *biodynamics* precipitated into war as "ultimate and decisive phase in all political processes."[85] The poet Aimé Césaire understood it from a completely different place as the *inevitable* fruit of colonization which worked "to decivilize the colonizer" by ensuring that "slowly but surely," Europe "proceeds towards *savagery*." The reason Hitler cannot be forgiven "is not *the crime* in itself, *the crime against man*, it is not *the humiliation of man as such*, it is the crime against the white man, and the fact that he applied to Europe colonialist procedures which until then had been reserved exclusively for the Arabs of Algeria, the "coolies" of India, and the 'niggers' of Africa."[86]

2.7 War of/in the World-Economy

It is therefore not surprising that the authors associated with research on the world-economy are completing and enriching the analysis of the transformations of war and the ways it is waged in direct relationship with nascent capitalism and the colonies. And in fact, "primitive accumulation" provides the crucible for all the functions that war would later develop: establishment of disciplinary apparatuses (*dispositifs*) of power, rationalization and acceleration of production, terrain for testing and perfecting new technologies, and biopolitical management of productive force itself. Most of all, war plays a leading role in the "governmentality" of the multiplicity of modes of production, social formations, and apparatuses of power that coexist in capitalism at the global scale. It is not limited to being the continuation on the strategic level of the (foreign) policy of states. It contributes to producing and holding together the differentials that define the divisions of labor, sexes, and races without which capitalism could not feed on the inequalities it unleashes.

Fernand Braudel notes that war, "rejuvenated by technology, the midwife of modern times," worked to accelerate the establishment of capitalism: "By the sixteenth century, advanced warfare was furiously engaging money, intelligence, the ingenuity of technicians, so that it was said that it changed its nature from year to year."[87] For Immanuel Wallerstein, in reference to the same period, war was both a source of employment for the poor and a productive force of great importance in stimulating credit. "[I]ncreased military expenditure has often stimulated more production of other kinds so that the amount of surplus rose in time of war." Military logistics not only engaged commerce and production, "[t]he system was credit-creating. For not only did princes borrow from bankers; so did the military entrepreneurs."[88]

Reminding us that "war in Brazil simply could not be fought like the war in Flanders," Braudel gives another important indication about how primitive accumulation imposes profound changes on the way war is waged by shifting it towards *guerrilla* warfare, for which Carl Schmitt dated the emergence much later, according to a European calendar that has him privilege the forms of resistance elicited by the Napoleonic wars, in particular in Spain.

War, "daughter and mother of progress," which accompanies the nation-state like its shadow and contributes to the rise of the "civilization" of capitalism, only exists on the central stage of the world-economy. On the periphery, in the colonies, a *poor war (guerre de pauvres)* is fought against *barbarians*, the only war adapted to their "means." To the great confusion of professional soldiers sent to the "Americas," it was impossible to wage war in Africa, Brazil, or Canada according to the customary European rules ("the laws of war"). The *guerra do mato* (forest war) or *guerre volante* carried out by troops recruited on location (the *soldatos da terra*) in the Brazilian Nordeste, was therefore less a tactical innovation than a type of strategic revolution in the "Western" art of war, which the colonial wars and state racism that accompanied them would continue to repeat and expand.

2.8 Primitive Accumulation Under Debate

Primitive accumulation constitutes the true "womb" of capitalism, but only on the condition of carrying out deep changes to the framework traced by Marx in *Capital*. In the Marxian analysis of the transition, we can see two "limits" that affect the entire analysis of capitalism.

First, there is the reduction of the multiplicity of wars of sexes, races, subjectivities, civilizations, etc. structuring the social division of labor to the single relationship of capital/labor. For our part, we have wanted to show that primitive accumulation, from the start, is a continuous creation/destruction carrying the *real* functioning of the global market in its production and reproduction of the differentials between a multiplicity of modes of production and exploitation of labor, social formations, power and domination apparatuses (*dispositifs*) that cannot be reduced solely to "mode of production."

Then there is the progressive, evolutive, linear idea of time and history that tends to "frame" any analysis of primitive accumulation and that prohibits in large part the *political* development of the historical analyses proposed by Marx.[89] What Marx calls "primitive accumulation" does not take place once and for all. It is repeated, according to Deleuze and Guattari, with each new assembly of an apparatus of capture in relationship with the possible figures of capitalism. With financial capitalism, the contemporaneity of "primitive accumulation" imposes itself, conquest and exploration acting *under the cover* of "trade" with the most modern productive processes.

This definition of primitive accumulation as a process essentially connected to the development of capitalism (and not its prehistory) is not new. It was established at the beginning of the twentieth century with the new wave of colonization under the impetus of financial capital that leads to the belief that imperialism is not one option among others for capitalism. Rosa Luxemburg is probably the first to see primitive accumulation as less a "historical" than a *contemporary* phenomenon of capitalism, which continued in the twentieth century in its imperialist form. While accumulation does not stop producing and reproducing itself, it only involves the "exterior" of industrial capitalism and operates on the periphery, subject to the violence of annexation of new territories ("land-grabbing": *landnahme*), while the center remains "pacified."

The accumulation of capital thus has two aspects. "One concerns the commodity market and the place where surplus value is produced—the factory, the mines, the agricultural estate. Regarded in this light, accumulation is a purely economic process, with its most important phase a transaction between the capitalist and wage laborer. [...] Here, in form at any rate, peace, property and equality prevail." This first side of accumulation takes place in the "North," while the second side, its unmentionable part, concerns the relationship of capital with the "South" and its non-capitalist modes of production. "Its predominant methods are colonial policy, an international loan system—a policy of spheres of interest—and war. Force, fraud, oppression, looting are openly displayed without any attempt at concealment, and it requires an effort to discover within this tangle of political violence and contests of power the stern laws of the economic process."[91]

While the two faces of accumulation constitute the "same organic phenomenon," they refer to an "inside" and an "outside" of Capital as such, in a time when the non-capitalist sector "represents [geographically] today the majority of the globe," and when non-capitalist economies remain in large portions of Europe itself.

Contemporary globalization has erased the spatial "outside" to be conquered that Rosa Luxemburg saw as the condition for capitalism's survival. Violence, fraud, oppression, and war are also used *against* the wage laborers in the "wealthy" North, which until then had benefitted, in one way or another, from the pillaging of the "Third World." Contemporary financial capitalism has brought back to the fore the critique of primitive accumulation initiated by Rosa Luxemburg. The most visible one, by David Harvey, with his concept of "accumulation by dispossession," hopes to distinguish itself from the reduction of primitive accumulation to an "original stage" to be surpassed (Marx) or its projection into the "external" reality at the center of capitalism (Rosa Luxemburg). Harvey stays in the framework of Marxist analysis since he accepts the "progressist" function of capital, identified as industrial capital and the primitive accumulation that opens the path for it. The "accumulation by dispossession" carried out by financial capital and based on the expropriation of the "holders of resources" is on the contrary denounced to the extent that it attacks industrial development.

"While the class violence was abhorrent," primitive accumulation *nonetheless* represents the possibility to "liberate creative energies, open up society to strong currents of technological and organizational change, and overcome a world based on superstition and ignorance and replace it with a world of scientific enlightenment with the potentiality to liberate people from material want and need."[92] This is reminiscent of a famous passage of the *Communist Manifesto*, which has been brought back into fashion by the "Accelerationists." In particular since these "positive aspects" of primitive accumulation are still being verified in the contemporary world, where it is still directly at work. Thus, in the 1980s, the industrialization of a country like Indonesia would have opened "opportunities" for the population that de-industrialization, triggered by the financial crisis of 1997–1998, in large part destroyed. Which "did far more damage to the long-term hopes, aspirations, and possibilities" of this country: does primitive accumulation lead to industrialization or financial de-industrialization?, asks Harvey. While he recognizes their correlation, primitive accumulation bringing "more positive change" remains one thing and "accumulation by dispossession that disrupts and destroys a path already opened up is quite another."[93] What Harvey calls "de-industrialization" is in reality a complete reconfiguration of the international division of labor, of which financial capital was the strategic head, and not the "parasite." This "fictive capital" brought home the new regime of accumulation where dispossession of the "holders of resources" and the exploitation of wage labor, war, violence, pillage, and the most real economy coexist at an unprecedented level.

The true war machine of capital is financialization, of which "industrial" capital is only a component, completely restructured and subordinate to the demands of "fictive" capital. Contemporary capitalism reverses Marx's formula where rent is a part of profit, since it is in fact profit that is derived from rent. For this reason, the Marxist analysis of contemporary capitalism developed by Harvey leads to particularly weak political propositions. By preserving the most classic distinction between industrial capital and financial capital, Harvey is forced to invent a political dialectic to reunite what he first separated, the "struggles in the field of expanded reproduction,"[94] in other words the classical struggles of the labor movement, and the struggles against accumulation by dispossession carried out by the "alter-globalist" movements. Avoiding the political question imposed by the hegemony of financial capital, in other words, the impossibility of distinguishing between accumulation by exploitation and "accumulation by dispossession" is the same as disregarding the war of/in the economy.

Not a Marxist, and therefore reticent towards the progressism of capital, Hannah Arendt gave an appraisal of imperialism, from the colonial wars of the nineteenth century to the total wars of the first half of the twentieth century, which was revealed by the hegemony of financial capital:

The decisive point about the depressions of the sixties and seventies, which initiated the era of imperialism, was that they forced the bourgeoisie to realize for the first time that the original sin of simple robbery, which centuries ago have made possible the "original accumulation of capital" (Marx) and had started all further accumulation, had eventually to be repeated lest the motor of accumulation suddenly die down. In the face of this danger, which threatened not only the bourgeoisie but the whole nation with a catastrophic breakdown in production, capitalist producers understood that the forms and laws of their production system "from the beginning had been calculated for the whole earth" (Rosa Luxemburg).[95]

3

APPROPRIATION OF THE WAR MACHINE

Contrary to what the liberals assert, state sovereignty was a vital condition for the formation of capitalism. For at least two reasons. First, because capital, to solidify its power over the world-economy, needed, for a long time, certainly until the 1970s, the territories of the nation-state. The second reason, however, is even more decisive since it fell to no one other than the state to order the expropriation and reorganization of the war machines of the feudal period, and as such to engage in what should be called, following Foucault, the "statification of war." The state centralizes, controls, and professionalizes the practices and institutions of war between states; it prohibits the confrontations of "private war,"[1] to the point of holding the monopoly on external war between states and securing control of civil war inside its borders. The analyses of Deleuze-Guattari and Foucault converge at this very point: the appropriation, institutionalization, and professionalization of the war machine were done by the state.

3.1 State of War

Why did the constitution of Capital pass through the state-form, asks Deleuze. Its development could have passed through the cities, when everything, or almost, as the liberals ceaselessly repeat, seemed to oppose Capital and State. Fernand Braudel notes that cities, at the beginning, were one of the most decisive factors in the development of capitalism: banking cities, trading cities, city-states. Unlike Asia where cities were subordinate to the state, in Europe, the cities and states were opposed and engaged in latent or bloody struggle from which the state apparatuses emerged victorious by seizing their "city-dwelling" adversaries.

To describe the nature of this struggle, Braudel uses the image of a race between two runners: the hare represents the city and the tortoise, the state. They advance at different speeds, since the city has a greater power of deterritorialization than the state. We can think here of the network structure of negotiating bills of exchange superposed over the economy of cities with the private banks that support large-scale trade, constitute the nerve center of markets and trade, regulate the circulation of precious metals throughout Europe... How then can we explain that the state-form defeated the city-form? Why did the least "dynamic" deterritorialization triumph, when the power of capitalistic projection of commercial capitalism, which is also manufacturing capitalism, was so strong, and when cities were the very basis of the European Renaissance?

According to Deleuze, who read the historians closely, the determining factor depended on the fact that "the city-form is not a good instrument of appropriation for the war machine. It essentially needs quick wars using mercenaries. The city cannot make heavy investments in war."[2] Moreover, between the fifteenth and eighteenth centuries, war underwent a *military revolution* which was at one and the same time technological, tactical, strategic, and conceptual. It would take place on land and sea by mobilizing concentrations of people and materials that had never been seen before. The qualitative and quantitative progress in artillery (muskets, molded bronze or forged iron cannons...) combined with the growing importance of firepower on the battlefield (musket salvos, mobile field cannons, siege artillery) would impose the primacy of infantry over cavalry by bringing an end to the reign of medieval chivalry. They also transformed the architecture of fortresses by imposing much larger (thicker, lower, broader) fortifications (in geometrical shapes) defended by "corner bastions" armed with several artillery pieces (the "artillery fortress") and which then led to the construction of an entire chain of siege engines accompanied by solid and wide lines of defense to protect assailants and guarantee their supplies. Thus the principle of *siege warfare* which *installed* this contradictory militarization of territory along with the parceling out of space (creation of permanent armies, construction of garrisons to house and watch them, organization of the logistics necessary for feeding the growth of troops, development of paths of communication) by infinitely extending the time of war in a strategy of attrition with "patient accumulation of minor victories" aimed at the "slow erosion of the enemy's economic base."[3] According to the observation of Robert Boyle, author of a *Treatise on the Art of War*, published in London in 1677: "Battells do not now decide national quarrels [...], as formerly. For we make war more like foxes, than like lyons; and you will have twenty sieges for one battell." His observation can be related to the commentary of a Grandee of Spain, the Marquis of Aytona, in 1630: "The manner of making war at the present time is reduced to a sort of traffic or commerce, in which he who has the most money wins."[4]

Yet while the victorious tortoise borrows the characteristics of the *silver fox* who is capable of undergoing the financial test of strength of military power[5] and imposing it on the population (with its lot of "subsistence crises"), it is still necessary for its *coulée* (since that is the name in French of the network of paths regularly frequented by the animal) to lead outside the European continent and its strategic impasse to spread into the sea—and overseas. "'In the present state of Europe,' wrote the Duke of Choiseul, chief minister of France in the 1760s, 'it is colonies, trade and, in consequence, sea power which must determine the balance of power upon the continent.'"[6] The military revolution also allowed mastery of the seas (sea power), with the appearance of large warships heavily armed with cannons (muzzle-fed and no longer breech-fed,[7] and placed on carriages) deployed in batteries and on several levels along the entire ship: they were veritable "floating fortresses," which could be reduced in size to increase their mobility. The economic-strategic-political rise of naval construction elicited the installation of heavily fortified and armed naval bases on the continent and overseas, without which the protection of maritime routes towards the colonies of America and Asia would not be ensured, and from which *commerce raiding*,[8] the sharpest tool of the "fleet in being," could be launched. While the sea is "principal among smooth spaces,"[9] bringing a power of deterritorialization invested since Antiquity by trading cities, one can also understand that only states could successfully carry out the military-merchant striation of the seas by raising it to the level of a first imperialist globalization that involved the permanent presence of ocean fleets. Their costs were so exorbitant that they could only engage the Atlantic states of Europe by maintaining their fierce rivalry—until the most maritime nation, for which "there was no short cut to supreme naval power,"[10] won the decisive victory that would allow the military revolution to be continued into the industrial revolution.

This economic war of "infrastructures" and "services," these investments in war required by the defensive and offensive arms race imposed nothing less than the absolutist figure of the modern state to finance and administer them. The military establishment of the state requires a "career" army (with a formation in *units, mass* training, a new military hierarchy privileging combat effectiveness) and a permanent administration, a codified legislation concerning private property which is given a legally unconditional character and which is "administered," and finally a market unified by territorial integration allowing an apparatus for imposing national taxes, such as the *taille royale* aimed at financing the first regular military units in Europe (it was the first national tax collected in France). If what Marx called "the well-regulated plan of a government [where] work is subdivided and centralized as in the factory"[11] was constituted at the time of absolute monarchy by distributing throughout the territory the attributes of a state of police, a military state, a fiscal state, an administrative state, a manufacturer-entrepreneur state of major public works, and a colonial state, the reason is that the mercantilist state caught in an "international system of states" (to use Porchnev's expression) is above all the effect of the military revolution which seals the new indistinction between economy and politics by victory over the city that it *subordinates (inféode) at the national level.* Or to put it another way, in relation with the question of feudalism and the "classical" Marxist position (in truth more Engelsian than properly Marxian) it remains prisoner of the thesis of "feudal absolutism" (also found up until Althusser) given the fact of the supposed "archaic rationality," essentially feudal, of the *absolutist* function of war[12]: the state subordinates and "nationalizes" cities by *militarizing war*, which deterritorializes and reterritorializaes at an unprecedented level the organic unity of the economy and politics of feudalism, which the cities had "escaped." From there, the state-tortoise, which becomes a fox and then a water-fox, can *surpass* the city-hare that owed its existence to "the unique 'detotalization' of sovereignty within the politico-economic order of feudalism."[13] Here we have reached the logic of power and potency of mercantilism, which is perfectly summarized by Giovanni Arrighi: "War-making and state-making were becoming an increasingly roundabout business which involved an ever-growing number, range, and variety of seemingly unrelated activities."[14]

Thus states appropriated the war machine by transforming war into war of materiel and by organizing "national conscription," in other words the generalized disciplinarization of "men" on the basis of personal military service corresponding to obligations that are no longer collective, placed under the sole authority of intermediate bodies (provinces, cities, trades), but individual. Through this new economy of power which, with the surveillance of the territory that comes with it, passes through the development of the military institution, the tortoise finally catches and knocks out the hare. Investments in the war industry are revealed to be of primary importance from a capitalist point of view: not only because they are quickly confirmed as one of the most important sources of technological and scientific innovation after having imposed the "uniformization" of arms production throughout the seventeenth century, but also in that they are vital to the "realization of surplus value." The war machine is in fact a machine of anti-production without which capitalism would collapse, from both the political and economic point of view. From this dual perspective, capitalism is consubstantially a war economy because all of the analytics of war and its multi-part machinery are necessary to close the "cycle of surplus value" from the workshop subject to military disciplinarization of its activity to the tax income of the state which feeds the colonial enterprises and allows land-use planning.

Foucault, who mentions without developing it a difference in nature between the "*militaire*" and "*homme de guerre*" that is similar to the distinction between the war machine and the state-military institution for Deleuze and Guattari, adds an important precision: between the seventeenth and eighteenth centuries, the goal of the war machine was not only war but also "peace," in other words the production of wealth, the organization of cities, territories, etc. In the major European states subject to permanent sedition, the army ensured civil peace by the constant threat of the use of force, "but also because it was a technique and a body of knowledge that could project their schema over the social body."

The hesitations, the doubts, the reversals of Foucault in thinking that war could constitute the "cypher" of power relationships are very instructive in that they require him to multiply the different versions of reversal. "It may be that war as strategy is a continuation of politics. But it must not be forgotten that 'politics' has been conceived as a continuation, if not exactly and directly of war, at least of the military model as a fundamental means of preventing civil disorder. Politics, as a technique of internal peace and order, sought to implement the mechanism of the perfect army, of the disciplined mass [...]."[15]

The army and the military institution were established "at the point of junction between war and the noise of battle on the one hand, and order and silence, subservient to peace, on the other."[16] The military institution thus constitutes a two-fold technique of power: it guarantees and maintains the equilibrium between European states (war as continuation of politics passing through the confrontation of the economic and demographic forces of nations), while it ensures discipline and order within each state (politics as continuation of war by other means).

While at the time of professionalization of the army, the first disciplinary techniques were put in place in Europe, during the Classical Age, the "disciplinary system of the army" organized the "general confiscation of the body, time and life" by means of "exercises that rationalize and discipline both individual movements using weapons and collective movements on the battlefield."[17] After being subject to a tabular arithmetic in treatises on strategy,[18] these treatises produced "a geometry of divisible segments whose basic unity was the mobile soldier with his rifle; and [...] below the soldier himself, the minimal gestures, the elementary stages of action, the fragments of spaces occupied or traversed."[19] It was therefore a question—Foucault insists—of inventing a *machinery* that could be built on for "constituting a productive force whose effect had to be superior to the sum of the elementary forces that composed it."[20]

Disciplinary techniques are unthinkable without the army, without the discipline carried by the military institution and the knowledge of those it "administered," which opened the way to the modes of operation of an economic administrative power in the very forms of the architecture of military power. "While jurists or philosophers were seeking in the pact a primal model for the construction or reconstruction of the social body, the soldiers and with them the technicians of discipline were elaborating procedures for the individual and collective coercion of bodies."[21]

3.2 The Art and Manner of War in Adam Smith

It fell to Adam Smith, and not Marx, to be the first to thematize the relationship between "wealth," "power," and centralization of the use of armed force by the state. A *strong* state. Go figure then why this man of the Scottish Enlightenment is considered the great theorist of *soft commerce (le doux commerce)* and the "fundamental pacifism" of the liberal tradition that is attached to him all the way to Schumpeter... Here, it will be enough for us to follow the military march of his demonstration performed wholeheartedly in the *Wealth of Nations.*

As the condition of a "civilized and opulent" nation, the law of the Sovereign must first and foremost bring about the centralization of power and the army. Definitive control by the state of the permanent war waged in society, the bringing in line of the *militias*,[22] and the institutionalization of the war machines inherited from feudalism into "a well-regulated standing army" are at the heart of this process of centralization. The historical accuracy of the reconstitution is less important than the arrangement it allows between the "division of labor" (present in manufacturing and trade *as in the art of war*) and power. The conclusion of this process is decisive for the accumulation of wealth: modern wars create a synergy between "power and wealth," between the military domain and industry which establishes an asymmetry of power between wealthy and poor nations, condition and cause of the accumulation of "great properties" in the first at the expense of the latter (colonialism, imperialism).

"In ancient times" characterized by being "almost in a continual state of war,"[23] "feudal law" established a first "regular subordination, accompanied with a long train of services and duties, from the king down to the smallest proprietor." Yet authority remained "too weak in the head and too strong in the inferior members," such that these members "continued to make war according to their own discretion, almost continually upon one another, and very frequently upon the king; and the open country still continued to be a scene of violence, rapine, and disorder."

Trade and manufacturing "gradually introduced order and good government, and with them, the liberty and security of individuals"[24] where feudal law had failed. This should not lead us to believe, as the liberals would have it, that this process was guided by the invisible hand of the market. It can only be brought about by the state since its duty to protect liberty and security "can only be performed by means of a [*sovereign*] military force." In ancient times, "every man [...] either is a warrior, or easily becomes such,"[25] while in "a more advanced state of society, [...] the progress of manufactures and the improvement in the art of war"[26] made necessary the specialization of an army under the orders of the state.

In each case, the "division of labor" is involved, but in different ways in the case of manufacturing and in the case of war. An "artificer, a smith, a carpenter, or a weaver" cannot make good soldiers because they are completely absorbed in work and "so very expensive and tedious a service would otherwise be far too heavy a burden upon them." Yet "the art of war, however, as it is certainly the noblest of all arts, so in the progress of improvement it necessarily becomes one of the most complicated among them. The state of the mechanical, as well as some other arts, with which it is necessarily connected" requires that the art of war "become the sole or principal occupation of a particular class of citizens, and the division of labor is as necessary for this, as of every other art." In conclusion: the division of labor in the art of war can only be ensured by "the state only which can render the trade of a soldier a particular trade separate and distinct from all others," while "into the other arts the division of labor is naturally introduced by the prudence of individuals." In a nation worthy of this name, the creation of a "well-regulated standing army" is indispensable to establishing "with an irresistible force, the law of the sovereign through the remotest provinces of the empire, and maintains some degree of regular government in countries which could not otherwise admit of any."[27]

Military law and the law of civil government must ward off civil wars internally and pursue imperialist wars externally that are required by the accumulation of wealth, power, and force. Adam Smith does not express himself in this way, of course, but he develops this logic in a scarcely more concealed (or "homeopathic," to use the term Marx used to describe it) manner.

The civil code and the military code maintain "some degree of regular government," not to defend "liberty and security" in general, but the property and property owners both inside and outside the sovereign state. "Wherever there is great property there is great inequality. For one very rich man there must be at least five hundred poor, and the affluence of the few supposes the indigence of the many." This inevitably leads to the *envy* of the poor and their limitless desire to take for themselves the goods of the wealthy which can only be preserved by civil government and the military force serving it. "It is only under the shelter of the civil magistrate that the owner of that valuable property [...] can sleep a single night in security. He is at all times surrounded by unknown enemies" and will be "protected only by the powerful arm of the civil magistrate continually held up to chastise it. [...] Where there is no property, or at least none that exceeds the value of two or three days labor, civil government is not so necessary."[28]

We could not have said it better: it is not the (Hobbesian) "nature" of people that is the cause of civil war but property and the social division of labor which are neither "fair" nor "equal." Or in other words: the "serenity of [the] happiness" of the rich must be protected against the "misery and distress" of the poor."[29] Public education of the "working poor" as promoted by Adam Smith had no other goal than to *force the multitude to follow reason* by cutting it off from its "most extravagant and groundless pretensions."[30]

The accumulation of great wealth does not only occur by exploiting the labor of others in manufactures, but also through the expropriation, pillage, and predation of the poorest and most "barbarous" nations. This indissociably colonial and imperialist capitalization is no less economic than political and military. It is not for nothing that Adam Smith engages the state and its army in the service of the "wealth of nations"! The mechanization and industrialization of war (with the large-scale use of the latest generation of "war machines") are an essential component of "colonial" accumulation, since they create the differences in power between rich and poor nations that translate into differences in wealth.

> In modern wars, the great expense of firearms gives an evident advantage to the nation which can best afford that expense, and consequently to an opulent and civilized over a poor and barbarous nation. In ancient times, the opulent and civilized found it difficult to defend themselves against the poor and barbarous nations. In modern times, the poor and barbarous find it difficult to defend themselves against the opulent and civilized. The invention of firearms, an invention which at first sight appears to be so pernicious, is certainly favorable both to the permanency and to the extension of civilization.[31]

The reasoning here is the same as for the division of labor: despite the inequality that it creates, it is supposed to produce a general opulence that will end up spreading even to the "lowest members of society." Colonialism is the historical truth of this entire process which, lest we forget, is that of primitive accumulation continued in "industrial capitalism" under military preparation. The "civilization of peoples" is nothing other than the accumulation of Capital. Thanks to military asymmetry, it never stopped being exercised as the use of the most "modern" armed force at the expense of nations that were the least modern. Militarized protector of the wealth of accumulation, internal security becomes *militarist* under the sustained barrage of its projection on the outside.

While spending on the army and war financed by manufacturing and trade were continuously augmented, Adam Smith still considered them "unproductive." Knowing that "military Keynesianism" has been a constant component of accumulation since the Italian city-states,[32] it is interesting that he does not consider military spending by the state as a productive investment multiplying wealth for the unequal trade of the British Empire. As paradoxical as it might seem, the explanation refers to the stratification of "military force" that underpins the imperialist demonstration of the wealth of nations for which the "modernity" no longer passes through Italian cities. Our debt to the late Giovanni Arrighi and his *post-Marxist reading* of Adam Smith should be clear to see.

4

TWO HISTORIES OF THE FRENCH REVOLUTION

4.1 Clausewitz's French Revolution

The first sequence of exercising the armed violence of/in internal and external colonization ended with the French Revolution. From the perspective of the war machine, Clausewitz is the one who was the most rigorous in seizing on this event: European equilibrium, the way to wage war and organize the army to guarantee international order, and legal-military administration in civil peace in each nation were definitively rebuked by the Revolution. Revolutionary events confirmed the difference in nature between the state and the war machine, since the latter escaped, for a brief moment, from state control—validating the hypothesis that it is always possible for the war machine to turn against the state.

Starting with the French Revolution, a second political sequence began. New social forces, workers and capitalists, attempted to appropriate the war machine and the state for themselves. The post-Revolution was first characterized by the success of the bourgeoisie in reorganizing both the state and the war machine around the interests of capital and then by the failure of the revolutionary movements that attempted to appropriate and transform the war machine and the state throughout the nineteenth century.

Let's go back to the turning point between the first and second sequences represented by the French Revolution. "This was the state of affairs at the outbreak of the French Revolution. [...] in 1793 a force appeared that beggared all imagination. Suddenly war again became the business of the people—a people of thirty millions, all of whom considered themselves to be citizens. [...] The resources and efforts now available for use surpassed all conventional limits."[1]

The war machine was no longer of "cabinets and armies," it was no longer the army of the Prince or King, "of these heralded generals and kings [...] at the head of equally heralded armies" in which "violence gradually faded away,"[2] but "army of the people, of the nation." While "very few of the new manifestations in war can be ascribed to new inventions or new departures in ideas [...] they result mainly from the transformation of society and new social conditions," as Clausewitz heavily emphasizes,[3] Napoleon is the marker that takes the Revolution back in hand, passing through the investment of revolutionary energy in the "Grande Armée." He exploited the revolutionary mobilization to turn the art of war and the balance of European states upside down, and enclose the momentum of the revolution in the new form of the nation-state that he *mobilizes*. War no longer has limits, not for immanent reasons, as René Girard believes (the "rise to extremism" having as its cause the mimeticism of the armies in conflict),[4] but because the conflict is invested by new political forces—in the sense, Clausewitz underlines, of "the new political conditions which the French Revolution created both in France and in Europe as a whole."[5] The new army resulting from the Revolution brings war closer to its pure concept ("absolute war") by bringing a fusion between politics and war in favor of an escalation of a first *imperialist politics of national war*, "waged without respite until the enemy succumbed" and based on "the peoples' new share in these great affairs of state."[6] "Since Bonaparte, then, war, first among the French and subsequently among their enemies, again became the concern of the people as a whole, took on an entirely different character, or rather closely approached its true character, its absolute perfection. There seemed no end to the resources mobilized; all limits disappeared in the vigor and enthusiasm shown by governments and their subjects."[7]

The difficulty of imposing limits starts to appear as much in the balance between states in Europe as in liberal economic regulation and in war, *which diverges at the same time from its (presumed) classical political regulation* inscribed in the meeting point between the military objective and the political goal constituted by the modality of returning to peace (war as "merely the continuation of policy by other means,"[8] according to the Formula of the *political goal of war*). For this reason, Clausewitz wanted to reinsert it in the Kantian perspective of a *Critique of Military Reason* to attempt to submit the "rise to extremes" to "the intelligence of the state personified"[9] which named the political representative of the interests of the entire community ("It can be taken that the aim of policy is to unify and reconcile all aspects of internal administration as well as spiritual values, and whatever else the moral philosopher may care to add. Policy, of course, is nothing in itself; it is simply the trustee for all these interests against other states").[10] An empty hypothesis, since beyond the defeat of the "God of War himself,"[11] the movement to surpass all limits seals the impossibility of founding limits in reason in the domain of "social existence" that includes war, which can be compared by Clausewitz to "commerce" (isn't it also a "conflict of human interests and activities"?).[12] If there is commerce, it is a commerce of the unlimited. It would spread to the entire *socius* with the advent of industrial capital, and gathered even more speed in the 1870s under the hegemony of financial capital, leading to "total war." While this concept and reality are undoubtedly much different than the "absolute war" of Clausewitz, since its emergence depended for him, the one defeated in the Battle of Jena, on the "monstrous effects [*ungeheueren Wirkungen*]" of the energies liberated by revolutionary politics and the Napoleonic administration of the intensities of the state of war. Clausewitz wants to think that these "absolute energies" will not necessarily condition the condition of subsequent wars and that they will return to the pre-Bonapartist status quo between "civilized nations" where "destruction of the enemy cannot be the military aim."

"Just in time, the reaction set in. The Spanish War spontaneously became the concern of the people."[13] The techniques of the offensive wars of the Great Army—that some have called "motorized" before its time, with its "reservoir" of human resources and "multivalent" soldiers integrated into relatively autonomous columns[14]—would in fact elicit new forms of resistance ("*guerrilla*") and especially a new *function for popular resistance* that Clausewitz, before Schmitt, considers to be such an absolute novelty from his Eurocentric perspective[15] that it redefines the goal of war: "his *immediate* aim is to *throw* his opponent in order to make him incapable of further resistance."[16] Thus the "character of modern [absolute] war" distinguishes itself strategically between, on the one hand, the Bonapartist revolution of "all the conventional ancient methods" of the art of war by militarization of the people in arms and, on the other hand, the resistance (*Widerstand*) of popular war (*Volkskrieg*) of the Spanish which is the consequence[17] of the first and that must be integrated, with its "moral factor," in the new *plan of war.* "When a whole nation renders armed resistance, the question then is no longer, 'Of what value is this to the people,' but 'what is its potential value, what are the conditions that it requires, and how is it to be utilized.'"[18]

With its "vaporous" and "fluid" component, which leads to a veritable *Treatise on Resistance* in Clausewitz, "guerrilla" opens the perspective of popular war through which communists, anarchists, and socialists would long consider the possibility of revolution.

4.2 The Haitian Revolution

Clausewitz's astuteness is undermined by one of the major political and military events of the French Revolution: the Haitian Revolution that captured the jewel of the French colonial empire, Saint-Domingue. It was also the wealthiest and most prosperous colony in the world.[19] Nothing less. Thus it could also be the most *fundamental* "event" of the Revolution[20] by the power of "ungrounding (*effondement*)" (to speak Deleuzian) that appears there: the *unthinkable* broke into History, which became *global* from a revolutionary perspective.

The first victorious proletarian revolution was a slave revolution. After the French Republic was obliged to accept it as a *fait accompli*, the revolution not only resisted the troops sent to the island in 1801 by Napoleon to reestablish order and slavery under the *Code noir*, it crushed them (inflicting 50,000 casualties— or much more than the French losses at Waterloo), just as it had crushed the Spanish and English armies. From the first revolt of 1791 to the declaration of independence on January 1, 1804, over a period of twelve years, the revolution of the 500,000 slaves of Saint-Domingue, which became Haiti, emerged politically and militarily victorious from confrontations with the three dominant colonial powers of the world-economy. Long before the Red Soviet and Chinese armies, the "Black army" was the first proletarian force to profoundly revolutionize the art of war. "They had the organization and discipline of a trained army, and at the same time all the tricks and dodges of guerrillas. [...] When the French sent large expeditions against them they disappeared in the mountains, leaving a trail of flames behind them, returning when the weary French retreated, to destroy still more plantations and carry their attacks into the French lines."[21] The very Clausewitzian style used by C.L.R. James should not blind us to the fact that we are touching something here that was unthinkable for the Prussian officer, who was able to measure the Spanish resistance in European geopolitics. It goes beyond his understanding that uneducated slaves "constitutionally incapable of discipline and freedom," were able to learn the most sophisticated techniques of war quickly and place them at the service of a relentless guerrilla after performing Voodoo rituals![22]

The "slaves" invented revolutionary war as war of the people by appropriating the conditions and modalities of the Napoleonic wars described by Clausewitz to reverse their process of "involution" and fight the *Code noir* (it was reestablished by Napoleon in 1802 in the French colonies, without major opposition in metropolitan France and to the great relief of England and the United States). "Generals," "officers," and "soldiers" were all part of the same, *new* social class, that of the "people" of slave-combatants who were all equally "leaders." (After Napoleon had Toussaint L'Ouverture arrested: *"Taking Toussaint is not enough; there are 2000 chiefs to capture here"*). They overturned the essence of colonial war, the genocidal/total war against the population, by asserting (and composing) the principle of existence of the latter as revolutionary force raised against the "people's army" of the new imperialism. "It was a war not so much of armies as of the people."[23]

Clausewitz's perspective on the new nature of Napoleon's armies guides the analysis of C.L.R. James *up to a point*: their force "did not fall from the sky, nor were his soldiers entirely the product of [Napoleon's] own unparalleled genius for military command. [...] Their irresistible élan, their intelligence, their endurance and morale, sprang from the new social freedom."[24] The slaves had indeed been at the French revolutionary school, but unlike the Napoleonic armies, they did not represent the leading edge of the retaking of control of the revolution by the bourgeoisie, nor the war machine of counter-revolution. They were able to establish a strategy to break with every offer of new governmentality in which the tactical maneuvers of the insurgent "headquarters" under the command of Toussaint sought to insert itself.[25]

While the Black revolution of Saint-Domingue found its roots in the French Revolution, and while the former's success would have been impossible without the latter, the slave revolution was no less a critique in action of Enlightenment ideals. The slave struggles were able to extract the principles of "liberty and equality" from the illusory universality of bourgeois liberty and equality. In the first constitution of Haiti (1805), *all Haitians*, no matter what the color of their skin or their origin, were declared *Black* (including the Germans and Polish who had fought Napoleon's armies alongside the insurgents). We should note in passing that such a *revolution of the subject* uniquely relativizes the long-debated question of "the" difference between the American and English revolutions on the one hand, and the French Revolution on the other. Hannah Arendt distinguishes the primacy of "politics" in the American Revolution as opposed to the "social" nature of the French Revolution; Foucault adjusts this by borrowing from Furet: the freedom of the "governed" from the governing would be the distinctive aspect of the American Revolution, while the French one would be characterized by the centralizing axiomatic of "human rights." In fact, the question of slavery, which underpinned the entire world-economy, indicates *the zone in which both only exist in the form of an idea* (of freedom).

As Susan Buck-Morris has noted in her remarkable *Hegel, Haiti and Universal History*, the Enlightenment critique of slavery addresses it as an institution, not as the reality of its exploitation and enslavement of millions of men, women, and children. "The paradox between the discourse of freedom and the practice of slavery marked the ascendancy of a succession of Western nations within the early modern global economy."[26] From Holland of the sixteenth century to the Franco-British seventeenth century, slavery became such a strategic metaphor for expressing all of the forms of domination *in Europe* that it could coexist without any difficulty with its practice *in the colonies* (Locke) of "opulent and civilized" nations (Adam Smith). The "naturalness" of slavery was just as "natural" as the liberty of "man" for the thinkers of the Enlightenment (including Rousseau), as Susan Buck-Morris observes. The abolition of slavery was not an application of principles or even a "dynamic" within the French Revolution: "while even the most ardent opponents of slavery within France dragged their feet, the half-million slaves in Saint-Domingue [...] took the struggle for liberty into their own hands."[27]

The fascinating (and rigorously documented) thesis of *Hegel, Haiti and Universal History* according to which the master-slave dialectic stems from reflection on the Black revolution of Haiti may be subject to debate. Yet the essential point lies elsewhere: the fact that for Marx the "struggle between master and slave" was not used literally, but only as a metaphor of class struggle was unquestionably a missed opportunity for removing Marxism from the eurocentrism found in the "Mancunian" definition of Capital (Susan Buck-Morris goes even further: "There is an element of racism implicit in official Marxism").[28]

While Marx analyzed and *problematized* this revolution, the many impasses into which the labor movement fell could have been, if not avoided, then at least confronted according to a completely different configuration of the *reality of possibilities*. The lesson could have been learned that the first victorious proletarian revolution was the act of a "race war" carried out by "non-salaried" workers. Then, including the "non-salaried" without forgetting the work of women would have allowed all "free" and non-salaried labor to be the source of collective inventions contributing to detaching the theory of the "value" of Capital from the all-too-visible mark that bourgeois political economy had imprinted on it. This narrow point of view, focused on salaried labor and capitalist enterprise, continues to weigh heavily on the way the struggles and development of political strategies of emancipation take place.

The Haitian Revolution, *like all revolutions that succeed*, did not take place at the most technologically advanced point of capitalist development, but where it was "behind" in its intrinsic transformations and contradictions, in "colonies" (since China and Russia of the revolutionary period could be considered "semi-colonies"). The "progressist" and "revolutionary" concept of capitalism and the bourgeoisie could have been seriously challenged, as the very existence of the slave colonies makes them unintelligible (or all too intelligible).

Taking the point of view of the "social division of labor" and not that of the organization of labor alone, the "great experiment" in Haiti becomes even more important. The "race war" at the foundation of the world-economy of capital since primitive accumulation was won by slaves by opening the global political action to the rallying cry of "Proletarians of every nation, unite!" Only on the condition that "of every nation" reaches beyond the borders of Europe and deploys its "internationalism." The abolition of slavery did not abolish race war, which has on the contrary continued until today "by other means" (like slavery itself). Its power of "racist" division is manifested in each "crisis" of capitalism (as we said in the introduction: racism is not a "biopolitical" creation of "modernity" but of the oldest primitive accumulation in its infinite continuity).

They say Lenin celebrated the day when the Russian Revolution had lasted longer than the few weeks of existence of the Paris Commune. What could be said then of a process of revolutionary insurrection over twelve years? Even today, Alain Badiou refers to Spartacus to thematize the revolt of slave-combatants and celebrate in Toussaint—the "Black Spartacus"—the resurrection of an "eternal truth." Except this one turns *historically* against the precedent of Thracian slaves wanting to *return home*, as opposed to the Haitian revolutionaries who wanted to *destroy the entire world of slave plantations.*[29]

"Forgotten" by European revolutionaries of the working class, the Haitian Revolution was brought back to the fore by anticolonialist militants as the *momentum* of emancipation of Blacks, African regeneration, and the revolutionary politics of decolonization. "By making an intentional anachronism, we could say that the Third World started to form in Saint-Domingue. Our inspiration here comes from the idea of

Sauvy—who compared the Third World to the Tiers État because it was 'ignored, exploited, disdained' like it. The planet being divided into First, Second, and Third Worlds, with this Third World also wanting to 'become something.'"[30] Because things always happen *late or early* (think here of the "modern proletariat" of giant sugar cane "factories," more proletarian and more modern than "any group of workers at the time," according to C.L.R. James), *nothing developed there* in the sense of a Marxism whose meaning would be given relative to the (teleo-)logic of the capitalist process. *Black Marxism.* Toussaint—or *the opening* (l'ouverture) *and the breach* in the multiplicity of wars of exploitation, domination, and subjection that institute the biopolitical regime of continuous accumulation of Capital.

5

BIOPOLITICS OF PERMANENT CIVIL WAR

5.1 The Temporal Sequestration of the Working Class (and Society as a Whole)

Sheltered from the dangers of the Revolution, placed under the auspices of the Restauration, did capital develop "peacefully"? For liberal ideology, the response is in the affirmative, without hesitation. In 1814, year of the defeat of Napoleon's armies that for Carl Schmitt coincides with the "victory of the Industrial Revolution," Benjamin Constant uttered one of the first refrains of liberalism: "We have arrived in the era of commerce, a time that must necessarily replace the era of war, just as the era of war replaced the one before it."[1]

The history of the nineteenth and twentieth centuries shows that he was wrong. Throughout the nineteenth century, the "civilized calculation" of economics in no way replaced the "savage impulse" of war; on the contrary, it triggered civil war to transform the proletariat into a submissive labor force and thrust the nation-state into a new type of war: *total* imperialist war, which is at one and the same time interstate war, economic war, civil war, and colonial war.

The continuation of "primitive accumulation" in the so-called post-revolutionary period is found in the intensification of internal colonization (formation of the industrial labor force involving generalized civil wars and new wars of subjectivity) and of external colonization (the long century of the repeal of slavery coincided with an extension of colonization to cover almost the entire planet). Coupled with the power of industrial Capital and the development of science and technology, the multiple violence of racial, sexual, and class divisions and the wars to which they led crossed a new threshold.

In the nineteenth century, the "subjective" training (*dressage*) of proletarians to attach them to the apparatus of production by normalizing their behavior and their ways of life in order to transform a lifetime into "labor time" could only take place with the start of a "generalized civil war." We prefer the term "civil war," with Foucault, over that of "class struggle" because "permanent civil war," "generalized civil war," the denial of which is one of the first axioms of the exercise of power, implies a series of powers and knowledge, but also forces and institutions that cannot be reduced to the conflict between workers and capitalists inside the factory, *even though they are a constitutive element of the mode of production.*

Biopower acts on a population that has already been subjected to a first wave of training by means of disciplinary and biopolitical techniques, which are historically indistinguishable from all the demonstrations of force of the primitive war of accumulation. This first modeling of behaviors revealed itself to be insufficient. By giving rise to forms of resistance and bitter struggles in the context of social crises and popular uprisings, the apparatuses of power and the wars of subjectivity in this sequence were far from ensuring a strong enough submission to the new world order of labor. The multiplication of measures of coercion in which savagery competes with *rigorous* economism bears witness to this at the end of the Classical Era, where the growth of wealth and goods encouraged the "need for security" at a time of strong expansion of the urban fabric that saw the proliferation of the urban proletariat. For the Physiocrats, the vagabond thus becomes a figure of the devil of anti-production that needs to be hunted, marked, placed in forced labor, reduced to slavery, and more. The explanation is that the danger the vagabond represents for the *political economy* of production is that of "enemy troops spreading over the surface of the territory, living as they wish, as in a conquered country, exacting levies under the name of alms."[2] According to another version, only a few years later, which presages the famous expression about proletarians having "nothing to lose but their chains," vagabonds are beings "avid for novelty, audacious, and similarly more enterprising insofar as they have nothing to lose and are habituated to the idea of punishment that they merit each day; interested in revolution of the state, which alone can change their situation, they fervently take any opportunity to incite a disturbance."[3] As the exclusively disciplinary structure of the negative paradigm of the vagabond was not enough, the need was seen to adjust the mechanisms of power to have them take charge of daily conduct and place it under surveillance in a tighter structuring of the social body without which the *salary-form* cannot frame the entire *socius*.

In the nineteenth century, the power apparatuses *(dispositifs)* that ensure the production, reproduction, and governmentality of the working class were fundamentally two in number: family, and what Foucault calls "institutions of temporal sequestration." "Sequestration" is a concept that helps distinguish the nineteenth century from the Classical era of the "great confinement," as sequestration is less a question of space (by fixation in a closed system) than time (by controlling existence) which gives internal colonization a new impetus and a new hold, allowing the production of the labor force as an adequate subjective disposition for *the necessity for the freedom of labor.*[4]

For this reason, internal colonization did not focus on the disciplinarization of workers without combining it with a biopolitics that implicated women, children, beggars, criminals, the infirm, in other words, the entire population of the poor that had to be moralized and normalized by subjecting them to the "penalization of existence."[5] "Biopolitics" appears there as the apparatus multiplying power in the generalized civil war that it administrates and of which the object is the subject, in other words life. Not "naked life," but life in its increasingly qualified articulations and passages: family life, military life, school life, work life, hospital life, prison life, etc. The entire biopolitical economy of *equipped life* is traced here with its productive instances of "surplus-power" renewing in intensity as well as in extension the disciplinary model of the state structure deployed at present through all social mechanisms. Thus, the institution of work time presupposes the biopolitical control and disciplinarization of *all* temporalities. To restrict to "work time," the time of "life" must be disciplined, from birth until death. To impose the rhythms of production, *all* rhythms of life must be controlled, integrated, normalized, and moralized. "It was necessary to hunt down festive revelry, absenteeism, gambling, and notably the lottery as a bad relationship to time in expecting money from the discontinuity of chance rather than from the continuity of work. The worker had to be made to master chance in his life: illness, unemployment. To make him responsible for himself until death, he had to be taught the quality called foresight by offering him savings banks."[6]

The continuity between the "workshop clock, production line stopwatch, and prison calendar,"[7] which constitute the training of the labor force in the strict sense, implies a transversal disciplinarization to the time of production alongside the time of savings, the time of reproduction, and "free time." Time being the only "good" owned by proletarians, the worker exchanges (work) time for salary, while the "criminal" is constrained to exchange time (of freedom) to pay for a "crime" (most often against property). Marxism, up to the most innovative heterodoxic Marxism, moves in the opposite direction: capital first appropriates working time and then—after a long path leading in the end to the Second World War—exploit the time of life in "consumer society," and more intensely and diffusely in "post-Fordism."

With the Industrial revolution, we pass from the localization of individuals, in other words their attachment to a land (space) on which sovereignty can be exercised and from which rent can be taken, to a "temporal sequestration." "Sequestration" is a "temporal cycle" that captures individuals in a way that their life is always subject to the homogenizing time of capital, and that it is as a result thoroughly *socialized*. To think "temporal sequestration," we cannot look only at the spatialized apparatuses like the factory, school, hospital, etc. even if time regulates discipline there, or remain with the sole question of the "internalization" of the discipline of time.[8] "Savings banks, contingency funds" (related to what in the twentieth century would be called "welfare") represent apparatuses of control, disciplinarization, and production of social norms that attach proletarians to the temporalities and rhythms of capitalism while taking it in "a discursivity that takes up the quotidian, the individual, the personal, the body, and the sexual in a space defined by instances of sequestration. It is always from the point of view of the totality of time that the individual's life will be scoured and dominated."[9]

The institutions of temporal sequestration would be called "indiscreet" in that they involve things that do not concern them directly. They are also "syncretic," like in the example of the silk factories employing women analyzed by Foucault, since they impose behaviors that only seem to concern production indirectly: no interactions or working alongside men in the factory, but also no going out on Sunday... At the center of the activity in these institutions, there is always life in its entirety—in which work is caught and subjected to *a relationship of production that is first a power over life, taking power over existence.* To repeat: from this point of view, the social form of production and reproduction extended to society as a whole in its "real subsumption" is not, as such, an invention of post-Fordism.

"These institutions take responsibility for the direct or indirect control of existence. They fix on a certain number of points in existence, which are, generally, the body, sexuality, and relationships between individuals."[10] The institutions of temporal sequestration are apparatuses of power generated by the generalized civil war that, by continuing war by other means, ensures a relatively stable, predictable, regular governmentality of behavior valid for fabrication of the social and "defense of society"—capitalist society, it goes without saying.

In conclusion, while "time management" passes through the military discipline of the factory, it also participates in a more global apparatus where "it is offensive for the labor force merely to 'pass the time.'"[11] The *value* of the war on time launched by capitalism against society as a whole comes from here.

5.2 Formation of the Family Cell

Generalized civil war, the condition and consequence of the formation of the labor force, is at the same time a "war of subjectivities." The production of subjectivity is simultaneously the first capitalist production and one of the main modalities of war, and civil war.

The struggle against proletarian illegalities in order to quash the refusal to submit to disciplines and to the model of subjectivation of the salaried laborer therefore implies not only the classic apparatuses of civil war; in a liberal society indexed on private property, proletarians are not attached to the apparatus of production by economic constraints alone; their subjection is not maintained with the "discipline of hunger" and the threat of prison; their behavior is not "regularized" by pure and simple repression (vice squad) or by the brutal imposition of new norms.

As soon as the passage from the condition of expropriated proletarian to salaried laborer is far from automatic, the encounter between the "man with the money" and workers which defines industrial capitalism requires the long work of converting subjectivity. During colonization, entire peoples, after having been expropriated from their "life as savages," let themselves die off rather than fall into a slavery that could include the option of "free labor." "Free labor" that the practice of *working to death* in workshops and manufactures brings so close to slavery *itself* that the *Morning Star*—the organ of the English free-traders—could exclaim: "Our *white slaves*, who are toiled into the grave, for the most part silently pine and die."[12] Extermination by labor thus becomes the absolute truth of the *global war* of primitive accumulation that transforms industrial cities into *black continents* of slums and workshops crowded with people—the only limit seeming to be the revolt of the poor reduced to the state of "flesh for the machine."[13] The immediate replacement of those who perished could only be explained by the rise of pauperism, which would soon be seen as contributing to proletarian nomadism and illegality while threatening liberal society with "cataclysmic conflicts," with a "barbarian populace that haunted the cities more than they inhabited them."[14] A state of emergency in the form of "laboring classes, dangerous classes" that make Paris resemble a "nomad camp" (Lecouturier), and where there is the threat of a *colonial-style war to the death* with an outcome so uncertain that it is the victorious insurrection of Saint-Domingue reemerging in the heart of the working-class suburbs. Take, for example, this text published in December 1831 in the *Journal des débats* the day after the revolt of the silkworkers of Lyon: "Each resident lives in the factory like planters of the colonies in the middle of their slaves; the sedition in Lyon is a kind of Saint-Domingue insurrection. [...] Barbarians who threaten society [...] are in the outskirts of our manufacturing cities. [...] The middle class must know how things are; it must recognize its position." The science of the labor force and the reproduction of working class labor would therefore have to spread to the entire urban territory by making population management the object of new collective systems. The "positive" powers that they exercise (schools, housing policies, public hygiene, medicalization of populations...) are at the heart of the economic-liberal redefinition of the state.

The awareness that grows over the course of the long nineteenth century, age of rationalization of mass labor, is that capitalist development is unthinkable without the training of bodies and minds for new productive and subjective functions required by the accumulation of capital. Or to express it better, it is understood that there is no *lasting* and *sustainable* (somatic) training of bodies without a moral training of minds that is fully part of the disciplinary transversality of the biopolitical science of populations. *Social action* thus conditions the renewal of the mercantilist criteria of output in a *laissez-faire* (the "freedom of labor") that scarcely characterizes the management of power as to this same labor force that is "to be 'cultivated' in the literal sense of the word. That is, to work in order to make them work, so as to create, drive, and reap that which labor brings along with it: namely social wealth."[15] And this "culture" could not be without a *general culture* of the division of liberal society.

The constitution of the small family, with its sexual identities and the distribution of powers and functions they imply ("productive" labor for men and "reproductive," unpaid labor for women), without forgetting the control of incestuous affects and desire that circulate there, is the product of a war (of production) of subjectivity that concerns in different ways the proletariat and the bourgeoisie. Yet here and there it targets women most specifically, to the extent that the crisis of sovereign patriarchal power and its exercise in organic groups tending to break apart is the first reason for the constitution of the small family. All too often neglected in the history of capitalism, the formation of the conjugal family depended on the transformation of the domination of women by the intermediary of an *interior domestication* that is paradigmatic of this "war of subjectivity" that must decidedly be reinscribed on the horizon of the emancipation of *private man*.

The "campaign against masturbation" by children, which mobilized so many doctors and educators from the end of the eighteenth century to the end of the nineteenth century, encouraged the bourgeois family to eliminate all intermediaries (preceptors and nannies), to remove, if possible, domestic workers (including wet-nurses), and transform the family space into a space for constant education and surveillance. While benefitting the spread of domestic medicine (masturbation is an "illness") the body of the child was supposed to become the object of permanent attention from parents (Locke's *Some Thoughts Concerning Education* is one of the first systematic examples). With all of the practical instructions it included, this veritable crusade "was a means of compressing family relationships and closing up the central parent-child rectangle into a substantial, close-knit, and emotionally saturated unit."[16] The transformation of the large family caught in a complex web of relationships of dependence and membership into the narrow, cellular, conjugal, and parental family as it is known today in its economic-moral autonomy is due to this government of children which in turn conditions the formation of the bourgeois figure of the spouse and the "mother of the family." The fact that on the outside, there is no longer anything for her except to perform charitable acts and educative missions confirms how essential it is for the cycle of bourgeois normalization to maintain itself by connecting the entire series of elements composing it in a circuit. Women are thus attached to this production of subjectivity combining valorization of the child's body by the family cell (restricted as a result to the parental nucleus) with an infiltration of sexuality by a technology of medical power, collaborating in the economic and affective valorization of the child by the state that can then take charge of the technical formation of its normalization through specialized pedagogical institutions. The child's sexuality is thus revealed as the ploy of incest (from the incestuous indiscretion of the parents to its *transference* in the incestuous desire of the children) through which parents leave to the state its "instrument of performance"...[17]

The conditions and modalities of intervention on working-class environments were much different. With the transformation of the European proletariat into a "productive force," the conditions of labor, housing, mobility, and insecurity "all made family relationships increasingly fragile and disabled the family structure"[18] in favor of *free union*. The question of the vagabondage of individuals and children returns with singular emphasis in the first half of the nineteenth century through the uncontrolled urbanization linked to industrialization, the demographic explosion, and the development of pauperism. The struggle against these social plagues, to which were added pathological designations (contagion, epidemics) and hygienic interests, imposed the renewal of the old regime of alliances and affiliation in favor of a new alliance of state order and family order into which *private initiative* (managerial order, assisted by the Church) was inserted, the first *interested* party in the moralization of workers' ways of life and their habitat. This was the great campaign aimed at "moralizing the poor classes."

The family strategy aimed at the proletariat by the many philanthropical societies, unlike the one aimed at the bourgeois sphere, was a campaign to reestablish marriage and promote family life: "Get married. Do not have children first only to abandon them later [to the charge of the state]. The whole campaign is directed against free unions, against concubinage, and against extra- or parafamilial fluidity."[19] Replacing the dowry with unpaid domestic labor contributes to the regularization of behaviors in a domestic space where the social economy consisted of giving a new foundation to patriarchal power by subjecting the entry of women into the labor market to male control but also by encouraging surveillance of men (and children) by *domesticated* women in their *household.*

Starting in the years 1820–1825, executives, philanthropists, and public powers spent considerable energy to house families in a new domestic habitat, of which the paradigmatic example is the *cité ouvrière* (working-class housing project). It was announced as being the "tomb of the riot" led by the insurgents of 1848 and that it would "end the era of revolutions"[20] of the people in arms with its pavilion model and separation into three rooms. While the "bourgeois family was constituted by means of a *tactical constriction* of its members aimed at suppressing or controlling an internal enemy, the domestic servants"[21] (they take the place of the desire that is spied on and under surveillance), proletarians on the contrary were asked to divide their bodies in a strategic space of separation (one room for the parents, one room for the children, and one common room: the model appeared around 1830 in the plans for the first *cités ouvrières*) to avoid "sickening promiscuity," while excluding the stranger, the "sleeper," in other words the "lodged" bachelor who opened the familial space onto a social field where desire is not absent. The working-class family and workers' housing were therefore both projected against the conditions of reality of potential adult incest and raised up against "external temptations" (leading to the "cabaret" or the "street"). The housed family would thus see all its members fall under a regime of *liberty and residence under surveillance* by the collective structures of managerial disciplinarization which are the very principle of the biopolitics of a liberal society towards the working-class population which is to be *settled* in this manner.

If the good worker is the *pater familias* (he is the *anti-sublime*),[22] it is easy to understand the economy that pushes workers to become home owners. In the August 1886 edition of the *Revue d'Hygiène*, it states: "He does not own his house; soon his house owns him. It performs a complete transformation on him."[23] Yet this transformation also has the result of creating an intimacy that is not limited to the function of demographic womb: besides the conjugalization of desire, objectively placed under the Law of the factory which itself depends on it (wasn't it born in the separation of the place of residence and the space reserved for work?), the house participates directly in the *subjective production of individual habits*. Habit, write Lion Murard and Patrick Zylberman, is "*the missing link of the entire apparatus*: incapable of being reduced to the profession, going beyond the social field, it offers a hold on a microscopic, infinitely multiplied pedagogy."[24] It has the role of joining in intensity the two separate territories of productive time and free time by making the *total life* of the worker the object and *subject of power*. As idealized as it may have been by charitable organizations, this "proto-welfare" gives rise to a disciplinary intimacy reliant on a strategy of behavior and a tactics of feelings that are presented as *the pursuit of war by the regulatory means of a biopolitics of intimacy*. This does not mean that the managerial dictatorship of "workfare" and the military regime of organization of industrial labor stop ("in the workshop, I am the leader, you are my soldiers. I give the orders; you must obey"), but obedience becomes the object of a science of behavior that seals the biopolitical conjunction of disciplines and liberalism. A Human Science as much as a science of class.

These two politics of production of subjectivity led to an "inter-classist" family model based on what was called at the time, in reference to the working-class world, "the house inhabited in a bourgeois manner," even though it articulates in a very different way the common prohibition in relation to the unhappy games of sexuality and alliance that haunt the modern family ark. Implicated here is no less than the dualism between a medical surveillance of child sexuality and a police-judiciary-style social control of adult sexuality in the dangerous classes. "There have been two types of constitution of the cellular family, two types of definition of incest, two descriptions of the fear of incest, and two clusters of institutions around this fear. I am not saying that there are two sexualities, one bourgeois and the other proletarian (or working-class), but I would say that there have been two modes of sexualization of the family or two modes of the familialization of sexuality, two family spaces of sexuality and sexual prohibition."[25]

In fact, while on the one hand, the domestic reorganization of the family around the judicially controlled danger of parent-child mixing was part of an "eugenics of the labor force" with the aid of new technologies of (disciplinary) training and (biopolitical) control with the aim of forging a *race of workers*,[26] on the other hand, the medically assisted drawdown of child sexuality by parents took part in forming a *class body* "with a health, hygiene, lineage, and race" bearing witness to what Foucault called a "dynamic racism." A *racism of expansion* that bore all its fruit in the second half of the nineteenth century.[27]

5.3 Subjective Training is not Ideological

The war of subjectivity is not ideological. It takes place through apparatuses, institutions, technologies, and knowledge that together frame individuals in a system of identities and functions without referring first to consciousness and its play of (false) representations, which on the contrary depend on it. To the extent that the family apparatus is actively caught in all of the real mechanisms of subjection, the family has remained, until now, at the center of the capitalistic organization of power over life and at the heart of the "subjective conflicts" it unleashes.

Its economy is not limited to placing the work of (affective and economic) reproduction freely at the disposition of "society;" it is also a relay and multiplier of power between all disciplinary institutions (school, army, factory, hospital) and between them and the new regulating apparatuses (savings banks or contingency funds, aid mechanisms, hygiene and medical services, among others) without which industrial capitalism could not function in a lasting manner.

During the Classical Era, the control and attachment of individuals to a function, role, and identity were obtained by their territorial belonging to castes, communities, and groups such as corporations and guilds, with which the vertical filiation of generations implied in the old regime of the family was closely articulated. Starting in the nineteenth century, due to the dislocation of these membership bodies and the disintegration of the old family model by fixation ("free labor") in factories, individuals are *attached and reattached* as if from the exterior to a multiplicity of apparatuses of "temporal sequestration" for which the continuum is nothing other than the *useful time of life*. "At birth they are placed in a crèche; in childhood they are sent to school; they go to the workshop; during their life they come under a charity office; they must deposit money in a savings bank; they end in a home. In short, throughout their life, people enter into a multiplicity of links with a multiplicity of institutions."[28]

The impulse that pushes people to enter and leave this network of disciplinary institutions and regulating apparatuses is given by the "reduced" family for which it stimulates the *conjugal re-foundation* by supporting it with all of its power (power operates in a network). There is no "progressive shrinking of the old family [...] whose original functions would be taken charge of by the [new] collective structures";[29] there is on the contrary a spread and intensification of power in a *new organ* destined to equip all individuals with a lateral alliance between spouses ("Get married!") that serves as the matrix of disciplines and the principle of regulations. For this to happen, the father has to conserve before the law the principle of sovereignty that integrates the new system of domination proper to the micromechanics of familial power: "Thanks to the civil code, the family preserve the schemas of sovereignty: dominations, membership, bonds of suzerainty, etcetera, but it limited them to the relationships between men and women and parents and children."[30] If the modern family fails to fulfill its functions of normalization guaranteed by the concrete arrangement of relationships of domination within it, if an individual is revealed to be incapable of following academic or factory discipline, that of the army or prison, then the "psy function" would intervene, in other words no longer directly a (disciplinary) power but a (medical) knowledge of pathologies of intimacy with the aim to correct behaviors. Another type of power or a "surplus power," of which the mechanisms contribute to the expanded reproduction of individuals as subjects *and as subject to discourses of truth*.

In the generalized civil war unleashed by liberalism to transform the proletariat into a labor force, knowledge represents a strategic weapon. The human sciences, the nascent social sciences occupied this function of apparatus to verify power remarkably well.

Every power formation requires a knowledge; *relationships of strategic power* have to be stabilized both in power apparatuses (disciplines, governmentality) and in knowledge (methods of observation, recording techniques, investigative and research procedures…) to be ready to "govern" behavior in a relatively stable and predictable manner. Thus, in parallel to the power exercised on and in the family, a "medical-psychiatric knowledge" was constituted that did not depend on it but that would be ineffective without it. Medical-psychiatric power is the proper of this "psy function" that continued to spread in the second half of the nineteenth century by functioning inside each apparatus of power: "If psychologists turn up in the school, the factory, in prisons, in the army, and elsewhere, it is because they entered precisely at the point when each of these institutions was obliged […] to assert the power exercised within them as reality."[31]

This power of knowledge is presented as the principle of reality from which the individual is instituted as subject and the subject is constituted as "object-effect" of an analytical investment that leads him or her to espouse a differential system of *development* related to a universal norm, for which the jurisprudence comes from clinical knowledge.

We should therefore understand "generalized civil war" here as the continuums of interventions that led from the most violent expropriation from the land and the freedoms of association that it arranged to the disciplinary training of bodies, to biopolitical campaigns for the nuclear family communicating the sovereign subjection of women and the promotion of the mother of the family with the constitution of new educative and medico-psychiatric knowledge, which collapses government by the family on the government of families. Between the formation of the labor force and its bloody repression in the riots and revolutions that erupted throughout the nineteenth century, the institutions of discipline, security, and sovereignty continued civil war by all of these means, bipolarizing the individuation of populations while favoring the *strategic (and not ideological)* connection of the working-class family to the bourgeois family.

6

THE NEW COLONIAL WAR

This War, as everyone knows, is unlike any other; recollections of European tactics are good for nothing and are often harmful.
    —Alexis de Toqueville, "Essay on Algeria" (October 1841)

Around us, the lights have been extinguished.
    —Alexis de Tocqueville, "First Report on Algeria" (1847)

Between the Napoleonic wars and the total wars of the twentieth century, a new wave of wars of colonization unfurled across the planet. What is politely referred to as the "second European expansion" and more properly as *capitalist enveloping of the Earth*[1] is directly connected to the Industrial Revolution and the industrialization of space and time, to the military supremacy that they augmented,[2] to the development of financial capital (the "new bank"), and to the first crises of overproduction... It is also related to the problems of governmentality posed by internal colonization that were unable to contain the rise of class struggle and the uprisings of the "populace." Ernest Renan would conclude that "a nation that does not colonize is irrevocably destined for socialism."[3]

Although it preceded the full rise of imperialism after 1870, France's war to conquer Algeria (1830–1871) interests us in particular because directly or indirectly, and through several angles, it transects the "social question" and the struggles of revolutionary movements in metropolitan France. Beyond the post-slavery policy of "assimilation" and the colony of population encouraging the expatriation of dangerous classes, the close connection of war and civil war in a colonial war described as a "small war" and tested in North Africa against "Arabs" provided military techniques used by the "Republic" to crush the June 1848 insurrection. Colonel Charles Callwell was not mistaken: in his book, the "repression" of "sedition" and "insurrection" in "civilized countries" by regular troops opens up the field of application of *small wars*, which could have been thought to apply only to campaigns of conquest ("when a Great Power adds the territory of barbarous races to its possessions") and punitive expeditions "against tribes bordering upon distant colonies."[4] Their definition as "partisan warfare" is there to disabuse us by reestablishing (starting in the introduction) the proper order of real war as *Civilized, barbarians, savages*. The French conquest of Algeria inevitably occupies a prominent place in what is considered to be the great, late-Victorian treatise on counter-insurrection.

Disqualifying any nostalgia for what Hannah Arendt called a "golden age of security" (which would only have been broken at the end of the nineteenth century by the racial thinking of the Boers),[5] these new wars of conquest reveal the continued aspect of primitive accumulation by the continuity of colonial racism in the industrial period. It quickly contributed to the "scientific" development of the imperialist formula "Expansion is everything" with the corollary that followed it like its shadow since the mid-nineteenth century: "Race is everything." Confirming our hypothesis: capitalism is consubstantially a "market" of global subsumption that includes, in its very reality, the continued and racially-based creation of "colonial" accumulation. The very concept of "industrial mode of production" must imperatively include as "productive forces" the imperialist violence of colonial predation and racism made bureaucratic in a "Government of the Subject Races,"[6] at the same level as labor, capital, and the "new bank" financing them all (under the protection of the state). This statement is, in truth, hardly Arendtian given the *a priori* underpinning her entire analysis of the Boer anomaly, and which is presented as if incidentally: "normal capitalist development" would seal the "normal end of race society."[7] The problem is that imperialist expansion comes (economically) from the former while including (historically) the latter in a racial thanatopolitics that could be described, as Olivier Le Cour Grandmaison has suggested, as "the pursuit of the objectives of biopolitics by other means"...

The new colonial war thus completely overturns the concept and reality of war as it was practiced in Europe. While Carl Schmitt, following Rosa Luxemburg, perfectly describes imperialism as "land appropriation" (and therefore mentions colonial expansion), he neglects the modalities of colonial war that anticipate and prepare "total war." In a similar way, Michel Foucault makes "race war" the means to reestablish, against the juridical-political power of the philosophers of sovereignty, the historical singularity of war at the horizon of what he calls "fundamental war"; however, he shows little interest in the heavily colonial aspect of "race wars." Yet, the "war of civilizations" to bring "progress" and "Enlightenment" to the "savages" is an old European practice. It took a new turn, as universalist, republican, and liberal, with the *civilizing mission* of post-revolutionary France standing against "oriental despotism," the barbarity of the Arab, and the warring fanaticism of the "religion of Mohammed" (the religion of the "glaive" denounced by Montesquieu is placed at the service of the colonial struggle between "two civilizations").[8]

On the side of both the colonized and the colonizer, the war of conquest and pacification could not be a "conventional war" aimed at the surrender of the sovereign and the capitulation of his armies. The colonized was not an enemy organized around a regular army obeying the centralized leadership of a state which, like in Europe, had been able to *monopolize* the war machine: free of any central power, the Arab tribes (nomads) and farmers (mainly Berber and Kabyle) had always been armed and jealously guarded their right to exercise force in the name of their "independence." Presented as a born pillager, the Algerian "native" was singularly equipped to engage in what had been called "guerrilla" since the Peninsular War, and which many French officers serving in Algeria knew only too well for having confronted this "veritable plague, leading cause of France's misfortune" (Napoleon to Las Cases).

On the strength of this experience, which threatened to repeat itself in Algeria, the Army of Africa, at the end of 1840, decided to "defeat the guerrilla with its own methods," in the shape of an all-out war and counter-guerrilla drawing all the consequences of the address made by Abdelkader, Emir of the "Arabs" ("a sort of Muslim Cromwell" according to Tocqueville), to General Thomas-Robert Bugeaud, governor of the colony: "When your army marches forward, we will pull back, but it will be forced to withdraw and we will return. We will fight when we deem it appropriate. Opposing the forces you drag behind you would be madness. But we will exhaust them, we will destroy them piece by piece."[9]

How can one "fight battles" according to the rules and law of "war between nations" with such an evasive enemy who is none other than the population mobilized against an army of conquest and occupation? The limits of space and time in conventional war are extended to the entire occupied territory and society, changing their nature profoundly and contesting the very principle of reaching a lasting peace that could never be decreed with the "Arabs." (Franz Fanon: "As if to illustrate the totalitarian nature of colonial exploitation the colonist turns the colonized into a kind of quintessence of evil.")[10] After defeating them, it was a question of exercising "total domination" to exploit the conquest and make it irreversible, according to the recommendation of the very liberal Alexis de Tocqueville in a report he wrote as a deputy specialized in colonial affairs. "Total domination" is the biopolitical name of a *new state of permanent war*.

As Tocqueville suggests in his "Essay on Algeria" (1841)—a *factum* to which those who hold the theory that "the problem of liberalism is that of governing the least possible" should turn their attention—colonial war should practice everything that was prohibited in conventional war by the "rights of people," something which is now known as a global strategy of terror and famine: ravage the economy of the occupied territory, "destroy everything that resembles a permanent aggregation of population or, in other words, a town," carry out raids, burn villages, take herds, "capture unarmed men, women, and children," make no distinction between civilians and military (without, however, systematically executing prisoners). As one who presents himself as a responsible proponent of the middle road, he explains that the action of the government on these populations should not "separate domination and colonization and vice versa." Bugeaud, a veteran of the Peninsular War, summed up the objectives of the war in this way: "The goal is not to chase after the Arabs, which is quite useless; it is to prevent the Arabs from sowing, harvesting, pasturing, [...] from benefitting from their fields [...]. Go burn their crops every year [...], or exterminate them down to the last one."[11] While Tocqueville opposes the last idea and prefers to "contain the Arabs," he agrees with Bugeaud on the need to adapt the army to these new types of counter-insurrectional combat by promoting procedures prefiguring the modular army organization that became widespread in the 1960s. Supporting the need to maintain "large expeditions" to show "there are no obstacles in the country that can stop us," he argues that "it would be worth more to have several small mobile corps constantly moving around fixed points than to have large armies." This would involve the "creation of a special African army" that would be uniquely qualified to fight "armed marauding" by turning their own "methods" against the "Barbarians."[12]

His approval of Bugeaud's military strategy against the Algerian populace (including "*enfumades*" or smoking out caves)[13] did not however extend to the general's project for paramilitary colonization of Algeria (colonization by veterans inspired by the Roman model and aimed at producing an army of workers).[14] For Tocqueville, every coercive method needed for "domination of the Arabs, without which there will be no safety for the European population nor progress in colonization"[15] has no other goal than to ratify the colonial exception through the "normalization" of the Algerian situation (pacification) under the general rule of liberalism ("that economic conditions are such [in Algeria] that one can easily attain comfort and often wealth") and "free trade" with France.[16] In other words the principle of a *liberal colonial government* basing the "liberty" of the colonists alone (the European population replacing the "indigenous element" by repressing and destroying it)[17] on apparatuses that could have been called, before their time, apparatuses of *wars of security*. Through these exceptional means, they extend (to the exterior) the liberal art of governing (in the interior) in its relationship of very close dependence on this "incredible range of governmental interventions" and the "strategies of security, which are, in a way—as Foucault duly noted—both liberalism's other face and its very condition."[18] This shines an entirely new light on Tocqueville's assertion that "it should not be said that social organization in Africa must be exceptional, except for a few similarities, but on the contrary, that things should be conducted in Africa as they are in France, but for a few exceptions."[19] Among these exceptions is the prohibition on trade for the "Arabs," which the liberal Tocqueville believed to be "the most effective means we can use to subjugate the tribes."[20]

When the revolution of February 1848 turned into a civil war in which the "working class" appeared for the first time as political subject of *class combat*[21] ("Woe to the June uprising!"), who was better suited than the African generals to fight not an army but "Bedouins of mainland France" fighting *without war cries, without leaders, and without flags*? Who was ready to operate not on a battlefield but in a city where the combat took place in the streets and house by house, if not those who carried out a "total" war against the "Arabs"—like Bugeaud who had participated in suppressing the uprising of April 13–14, 1834? He was also the author of *La Guerre des rues et des maisons* (The War of Streets and Houses) where the city was seen as a battlefield on the internal front of class struggle and should be reorganized as a result... Who could confront the "internal barbarians" better than those who had fought the "barbarians" of the colonies in similar situations? Who could crush this "rebellious rabble," these "brutish and fierce beasts" of the populace in revolt if not the "African Cavaignac," named governor of Algeria in February 1848, then Minister of War on May 17, acting "in Paris as he would have in the mountains of Kabylie" with his civil war army? Tocqueville, at first reticent ("by instinct more than by reflection") towards the "military dictatorship" put in place under the authority of Cavaignac, unreservedly supported the *programmed destruction* of the internal enemy using the military tactics of the "Coloniale" (a thousand deaths in combat, three thousand executions afterwards). In "The 23rd of June," Engels, who at times could repeat the racial refrain on the "very low [...] moral level" of the Kabyles and Arabs but not the *class racism* that haunted France of the 1840s, refers no less than three times to the war in Algeria to show that Parisian workers, despite their military experience, were not prepared to face "methods employed in Algeria" and "Algerian barbarity." How could they think that "this brand of Algerian warfare could be used right in the center of Paris" and that an entire population would be subject to a "war of extermination"? It was because "the bourgeoisie declared the workers to be not ordinary enemies who have to be defeated but *enemies of society* who must be destroyed."[22] The generals of the African army marked the "nature" of the Republic for all time with the Algerian crushing of the popular uprising, in which "women [...] took part as much as men."[23] Bugeaud, again: "A democratic republic, you have it; a social republic, you will never have! I am telling you now, mark my words." Far from being contradicted by the policy of colonial emigration aimed at making the proletariat a colonist-proprietor (*swords to ploughshares*), the racial hatred of the African generals immediately recognized the red thread connecting the "internal indigenes" and those of the colonies. This was something the French Left, with all its republican ardor, was never able to understand.

Yet the domination exercised by the model majority (colonizer)/minority (colonized) also "benefitted" European workers. Despite the exploitation they suffered in Europe, they shared the dividends of colonization with the capitalists, which led to their "embourgeoisement," to use Engels' term. As he noted in a particularly caustic letter addressed to Kautsky in 1882, "You ask me what the English workers think about colonial policy. Well, exactly the same as they think about politics in general: the same as what the bourgeois think. [...] The workers gaily share the feast of England's monopoly of the world market and the colonies."[24] It wasn't until 1920 that Lenin, in his report to the Second Congress of the Communist International, asserted that the struggle against imperialism would be victorious when the onslaught of "the exploited and oppressed workers in each country [...] merges with the revolutionary onslaught of hundreds of millions of people who have hitherto stood beyond the pale of history, and have been regarded merely as the object of history."[25]

"Racial" policies bring out the force of the divisions within the global proletariat and the weakness of workers' internationalism, which suffered fundamentally from the same limits as its liberal "brother" in terms of the universalism of its principle. In a curious back-and-forth, the first Socialist congresses held in Algiers at the end of the nineteenth and early twentieth century defended "French laborers" against Italian laborers, which was considered foreign; and while the French colonizers considered themselves "Algerian," the colonized were only "natives" or "Muslims."[26]

As with sexual hierarchies, power also passes through the dominated who reproduce it by conforming to it. Workers, the object of class racism throughout the eighteenth and nineteenth centuries, turned it against the colonized. The combination of class exploitation with the domination of the majoritarian model in *uniform* operates here as well. Think for example of the Napoleonic citizen-soldier as the *working-class* model of a very masculine civic virtue which, in the 1840s, was called on again from a more republican side (that of the *colonist-worker* or *colonist-laborer*) in French Algeria. Colonial war is at the same time a "war of subjectivity," because the establishment of the relationship of domination colonizer/colonized is also a relationship of subjection that would format the subjectivity of the colonizers, and the colonized, for a long time.

Political decolonization must therefore be accompanied by subjective decolonization, a conversion of subjectivity that, through a critical return to Marxist economism, would prohibit any projection of capitalism and its dialectical actors, "modern" bourgeoisie *and* "working classes of every civilized nation," in any "progress of civilization"—according to the modernist expression used by Engels in relation to the conquest of Algeria, when the "Arabian chief" was captured (to Engels' delight).[27]

THE LIMITS OF THE LIBERALISM OF FOUCAULT

[You know] Freud's quotation: *"Acheronta movebo."* Well, I would like to take the theme for this year's lectures from another, less well-known quotation from [...] the English Statesman Walpole, who, with reference to his way of governing, said: *"Quieta non movere,"* "Let sleeping dogs lie." In a sense, the opposite of Freud.

— Michel Foucault, *The Birth of Biopolitics*

Haunted by the thought of 1848 and the project of a "Republic that is democratic and social or not at all" (as the revolutionaries of 1848 said), the nineteenth century is the century of liberalism's triumph, with the spectacle of crises and working-class misery caused by the "freedom of commerce." It was supposed to take the place of war and the unlimited capture of a state *limited* to only defending the safety of goods and the people *owning* them, according to the very "Lockean" reasoning of Benjamin Constant. He therefore concluded that political rights should be limited to those who have "the leisure indispensable for the acquisition of understanding and sound judgment."[1] This indicates that the liberal management of freedom would only become the irreversible horizon of democratic societies by beginning to juxtapose the perspective of subversion of bourgeois society with the reality of civil war against "internal Bedouins." As part of the liberal order of things, the survivors of the June Rebellion and their families were deported by the thousands to Algeria with Tocqueville's approval. He explained the ruptures of 1848—using a theme the liberal would then constantly repeat—by the continued growth of the state, under the effect of revolutions, to the detriment of society which should be left to itself (*laisser faire*), the better to *defend* it...

However, our total inability to subscribe to Foucault's take on liberalism in his course at the Collège de France in 1978–1979, *The Birth of Biopolitics*, does not come solely from its denial of the history of colonization and the role famous liberals played in it by associating it with the social question. These lectures have been all too often reduced to an analysis of neoliberalism, although for Foucault it is only a *particular genre* of the *common species* that he analyzed as a "liberal art of governing" reaching back to the "mid-eighteenth century."

In the analysis of liberal governmentality, of which the first manifestations were carried out by Physiocrats that he takes literally (*laissez-faire* aimed at ending the grain shortage), Foucault buries war as a "cypher" for the relationship of power with the disciplinary hypothesis, for which he substitutes the development of a theory of limits imposed by political economy on governmentality. "In a narrower sense, liberalism is the solution that consists in the maximum limitation of the forms and domains of government action."[2] In the market economy, the modern form of governmentality, "instead of coming up against limits formalized by jurisdictions, it [gives] itself intrinsic limits." The limit is no longer external (law, state) but immanent, in the "self-limitation of governmental reason characteristic of 'liberalism,'" that should then be studied as the "general framework of biopolitics."[3] In this new framework, the philosopher privileges the correlation between the "invisible hand" and *homo œconomicus*, which he reinserts at the heart of liberalism as disqualification of the latest forms of sovereignty: economic *sovereignty* (since the economic world is a multiplicity all the more impossible to totalize in that it ensures the spontaneous convergence of perspectives) and political sovereignty (of a governmental reason that continues—as for the Physiocrats—to have the freedom of economic agents coincide with the existence of the sovereign). Following Foucault, the economy becomes an "atheistic discipline" with Adam Smith, a "discipline without totality," which would call into question the very principle of totalization in the form of a veritable "critique of governmental reason." He explains that this critique should be understood "in the specific, philosophical sense of the term"[4]— thus in the Kantian sense of a (transcendental) self-limitation of reason in a Critique which, one year previously, had been the subject of an important conference ("What is Critique?") placed entirely under the sign of *the art of not being too governed*, in "attempting to answer the question [...]: *Was ist Aufklärung?*"[5] As we know, this is the same title as Kant's text from 1784 on *Aufklärung*, and Foucault continues to return to it by making the German philosopher part of the great shift of liberalism. In *The Birth of Biopolitics*, it very logically falls to Adam Smith to provide the liberal veridiction on any past, present, or future *Aufklärung*... by giving the art of governing, "whose objective is its own self-limitation [...] pegged to the specificity of economic processes," a new field of reference, one that is inseparable from *homo œconomicus* and which is of course *civil society*.[6]

Centered on the history of the model of the *homo œconomicus*, the two final lectures of the course play an eminently "strategic" role in Foucault's work, insofar as liberalism is identified there with the problem of governing "society." The need for government is questioned "in the name of society," in other words, "in what respects can it be dispensed with, and in what areas its interventions are pointless or harmful."[7] The question directs the inquiry towards finding an internal break in governmental practice with law as the principle of "external limitation" of the *raison d'état*.

We will summarize Foucault's demonstration in these two lectures and present it in broad strokes. They provide the plane of consistency for the entire course, which begins, as we have seen, with the new concept of a "critical governmental reason" such that "the objection is no longer to the abuse of sovereignty but to excessive government."[8]

Capitalism brings out the irreducible heterogeneity between the economic subject (*homo œconomicus*) and the legal subject. While the legal subject is socialized by renouncing rights, which are transferred to a superior authority, the economic subject is socialized by a "spontaneous multiplication" of its interests that is so irreducible that it places the art of governing in an essential incapacity "to master the totality of the economic field." The "indefinite field of immanence" of the subject of interest dethrones sovereignty by making it blind to the totality of the economic process. The question then becomes: where can "a rational principle be found for limiting other than by right" and other than by "economic science" a governmentality that could take charge of the irreducible heterogeneity of the economic and juridical?

Seeking to define a technology of power that "manages civil society, the nation, society, the social,"[9] Foucault seeks to reconstruct the history of the concept of (civil) society over which government must be exercised starting with a "point of inflection" that he situates in the second half of the eighteenth century and that he understands as a rupture with the Lockean philosophy of civil society. This philosophy was still characterized, in his view, by the primacy of the juridical-political structure ("of political society or of civil society"...), whereas the new conception of civil society consists of giving a privileged place to the economic subject as vehicle of a new form of rationality without any transcendence.

With Adam Ferguson—Foucault emphasizes the proximity between his *An Essay on the History of Civil Society* and *The Wealth of Nations* ("the word 'nation' in Smith [...] having more or less the same meaning as civil society in Ferguson")[10]—an already diffuse position finds its expression, one that tends to assert a principle of continuity between civil society and the economic subject. Like the economic bond, the social bond forms spontaneously, without having to initiate it or without the need for self-initiation. Like the economy, civil society ensures the spontaneous synthesis of individuals without turning to an "explicit contract," a "pact of voluntary union," or a "renunciation of rights" that would have to be situated at the beginning of civil life.

Power relations do not have the political-juridical form of the "*pactum unionis*" and the "*pactum subjectionis*," since power (and the relationships of subordination that facilitate it) are spontaneously founded in "a *de facto* bond which links different concrete individuals to each other."[11] The juridical-political structure comes after the relationships of power that spontaneously formed in the play of differences between individuals. The complicity between economic subject and civil society is clearly established from that point since interest is the force of socialization in each case: "disinterested interests" (sympathy, compassion, repugnance, etc.) in the case of civil society and "egoist interests" in the case of *homo œconomicus*.

Egoist interests produce "no localization, no territoriality, no particular grouping" (the market is deterritorializing, universalizing, and its relationships are "abstract"), while disinterested interests produce community ties and thus territorialized, localized, singular groups. "Civil society is much more than the association of different economic subjects" since it is not a simple system of exchanges of rights or of economic exchanges. However, "economic egoism will be able to play its role within it" (by territorializing itself, locating itself in singular groups), a positive role of rupture and innovation as an agent of change in society. The spontaneous synthesis of "egoist interests" (the *market*) constantly threatens the equally spontaneous synthesis of the "disinterested interests" of civil society; it "constantly tends to undo what the spontaneous bond of civil society has joined together."[12] Yet the "dissociative" economic bond, since it is egoist, abstract, deterritorialized, and deterritorializing, constitutes at the same time a positive principle of "historical transformation," of "constant transformation" of civil society. To say it with Adam Smith, "Every man [...] becomes in some measure a merchant."[13] Thus civil society and economic subject are part of a same whole that participates in a "transactional reality."[14] As Foucault concludes, "civil society is the concrete ensemble within which these ideal points, economic men, must be placed so that they can be appropriately managed."[15]

It is easier to understand why liberalism was of interest to Foucault when reconfigured in this way, starting with a utilitarianism for which the immanence is shifted to a new technology of government. It combines all of his themes in a very profound way: critique of the juridical-political form, critique of sovereignty, non-juridical genealogy of power, "collective and political units constituted by social bonds between individuals which go beyond the purely economic bond, yet without being purely juridical."[16] While civil society existed with its phenomena of spontaneous power before the juridical-political form, the problem that determines an entirely *new art of governing* "is simply how to regulate and limit power within a society in which subordination is already at work"[17] by disqualifying political reason "indexed to the state," including its non-despotic version.

Foucault therefore returns to the difference between: Germany, where civil society has value in function of its ability to "support a state" (the lineage from Kant to Hegel); France, which, with the *Déclaration des droits de l'homme*, was stretched between "the juridical idea of a natural right that it is the function of the political pact to guarantee" (after Rousseau) and the conditions that the bourgeoisie imposes on the state; and finally England, *which did not experience the problem of the state* because of the "internal governmentality"[18] of civil society, making each government a *dangerous supplement*... In passing, in an illustration of the invisible hand that spontaneously combines interests, Foucault borrows from Ferguson the comparative analysis of French and English modes of colonization. "The French arrived with projects, administration, and their definition of what would be best for their American colonies," and these colonies collapsed, showing the paucity of resources of their "men of state." Ferguson-Foucault (a Ferguson shorn of any *republican virtue*, the better to *liberalize* him) continues: "The English [...] arrived with 'limited views.' They had no other project than the immediate advantage of each, or rather, each had in mind only the limited view of their own project. As a result, industry was active and settlements flourished."[19] Preventing any "overarching" position, it is in fact through the *Enlightenment* of Adam Smith that "in the middle of the eighteenth century, political economy denounces the paralogism of political totalization of the economic process."[20] Foucault, however, is not unaware that the Vienna treaty (1815) sealed the political-military domination of England which, through its economic power and maritime supremacy, imposed free circulation of the seas (the sea as space of free competition) *controlled by England*, by leading for its benefit an *unlimited* "commercial planetarization," *implying "everything in the world* that can be put on the market."[21] In short, this supposed "Europe of collective enrichment" as "a region of unlimited economic development in relation to a world market" that Foucault calls liberalism without ever pursuing its imperialist characteristics would further merit additional development on the exact nature of the "role [of England] as economic mediator between Europe and the world market."[22]

Throughout his lectures on the birth of biopolitics, Foucault is mindful of the most significant forms of government after the Second World War (German ordo-liberalism and American neo-liberalism), which he analyzes as governmentality of society. Yet his reading here remains highly problematic and, it could be said, eminently *acritical*.

This idea, this *ideation* of a "civil society" neutralizing at one and the same time the state, war (and civil war), and Capital does not get past the second half of the nineteenth century. Yet Foucault does not question the reasons for its failure, nor the disasters that it brought with it. Everything the liberal doctrine repressed (war, state, and capital) returns with an unprecedented destructive force. Which Foucault recognizes ("In fact, with the nineteenth century we enter the worst period of customs barriers, forms of economic protectionism, of national economies and political nationalism, and the biggest wars the world has ever known")[23] but he relegates it to a strictly historical plane—that of the crises of the economy of capitalism. War here is only the demonstration *ab absurdo* of the "fundamental incompatibility between the optimal development of the economic process and a maximization of governmental procedures."[24] Hayekian in inspiration and tone, this thesis has a deep influence on the analysis of the "Classics" (Locke, Smith, Ferguson, Hume) that Foucault proposes in *The Birth of Biopolitics*.

The commentary on Kant's work, *Perpetual Peace: A Philosophical Sketch* (1795), purged of its relationship to war the better to ensure perpetual peace through commercial globalization alone,[25] is both necessary here and… problematic in its very aim. Necessary because it is a question of asserting, with Kant and all the liberals the essential incompatibility between the *commercial spirit* and war. From there ensues the curious republicanism that Foucault calls the "*phenomenal republic of interests*" to indicate clearly that the new liberal regime of government "is basically no longer to be exercised over subjects and other things subjected through these subjects"[26] as in a police state. Problematic because it contributes to giving a basis in reason to *the irreducibility of the crises of liberalism to the crises of the economy of capitalism* to argue in favor of a "crisis of the general apparatus [*dispositif*] of governmentality"[27] for which liberalism would offer, in the name of self-limitation of governmental reason, the first and only response known to this day in a society where "exchange determines the true value of things" and thus problematizes the "use value" of government.[28] In light of this narrative, which could almost be called *transcendental* in the sense of the transcendental economy of liberalism that it mobilizes and that supports it, the nineteenth century prepared a completely different result by sketching a radically different portrait of liberalism. The "non-totalizable multiplicity" is crushed and centralized by monopolies under pressure from the most abstract form of capital, financial capital, which literally explodes every "limit" by making the "synthesis" of interests impossible and by opening the way for imperialist and colonial wars. War comes to operate the closing of the "economic table" that no "self-regulation" ensures. No longer capable of being carried out by sovereignty, totalization is carried out by its "opposite," war and the state war machine. Such that while economic competition replaces war, as the liberals would have it, it only leads all the more inexorably to war.

Foucault also remains silent on the continuity of the liberal regime of civil society with the reality of its Lockean "prehistory," even though liberalism, throughout the nineteenth century, builds on the *civil society of owners-shareholders*. In passing, we can note Tawney's explanation of how, for Locke, "*society* [...] *is a joint-stock company*" into which the shareholders enter to "insure the rights already vested in them by the immutable laws of nature" and where the state, "a matter of convenience, not of supernatural sanctions [...] secures full scope for their unfettered exercise"[29] that is the most mercantile based on the intensification of wars of accumulation. Continuing this path, we find Adam Smith's liberal art of war and what Marx calls, at the very end of Book I of *Capital* (and of section VIII on "primitive accumulation"), which he places under the sign of "the modern theory of colonization," "the secret discovered in the

New World by the political economy of the Old World, and loudly proclaimed by it." Here is that secret: "*the capitalist mode of production and accumulation, and therefore capitalist private property as well, have for their fundamental condition the annihilation of that private property which rests on the labor of the individual himself; in other words, the expropriation of the worker.*"[30] Colonialism thus leads in the end to the truth of class war as vector of liberal "governmentality" of which the critique crosses out this time the modernism of the dual mission of the bourgeoisie, both destructive and creative, in colonized countries.[31] That we find ourselves faced here with what might appear to be the *original colonial version* of Schumpeter's famous pronouncement on the "creative destruction" of capitalism is already an indication of what Foucault missed so terribly in his course on liberalism.

Let us return to the moment when, starting with the liberal movement, Foucault sees the emergence of two heterogeneous principles of governmentality: "the revolutionary axiomatic, of public law and the rights of man, and that of the empirical and utilitarian approach which defines the sphere of independence of the governed" in relation to those who govern.[32] While there is recognition of "a whole series of bridges, transits, and joints" between the two principles, only the latter redefines the question of governmentality from the perspective of its utility (or inutility?) at the horizon of a utilitarian radicalism indexed on this single principle made consistent with exchange and such that the market, from the start, in a complex interplay of individual and collective interests, determines individual and collective utility.

What does it mean in fact for this governmentality that poses the question "Why govern?" when exercised in reality?

Did governing in the nineteenth century follow the principles of the "independence of the governed in relation to those who govern" in the chosen lands of liberalism?

In a famous polemic between liberals on both sides of the Atlantic, the English mocked the use of the word "liberty" in the mouths of those who supported slavery. The American "liberals" replied that in England, the workers, the poor, and the indigent were treated worse than their slaves. Which is absolutely correct *in both cases*... Liberals would never adopt the principle of "the independence of the governed in relation to those who govern" to "govern" the masses of non-property owners kept in a state of servitude, exploitation, and misery. This humanity, which is not considered human (the French liberal Sieyès imagined breeding "monkeys and negroes" to create a new race of servants), is subject to a governmentality of civil war that is the precise opposite of "governing the least possible." It exercises a domination without limits. Object of and subject to the governmentality of a police state that does not disappear with Locke's "mercantilism," the "population" is in this sense a euphemism participating in the *soft commerce* condemned by Marx. The independence of the governed in relation to those who govern only concerns the "people of means" and it especially aims for no "sovereign" power to limit the enjoyment of liberty by property owners, which is first the liberty to exercise their power over slaves or semi-slaves, the poor, workers, their women, and their children...[33]

In his *Liberalism: A Counter-History*, Domenico Losurdo patiently lists the definitions proposed by historians to grasp the nature of the system of liberal power in relation to its colonial infrastructure: "white plantocracy," "planter democracy," "*Herrenvolk* democracy" (democracy for the "people of the rulers"), "segregationist liberalism," "aristocratic republicanism," "Hellenic democracy" (based on slavery), "white democracy," and simply "aristocracy."[34] On this topic, Losurdo notes that the very definition of a "property-owning individualism" or a "possessive individualism" (MacPherson) does not fully grasp the contours of this liberalism, which even in the nineteenth century operated by expropriation, dispossession, forced enlistment, and forced labor borrowing the fiercest aspects of civil war against non-property owners, as a direct continuation of practices which did not bother "liberal sensibilities" because they had been, since Locke, the foundation of the self-government of civil society.

In *The Birth of Biopolitics*, Foucault sufficiently connects the problems of governmentality of this post-Lockean "civil society" directly to the government of "society" by German ordoliberalism (and American neoliberalism of the Chicago School) to take the risk of digging a black hole of a century. Yet post-war "society" is radically different from the "civil society" of the nineteenth century, since it is the result of a dual process that Foucault does not reconstruct. It is first the result of the struggle of slaves, workers, the poor, and women to depose the "liberty" of property owners, which operates as a "liberty" to exploit and dominate them while excluding them from civil and political rights. During the entire nineteenth century, non-property owners shook the walls of tax-based "democracy" behind which there were only property owners by demanding equality and liberty *for all*. "Universal" suffrage (excluding women) was the first demand of the nascent workers' movement. It was won on the barricades of June 1848 in France, while the position of liberals was in favor of tax-based voting (remember that in liberal England of the early twentieth century, paupers, domestic workers, non "established" workers, and women were not allowed to vote). Freedom of the press, of gathering, and of association were also won after intense struggle. And then, do we need to mention that post-war "society" was created by the two world wars that mobilized the "population" as a whole, by reversing the demand for equality of the nineteenth-century revolutionary movements into an equality of the involvement of *everyone* in war? Without this dual rupture with the civil society of property owners, it is impossible to understand the reality of "society" and the new liberalism that "governs" it.

In April 1983, Foucault reflected on the function of liberalism in his work. Won from the domination of absolute monarchy and against the bureaucratization and "excesses of power" of the "administrative states" of the eighteenth century, the "liberty" of the liberals—he explains—should be able to problematize the bureaucratization and contemporary excesses of administrative power, in particular "welfare." He thus proposes a reevaluation not so much of liberal thought than of its problematizations. "I believe I have reactivated these problems to some extent, not at all to take them up under the same terms or return to John Stuart Mill, but to take up the questions that were those of Benjamin Constant, Tocqueville," questions "that have to be asked of any socialist regime."[35]

But shouldn't we begin by responding to the critique Josiah Tucker made of Locke and the American colonists rebelling against England, a critique that does not spare the liberalism of Tocqueville and Constant? "All Republicans ancient and modern suggest no other Schemes but those of pulling down and leveling all Distinctions above them, and of tyrannizing over those miserable Beings, who are unfortunately placed below them."[36] For this reason, this theory of the limit that the economy would introduce into politics by imposing on the sovereign and the state the "critical" principle of "there is always too much governing" seems decidedly incapable of accounting for the historical actions of liberalism—in other words, its *practices*, as Foucault mentions and claims for his own inquiries.

Behind Locke and liberal civil society, there is always the figure of Hobbes, the state, and the war machine, since "society" is always ruled by maintaining deep divisions. Starting in 1977, Foucault seems to set aside the analyses he developed in the 1972–1973 course (*The Punitive Society*) *against* the concept of "society" in the name of which liberal government questions its own usefulness. We need to look back at these pages, since governmentality has never stopped being exercised not over society in general, as the last Foucault would have it, but in and through its divisions.

From the relationship between habit, discipline, property, and society, Foucault draws a radical critique of liberalism and its concept of "civil society," one that is unfortunately later *forgotten*. Political philosophy of the eighteenth century, he remarks, strips down the tradition of sovereignty by making habit its foundation. One obeys the law and institutions by habit and it is always by habit that one respects authority. Hume makes habit a result, not an origin, so that there is something irredeemably artificial and thus fabricated in it. In the eighteenth century, this notion is used "in order to get away from anything of the order of traditional obligations founded on a transcendence, and to replace these obligations with the pure and simple obligation of the contract."[37] The use made of it by the nineteenth century, however, was different. Habit is "conceptualized as complementary to the contract." Habit is transmitted and learned, and thus constitutes the principle of the functioning of disciplinary techniques. The apparatus of "temporal sequestration" attaches individuals to the apparatus of production by producing both "a fabric of habits through which the social membership of individuals to society is defined"—and norms that have the function of producing "normals."

In the 19th century, habit and contracts are seen both as complementary and as what deeply divides society in that they imply an essential inequality in the face of property.

> The contract is the link between individuals and their property, or the link between individuals through their property. Habit, on the other hand, is what links individuals, not to their property, since this is the role of the contract, but to the production apparatus. It is what binds those who are not property owners to an apparatus they do not own; it is what links them to each other as members, not of a class, but of society as a whole.[38]

Property connects individuals in "civil society," while habit/discipline connects them in "society as a whole" by subjecting them "to an order of things," "to an order of time and a political order" that erases divisions and class membership. The first function of the social sciences is to neutralize this division between property owners and non-property owners precisely through the concept of the "social" and "society." Durkheim's sociology represents the very accomplishment of this insidious, daily, habitual work of disciplines and the norm. "Power is exercised through the medium of the system of disciplines, but so that it is concealed and appears as that reality called society, the object of sociology."[39]

Starting with the work on governmentality (1977–1978), the difference between the society of property owners, regulated by contract, and the society of non-property owners, regulated by the habit of disciplines, disappears and with it the division of society. "Society" now represents a "natural" and "spontaneous" order of people amongst each other when they exchange, produce, cohabit. Governmentality is exercised on this "intrinsic naturality" of society. "The state has responsibility for a society, a civil society, and the state must see to the management of this civil society."[40] In such a *naturally immanent* way that you could search in vain for any trace of the "management" of social division and the unequal exchange that they promote (between land owners and day-laborers, manufacturers and workers, or between the merchant and the public) in the two courses on classical liberalism: something that Adam Smith still recognized by emphasizing the de facto difference between "the general interest of society" and the pure expression of the private interests of the dominant classes.[41]

It is true that between 1972 and 1973, Foucault shifted from the analysis of disciplines to the analysis of security techniques. But did private property and the division of "society" that it determines disappear as well? Security techniques manage the same problem in another way and in another context. They do not govern society but the divisions carved out by property. They produce, incite, solicit, and reproduce the existence of property owners and non-property owners. These are the techniques that, until today, were capable of managing a civil war that had taken on a more abstract, more deterritorialized form: that of creditors and debtors.

THE PRIMACY OF CAPTURE,

BETWEEN SCHMITT AND LENIN

To conclude the analysis of the 1870–1914 sequence and the turn it represents, we will contrast the readings of imperialism carried out by Lenin and Carl Schmitt to complete each one according to the principle of mutual critique. This approach is justified by a certain number of connections between the economic-political analysis of modern imperialism by the German constitutionalist and the Leninist theory of imperialism, the sources with which Schmitt had some familiarity: Engels' theory of the economy of war in the *longue durée* of the history of capitalism (up to the final crisis),[1] *Imperialism. A Study* (1902) by John A. Hobson (the global economy of colonialism is at the heart of his critique of imperialism),[2] and *Finance Capital* (1910) by Rudolf Hilferding.

If we follow Carl Schmitt, taking him from the middle of his trajectory marked by the forced abandon of his sovereignist thought, and taking his major work from the end, which is its true beginning (*The·Nomos of the Earth* was started under Anglo-American bombardments), imperialism borrows the economic-global forms of "'englobing/enclosing' the national by the international"[3] at the end of the nineteenth century. These forms do not take possession of the nation-state without revealing its real economic history, which they appropriate *by liberalizing it to monopolize it better.* This liberalization passed through the "confusion of intrastate sovereignty and suprastate free economy" through "an order penetrating the market, the economy, and foreign law"[4] freed of all the limits of the old spatial order of the Earth that were based on interstate territorial capture in the New World and its distinction with the "theater of war" (*theatrum belli*) on European soil. It is not only that Schmitt sees the New World as the real condition of the limited war in European space (the "great reservoir through which European peoples balance out their conflicts" by "the compensations and impunity that it offers"),[5] it is also that imperialism becomes *the European way to overcome civil war by "war in [inter]state form."*[6] If colonies thus defined are "the fundamental spatial fact [*raumhafte Grundtatsache*] of international European law as it developed"[7] by ensuring this essential difference in regime between intra-European war between states and extra-European colonial wars, then we are given to understand that the renaissance of colonial companies in the nineteenth century, contemporary to the transformation of colonies into state territory, could only mean for Schmitt the advent of a global economy of unlimited war mixing the regime of surplus value with the transformation of world politics (*Weltpolitik*) into a "world police" (*Weltpolizei*). This expression can be found in the last text he published in 1978 ("The Legal World Revolution") as a "political surplus value" that must be grasped as the final corollary of the "new nomos of the earth"[8] that can no longer go without the reference to Marxism. Yet this reference is quite present in a mode of permanent confrontation that makes its original terminology change in the retroactive premises of *Nomos of the Earth*. As Céline Jouin has recently shown, Schmitt systematically refers to the work of Carl Brinckmann[9] on the question of imperialism, which openly posits the unavoidable aspect of Marxist analysis (Hilferding, Rosa Luxemburg) on the question of the relationship between economy and war. The critique of Schumpeter's *The Sociology of Imperialism* which concludes *The Concept of the Political* (1932) confirms this point: an "imperialism based on pure economic power" is not foreign to either politics or war. And once "economics has become political," it is "erroneous to believe that a political position founded on economic superiority is 'essentially unwarlike.'"[10] The proof can be found in World War I and what Schmitt calls in *The Nomos of the Earth* the "transformation of the meaning of war." For his part, Lenin understood the politics of "imperialist peace" on the horizon of secret negotiations as a *continuation of imperialist war by other means.*[11] Reversing the Clausewitzian formula that he had used until then.

In his 1953 article, "Appropriation/Distribution/Production: An Attempt to Determine from *Nomos* the Basic Questions of Every Social and Economic Order," where he refers to Lenin *explicitly* for the first time, Schmitt underlines a trait that first appears as strategic in capitalism by emphasizing that imperialism and its project of colonial expansion results from prioritizing appropriation (*nehmen*) over distribution (*teilen*) and over production (*weiden*). Imperialist accumulation is "land-appropriation" (*Landnahme*), colonial appropriation ("land appropriation of a new world") supported by "sea-appropriations" (*Seenahme*) that occur through conquest, occupation, and pillage and that are continued in a *world industry-appropriation* (*Industrienahme*). Schmitt not only critiques the primacy that liberals attribute to "production" but also the Marxists' belief in its "progressist" nature. According to his demonstration, socialism and liberalism fundamentally agree on the idea that "Progress and economic freedom consist of freeing productive powers, whereby such an increase in production and in the mass of consumer goods brings appropriation to an end, so that even distribution becomes an independent problem."[12] Schmitt makes reference here to the arguments of the *Ordoliberalen* in Germany concerning the "social market economy" in a sense that could not be more diametrically opposed to Foucault's analysis. Schmitt endeavors to demonstrate that shifting "attention away from appropriation and distribution to production"[13] is characteristic of the economy and liberalism, which have always tried to contain the violent and warlike modalities of expropriation in a type of prehistory—or a very "primitive" and original accumulation that the new regulations of social capitalism could repress in people's memories. Capitalism would thus only appropriate what it has created, or contributed to creating. This would still be the point of view of Marxists and Lenin himself, to the extent that they add the appropriation by the capitalist of the surplus-value produced by the worker. Seen as a "contradictory state of distribution," the question of appropriation would be resolved in the end by the dialectic of History with the full development of productive forces and expropriation of the expropriators who limit its enjoyment. This doubly pure production leaves unquestioned "the strongest imperialism, because it is the most modern"[14] that begins by referring back to a state that is "medieval, even atavistic, reactionary, opposed to progress" in the fact that "imperialist expansion, i.e., appropriation, especially land-appropriation, should precede distribution and production." Against "such a reactionary opponent, who would take something away from other people, Lenin's own efforts were directed at unchaining the powers of production and electrifying the earth."[15] Need we remind you that even today the political problem of the "social question" is used in reference to the same magic word of "growth" and to belief in the "principle of technological progress" shared by liberals and a good number of Marxists who have also forgotten to be Engelsians? In more concise form, Schmitt does not shy from noting that "Marx adopted and emphasized the progressivist claim to the unlimited increase in production essential to progressive liberalism."[16]

The pillage, theft, rapine, and conquest, in other words the unmediated appropriation, by force, of "production" are not anachronisms or vestiges of past eras destined to be left behind by modernization of the appropriation apparatus through technological development, rational organization of labor, and science. Appropriation does not only come "at the beginning," it also operates, even in its most "medieval" forms, in the most highly developed capitalism.

The two definitions of capitalism proposed by Kojève in a 1957 lecture in Düsseldorf (addressing representatives of "Rhine capitalism")—immediately recorded by Schmitt in one of the commentaries he added the same year to the publication in a collected volume of "Appropriation/Distribution/Production"—can help us grasp the meaning of the "primacy of appropriation" by removing some of the ambiguities and misunderstandings introduced by "Fordism" into the understanding of the nature of capital. Referring to what he calls "one of the most brilliant articles I have read in my life,"[17] the Hegelian philosopher and senior French government official proposed a fourth root for the modern *nomos* in the shape of the "gift" (*don*), which is immediately identified with the "root of the economic and sociopolitical law of the modern Western world" to make a distinction (in a critique of Schmitt) between a "taking capitalism" and a "giving capitalism." The latter is "modern, Fordist, and enlightened [capitalism], turned towards increasing the buying power of workers," while the "taking capitalism" that preceded it ("primitive capitalism," "classic capitalism," giving as little as possible to the working masses) would be Fordistly surpassed in an "*Aufhebung*" making the End of History (the global Americanization of the world) in law and in fact.[18] It is easy to understand the title chosen by the very liberal review *Commentaire* to introduce Kojève's article: "Capitalism and Socialism. Marx is God, Ford is His Prophet." According to Kojève's reasoning, Ford would be the only authentic Marxist of the twentieth century, through whom capitalism removed its internal contradictions in a "pacific and democratic" manner, substituting "distribution" ("giving capitalism") for "appropriation" ("taking capitalism") ... Other than Soviet socialism, which only augured that the revolutionary overthrow of a police state for the administration of poverty would lead to the same end, the final terrain of the Marxism of "appropriation" is economic colonialism, to which Kojève sought to apply the same recipe in the form of a "*giving colonialism*"(!), inspired by the speeches of President Truman: industrialized nations are called on to contribute to the development of non-industrialized nations...

In the commentary where he alludes to Kojève's conference, Schmitt stages himself as a fictional interlocutor responding that "No man can give, divide, and distribute without taking. Only a god, who created the world from nothing, can give and distribute without taking."[19] For Schmitt, it is impossible to give without taking and it is imperative to assert, against the economists, that separating war from economics is an "ideological" attempt to hide the reality of the economy as the continuation of war by other means. As for the positions of distributor and redistributor adopted by "welfare" (for which the ordoliberal version is stated in good German: *Verwaltungsstaat der Massen-Daseinvorsorge* or Administrative State of Mass Social Protection), they are "positions of power that are themselves the object of an appropriation and a distribution."[20]

We can better articulate the primacy of appropriation over distribution and production by starting from the Leninist analysis of imperialism. It allows us to observe that so-called "giving capitalism" was only a brief and exceptional strategic parenthesis in the very long history of "taking capitalism," which has continued since the mid-1970s with the conquering captures of neoliberalism.

For Lenin, imperialism is inseparable from the financial capital that imposed itself as the direction and leadership of industrial and commercial capital from the 1860s. Financial capital is not a perversion or an anomaly of the supposedly industrial nature of capitalism but its realization. It is only fully accomplished when its hegemony in A-A' is ready to realize all of its "political surplus values." The particularity of the apparatus of capture of financial capital is that it is not "limited" to exercising its "appropriation" over properly capitalist "production" and wage labor, since it makes no distinction between forms of production (modern, hypermodern, traditional, or archaic). It appropriates in the same way the production of so-called "cognitive" workers and the production of the slaves of the textile industry brought up to the modern era of the "fixed-term contract" by its most "immaterial" actions.

Despite the remarkable reversal of economic logic that he performs, Carl Schmitt remains faithful to an industrialist conception of capitalism. The final "nomos of the earth" is industry, and its appropriation, an "industrial appropriation" at the start of which economic war becomes "total war," while financial capital and the englobing specificity of its appropriation on a global scale have in fact been at the center of the continued accumulation of capital since the end of the nineteenth century. This is the very meaning of the Leninist analysis into which we must insert Schmitt's views to do justice to his observation that the new decisive division is situated between debtor and creditor peoples.[21]

The history of capitalism fully confirms the Schmittian perspective on appropriation and our hypothesis on the hegemony of financial capital. While the three major moments into which we can divide the development of capital in the twentieth century always begin with a capture, financial capital is the "subject" of this capture, and not the industrial capital that already fused with it. The imperialist sequence begins with colonial "land appropriations" and their development into global "industry appropriations" under the domination of financial capital, which until the Great Depression of 1929, controlled and monopolized the "free global economy" as government of industrial capital and political science of Capital's rule of law.

In relation to this political-financial hegemony, the New Deal of "Fordism" figures twice rather than once as *an exception proving the rule*—"by reasoned experiment within the framework of the existing social system," as punctiliously explained by Keynes.[22] Except that Keynes' reasoning is only viable on the horizon of *economic war* threatening the foundation of all institutions[23] on the national and international level, as seen in the global extension of the crisis, not without awakening the impact of the October Revolution and the perspective of a "final civil war."[24] As a result, the "entire structure"[25] of American capitalism must be reevaluated according to the retrospective lesson of

Keynes in *The General Theory of Employment, Interest and Money*: "pushing monetary theory back to becoming a theory of output as a whole."

From there, the "appropriation" of Fordism can have as its object financial capital itself and be accompanied by the very temporary supervision of industries, banks, and insurance companies in the context of the "welfare state." Keynesian euthanasia of the rentier is the expropriation of rent and finance that allowed, in the context of the "bankruptcy" and total crisis of the "system," and in a very political manner (the "opportunistic virtuosity" of Roosevelt),[26] a very brief capitalist sequence in the center of which there were not only major corporations but also, and first and foremost, the accelerated constitution of a new state-form: the Plan-state. Only the Plan-state was capable of announcing, as its birth certificate, the National Recovery Act (1933) confirming its leadership over private enterprise, banks (Emergency Banking Act, with a moratorium on bank payments), and the stock market (Securities Act).[27]

In Fordism, therefore, the strategic weapon is no longer finance but, under the supervision of a National Resources Planning Board, the *productive administration* of money generated by taxation: this is the sequence opened by the abandon of the gold standard in 1933 which led, after the Second World War and the Bretton Woods Accords, to the supremacy of the dollar as the currency commanding the New Deal/*New Liberalism* of global capitalism: Pax Americana, Marshall Plan. Determined not by the immanent laws of accumulation of capital but by "*la rebelión de las masas*" (Ortega y Gasset) and strategic relationships between classes (in the context of the National Labor Relations Act promoting unions and their representation in salary negotiations), the subordination of finance to the constitutional principle of "social welfare" (formalized in the Social Security Act) would be temporary: it would strictly coincide with what has been called "the proletarian period in class politics" (David Greenstone). The social state of capital responded to it, in other words to the reformism recognizing labor demands as engine of the socialization of production in a reasoned exploitation with recovery through consumption. Negri defined it as "the painful process whereby the working class became internalized within the life of the state," which can therefore "descend" into society.[28] In the United States itself, the cards were significantly reshuffled by its entry into war and the establishment of a *war capitalism* (led by the War Production Board and the War Labor Board), revealing the violence necessary to accomplish the project of a *society-factory*, while opportunely removing the signs pointing to a new depression.[29] Making Keynes right once again: "It seems politically impossible for a capitalist democracy to organize expenditure on the scale necessary to make the grand experiment which would prove my case—except in war conditions."[30]

9

TOTAL WARS

What's essential is not what we fight for but how.
　　　—Ernst Jünger, *Combat as an Inner Experience*

The World War was one of the most popular wars
known to history.
　　　　　　—Ernst Jünger, *Total Mobilization*

War is the health of the state.
　　　　　—Randolph Bourne, 1918

"The First and Second World Wars are connected like two fiery continents, linked rather than separated by a chain of volcanoes."[1] Preceded by "wars of observation" for the European powers (the South African War of 1899–1902, the Russo-Japanese War of 1904–1905, the Balkan Wars of 1912–1913), the total wars of the first half of the twentieth century represent, despite the interruptions, a single world war that caused profound changes for Capital and the state in the *unlimited totalization of war*. The "sovereign" function of the state ("imposing limits on interstate war and subduing civil war," according to Carl Schmitt's definition) and the legitimate monopoly on force behind it could no longer function like in the eighteenth and nineteenth centuries. So-called total war abolishes any distinction between civil war (internal) and major war (exterior), major and minor war (colonial), military war and non-military war (economic, propaganda, subjective), between combatants and non-combatants, between war and peace.

The thesis is well-known and recognized at the intersection of war and revolution. But there is some uncertainty over its semantic history between Germany, where it is thought to come from, and France, since Léon Daudet, in 1918 and in the name of *Action Française*, helped forge the term "total war." It was then taken up in 1935 by Ludendorff, Field Marshal of the German Army, in reference to the "racial policy" of the Reich.[2] "What is *total* war?" wrote Daudet, "not as a polemicist, but as a historian concerned with making a convincing argument [...]. It is the extension of struggle, in its most acute and its most chronic phases, to the political, economic, commercial, industrial, intellectual, juridical, and financial domains. Not only armies fight but also traditions, institutions, customs, codes, mindsets, and especially banks."[3] While the author of these lines is obsessed with "German gold" and the operations of "internal dissociation" that it allows behind the front lines (Ludendorff also emphasizes "financial mobilization" and "German financial weapons"),[4] we would like to introduce the perspective of Capital and the war machine as the constitutive perspective of total war.

Commanding the totalization of the two world wars, the results of which threatened the very existence of capitalism, is the appropriation of the war machine by Capital, which integrates and *reformats* the state as one of its components. This appropriation and integration, without which we could not think of war as *state*, and total war as *state of a new governmentality*, operate under the pressure of three processes that grew in intensity throughout the nineteenth and twentieth centuries. They are the emergence of class struggle (1830–1848) and its repeated attempts to construct its own war machine to transform "generalized civil war" into revolution; the failure of liberalism for which the principle of free competition, far from producing its own self-regulation, led to the concentration and centralization of industrial power (monopolies), pushing national imperialisms into armed confrontation for the domination of world markets; and finally the intensification of colonization, covering a large part of the planet at the end of the nineteenth century (the "race to divide the world"). As for the rise to extremism on the front-line of wars of subjectivity, since the First World War, the *nationalization of the masses* became the principle of totalizing management of societies whose forces can only be entirely mobilized in war through "dissociation" from the international solidarity of the proletariat. The national community of the labor soldier of industrial war therefore passes through the *de-proleta-rization of the people* and a "worker" who, before taking on its totalitarian meaning in Jünger (*Der Arbeiter*, 1932),[5] is subjected to a reverse trend aimed at negating a history expressed in the language of Marx. Ludendorff can thus explain that "introduction to the work of war, through obligatory service, had the *major moral importance* of placing all Germans, in these serious times, in the service of the fatherland."[6]

These three processes constitute the triple matrix of total wars in the following cases:

1/ war and production overlap so absolutely that *production* and *destruction* become identified in a process of rationalization—that of industrial war—that can be seen as a challenge to political economy and Marxism;

2/ no longer the sole affair of armed forces but of entire nations and peoples whose existence is threatened, total war means that the extreme violence of colonial "small wars," which have always been wars against populations, comes back home to the colonizers;

3/ as total war is at the same time civil war, the struggle between imperialisms takes place at the intersection of war and class struggle, before being "overdetermined" by the Soviet Revolution, which proposed to transform imperialist war into *global civil war*. It was rapidly led by *others* in the mode of a daunting counter-effectuation of "revolution."

9.1 Total War as Reversibility of Internal and External Colonizations

Total war establishes a reversibility between colonial war and interstate war to the extent that the characteristics of the former come to redefine, in a *continuum* of extreme violence, the realities of the latter, which until then had been incompatible with a "nightmare of pure destruction" (Jünger), extending to civilians the negation of any *jus in bello*.

It is therefore not by chance that Ludendorff begins his work on total war with a refutation of the "master of the art of war": Clausewitz. Ludendorff argues that Clausewitz *limits* his reasoning to "the annihilation of military forces alone," contradicting in that way his own understanding of the newness of Napoleonic armies that resided in the "popular forces" mobilized by the French Revolution and integrated into a first *Volkskrieg* (the "*levée en masse*," citizen army, army of citizen soldiers). It is true that Napoleon himself, with his army corps "*en masse*" only proposed to destroy the opposing army in a decisive battle in *flat country*. Thus "war had not yet realized, to talk like Clausewitz, its *abstract* or *absolute* form"[7]—unlike world war, war in which "it was hard to tell where the armed force itself began and where the people ended. People and army were as one" in the "war of peoples." It follows that "all of Clausewitz's theories need to be replaced." This need can be seen in the unfortunate influence they long retained among German commanders, where they contributed to maintaining the outdated idea of war as "instrument of external policies" of states. Now, *politics must serve war*[8] in a radical transformation of each, taken to the point of fusion of interior and exterior that eliminates the distinction between combatants and non-combatants in *total politics and total war*.[9]

"Without total war," Daudet explains punctiliously, "the blockade with which the allied nations rightly claimed—at least until the Russian defection—to encircle and starve Germany was and could only be just words."[10] In response there was the "total submarine war" against ships of the merchant marine of the Allied forces—and even "those flying a neutral flag"—that could be no more disputed than the bombardment of civilian populations, since they both suited the "demands of total war,"[11] this time according to Ludendorff. Italian general Giulio Douhet, to whom we owe the first theory of strategic bombing, observed that "the distinction between belligerents and non-belligerents no longer exists, since everyone works for war and the loss of a worker may be more serious than the loss of a soldier."[12] He explains that "aerial targets are therefore, in general, surfaces of a given area on which stand normal buildings, habitations, establishments, etc. and a given population." Since "there can no longer exist any zone in which life can continue in total security and relative tranquility. The battlefield can no longer be limited: it will only be defined by the borders of the nations fighting:

everyone becomes a combatant because everyone is exposed to direct strikes from the enemy."[13]

To attain victory, it is necessary to attack the material and "moral" (or subjective)[14] sources of the nation and population mobilized in its entirety. Because it is industrial war, industry and the working class must be mobilized by ensuring the subjective adhesion of the population to the nationalist project of the total war economy where—as Ludendorff repeats without false modesty—"the law of the strongest decides what is and is not 'law and use.'"[15]

It is easier to understand why Ludendorff pays attention to "colonial wars" (in quotation marks) in his first chapter on the "Characteristics of Total War," even if they "do not deserve the noble and serious designation of *war*." "Through its very existence, total war cannot be waged unless the entire people is threatened and it is decided to take charge of them"[16]: this is immediately the case of colonial war *from the point of view of the colonized*. In the colonies, as we have seen, this type of "total" war has always been waged and merges with colonization as its condition of reality. To fight the irregular action of guerrilla (and that "popular war [...] carried out behind the back of a victorious army," which Ludendorff recognizes in the European theater alone),[17] one must attack, as Tocqueville argued, the harvests, livestock, trade, lodgings, and cities… since the entire population supports and assists the combatants. Having never benefitted from the law of war between European states based on the strategic demand of preserving the power of Nations, the colonies could only be subject to a regime of "total war"—before its time in its mobilization in an apparatus (*dispositif*) of enframing that was imposed on all Europeans in World War I and in its "battles for materiel." ("We are the first-choice materiel," writes Jünger in

Combat as an Inner Experience.) "Colonial war is not a war against an overarching entity called 'government,' it is a war of everyone against everyone else. [...] It is precisely in this way that colonial war constitutes the historical matrix of the evolution of war."[18]

The distinctions between peace and war, between regular war and irregular war, between military and civilians that total wars abolish in what has been seen as a process of "de-civilization" (Norbert Elias), never occurred in the colonies. The colony was the *dehumanized* space where states subjected to the "law of people" in the European theater of operations could, had to participate in the most savage and reasoned brutality, with no "anthropological" limit, with no "sense of warrior's honor" or individual heroism. The passage from one field to the other is that of the *expeditions* that Ludendorff calls "the most immoral acts," "provoked by the love of profit," not deserving "in any way the noble and serious designation of *war*" ... to a total war that includes all practices in its *war machines* by unlimiting them in the order of reasons of their globalization.

To overcome the resistance that inevitably follows the application of the techniques and teachings of "small wars" to European wars, the state itself has to be transformed into an economic war machine, while military command passes from the hands of the aristocracy of career generals to a more restricted general staff whose main task is to develop the tactics of mass industrial war managed by the state. Thus Lieutenant-Colonel J.F.C. Fuller was still severely criticized in January 1914 for producing a document where he asserts that tactics must be based not on military history but on "weapon power," and that, as a result, every strategy should be rethought. The offensive charge, caricatured in its "charge with bayonet," had to give way to quick-loading field cannons and especially machine guns, which were still dismissed by European armies—except for the Germans.[19] However, as argued by the American inventor of the first "performing" model of machine gun (the Gatling Gun), it "bears the same relationship to other firearms that [...] the sewing machine [does] to the common needle."[20] *Industrial death, mass death*, confirmed by the law of big numbers (more than two-thirds of those who died in combat during the First World War were cut down by machine guns) and by the "inner experience" of storms of steel by the combatant Ernst Jünger: "It is nonetheless miserable. If the preparation does not crush everything, if there is even one machine gun still intact on the other side, these splendid men will be shot like a herd of deer when they charge across the no man's land. [...] A machine gun, a simple band that unfurls a few seconds in time—and those twenty-five men, with whom you could farm a broad island, hang on the barbed wire like bundles of rags...."[21] The continental and proto-colonial image of a cultivated island that peeks through Jünger's prose reminds us that colonization in Africa in the late nineteenth century was precisely done *at the end of a machine gun. Making the Map Red.* The Battle of Omdurman, in Sudan, on September 2, 1898, gave a measure of its efficacy: General Kitchener lost 48 men, while the Sudanese left 11,000 dead and 16,000 wounded on the battlefield.[22] Asia was not spared either, notably during a punitive expedition by the British in Tibet: there was no battle but a mass execution carried out with the best cost/benefit ratio by... executors. The experience in the European theater was reduced to the defensive by the failure of wave of assault. "It was as simple as this: three men and a machine gun can stop a battalion of heroes."[23]

Aimé Césaire repeatedly made this point: colonial violence, which was banned from the Western art of war, would end up turned against the European populations. After pillaging the entire planet, Europe unleashed methods first tested in the colonies against itself. The list is long: from the double genocide in the Americas to the German ordering of the "final solution" in 1904 against the Hereros in their southwest African colony or to the concentration camps invented by the English during the Boer War; from the first aerial bombardments improvised in Libya on an Italian colony to the widespread use of machine guns, without which the British South Africa Company would have lost Rhodesia... The promethean force aimed at civilizing "barbarians" was turned back against the capitalist "North" by applying *the same science* to the rationality of production and to the production of destruction. Which only fully—and technologically—makes sense because the colonies, up until the start of the First World War, served as the test laboratory for the new arms systems that would impose the "quantitative" theory of industrial war on enemy nations and the *new barbarity* they incarnated on each side. "A barbarian destroyed our churches," they would say in France in 1914. While racial or racialist representations fed the theme of the "barbarian" that could be machine-gunned, bombarded ("saturation bombing"), and gassed, industrialization maintained the threat of civil war whose instigators (the "populace" in the language of *L'Action Française*, "masses of malcontents" to use Ludendorff's euphemism, union members resistant to the war effort, and Bolsheviks) could be subject to the same treatment.[24] *And in any case, the primary aim was workers, combatants, and non-combatants.* "At the same time, the old spatial separation between the center (area of peace and law) and the periphery (area of violence and war) started to be erased. The frontier between interior and exterior was no longer necessarily a geographical border."[25]

In the impossible peace between the two World Wars dominated by the Treaty of Versailles, the threat of communism, and the anti-colonial struggles that reached the heart of allied Europe,[26] Carl Schmitt attacked the distinction cherished by "liberal ideology" between economy and politics. If "economic antagonisms can become political," as he writes in *The Concept of the Political*, it is "also erroneous to believe that a political position founded on economic superiority is 'essentially unwarlike.'"[27] It is also not so much "production" (as understood by economists) that is at stake in the economy than class struggle. Which means that from a revolutionary perspective, *class war* must take the place of economic crisis (and parliamentary battles). Following Schmitt again—albeit this time from his major post-war book, *Theory of the Partisan*, with the subtitle, *Intermediate Commentary on the Concept of the Political*—it fell to Lenin to define class struggle as "absolute hostility" (against the class *enemy*), a strategic confrontation that through the introduction of "irregular" forms of combat subverted the limited configuration of war and the political equilibrium that it had guaranteed until then on European soil. "The irregularity of class struggle calls not just the military line but the whole edifice of political and social order into question. [...] The alliances of philosophy with the partisan, established by Lenin, unleashed unexpected new, explosive forces. It produced nothing less than the demolition of the whole Eurocentric world, which Napoleon had tried to save and the Congress of Vienna had hoped to restore."[28]

While Carl Schmitt emphasizes that with Western capitalism and Eastern bolshevism "war became absolute war" by transforming what "began as a conventional state war of European international law and ended as an international civil war of revolutionary class enmity,"[29] he does not take sufficiently into account the fact that the "small wars" against colonized populations were the first form of total war—and that from this fact, Leninist absolutization of class struggle is not solely the "Clausewitzian" heritage of the Spanish guerrilla against Napoleon's armies of occupation. Schmitt is close to admitting it when he notes that "two kinds of war are particularly important and in a sense even related to partisanship: civil war and colonial war."[30]

Lenin surely delivered the most acute interpretation of the colonial matrix of World War I. In 1915, he defined the ongoing war as "War between the biggest slave-owners for preserving and fortifying slavery." This aspect of the First World War is largely overlooked. Yet it would have such important consequences that they can still be felt today—in the reestablishment of global order or, on the contrary, in the possibilities of new revolutionary initiatives.

> Six powers are enslaving over *half a billion* (521 million) inhabitants of colonies. For every four inhabitants of the "great" powers there are five inhabitants of "their" colonies. [...] The Anglo-French bourgeoisie are deceiving the people when they say that they are waging war for the freedom of nations and for Belgium; actually they are waging war for the purpose of retaining the colonies they have inordinately grabbed. The German imperialists would free Belgium, etc., at once if the British and French would agree "fairly" to share their colonies with them. The peculiarity of the situation lies in that in this war the fate of the colonies is being decided by war on the Continent.[31]

At the end of the war, the victorious imperial powers (France and England) divided up the "cake" of colonized countries and populations. The Bolsheviks, despite being ideologically faithful to the Marxist axiom that revolution *must* occur at capitalism's highest point of development, were then forced to take an interest in the part of the world (in particular "the Orient") which, like Russia, was "behind in development." They therefore carried out an important shift in the Eurocentric point of view that still constituted official Marxism.

World War I marked a fundamental moment in the political history of the world, one that Lenin did not fail to emphasize, with the arrival of colonized peoples into the struggle against imperialism and capitalism. The de-colonial Event continued throughout the twentieth century and is far from having ended with the new century.

> [P]recisely as a result of the first imperialist war, the East has been definitely drawn into the revolutionary movement, has been definitely drawn into the general maelstrom of the world revolutionary movement. [...] In the last analysis, the outcome of the struggle will be determined by the fact that Russia, India, China, etc., account for the overwhelming majority of the population of the globe. And during the past few years it is this majority that has been drawn into the struggle for emancipation with extraordinary rapidity.[32]

The Communist International gathered in Moscow in the summer of 1920, but the participating delegates were mostly European. In September, the "First Congress of the Peoples of the East" was held in Baku, which Zinoviev, at the time the President of the Comintern, called "the second half of the Congress of the International." 1,891 delegates from different countries of the "oppressed East" took part (including 100

Georgians, 157 Armenians, 235 Turks, 192 Persians, 82 Chechens, 14 Hindus, and 8 Chinese), of which 1,273 were communists. A witness of the event described the room as "extremely picturesque; all of the costumes of the East together made a stunning and richly colorful tableau."[33]

The strategic intuition was remarkable, even if it was more of a gathering than a congress. The colonial question and the Muslim question were at the heart of the discussions. Speaking to delegates who were in the majority Muslim, Zinoviev believed he had to speak their language and, full of enthusiasm, affirmed that the political objective was to "raise a veritable holy war (*jihad*) against English and French capitalists." Duly noted!

Although it was not translated into a proper political platform, the clairvoyance of these statements deserves attention. Zinoviev seems to anticipate the most common lot of decolonization: "The great importance of the revolution that is beginning in the East does not consist of chasing the English imperialists feasting at the table only to replace them with rich Muslims [...]. We want the world to be governed by the calloused hands of workers."

The statements of a Turkish woman are particularly representative of the changes brought about by revolution, since it shows the "war between the sexes" at work in a "revolutionary" assembly largely penetrated by patriarchal culture (55 women out of almost 2000 delegates, with strong opposition to the election of three women as officers of the congress). It also has the merit of reminding us that some questions do not stop at the borders of the colonized peoples, since they continue to disturb, in a France that is said to be lacking "integration," the good conscience of secular republicans "on the left." *In extenso*:

The women of the East are not merely fighting for the right to walk in the street without wearing the *chadra*, as many people suppose. For the women of the East, with their high moral ideals, the question of the *chadra*, it can be said, is of the least importance. If the women who form half of every community are opposed to the men and do not have the same rights as they have, then it is obviously impossible for society to progress [...]. But we know, too, that the position of our sisters in Persia, Bukhara, Khiva, Turkestan, India and other Moslem countries is even worse. [...] If you want to bring about your own emancipation, listen to our demands and render us real help and co-operation: Complete equality of rights; Ensuring for women unconditional opportunity to make use of the educational and vocational-training institutions established for men; Equality of rights of both parties to marriage; Unconditional abolition of polygamy; Unconditional admission of women to employment in legislative and administrative institutions; Everywhere, in cities, towns and villages, committees for the rights and protection of women to be established.[34]

Lenin was quickly convinced that revolution in Europe had failed. He observed that imperialist forces had succeeded in blocking its expansion and in isolating Russia. Yet the causes of this failure were also internal to the working class, since the labor aristocracy of capitalist countries was an accomplice of the victors: "it was by helping their 'own' bourgeoisie to conquer and strangle the whole world by imperialist methods, with the aim of thereby ensuring better pay for themselves, that the labor aristocracy developed."[35] Colonized peoples therefore had to become allies to allow the revolution to retake the initiative.

The Congress of the Peoples of the East was not without effect. The "awakening of Asia" pointed to by Lenin in the wake of the Russian Revolution of 1905 would come to represent, in the words of Geoffrey Barraclough, "the most important theme" of the twentieth century, "that of revolt against the West." A revolt that was at the origins of the decline of Europe and the reshaping of the West in general. "As the twentieth century opened, European power in Asia and Africa stood at its zenith [...]. Sixty years later, only the vestiges of European domination remain."[36] Barraclough comes to consider that the pressure from the revolt of the South against the West was just as important, if not more so, than the conflicts over wages by the working classes of the North in triggering, in the 1960s, the crisis in the model of accumulation that resulted from the Second World War. Zinoviev had reached the same conclusions in the 1920s: "When the East truly moves, Russia and all of Europe will only occupy a small corner of this vast tableau."[37]

9.2 Total War as Industrial War

Capital is the second matrix of total wars where war and production tend to overlap completely. Total wars bring irreversible changes, not only in the way to wage war and civil war but also in the capitalist organization of production, for the economic and political functions of "labor" and the governmentality of populations. Winning the war is no longer simply a military question or problem: *above all*, the war of industries, the war of labor, the war of science and technology, the war of communications and communication, the war of production and subjectivity must be won... Limited to the battlefield until the Napoleonic Wars, the space-time of war overflows into society by invading it like radio waves (wireless transmissions of energy), introducing the fourth dimension into war by abolishing *the thread of space and time*. From the point of view of "production," the word "total" refers to the subordination of society as a whole to the war economy through which capital *reorganizes itself.*

To put it another way: what the Marxists call the "real subsumption" of society in capital found a precedent and was anticipated in the First World War. Or better yet: the subordination of society to production is conditioned by this new regime of "total" war where it is quickly understood that "it is the interest of efficient warfare to *militarize peace*"[38] in a new technology of power. As Hans Speier and Alfred Kähler explain from their exile in America, on the brink of the Second World War, it is connected with the *technologicalization* of the machinery of destruction that "tightens the grip which modern war has on the common man's life."

The "peaceful" deployment of real subsumption after the defeat of Nazism was only a consequence of this large-scale experimentation that times of "peace" could never reproduce with the same intensity, despite the rapid transformation of the American economy into a "permanent war economy." While capitalists have long dreamed of the reestablishment of this "general mobilization" for "production" (the "wild energies of expansion"…), the neoliberals were the ones to adapt some of its modalities (modular "armies" of free-forced labor, explosion in military spending…) in their political program.

"Total" war should be understood as a war that mobilizes all productive (labor, science, technology, organization, production), social, and subjective forces of a nation for the first time, bringing an end to the time when "it was enough to send into combat hundreds of thousands of subjects who were recruited and given clear leadership."[39]

Total war is the model for full use of all productive forces mobilized in the sense of an *extension of the domain of production.* This was Ludendorff's obsession, explaining that war "forced us to display and use all of our human forces."[40] At the end of the war, as Jünger confirms, "there was no longer any activity—be it a domestic worker working with a sewing machine—that was not production destined, at least indirectly, to the war economy."[41] Yet total war is also an opportunity for the intensification and rationalization of the domain of production. It gives rise to the first planning of the organization of labor and control of its productivity on a national scale. Lenin, as we know, was sensitive to the dialectic of history motorized by war, which accelerates "the way monopoly capitalism develops into state-monopoly capitalism," which he considered to be "a complete *material* preparation for socialism"[42]; and Russia becoming Soviet in a globalized civil war of fourteen countries would have to draw on the organization of the war economy of Germany, theorized and implemented by the industrialist Rathenau, the architect of German planning of arms production, to organize *production campaigns* of five-year "plans." The plan first concerns labor, which is made "obligatory for the entire population" and instituted as the regulating principle not only of industrial production but also German society as a whole. As Lenin wrote in March 1918: "German imperialism [...] has incidentally given proof of its economic progressiveness by being the first country to introduce labor conscription."[43] Also by following the creations of Moellendorf, a mechanical engineer by training, technical advisor for weapons at the Ministry of War and right arm of Rathenau, industrial mobilization becomes the corollary of a project of global planning of which the "Labor Bureau," tasked with controlling the entire labor force of the Empire, was the central organ. "All activity was required to follow the orders of the Labor Bureau."[44] Historians have disputed the economic efficacy of this *absolute* militarization of production which, in Germany, still depended on an order that was still too strictly corporatist and autocratic to reverse the trend and win the war when Ludendorff obtained full powers in July 1917. However, all the European powers would, if not adopt but *adapt* this first model of state-plan based on the total mobilization of the population by promoting the "soldier of labor." It took hold as a veritable *collective subject* of total war in the mass production it promoted and that changed the management of armed forces by taking as its model the "scientific" control of production adjusted to the militarization of civil society.

With the introduction of the first assembly lines in the arms industry and mechanical construction (in particular, automobile manufacturing), the war economy gave impetus and depth to the *principles* of Taylorist organization of labor associated with standardization and serial production. It had been relatively limited before the war due to the fragmentation of industrial structures and labor resistance to the law of the time clock and the incentive wages found in the new discipline of the factory.[45] In France, the progress in metallurgical productivity reached 50% thanks to Taylorism; in Great Britain, "national factories" were privileged, going from 70 in 1915 to more than 200 at the end of the war; in the United States, after the introduction of the "Taylor System" at the Watertown Arsenal (1909–1911), naval construction was rationalized and developed to meet the needs of the Allies (with assembly of cargo ships from standardized prefabricated elements). George Babcock, member of the Society to Promote the Science of

Management and Lieutenant-Colonel during the war, declared to an auditorium composed mostly of engineers in Boston in 1919: "one of the biggest lessons of the war which we have learned, is that the expansion and further study of the principles of industrial management, promulgated and carried on under the Taylor principles of scientific management, have been justified in practice under one of the heaviest burdens ever placed upon them."[46]

Starting, therefore, with the United States, where "from one day to the next, during the Great War, scientific management was widely adopted: new systems of automatic wage calculation, precise recording of productivity, standardization, and the organization of work around 'functional' supervisors became general practice in military establishments and the war industries under the authority of the federal government."[47] The phenomenon spread further after the war, a period characterized both by the development of mass consumerism and the disciplining of labor struggles in an extreme anti-communism without which Taylor and his managerial regime of *enforcing (forçage)* would never have become the heroes of the "new factory."[48]

Yet the defeat of the labor movement following the First World War was also the result of the "collaboration between capital and labor." It presided over the negotiated incorporation of workers into the national state of total war throughout Europe. Before leading to its Italian-fascist and German-Nazi reconfiguration, the reformist France of Albert Thomas, Socialist Deputy and early member of the "Union sacrée" who was given the mission of arming France as Minister of Munitions, and of Léon Jouhaux, at the time General Secretary of the CGT, emphasized new forms of organization of labor and social discipline that could replace the pre-war class struggles with national unity for economic progress. By promoting "every means of coming together, understanding, and collaboration" between "industrialists and workers," it was proposed the "the effort made for the war also serve as fully as possible in arming the country for peaceful struggles on the field of industry."[49] In the early 1920s, in the more liberal context of the United States and "cooperative competition," or "coopertition," it is quickly recognized that it only represented an "American variation on the efforts undertaken by Europeans to transcend class struggle and build a 'functional democracy.'"[50] From the very fact that work reveals itself to be even in the post-war reconstruction a formidable vector and instrument of the war of subjectivity (or according to the vocabulary used by the French socialist and syndicalist of the "war mind," which is also a "war of the mind"), the considerable "progress" in the scientific-engineering application of these disciplinary techniques to the war of labor are revealed to depend on their extension and their biopolitical intensification to society as a whole, also engaging an entire *domestic front*.

The opening of this domestic front was also commanded by the first great feminization of labor that took place in the Great War (the "munitionnettes"). The war of women contributed to the new Taylorist management of the labor force (unskilled or unqualified) by thoroughly renewing the oldest manufacturing practice of the labor of women when arms are lacking ("vagabondage" and worker's instability, periods of planting and harvest, military requisition). It is good to remember that in the 1960s, there were less women working than in the last war. (In the case of the United States, other than the half-million women mobilized in the armed forces, five million were employed in the defense industries out of a total of six million working women.) The full employment of the Fordist period is above all an affair of men. *Rosie the Riveter*, from the famous poster by Howard

Miller, lost her place. And in more than one sense, the underlying causes for it were found in the First World War and in the first defeats of the feminist movement by the war.

The emancipation struggles of these women that were on the "front line" and number of whom became widows,[51] stumbled in France—despite the strength of the feminist movement until 1914—with the failure to obtain the right to vote in the post-war: approved by the National Assembly, it was finally rejected by the Senate in 1922, for the reason that women could bring a "new Bonaparte" to power or favor a "Bolshevist revolution." (The right to vote would only be granted to them by a ruling of the French Committee of National Liberation (Comité français de Libération nationale) in 1944, for services rendered during the Resistance.) The same misadventure took place in Italy which had in the meantime come under Mussolini. In Belgium, only the mothers and wives of men fallen at the front were authorized to vote: the *suffrage of the dead* was established in 1920. The most interesting situation was undoubtedly that of England, where the reward for services rendered to the nation played a role in giving the right to vote to women in 1918, but it was accompanied by the decision to tie women's rights to those of their husbands and an age limit (over thirty) which summarily excluded the young women who worked in the munitions factories ("women war workers"), or joined the army auxiliary services… Moreover, the question of women's suffrage was only a "late addition" to a project aimed at expanding the male electorate, and it was also the only one of the proposals of the "Speaker's Conference" that did not receive a unanimous vote. "Women, even those with the right to vote, remained above all mothers and spouses (which was expected of women over thirty) while the young women that the war had made more independent, who would soon be called 'flappers,' were refused any say in the reconstruction of the country."[52] It was only in 1928 that the minimum voting age for women was aligned in England with that of men. As the German feminist Helene Lange said as early as 1896: "Men will not accord women the right to vote until it serves their interests." Including their *class interests*. (In the context of the 1918 revolution and the new constitution of the Weimar Republic, women obtained the right to vote in Germany.) More generally, many feminist works put forward the principle of a "double helix" where the social integration of women in the war was a parenthesis just as quickly closed by the return of men as the war of the sexes was largely suspended on the "Homefront" during the conflict. "Women *when named as a sex* by the formulations of social policy cannot escape being the incarnation of gender as strange or temporary workers; nor can they escape being seen as hovering on the edge of maternity."[53] War thus leads back to the *work of the war against women* until their enslavement to the order of production. The capitalist or socialist version.

Total wars were in effect the occasion of a rise in the militant ideology of productivism in Europe, and even more in the Soviet Union, where the ideal of a *proletarian Taylorism* was developed, transforming into "Stakhanovism" what Leninism considered to be a "great progress in science." Science that he claimed to dissociate from its function of capitalist exploitation, which limited "rationalization" to the sole process of labor to extend its principles to society as a whole. It is very exactly the enterprise of total war, which Lenin can only claim to "collectivize" because he did not grasp its real (bio-)political dynamic, which was nonetheless exercised in the "slogan of 'census and control' repeated [by him] during this entire period."[54]

The critique of work that had marked the proletarian struggles of the nineteenth century made way for a "sanctification," the deleterious effects of which on the labor movement would only be fully felt after the Second World War. Separated from the "revolutionary mobilization of workers" that Lenin called for, emancipation depended on the "discipline of labor," before becoming an affair of growth and economic productivity as the sole objective of the labor movement. The lesson here is once again Taylorian.

The ambiguity that Marx himself maintained by making work both the generic essence of man and the very place of exploitation is erased by total war. The image of war "as an armed action increasingly fades in favor of a much broader representation of it as a gigantic labor process."[55] This explains how the conversion of internationalist workers into nationalist soldiers occurred almost instantaneously: the organization of war and the organization of work became homogenous with the *work of war*. On the most immediate front of the militarization of work, there were on the one side the "shock workers" and on the other "workers of destruction" of troops that were not all shock troops... Like a machine-tool on the assembly line, as Massimiliano Guareschi remarks following a line of thought that bears repeating:

> soldiers in the trenches represented human material with replaceable parts: for the first time, medicine turned to a more widespread use of prostheses to alter destroyed members or even to reconstruct disfigured faces. But worker-soldiers were equally interchangeable as a whole. In their work, be it in a factory or at war, any relationship with the arts from which these activities came was annihilated. Serial production on the

assembly line took place in the form of anonymous production of death in battles of materials. In 1930, Friedrich Georg Jünger in *Kreig und Krieger*, and his brother Ernst in *Die totale Mobilmachung* clearly showed the anonymous aspect of serial production on the level of war labor and defined it as one of the fundamental characteristics of world war.[56]

Through confrontation that had become less inter-state than inter-imperialist, flows of financial capital and flows of war progressively lost their respective limits by crossing another threshold of deterritorialization together. War frees "production" from the necessity of the "market" to the extent that its aim is no longer "profitability" and "profit" (even if the capitalists were enriching themselves more than ever)[57] but the unlimited production of the "means of destruction" around which every economic machine and every society is mobilized in a machinic discipline under a single reticular command. (To paraphrase David Noble: "The military term for management is command; the business term for command is management.") Simultaneously, the transformation of class struggle, defeated on the internal front, into revolutionary civil war carried out by the Soviet Revolution, on a reversed front, freed the war on the space-time limits established by the *Jus publicum Europaeum* that had framed its *raison d'état*. Total war is not only global by extension, it is also *by intension* by making the frontiers between civil space and military space porous.

By freeing war and production from *all* their limits, imperialist war and revolutionary civil war brought forth *total* production and *total* war, for which the condition of possibility is given by destruction: destruction of the national enemy, the class enemy, but also, with Nazism, absolute or *total destruction*.

Between the two wars, Karl Korsch ran afoul of the Bolshevik party by drawing attention to the upheaval brought about by total war, the effects of which he saw as largely overlooked by the Marxists. Production distinguished from destruction, he argued, loses its progressive aspect when the *destructive forces* of mechanized modern war become an integral part of the "productive forces" of the war machine of capital. Or to put it more *economically*: "The gains in productivity and gains in destructiveness followed the same trend: the cost of destruction continued to decline throughout the eighteenth and nineteenth centuries. In terms of its destructive power, military technology had never been cheaper."[58] Everything took place as if consumption and production could only tend *to the infinite* through destruction. Which was largely realized by total war, and in particular the Second World War, the great preparation for the global society of mass consumption.

This reversibility of production/consumption/destruction implied by the general mobilization of productive forces (work, science, technology, population) challenges and calls into question the capability of the categories of political economy, but also its critique, to grasp the nature of capitalist production, while the (liberal) illusion of replacing war with the economy was contradicted by the facts, and war was no longer only to "engage in the conflict of competition [*der Konkurrenzkampf durch Kriege*]." How can we define capital and labor in total war? Can the concept of capital be enclosed in an "economic" definition with, as its only alternative, the opposition of "productive capital" with "fictive capital" and with "parasitic capital"? After the total wars, what can be the sense of academic dispute over the distinction between productive and non-productive labor? How can the enormous quantity of work engaged in and released by "general mobilization" be defined? How do we account for the fact that the greatest advances in science and technology were stimulated by military research and placed in the service of "energetic equipment programs" that can no longer be distinguished from *means of destruction*, thus reaching a power unknown to any other "civilization"?

The entire Marxist conception of capitalism and the productive forces it frees (work, science, technology) as force of "progress," as forces *tending* to create conditions for the extinction of capitalism and the rise of communism is jeopardized by total war. The progressive function of the bourgeoisie and the entrepreneur is extinguished at the same time as the "electric instruction of the masses" (Lenin). Without the introduction of *strategic relationships of power* at the most constitutive level, the very "nature" of capital escapes it most resolute adversaries. War becomes a parenthesis, an interruption or a crisis mode of the normal course of (economic) affairs, after which capital returns to its path and its "productive" history as "condition of the emancipation" of humanity—even if "*the proletariat [would have] disappeared*" (according to the famous statement by Lenin, which continues to apply outside the Soviet context of 1921). The shock to the generation of the war was definitively expressed by Walter Benjamin, for whom the *very possibility* of belief in the progress, science, technology, and discipline of salaried labor came to an end under the "storms of steel" and the combat gases of the Great War, subsequently converted into pesticides.

Surprisingly, after the Second World War, which saw American industry grow faster than in any other period of history by financing (like in the first conflict) the Allied mobilization, production was again separated from destruction, and capitalism from war, as if their relationship was only contextual. Proof if there ever was that it is decidedly difficult for Marxism to get away from its progressive conception of capital, wage labor, technology, and science despite the tragic verification of their destructive function in the total wars. It continues to feed orthodox and heterodox Marxism, up to the surprising theory known as "accelerationist" that gives a *techno* beat to recycling the progressist sensibility of nineteenth-century socialism and its dialectical replacement in (neo-)Leninist planning of "(post-) proletarian management."

Less comically, in the long post-war of Fordism, the most heterodox theories divided the Marxist definition of Capital as if the total wars had not taken place, as if, in the machine-gunning of hammer-revolvers, total war had not *already* realized the most real subsumption possible of society as a whole in the war machine of capital. "To the tensest nerve" and to "the child in the cradle," the entire "physics and metaphysics of exchange" find themselves mobilized "in times of peace as in times of war"— since the "war of workers" mobilizing "engines, airplanes, metropolises with millions of inhabitants" means that there is no longer "any atom *outside work*."[59]

9.3 The War and Civil War Against Socialism (and Communism)

Probably the most important matrix of total wars is the civil war between capitalism and socialism. The "small wars" against Parisian workers in 1848 and the Communards ("internal Bedouins") were no longer enough when socialism was presented as a global alternative to capitalism. Following the Russian Revolution of 1905 and its bloody suppression, which "brought to the stage actors who would then become the protagonists of the war of 1914,"[60] up to the eve of the conflict, socialism was causing capitalism to quake. The alert level had also been reached in the United States with the growing attraction of the Socialist Party for a large swath of the union movement.[61]

In his very valuable *1914*, Luciano Canfora quotes a page from the liberal English historian Herbert A. L. Fisher's *A History of Europe*, published in 1936: "A serious strike in the Saint Petersburg factories which broke out on July 8, 1914, and led to barricades and fighting in the streets, seemed to show that in the race between war and revolution it was revolution which would outstrip its rival and just pass the post." He also offers this passage from Braudel: "without exaggerating the strength of the Second International, we can still say that the West, in 1914, *while being on the verge of war, was just as much on the verge of socialism*. Socialism was on the point of taking power, to create a Europe that was just as modern, if not more so, than the one now. In a few days, in a few hours, the war ruined these hopes."[62]

It is an axiom: when "politics" threatens to transform into civil war attacking the very existence of capital, capital always responds with war. In this first or "original" sense, (virtual-real) civil war precedes total war *that sets the masses in motion against themselves*. The corollary follows: goaded by financial capital, supported by liberals and interventionists, Empires and States plunged Europe into the massacre of the First World War with no second thoughts. When the "internal Bedouins" number in the millions, when socialism is no longer only a specter because it becomes a possibility for all of Europe, the "great war" has to take on the exterminatory modalities of "small war" to eradicate them. Its extreme violence is *massified* by the industrial mobilization of nations transformed into "giant factories producing armies on the line to be ready to send them, twenty-four hours a day, to the front lines where a bloody process of consumption, once again completely mechanized, plays the role of the market."[63] Do we need a reminder that liberal democracies had "the dubious but considerable distinction of having sparked off the hell of the twentieth century"?[64] Once they realized that war did not succeed in finishing off socialism, and that the danger of communism had become incarnate in the Soviet Revolution that was introduced on the internal and external front, the liberal elite did not hesitate to enter fully into the era of *great* European civil *wars*. *Global civil war* began by turning against the (Russian) Revolution what Schmitt still called (reserved for the United States!) *the discriminatory concept of war* (war against a total enemy).[65] The late emergence of the notion of *Weltbürgerkrieg* in conservative and counter-revolutionary literature is not a *détournement* (and *reversal*) of Leninist "revolutionary civil war" for no reason...

Between the two wars, questions start to be asked about the meaning of the changes brought about by "total war" in relation to the civil war won by the Soviets and that long threatened to carry Germany into the revolutionary upheaval. In Italy, Mussolini was vigilant in seeking to stop the risk of contagion. Outside the Soviet Union, the thrust of "the militant ideology or productivism" was broken by the multiplication of labor strikes while rearmament was the order of business. The distinction in principle between war and civil war started to become vague, even to the point of disappearing. Ernst Jünger is a key witness here: "Between these two phenomena, World War and civil war, there exists a greater interconnection than it would seem at first glance; they are the two sides of a same event of planetary significance."[66] On the other end, Hannah Arendt also connected inter-imperialist war to the question of revolution and civil war: "a world war appears like the consequences of revolution, a kind of civil war raging all over the earth as even the Second World War was considered by a sizeable portion of public opinion and with considerable justification."[67] This would be enough to justify the meaning Lenin gave to total war when he asserted, in 1914, that in the situation of globalized capitalism, there was only one type of "just war": (civil) war against (imperialist) war.

As the spear tip of the Sacred Union on which the European socialist parties faltered, nationalism, which represented the subjective force of motivation for war, along with racism, was the first response to the intensifying social conflict and the threat of civil war. As Thomas Hippler notes, "war is only national to the extent that the warring nations are able to contain the underlying social conflict; war is only national to the extent that the social problem is absorbed into the national problem." Which amounts to saying that "war between nations hides class warfare. [...] This latent war works [...] nations from the inside."[68]

While Foucault is the one who shows that power is not first repression but production, incitation, solicitation, "action on actions" according to the consecrated phrase, this matter of fact should not be forgotten: when the political existence of Capital was threatened by socialism and communism, capitalism responded with repression, the "brutalization" of populations, and war. Only after victory was obtained over revolution in Europe did a political response emerge with the New Deal (substantially the same one in the democratic United States, fascist Italy, and Nazi Germany). It therefore took total war, the 1929 crisis, and European civil wars for Capital to start to consolidate for a time this global "economic-political" response where power showed its most "democratic" face without abandoning the most bellicose mobilization possible. "If we are to go forward," declared Roosevelt in his 1933 inaugural address, "we must move as a trained and loyal army willing to sacrifice for the good of a common discipline. [...] With this pledge taken, I assume unhesitatingly the leadership of this great army of our people dedicated to a disciplined attack upon our common problems." We could find no better way to say that the New Deal is the continuation of war by other means... renewing the National Recovery Act (NRA) for the War Industries Board established by Wilson in 1917 that served as its model.

The involvement of the industrial proletariat and the population in total war had been followed by a growing disorder in capitalist development disconnecting the (Taylorian-Fordist) organization of labor from the organization of markets. It would lead to the collapse of American financial capital (the Great Depression of 1929). Sealing the fate of liberalism while rekindling the risks of civil war, it forced "democratic" regimes and fascist regimes to take charge of the "social question" by reinforcing, by *universalizing* the role of the state in economic management and in societal control. From there, "the national state, as it was formed starting in the nineteenth century, progressively evolved into a 'national-social state.'"[69] It quickly drew criticism from American liberals and Marxists due to the similarities between the New Deal and Mussolini's corporatist state and Hitler's totalitarian state (liberals did not fail to add "state socialism" to this list).[70] Since "fascism" was more or less a synonym for an economy directed by a *strong state*, the New Deal was commonly assimilated—and not always critically[71]—with *economic fascism*.

The intense debate that took place at the time when the German constitution was composed following the Second World War concerning the definition of the "social" state, and which both Schmitt and Foucault discussed, in different ways, took place against the backdrop of the major problem of dis-continuity between democratic *social policies* and the measures taken in the 1930s, not only in the USA, but also in Italy and Germany. We could also think of the last Franco-German dialogue—the "Walter Lippmann Colloquium"—which took place in Paris in 1939, and where some of the participants who had fled Germany or been reduced to silence placed the (interventionist) idea that "the state should dominate economic development" (Franz Böhm)[72] under the auspices of a *social liberalism.*

Going beyond the sole disciplinary principle of the *factory-society,* the social polices deployed transversally in American democracy, fascism, and Nazism, exceed Foucault's definition of biopower (taking charge of birth rates, health administration, insurance system against work-related risks...). In fact, they were not limited to the "biological" life of populations and giving them "security." They concerned much more the entire *equipment of modernized life* by opening the way to mass consumption as a new form of control: programs of "motorization" in Germany (creation of the first highway network and launch of the first people's car: *Autobahn, Volkswagen*) and "electrification" in the US (hydraulic program of the Tennessee Valley Authority [TVA], including land improvement in a veritable land management project, or the "New Deal Landscape"), invention (and Taylorization) of "hobbies," of dopolavoro (Opera Nazionale *Dopolavoro*) and of Kraft durch Freude (Strength through Joy), widespread use of the radio ("Electric Eden, where the self is absorbed by technology," according to the famous expression by McLuhan) and film, development of propaganda and control... On this subject, we should also mention the Blue Eagle Campaign by the NRA, based on the war mobilization of

1917–1918, through which each citizen, each consumer, each employee, and each employer pledged as NRA members to *personally and publicly* support all of the emergency measures of the New Deal: "WE DO OUR PART," "Those who are not with us are against us." Knowing that Hitler quickly understood that the material and mental pauperization of the working class freed of its "bonzes" (*Bonzen*) and its Marxist unions would not play in favor of the new regime and the new spirit of national and social union, any resemblance between the "people" evoked here (the people, the common American) and the *Volksgemeinschaft* is not... accidental. If it needs to be highlighted: through intermediaries that were not solely diplomatic, for several years, before History accelerated decisively in the direction of "axial" expansionism, *exchanges* were constant between Mussolini's fascism, Roosevelt's New Deal, and Hitler's Nazism.

The goal of the social policies of the 1930s was to ward off the danger of bolshevist "collectivism" and to take under supervision the suicidal individualism of liberal and financial "capitalism." The New Deal, fascism, and Nazism were therefore considered by American and European "observers" as three modes of *post-liberal governmentality* of which the objective was to plan the economy under the direction of the state, which had the role of *protecting—and to protect the interests of capital against itself and against the people by nationalizing them both* after the violent death of "*laissez faire*." (After all, hadn't it led to the Great War, and from the Great War to the Great Depression?) Thus, a *national-social* state. "What ought to be called national-socialism—asserts a respectable professor from the University of Chicago and author of the weighty tome titled *The Pursuit of Power*—if Hitler had not preempted the term, emerged from the barracks and purchasing offices of the European armed services and, with the help of a coalition of administrative elites drawn from big business, big labor, academia, and big government, made European society over in amazingly short time."[73] All things equal, the Stalinist turn to "build socialist society in one country" (1924) and the renunciation of international proletarianism can also be called *national-socialist before its time.* Outside the combative interest in his experience with planning, Stuart Chase, the star journalist of the Democrats who is credited with the term "New Deal," concluded his column "A New Deal for America" on a note of very British humor: "Why should we let the Russians have all the fun remaking a world?"[74]

9.4 The "Paradox" of Biopower

The two world wars, civil wars, and the 1929 crisis carried out an unprecedented generalization and totalization of biopolitical and disciplinary technologies. They introduced a radical break in their evolution, one of which Foucault is far from taking the measure. Between the two wars, biopower and disciplines were completely reconfigured with respect to the class struggles and civil wars that were unfolding in Europe. They took on such importance that the 1914–1945 sequence has been called a single "European civil war."[75]

Foucault perfectly describes the generalization of the new mechanisms of power that reached their climax in Nazism: "No society could be more disciplinary or more concerned with providing insurance," he asserts on the subject. The development of "this society in which insurance and reassurance were universal, this universally disciplinary and regulatory society" is immediately referred to the realization of a trend "inscribed in the workings of the modern state."[76] Is it possible, however, to account for the generalization of biopower and disciplines without problema-tizing the "war machine" of Capital at the dawn of its new *organization* where it is energetically placing so much value on its *social* aspect? We have mentioned how in the First World War the extension of disciplines depended strictly on the war economy and the not only disciplinary but biopolitical distribution of *labor-value* as the principle of organization of "total mobiliza-tion." The unexpected success of the Russian Revolution and the failure of European revolutions, on the one hand, and the finan-cial crisis of 1929, on the other, made a complete reconfiguration of biopower necessary to neutralize "class struggle" and global civil war. In the absence of a strategic framework, fascism, Nazism, and the generalization of technologies of power, with the "right to kill" that comes along with them, are incomprehensible.

According to the final lesson of "*Society Must Be Defended*," the generalization of biopower leads to a "paradox": power that has as its object the administration of life can also eliminate it, and thus eliminate itself as biopower. Atomic power is the absolute paradigm of this paradox since the atomic bomb has the power to annihilate the population of which biopower is sup-posed to take charge. At this stage, the old privilege of sovereign power, the decision to put subjects to death ("the right to kill"), is shaken (how can a power that ensures life order death?). The only way to escape this paradox for Foucault, as we remember, is "state racism." "Of course, Nazism alone took the play between the sovereign right to kill and the mechanisms of biopower to this paroxysmal point. But this play is in fact inscribed in the workings of all states."[77]

With biopower "entire populations are mobilized for the pur-pose of wholesale slaughter in the name of life necessity." In this sense, "massacres have become vital." Yet does one still have to introduce race as the determining factor of the "naked question of survival"?[78] Doesn't this mean abstracting oneself from the stubborn presence of class warfare (to which, since primitive accumulation, we have traced race war as one of its articulations) that threatens to sabotage imperialist war to conquer global markets and where the belligerents can long remain "political" enemies up to the unlimitedness of total war? They only become "biological enemies" under certain conditions, in particular in Nazi Germany, which can be shared (unequally, with the help of colonization) but without *always* depending on the exclusive action of "biopower."

A few years later, Foucault would critique his theory of the "paradox" since the greatest "butchery" of history that took place during the Second World War was accompanied by the implementation by all protagonists of "great welfare, public health, and medical assistance programs" (Foucault is referring to the Beveridge program, English "social security"). Thus "large destructive mechanisms" coexisted with "institutions oriented toward the care of individual life." Although it is in the "nature" of capitalism to be both a "mode of production" and a "mode of destruction," Foucault only sees this dual dimension forming in the twentieth century, and always with the advent of the welfare state: "One could symbolize such a coincidence by a slogan: Go get slaughtered and we promise you a long and pleasant life. Life insurance is connected with a death command."[79] In this context, Foucault introduces the concept of *thanatopolitics* as the "reverse of biopolitics." The population, the object of biopower, "is nothing more than what the state takes care of for its own sake, of course, the state is entitled to slaughter it, if necessary."[80]

Foucault's concepts seem to shy away from this terrible sequence in the history of the West, since once the "paradox" is lifted, there remains no real explanation for racism. Just as the right to kill of biopower was taken to an extreme point of coalescence. It is therefore of particular interest that Foucault, returning to Nazism in *The Birth of Biopolitics* in his analysis of ordoliberalism, relates it to "the organization of an economic system in which protectionist economics, the economics of state aid, the planned economy, and Keynesian economics formed a firmly secured whole in which the different parts were bound together by the economic administration that was set up."[81] There is the transversality of the three "New Dealers" (Roosevelt, Hitler, and Mussolini) that we quickly mentioned, and to whom Foucault adds England and its total mobilization against the Third Reich by lending its voice to the ordoliberal critique: "English Labour party socialism will lead you to German-style Nazism. The Beveridge plan will lead you to the Göring plan, to the four-year plan of 1936.[82] Yet, as he recognizes himself, "Nazism as the extreme solution cannot serve as analytical model for general history, or at any rate for the past history of capitalism in Europe."[83]

9.5 The War Machine and the Generalization of the Right to Kill

Total wars and the European civil wars that they integrated and that threaten to *disintegrate* them are marked by a ferocious struggle between the war machine of capital and the revolutionary war machines mobilized against capitalism. In this merciless combat, the elites, the industrial and financial capitalists slowly removed all credit from the democratic-liberal parties in power and largely opted, after the First World War, for fascism, witnessing the impotence of parliamentary democracy in the face of the "Bolshevik" danger that took hold in Germany after the strikes of 1918 and the Spartakist split with the SPD. They thus favored the rise of fascist war machines that, seeming to respond better than liberal democracies to the dual challenge of political crisis (Russian Revolution) and the economic crisis culminating in 1929, nonetheless risked becoming autonomous and pursue goals contradicting the interests of capital. It is therefore in the context of *European Civil War* that we must analyze the transformations of disciplinary/security (or biopolitical) techniques and the generalization of the "right to kill" responding to the strategic aims of class struggle *on the global level imposed by Capital*. For Foucault, biopower seems on the contrary animated by an internal logic imposing its "paradoxes" on strategic forces.

To untangle these issues, we will reconstruct the relationship that Deleuze establishes in one of the courses alongside the writing of *A Thousand Plateaus*, between capital, war, and fascisms. He makes ample use of Clausewitzian concepts.

For Deleuze, as opposed to the liberal doxa, the "nature" of fascism is not foreign to that of capitalism. There is not only an instrumental relationship of repression or of "services rendered" to capitalists between them, but a dual complicity that implies the unlimited. That is where to search for the reasons for the generalization of the disciplines of biopower and the genealogy of the "right to kill." The latter is the direct and immediate consequence of capital's hold on war. The appropriation of the war machine by capital signifies that the infinite that animates production is transmitted to war by removing all limits from the "right to kill."

A tendency can be attributed to total war from the moment when capitalism takes hold of the war machine and gives it [...] a fundamental material development [...]. When war tends to become total, the objective [overcoming the adversary] and the goal [what the state aims for through realization of the objective] tend to enter into a sort of contradiction. There is a tension between the objective and the goal. Because as war becomes total, the objective, in other words, to use Clausewitz's term, overcoming the adversary, no longer has limits. The adversary can no longer be identified or assimilated with a fortress to capture, an enemy army to conquer but is the entire people and the entire land. In other words, the objective becomes unlimited and that is total war.[84]

In pre-industrial war, the goal and objective were aligned because the war machine was in the hands of the state: the military objective was subordinate to the political goal pursued by the state (war continuing politics by other means to establish its power). With total war, the military objective (overthrow the adversary) becomes unlimited (destroy the population and its environment) and the state is not able to impose a political goal on the endeavor. The state can no longer pursue its "political goal" because it is only a component of total war machines, such that it is not "its mechanics" (Foucault) that can explain the biopolitical totalization of disciplines and the generalization of the "right to kill." Fascisms resolve the contradiction between unlimited objective and limited goal by attributing to themselves the logic of production for production that they translate into the unlimitedness of destruction and the "right to kill," at the same time as they built a war machine to realize this objective. Yet another problem then arises: autonomous from the state, the fascist war machine risks becoming autonomous from Capital, even though it is not only a mode of production but also a mode of "destruction": destruction of a "part" of constant capital and variable capital in "economic" crises, and physical destruction of a "part" of the population during "political" crises. "Massacre," as Foucault demonstrated, is a mode of government of part of the population that operates *within certain limits* throughout the history of capitalism and that was progressively transferred from the colonies to the homelands.

Deleuze takes as his own the thesis of Hannah Arendt but turns it towards fascism alone, which he distinguishes from totalitarianism—albeit the focus of Arendt's major work of 1951—considered to be a *bad concept*.[85] "What fundamentally defines fascism is not a state apparatus, but the triggering of a movement that has no other end than movement, in other words the unlimited objective. A movement that has no other end than movement and therefore that has no other end than its own acceleration is precisely the movement of absolute destruction."[86] This diagnosis of fascism intersects "the texts of Hitler or his lieutenants, when they invoke a movement without destination or goal. The movement without destination or goal is the movement of pure destruction, the movement of total war. I am just saying that at that time, there was a type of autonomization of the war machine in relation to the state apparatus and it is very true that fascism is not a state apparatus."[87]

The generalization and intensification of the right to kill comes from "movement for movement" and the unlimited of "pure destruction" when the Nazi war machine becomes autonomous. But what does this mean if not that Nazism, by war *totally in act*, exacerbates the unlimited of production for production by giving ultimate consistency to the economy of its rational madness in pure *destructivism*: in this way Nazism carries into its death a simulacrum of a state apparatus, which is only for destruction. In the case of Nazism, Foucault also takes up the dynamic of war "without limit" but he seems to mistake the source when he assigns it to state biopower by wanting to ignore that "without limits" is a "law" of capital that introduces the infinite into production and, from there, into war, with what is first less a "right" (emanating from sovereign power) than a *power to kill*. It is this movement that escapes in fascism and constitutes its diagram of escape. The "racism of war" that Foucault talks about is unleashed by the same forces. How could the state free itself from its own *political conservation* in a *depopulation* as radical as the one pursued in the name and under the emblem of race by the Nazis? It seems that Foucault is turning around this question when he asserts, in the last lesson of "*Society Must Be Defended*":

They were also unleashed by the fact that war was explicitly defined as a political objective—and not simply as a basic political objective or as a means, but as a sort of ultimate and decisive phase in all political processes—politics had to lead to war, and war had to be the final decisive phase that would complete everything. The objective of the Nazi regime was therefore not really the destruction of other races. The destruction of other races was one aspect of the project, the other being to expose its own race to the absolute and universal threat of death. Risking one's life, being exposed to total destruction, was one of the principles inscribed in the basic duties of the obedient Nazi, and it was one of the essential objectives of Nazism's policies. It had to reach the point at which the entire population was exposed to death. Exposing the entire population to universal death was the only way it could truly constitute itself as a superior race and bring about its definitive regeneration once other races had been either exterminated or enslaved forever.[88]

Some have seen Deleuze's approach as being close to that of Foucault, but there is a chasm separating them. For Deleuze, the war machine and its tendency to subordinate states to its objectives explains Nazism and its reorganization of an equally disciplinary and suicidal biopower. It is impossible to account for it without introducing the infinite movement capital transmits to war, that its most "pure" machination transforms into a flow of absolute destruction in "the universal exposure to death." Biopower, like disciplines and the "right to kill," is only a component of the strategies implemented by the fascist war machines under the hold of unlimited movement and its totalization in the unlimited destruction of an enemy so absolute that any integration of a political goal, *and of politics as such*, in war becomes impossible, *including under the auspices of reversal of Clausewitz's formula*. This is contained *in nucleo* in the difference in nature between the war machine and the state when it engages, under the generic name of "fascism," all of the comprehension of Nazism.

In the totalitarian regime strictly speaking, the military often holds power, but it is by no means a machinic regime of war. On the contrary. It is a totalitarian regime in the sense of the minimum state. The fascist state, however, is something else altogether, and it is not for nothing that the fascists were not from the military. Military leaders, when they take over, they can make a totalitarian state. A fascist regime, it is not so certain. A fascist regime is such a twisted idea, it's not like the military. The German military leaders would have liked to have power, but they were beaten to it by Hitler [...] and you cannot say that fascism came from the German military leaders. It came from somewhere else entirely. This is where we see a war machine becoming autonomous from the state; about which Virilio had the very good idea to say the fascist state is a suicidal state. Of course, the idea is to kill others, but one's own death, that is the fascist theme of living death, as the crowning achievement of the death of others. You can see it in all the fascisms. Totalitarianism is not that at all. It is more petit bourgeois, it is much more conservative.[89]

Connecting biopolitical and disciplinary *techniques* with "industrialization" and "the economy" as Foucault does is entirely different than relating them to the "laws" of Capital and the war machine (distinct in nature from the state), as Deleuze proposes. The development of racism after the First World War gained momentum and became autonomous not from the techniques of biopower,[90] but from the Nazi *global war machine* which, by making itself autonomous in relation to the state and Capital, carries to its final solution the unlimitedness of annihilation of the enemy contained in total war.

If this "disturbing thing" appears here, leading biopower to the fascist coexistence of life and death, this "thing," far from coming, in a sort of continuous passage, from the history of the state, its own rationality, and its apparatuses, are instead subject to the contingency of "strategic relations" (which must be distinguished from the governing/governed relations and the *techniques of power* that manage them),[91] the discontinuities of class struggle, and the uncertain results of the deadly confrontation between capitalism and socialism. Here we can recall that the leader of the Labour opposition, Landsbury, declared one month after Churchill's "acting out" taking the "Roman genius" of Mussolini as its guide[92]: "I can see only two methods [of dealing with unemployment], and these have already been indicated by Mussolini: public works, or subsidies... If I were a dictator, I would do as Mussolini."[93]

Common in the beginning of the 1930s to the USA, fascist Italy, and Germany, these biopolitical measures subsequently diverge radically due to very different political and military strategies that command their respective economies. Still the relationships between Capital, the state, and the war machine take precedence.

Yet this becomes increasingly harder to perceive in Foucault's work at the end of the 1970s. The very rich theoretical articulation of the reality of capitalism tracing, within economic exploitation, disciplinary, security, and normalizing apparatuses of governmentality of the population failed to account for the dimension of class conflict that led to the European civil wars. Marxism, for its part, extracted social classes from the population and people, from which the Bolsheviks, in turn, extracted the avant-garde of the party to build the Bolshevik war machine from the "dictatorship of the proletariat" as *declaration of permanent revolution*.[94] To counter this politicization of the population according to a more warring than military class logic, total war reconstructs, first through the militarization of society, then through welfare, a "population" to mobilize inside it the resources of a "nationalist" people to which can always be administered "the racial antidote with the destructive effects of elements hostile to the popular community."[95]

On this point, Marx will be right against Foucault. *Especially* when Foucault, in the guise of a final approach to the reversal of Clausewitz's formula, is led to emphasize the *social-racism* afflicting a socialism that does not renounce "the problem of struggle, the struggle against the enemy, of the elimination of the enemy within capitalist society itself."[96] Since this remains our program, we still need to extract from the (category of) "population" the conditions of reality of a political *strategy*, even if it cannot be exclusively of classes in the strictest Marxist sense.

9.6 Warfare and Welfare

If the first objective of the generalization of techniques of biopower is to protect and ensure the life of the population while exposing it to death, the "paradox" of the "coexistence of life and death" brought forth by Foucault finds its point of application, explanation, and resolution in the relationship that should still be called constitutive between the biopolitical technologies of welfare and the techniques of warfare.

"From warfare state to welfare state," or "how the warfare state became the welfare state."[97] In a rigorous way, this should be understood in the sense where the matrix of welfare is the warfare of total wars, making the two notions inseparable in welfare *as continuation of* warfare *by other means.* This is the importance of the First World War: the response to the question "What is new in the New Deal?" refers to the attempt to construct a *neo-economy of war in times of peace.* As Marc Allen Eisner writes: "the New Deal is best understood as part of a larger history, one that dates back at least to US entry into World War I."[98]

The world wars that housed the Great European civil war determined a profound change of biopower that François Ewald's analyses of the welfare state, inspired by Foucault, only partially grasp. In fact, while "the welfare state accomplishes the dream of biopower,"[99] modern welfare did not come solely between the economics and the social of a right to *security* spreading to society as a whole an "insurance" logic of companies against all the "risks" inherent in productive activity (work accidents, unemployment, illness, retirement, etc.). It also comes from total war, and first as compensation for the population's and the industrial proletariat's involvement in the war effort. "The social state," observes Grégoire Chamayou, "was in part the product of the

World Wars, the price paid for cannon fodder, the counterpart to the blood tax, won in conflict. The 'cost' put in the balance of weapons for the 'political decision makers' is also calculated implicitly in terms of these expenses."[100] In France, one can think of the Order of October 4, 1945 and the Law of May 22, 1946 on the generalization of social security, "which guarantees workers and their families against risks of all nature that might reduce or remove their earning ability. It also covers maternity charges and family charges." Barbara Ehrenreich reached the same conclusion from the American situation, where the Social Security Act, passed in 1935, is an integral part of the New Deal: "In fact, modern welfare states [...] are in no small part the product of war—that is, of governments' attempts to appease soldiers and their families. In the U.S., for example, the Civil War led to the institution of widows' benefits, which were the predecessor of welfare in its Aid to Families with Dependent Children form."[101] We could add that the first disability pensions were paid to soldiers of the War of Independence and the first retirements also appeared after the Civil War, including the family members in a first "social welfare system."[102] Before the First World War, the system of military pensions can be seen as a first retirement plan for workers (the "respectable" working class).[103] It is not for no reason that the constitution of a "fiscal state" that finds its distant origin in civil war followed a series of wars before properly establishing itself to finance the First World War.[104]

Welfare is also a fundamental condition for the material and subjective production of soldiers for the wars of capital. Because births are needed to compensate for deaths and recruits must be able to fight! There follows a new *economy of life* that is combined with the citizen's right to death in a relationship of forces that is in principle more favorable than the one that presided over the first constitution of the labor force. The state now had to associate the "quality" of the population with its "quantity" beginning by including through a (natalist) politics of maternity as *national service* and *social work* deserving—in one form or another— "allocations" that make the mother giving and maintaining life the equivalent of the soldier risking death for defense of the *homeland*. "It was the military usefulness of human life that wrought the change. When a nation is fighting or preparing for another, [...] it must look to its future supplies of cannon fodder."[105] It goes without saying that neither the "equality" nor "difference" (nor "equality in difference") of the sexes were recognized as such... Yet it is not in the (masculine) logic of biopower alone that the paradoxical logic of a less than pacific "coexistence" should be sought; we should also look at the strategies of capital, its armies, and its war machines.

> In World War I, public health experts were shocked to find that one-third of conscripts were rejected as physically unfit for service; they were too weak and flabby or too damaged by work-related accidents. [...] Notions of social justice and fairness, or at least the fear of working class insurrections, certainly played a part in the development of twentieth century welfare states, but there was a pragmatic military motivation as well: if young people are to grow up to be effective troops, they need to be healthy, well-nourished, and reasonably well-educated.[106]

If there is no doubt a genealogy of welfare that passes the struggles for labor security at the factories and the right to life outside the factory into the "risk equation" of civil war, it fell to the total mobilization of society in the labor of war to impose the "universalization" of welfare on the entire population. And "where does this population come from?" responds Carole Pateman, echoing the feminist critiques of Foucault, that could here be put to work in reference to the diatribes of Roosevelt or Beveridge on the *mother soldier of life*. But she also shows how welfare tended to be substituted for the husband-family-provider, absent because of the draft (law on allocations to the wives of recruits, separation allowances): it is the *salary of the soldier* transferred to his *place holder* (woman as *private individual*)—instead of the social recognition of the woman "citizen," which still does not appear in the social security laws passed after World War II.[107] In the Beveridge Report of 1942, which presents the philosophy of the Family Allowance Act, and which is also the first act of the British welfare state and what would become the 1946 National Insurance Act, the liberal Keynesian explains: "the great majority of married women must be regarded as occupied on work which is vital though unpaid, without which their husbands could not do their paid work, and without which the nation could not continue."[108] A return to the starting blocks for the English suffragettes, who took up their refrain of 1914 published in *La Française*: "As long as the war lasts, the wives, sisters and mothers of the enemy will also be the enemy."[109] The same thing happened in France, where Marguerite de Witt-Schlumberger, president of the *Union française pour le Suffrage des Femmes* declared in 1916 that the women who refused to give a child to the homeland would be considered "*deserters*" (four years later she published a pamphlet entitled *Mothers of the Homeland or Traitors to the Homeland?*). However, it cannot be denied that maternal feminism corresponded to a wartime strategy.[110] In the country with the highest percentage of working women, it necessarily had to be combined with the measures taken by the Comité du Travail féminin [Women's Labor Committee], under the authority of the Ministry of War, and with the union struggles in the factory favorable to the development of a "social feminism" in the context of the welfare state under accelerated "welfarization."

In the United States, the creation of the National War Labor Board during the First World War anticipated the functioning of the National Labor Relation Act of the New Deal (the "Wagner Act") and encouraged the participation of unions (especially the American Federation of Labor) in the war effort[111]: the number of union members almost doubled between 1916 and 1919, while the average salary grew during the same years from \$765 to \$1272. Minimum wage, wage equality between men/women, and the eight-hour working day were all part of the intention to ensure "the subsistence of workers and their families in good health and reasonable comfort"—in exchange for the control of strikes by the unions (since the strikes exploded in an environment of full employment), limits on the right to strike, and the requisition of workers in strategic industries. At the end of the war, the AFL, in a much less favorable negotiating position, became the defender of sharing the profits of Taylorization and scientific management that seemed to have helped the "soldiers of labor." Against the order of worker's control, "Bolshevism, IWWism and red flagism in general,"[112] the AFL developed a politics of alliance with the "company unions" that proposed "profit sharing, stock bonuses, group insurance, old-age pensions, company housing, and clinics"[113] (welfare capitalism). As at least one union member remarked: "Is it not a close parallel to the Fascist trade unionism established by Mussolini in Italy? And if so, does it herald the dawn of an industrial and political dictatorship in America?"[114]

With total wars based on the mass conscription of the proletariat, the budget allocated to pay armies and other social payments to maintain soldiers (and veterans) in a corporatist welfare state has an obvious political function: it is a question of preventing the always present possibility of armed insurrection and social protests that the (mobilized or demobilized) draftees could join. Civil war is always lurking, and mutineers played a determinant role in the revolutions of the first half of the twentieth century. As Barbara Ehrenreich notes: "Ever since the introduction of mass armies in Europe in the seventeenth century, governments have generally understood that to underpay and underfeed one's troops—and the class of people that supplies them—is to risk having the guns pointed in the opposite direction from that which the officers recommend."[115]

More specific is the organization of American welfare—the most advanced organization that could be conceived at the time ("organization to the ultimate")—from the integration and *cooperation of "work"* in the model of totalization of the First World War. The modelling itself fell to none other than the former president of the War Industries Board (1917–1918) and close advisor of Roosevelt, Bernard Baruch, who confirmed it in a speech in May 1933: "We may find guidance in this crisis in the organization and the methods of the War Industries Board." As for labor, the rights of which were formalized in Section 7-a of the National Industrial Recovery Act (NIRA),[116] the conclusion was soon drawn on the union side:

> Under the new dispensation [...] unions are to survive not as militant organizations of workers, as in the past, but merely as the necessary machinery to insure that the arrangements entered into by labor leaders under central, government-dominated auspices will be observed by the millions of the rank and file [...]. It is not difficult to see in these developments the foreshadowing of an attempt to bring about universal compulsory

arbitration, for which machinery is already being evolved. Labor is to be fed—and tamed. It is to be given a comfortable cage, but its claws are to be clipped and its teeth filed.[117]

The "democratization of industry" should be read as the new *art of governing an industrial discipline*[118] exercised in priority on workers since business, which at first was to be "disciplined," would quickly be called to less coercive forms of cooperative self-government profiting large companies, overrepresented in the government agencies of a state that was in the end less anti-trust than compensatory... "The NRA," concludes Marc Allen Eisner, "was an experiment in compensatory state building, an effort to erect a system of government-supervised self-regulation plainly modeled on the War Industries Board."[119] The *strong* "Keynesian" program of the second New Deal, definitively adopted in 1938, arrived too late to seal the cracks of a war program in time of peace. It was left to the Second World War to resolve the problem. In proper English: "to provide the engine for economic recovery." There is no need to go into detail about how the transfer of the legislative to the executive of an administration engaged during the First World War (warfare) and pursued in the New Deal (welfare) would favor "the extreme delegation of power to business-dominated organizations and dollar-a-year men."[120] "Full employment" would be obtained under the Rooseveltian auspices of someone who was no longer "Dr. New Deal" but "Dr. Win the War," of a War Production Board dominated by businessmen more attentive to controlling wages than keeping down production costs, and of a drastic redefinition of the social redistribution of the welfare state. At the end of the war, only the "GI Bill of Rights" of 1944 proposed a real extension of the New Deal—exclusively to the benefit of "veterans" and under the governance of the Veterans Administration, which contributes, with its "100% Americanism," to the transformation of the welfare state in a National Security State of which the first characteristic was to erase the differences between time of peace and time of war. Presiding over the protection of American economic, political, and military interests throughout the world (Pax Americana), national security becomes the principle of governmentality of society and command of industrial planning turned to Research and Development (R&D).[121] The proclaimed industrial self-governance was largely steered by the Pentagon (which favored the aeronautics and electronics industries)[122] and its "government by contract." "To militarize is to governmentalize" asserted Harold Lasswell in his 1941 article on the "military state" (or "garrison state"). He argued that the state to come would be much less "rigid" than those in the past due to the chain of technology that presently linked the soldier to the manager.[123]

Thinking the constitution of the economic cycle not only starting from Capital but also in the constitutive relationship between Capital and war, the army, and the state leads us to propose a new hypothesis on the economic-political functions of welfare in the post-war period.

Total wars required an enormous conscription that concerned all countries of Europe: "60 million Europeans were mobilized. All social life was subordinated to military needs."[124] Between 1914 and 1945, European societies were entirely militarized. The American project of *welfare capitalism* in the post-World War II era must therefore be seen as an operation of new totalization aimed at integrating this immense militarization of Western societies into a new economic cycle that began with the largest strikes in the history of the United States (4,600,000 strikers in 1946).

On a very different scale, it resembles the situation of the "tyrant Cypselus" with whom we opened this book and who, to capture and transform the hoplitic war machine into a state force, carried out a "territorialization" of the army by integrating it into the economic circuit and making soldiers into "wage laborers." The construction of the economic circuit no longer took place by distributing land to soldiers but by distributing buying power (salary, subsidy, pension) and social rights (welfare) to the militarized population (industrial proletariat and military proletariat) in exchange for strict control of the right to strike by the unions (Taft-Harley Act, 1947),[125] by taxing the rich less than imposing on the poor (construction and modernization of the fiscal state, mass tax), by forgiving debts (in particular those of Germany), by developing the military-industrial complex and the financing sources of big business, and more. The "full employment" of the 1950s is the fruit of this reterritorialization of the deterritorialization produced by the total wars of the global civil war that had led the American economy, through creative destruction, to experience "the greatest expansion of capital in its history." If welfare is the transformation of the warfare that created it, the latter remains the active matrix of the first and imposes it as a *social recapitalization* of the state before absorbing it into the biopower of the military-industrial complex, "energized by the type of state building taken during World War II and by the attendant transformation of economic processes."[126]

The Marshall Plan carried out the reappropriation of war machines (fascists, revolutionaries, imperialists), with the objective, on the one hand, to establish a new regime of accumulation and, on the other, to build a new war machine "made in the USA," both a hegemonic military power and "great creditor" of the world.

9.7 The Keynesianism of War

Credited by Joan Robinson for discovering the *General Theory* before Keynes, the Polish Marxist economist of Jewish origin Michal Kalecki wrote two particularly important articles for the matter at hand: the first in 1935 on the economic policies of Nazi Germany, the second in 1943 on the "political cycle" of capital.[127] Taken together, they shed sharp light on the passage to the *Trente Glorieuses*, the thirty-year post-war boom, by accounting for the subordination of biopolitical and disciplinary techniques to the strategic interests of the capitalists and their war machine.

Kalecki's work follows that of another Polish Jew, Rosa Luxemburg, and her concept of war as "a pre-eminent means for the realization of surplus value,"[128] that is made to function as a fundamental economic-political element of the Cold War.[129]

In "Political Aspects of Full Employment" (1943), Kalecki lists the reasons for the aversion of "big capital" for the public spending policies financed by debt and finalized towards economic recovery through support for consumption and employment. Between the wars, the extreme reticence of employers for this Keynesian policy was shown in all capitalist countries, from the US of the New Deal to the France of the Popular Front, with the notable exception of Nazi Germany. However, and these are the last lines of his article, "The fight of the progressive forces for full employment is at the same time a way of *preventing* the recurrence of fascism."

Capitalist opposition only fell when public spending was mainly turned to arms production in preparation for World War II. Until then, a large part of major capital raised obstacles to state intervention arguing that it would reduce its autonomy and the spending towards consumption and employment would create relationships of force favorable to wage laborers. The hostility displayed was not economic, since profits would be higher in periods of full employment than under the "laissez-faire" regime. It was entirely political—giving a surprising description of the "political cycle" of capitalist accumulation, surprising because dominated by the strategic point of view. Kalecki is a rare case of an economist who is not an economicist.

He suggests a chain of three reasons to explain the phenomenon. First, financing by "mass consumption"; while it does not hinder entrepreneurial activity but stimulates it instead, it undermines the ethical basis of capital which orders to earn "one's daily bread with the sweat of one's brow." Second, under the conditions of full employment, firing no longer functions as a disciplinary measure at the sole discretion of the capitalist holding in his hands the fate of the worker. And everyone knows than when workers become "recalcitrant," the industrialists owe it to themselves to "teach them a lesson." Third, "'discipline in the factories' and 'political stability' are more appreciated than profits by business leaders. Their class instinct tells them that lasting full employment is unsound from their point of view, and that unemployment is an integral part of the 'normal' capitalist system."[130] Kalecki was frankly pessimistic on the capability of the capitalist system to promote a lasting *democratic* policy of full employment "by reasoned experiment within the framework of the existing social system" (according to the expression used by Keynes in a letter to Roosevelt in December 1933). Nazi Germany was the first to remove these objections to full employment by establishing a sort of model for big capital. Rejection of the financing of consumption was circumvented by concentrating public spending—in a manner until then unequaled in times of peace—on arms, which launched industrial production while controlling the rise in consumption by an increase in prices. Factory discipline and political stability were *totally* guaranteed by the new fascist regime (the panoply of interventions ranged from dissolving unions to concentration camps), while the state apparatus was placed under direct control of the new alliance between big capital and the Nazi Party.[131] The new Nazi war machine subordinated the state using new techniques of power (where political pressure replaced the economic pressure of unemployment).

The Nazi regime was the first to practice a successful "Keynesianism of war" in the strict sense (albeit *ante litteram*). Rearmament played a central political and economic role in reaching full employment and stimulating a cycle that had no other "outlet" than war. Reworked in the second New Deal (1937–1938) by Americans who take up the "total" scale, theorized in 1940 by Keynes himself in *How to Pay for War* [132] as the United States prepared to enter the war, military-industrial Keynesianism, far from being abandoned, was largely put to good use during the Cold War (with explicit reference to Germany of the 1930s by some economists linked to Stalinism, like Eugen Varga). In reality, however, rearmament policies had already provided a way out of the depression that threatened the world-economy after the financial crisis of 1907, the origin of which could already be found in the excess "laissez-faire" of the American financial system. Economic recovery by rearmament had led straight to World War I.

In parallel to the permanent economy of armament that it established—an economy that continued to grow until 1945, and that should be understood with Franz Neumann as a true "industrial revolution" (based on the chemical industry) financed by the National-Socialist state in favor of an unprecedented monopolization/cartelization/oligarchization[133]—Nazi Germany, while reducing the rights of the worker to nothing,[134] developed welfare like no other nation in the world. And it was by far its best weapon for internal propaganda.[135] "In total, the Third Reich spent 27.5 billion marks, an astonishing sum for this time, on family maintenance benefits during World War II. On average, family members of German soldiers had 72.8 percent of peacetime household income at their disposal. That is nearly double what families of American (36.7) and British soldiers (38.1) received." Budgetary policies called "population policy measures" also doubled between 1939 and 1941. In 1941, "pensions underwent an average increase of 15%." Higher education was free, along with access to healthcare. We could quote the highly surprising words of a British officer who, on his arrival in Germany, in 1945, observed that "the people did not fit the destruction. They looked good. They were rosy cheeked, happy, well groomed, and very well dressed. An economic system that had been propped up by millions of foreign hands and the total plunder of an entire part of the world was here displaying what it had achieved."[136]

Nevertheless, the suicidal non-durability of the capitalism of Nazi total war must be emphasized and situated in relation to the devastation of most German cities where there were only ghost-women and black silhouettes carrying bundles... There are also the reports by Victor Gollancz in autumn 1946 in the English-occupied zone[137] that scarcely fit with the officer's description above, as they reflect the destruction of an entire continent subjected to these extreme forms of "primitive accumulation" that were—insists Franz Neumann—the Germanization and Aryanization in which Western democracies made themselves complicit (before crushing the entire country under a carpet of bombs, "to destroy the morale of the enemy civil population and in particular of the industrial workers," according to Churchill's explanation in February 1942). Reason for the German people to lose belief in the liberal democracy of the status quo. Calling simultaneously for "conscious political action of the oppressed masses," for a political theory that proves "as efficient as National-Socialism" without sacrificing freedoms, and for the "potentialities of a unified Europe" that would bring welfare to all its inhabitants, the conclusion of Neumann's *Behemoth* is profoundly troubling.[138] We also know that warfare was and will continue to be the fundamental condition of mass consumption, to which the development programs of the Reich in favor of its *automobilized* population (the Nazi landscape) strongly contributed. This does not contradict the assertion of Kalecki in the early 1960s, who wrote that "experience has shown that fascism is not an indispensable system for armaments to play an important role in counteracting mass unemployment."

THE STRATEGY GAMES OF THE COLD WAR

> Whatever happens, the show must go on. And the United
> States must run the show.
>
> —Anonymous

The Cold War is often defined by the "arms race," as if it was specific to this period and to this phase of capitalist development. In response, it could be said that military Keynesianism in one form or another is the continued condition of the rise of capitalism. Or to put it another way, *war* has a strategic function that is directly economic, one that the Cold War only succeeded in making more obvious by contributing to its function of social control.

On the strength of his extended study of the pre- and post-war American economic context, Michal Kalecki asserts that "militarization of the economy" is an essential component of Keynesian "effective demand."[1] Following the teachings of Rosa Luxemburg, he sees military investments as the most effective means of resolving the contradiction represented by the realization of surplus value; they answer the problem of divergence between the development of productive forces and the market's ability to absorb them. Rearmament allows resolution of the contradiction by controlling it politically through war. Throughout the "Golden Age" of capitalism, military investments made it possible not to translate, in proportion to the increase of productivity,[2] the explosion of post-war industrial accumulation into mass consumerism and therefore into an increase in the quality of life of workers and the population. On the contrary, it made it possible to control its expansion and, where required, to reduce it in favor of the "part" of Big Business. "Full employment," Kalecki insists, was reached *thanks to the mass employment of soldiers and salaried workers in the war industries*. Without "war," be it cold or hot, there is no full employment. On this point, Keynes confirms the analysis of the Marxist Kalecki, who included the military underpinnings of the Marshall Plan (and more generally of all types of "external economic aid": *bases* and their contingents are never far). "Keynesianism" and the "liberal" militarization of society that supported it were applied with the same objectives and the same results to Germany and Japan, the two conquered (and officially demilitarized) powers of World War II. During the entire Cold War, according to this global perspective, growth in national revenue came first and foremost from increases in military spending, while the division of profits worked in favor of the proliferation of the arms industry. The major narrative of the *Trente Glorieuses*, the thirty years of post-war economic growth, is thus a chronicle of war. It should still be considered that the "militarization" of the Cold War is the major vector of the development and control of "scientific research." As we will see, Big Science made the connection between military and industry. They formed a single *complex of operational research* for all the "man-machine" systems of global capitalism that achieved its integration in the Cold War. A creation of the Cold War, "General

Intellect" is not the result of the generic development of communication, science, and technology, but of the vast military investments that shaped it as the brain of Integrated/ Integrating Global Capitalism.

Giovanni Arrighi draws even more general conclusions from the arms race when he criticizes Marx himself of neglecting the "economic" and "technological" function of war. The double "economist" and "technologist" limit putting a strain on the understanding of capitalism would be reproduced in the longer duration of the history of Marxism, even into its most acute metamorphoses (*Operaismo*). Marx's insistence on the "competitive superiority of capitalist production" over other economies made him write the shock—and oft-cited—formula wherein: "The cheap prices of its commodities are the heavy artillery with which [the bourgeoisie] batters down Chinese walls." Except that, as Arrighi objects, "insofar as China is concerned, actual military force rather than the metaphorical artillery of cheap commodities, was the key to the subjugation of East to West." And he concludes: "by focusing exclusively on the connection between capitalism and industrialism, Marx ends up by paying no attention to the close connection between both phenomena and militarism."[3]

The arms race has characterized the development of Capital since its origins. "So-called 'military Keynesianism'—the practice through which military expenditures boost the incomes of the citizens of the state that has made the expenditures—is no more a novelty of the twentieth century than finance capital and transnational business enterprise."[4] Italian city-states had already practiced a type of Keynesianism of war on a smaller scale.

The same Keynesianism of war is also at the basis of the functioning of the balance of power between European states following the Treaty of Westphalia (something Schmitt did not see in his analysis of "European equilibrium"). Pushing towards military competition, it required states to improve the production of their companies and their military techniques constantly to deepen the differences in power with the other parties in the world. It thus represents one of the keys to understanding colonial accumulation, of which the condition *sine qua non* was the accumulation of military force. Capitalism and militarism mutually reinforce each other at the expense of other economies. "The synergy between capitalism, industrialism, and militarism, driven by interstate competition, did indeed engender a virtuous circle of enrichment and empowerment for the peoples of European descent and a corresponding vicious circle of impoverishment and disempowerment for most other peoples."[5]

Arrighi therefore has grounds for seeing war as the source of technological innovations that spread and energize "production" and commerce. Isn't war the first social machinery, well before the factory, to make widespread use of large technological machines? The army is also the first institution to introduce, at the beginning of the seventeenth century, "scientific management" by standardizing the movements of soldiers, marching, charging, and using weapons (which did not escape Foucault). "Creative destruction," with all due respect to Schumpeter, is not only moved by entrepreneurial innovation, but first, and with even more dramatic consequences, by war.

Technological and scientific innovation depends on the social machine and, first of all, the war machine. It can blossom according to the "autonomous" logic of the machinic phylum, but its selection, implementation, perfecting, and application on a large scale to production and consumption are largely due to the war machine. Our analysis of the two total wars, and of what would continue under new means in the Cold War, corroborates the meaning of the observations of Arrighi about industrial revolution: "military demands on the British economy during the Napoleonic Wars in making the improvement of steam engines and such epoch-making innovations as the iron railway and iron ship possible at a time and under conditions which simply would not have existed without the wartime impetus to iron production. In this sense, the Industrial Revolution in the sectors that really mattered—i.e., the capital-goods industries—was largely a byproduct of the European armament race."[6]

The arms race that characterizes the entire twentieth century is revealed to be the irreversible inscription of industrial war at the heart of the mode of production, which is now just as irreversibly a "mode of destruction." "Industrial" wars are in no way a bloody parenthesis in economic development;[7] as industrial, they are like *the precipitate* of this development and the most coherent achievement of the capitalist mode of production. In this sense, the Cold War only continues and intensifies the inscription of war in Capital in the ultimate form of liberal-Keynesianism. "Under the new system, global military capabilities became an effective 'duopoly' of the United States and the USSR but the armament race continued with a vengeance, driven by a 'balance of terror' rather than a balance of power."[8] The destructive power of atomic humanity did not stop at Hiroshima. Hiroshima became the "technological breakthrough" of the Cold War leading to the installation, in the 1960s, of hundreds of thousands of long-range nuclear missiles aimed at the largest cities of the USA and the USSR. Far from ending the bipolar race, the SALT accords on the limitation of strategic weapons signed in 1972 only served to shift it "to other kinds of weapons not mentioned in the treaty for the good reason that they did not yet exist."[9] The principle of existence of the Cold War was only definitively damaged by the collapse of the USSR, which crowned the centralization of global military-industrial-scientific resources in the sole hands of the United States.

The history of the Cold War is an *American history* written from start to finish by the super power that emerged victorious from the two world wars. Overfed by full employment and the technological innovation of the war economy that increased productivity and mass consumption with the logistic militarization of society as a whole (*military subsumption*), the United States was confirmed as *creditor* power of the new global order resulting from the socialization and capitalization of total war. It took the form of an imperialism *so deterritorialized* that it can even be called "anti-imperialist," in the sense that it accelerated the disintegration of classic imperialism.[10] There is the deterritorialization of expansion, which is no longer territorial, *and the deterritorialization of war* that supports neocolonial decolonization and the geopolitics of economic aid: one and the other come from the investment of excess capital in the global protection of the Pax Americana market. But the Cold War was not only deterritorialization of interstate war aimed at "Soviet imperialism" and "communist slavery"; it was, at home and abroad, a new biopolitical regime of *endocolonization* for the entire population subject to the "American way of life" that must be decidedly inscribed at the heart of the war machine of capital. To summarize with Kissinger: "what is called globalization is really another name for the dominant role of the United States."

The historial fate of "class struggle" would therefore play out in the United States. Economically and politically strengthened by the "full employment" of the second industrial war, the working class was nonetheless defeated at the point of contact between the working subject and a new political fundamentalism that readjusted the rules of economic war by attacking *the very idea of communism* carried by the Russian Revolution. Even Marx and Lenin, who were called on in Detroit during the 1946 strikes, could not counter this result, and it represented a first victory of the Cold War in the immediate post-war period. But it was also the cycle of struggles for which 1968 was the global number and which started in the late 1950s in the USA, sounding the death knell of the political strength of "class." Confronted by Capital-Labor directly with the development of mass consumption, against the managerial institutionalization of "General Intellect," there were the struggles of the internally colonized, Blacks, women, proletarians not protected by the "enterprise system," students, and new subjectivities. These struggles without a central contradiction or general mediation were the first to explore the reality of a new anti-capitalist war machine of which the modalities were in all evidence no longer determined by the confrontation between "movement" and "organization" that ran throughout the 1960s.[11]

10.1 Cold War Cybernetics

The Cold War not only marked the entrance into the cyborg age of cybernetic communication and control, it was itself a manner of cyborg in the sense that its gray zone harbored the Great Transformation of the war machine of capital through feedback of all the "information" of industrially and scientifically organized total war, becoming the model for the development of the economy of *(non) peace*. From the studies on ways to fire anti-aircraft guns and their automation leading to the idea of feedback (and servomechanisms) to the digital simulations needed to build the atomic bomb, cybernetic thought was not only born of war—it continued war *by all means* in the management of a virtual-real planetary war allowing a permanent mobilization of all society submitted to calculations of optimization (in good American: "to get numbers out"). No science fiction here,[12] since the automatic factory, with the computer that "calculates" the best strategy to win atomic war, was the other entity of the cybernetic scenario. This constitutive relationship between the machine-to-make-war and the machine-to-produce gives cybernetics its most modern meaning (based on the Greek word *kubernetike*) of machine-to-govern and *capitalistic machination of the government of people*. It governs the management of war and the industrial management of society as a whole (even the systems of public health, urban development, organization of domestic space, and more), of which "one thinks to understand and control the dynamic by means of new instruments derived from the formalized sciences of engineers" and management techniques (understood in the broadest logistical sense, because there is no longer a "real" difference between technique and logistics, hardware and management).[13] The war machine of capital is the engine of this *science of organization* and of *operational research* tending to abolish the disciplinary frontiers by producing hybrids between "pure" mathematics (which are *fundamentalized*), hard science (with its monumental facilities that can only be shared: birth of "Big Science"), "engineering," and the social sciences (under the auspices of "behavioral sciences" and cognitive psychology: *behaviorism*). Promoted by the war of applied sciences that had just been won,[14] the engineering of complexity passes between (sciences of) Nature and Society with the invention of polymorphic tools built on mathematics, logic, and computers.[15]

Their modal and highly formalized approaches had names like "operational research, general systems theory, linear and non-linear programming, sequential analysis, mathematics of decision making, game theory, mathematical theory of optimization, cost-benefit analysis."[16] A first form of *transdisciplinarity* ensued (between logicians, mathematicians, statisticians, physicians, chemists, engineers, economists, sociologists, anthropologists, biologists, physiologists, geneticists, psychologists, game theorists, and operational researchers coming directly from the military) that was favored and financed by the American military (think tanks like the RAND Corporation, rightly considered to be "the institutional keystone of the Cold War in the United States,"[17] Summer Studies, universities) in constant coordination with major companies that it contracted to orient their development (economy of innovation). It was therefore an *entrepreneurial transdisciplinarity* where researchers, albeit directly funded by the military apparatus,[18] were led to arrange "networks of technologies, financers, and administrators to achieve their projects."[19] A new mode of *transversal governmentality* for all society also ensued, one that had scientific production "communicate" with the science of production in the factory while machining citizen-consumers according to the same procedural principle of optimization of control (for regulation of an open system taking into account the factor of uncertainty) and of the extension of the domain of circulation of "information." As a result, on this dual level, which involves the constitution of the *General Intellect* of Capital imposing "cybernetics" as the metaphysics of a "Theory of Everything" (Andy Pickering) informed by computers, the Cold War led to experimentation on the planetary scale in a global epistemology of the soviet enemy based on *simulation*. But that is not all: *it was the most intensive strategy for rational continuation of total war* defined by the inseparability of the "total domestic product" between the military and civilian domains, and by its incompatibility with every kind of *laissez-faire*. Which means that the Cold War was an American project of globalized social control driven by a cybernetics of the population.

This "internal production," this "interior" that proves the capability for global projection was the power that emerged victorious from the war at such unequaled levels in the military, industrial, technological, financial and other domains that it marked the end of European supremacy and its classically expansive forms of imperialism. The pre-war world was in ruins. While the wave of decolonization spreading across Europe at a time of social upheaval ("property is collaboration") contributed to the new forms that the global function of American power had to take, at home, this power had to face questions of demobilization and economic conversion as well as the labor power resulting from the "full employment" of war. Coinciding with the emergence of the question of "Blacks" and "minorities" (*racial wars* of *internal decolonization*), and with the "problem" of the place of women in society after their massive presence in factories (*war of the sexes* for equal wages threatening to affect the domestic economy),[20] the increase in strikes acutely posed the question of the transduction of *warfare* into an anti-communist *welfare*. To carry out the conversion of the "destructive forces" mobilized by the sciences and industries of death into the "productive forces" of the "American way of life" (the *world-welfare* of mass consumption rolling out the virtuous circle of wealth and power), *welfare* had to integrate the subjective conversion of the population militarized and socialized by the experience of total war into individualist workers supposed to lead the egoistic maximization of *homo oeconomicus* to the point of optimal tangency for the system between consumers and producers. The question of social production and the work of reproduction of the worker takes its place at the heart of the new cybernetic strategies of the war machine of capital. More investment than ever before had to be made in the "family unit" and the "feminine condition," and it was not for nothing that they were the *subject* of the famous "Kitchen Debate" between Richard Nixon and Nikita Khrushchev in 1959. It took place in Moscow during an international fair where the American pavilion consisted of a model home of six fully-furnished rooms over which a particularly "feminine" housewife was to reign... The war of missiles (the "missile gap") was joined by a "gendered" war of merchandise ("the commodity gap") emphasized by Nixon's rhetoric: "To us, diversity, the right to choose, [...] is the most impressive thing. We don't have one decision made at the top by one government official [...]. We have many different manufacturers and many different kinds of washing machines *so that the housewives have a choice* [...]. Would it not be better to compete in the relative merits of washing machines than in the strength of rockets?"[21] The theory of "rational choice" thus passes through consumption, which is no longer the frontier of future peace and prosperity, but the *limes* of the present designed, *designated* on the domestic front of the Cold War/Peace by the white line of electronic appliances.

The importance of communication can be found in the fact that this *Characteristically American* project had to be "sold"— according to the best-seller published in 1949 by a professor of philosophy at Harvard, Ralph Barton Perry—as an enterprise consolidating, starting with the couple, an "aggregate of spontaneities" in a "collective individualism" (two expressions of the same) of which the truth is a "scientific humanism" equated with the *social engineering of freedom itself* (Lyman Bryson, in another successful academic work published two years prior with the sober title *Science and Freedom*).[22] The arms race that allows the Keynesianism of war against the USSR reconfigured welfare into a *war of communication* contributing in turn to positing Intellect as an "instrument of national purpose, a component part of the 'military-industrial complex,'"[23] the power of which was also measured by the quality of its washing machines.

The source of the development of *human capital* was the integration of civil and military resources in a scientific-academic, military-industrial complex projecting Science to the level of an "endless frontier," according to the manifesto-title of Vannevar Bush's report in 1945 (*Science, the Endless Frontier*). This theme was quickly taken up by General Eisenhower in a memorandum of 1946:

> The armed forces could not have won the war alone. Scientists and business men contributed techniques and weapons which enabled us to outwit and overwhelm the enemy. [...] This pattern of integration must be translated into a peacetime counterpart which will not merely familiarize the Army with the progress made in science and industry, *but draw into our planning for national security all the civilian resources which can contribute to the defense of the country.* Success in this enterprise depends to a large degree on the cooperation which the nation as a whole is willing to contribute. However, the Army as one of the main agencies responsible for the defense of the nation has the duty to take the initiative in promoting closer relations between civilian and military interests. *It must*

*establish definite policies and administrative leadership which
will make possible even greater contributions from science, technology, and management than during the last war.*[24]

Military-civilian and civilian-military, permanent technological
war could only favor a global and systematic approach integrating
the new technologies of management of the social in the "soft-
ware" of "public welfare" commanded by a state that was less
administrative than "pro-ministrative" (the "pro-ministrative
state," to use Brian Balogh's concept).

The systemic genius of the Cold War that commanded its
C3I rationality (command, control, communications, and
information) involving the "fission of the social atom"[25] was
the invention of a "strange grey zone that is neither peace nor
completely war"[26] as the extreme *situation* where all forms of
social subjection start to depend *directly* on a machinic servitude to the system as such, even as it asserts its immanence in
the axiomatization of all its models of realization according to
purely functional relationships that make them infinite in
right. Or to say it with Deleuze and Guattari: the axiomatic is
immanent in the sense that it "finds in the domains it moves
through so many models, termed *models of realization.*"[27] For
us, there is therefore no "tension" between the will for axiomatization characteristic of the Cold War and "the practices first
developed with a sense of urgency, the very multiple and much
more pragmatic practices that then had to be extended,
expanded, formalized, and theorized."[28] Here, on the contrary,
we reach the *axiomatic engine* of the transdisciplinary practices
implemented in the laboratories of the Cold War (a *cold trans-
diciplinarity*). The war machine of capital would thus be able to
develop in the Cold War the immanent axiomatics of a new

capitalism, one of "human-machine systems," which imposed a system of generalized enslavement taking charge of subjection in "normalization, modulation, modeling, and information that bear on language, perception, desire, movement, etc., and which proceed by way of microassemblages."[29] In this sense and above all, the Cold War was a *war of subjectivation*, bringing with it what has rightly been called a veritable "behavioral revolution." It would be a synonym of unprecedented state intervention—a *state deterritorialization* that deterritorizlizes, mediatizes, and axiomatizes the state itself by putting it in a network in the entire *socius*—through which *peace and war are identical* in the "feedback" of the epistemology of the external enemy onto the ontology of the interior enemy, extending the imaginary field of the global proposition of the Cold War. "The rise of the TV 'sit-com' occupied Americans' living rooms while the building of a succession of ever-more-reinforced Situation Rooms occupied the White House basement. Across the newly emerging American behavioral sciences, sites of Cold War rationality, the situation took root"[30] and its explosion of *experts*. It also made communicate under a single term—that of *containment*—the psychology of the middle classes ("contain" one's emotions, "secure" one's home: *domestic containment*) and the strategy of "curbing" Soviet power.[31] The ins and outs of the situation lead back to the prediction made by Warren Weaver, the brains behind Operational Research (OR), "Grandmaster Cyborg," and "creator of transdisciplinary research networks": "The distinction between the military and the civilian in modern war is [...] a negligible distinction [...]. It may even be, for example, that the distinction between war and peace has gone by the board."[32]

10.2 Assembly (*Montage*) of the Cold War

"The problems of the United States can be summed up in two words: Russia abroad, labor at home,"[33] declared Charles E. Wilson in 1946. Former Executive Vice Chairman of the War Production Board, at the time head of the War Department Committee on Postwar Research, and future director of the Office of Defense Mobilization during the Korean War,[34] Wilson was the president of General Electric when he made this statement, the strategic concision of which undoubtedly comes from the multiple qualities of the person uttering it, and who by all evidence knew twice over what he was talking about. To the extent that we could even evoke a "General Electric"[35] that points to the military-industrial assembly of the subject of enunciation, as it prepares a symmetrical war on the dual external and internal front of the Cold War that programs it as such. Backed by one of the leading companies in industrial scientific research in a highly strategic sector for the armed forces, the entire economy of the Cold War correspondingly asks to be redefined: "Russia abroad, labor at home." Failing that, and according to a post-communist as much as post-cybernetic perspective, it seems difficult not to share the idea according to which the role of the Cold War was "from today's vantage point [...] really secondary" in relation to the "New Deal for the world" that would deploy its power, up to the postcolonial transformation of the Third World, "less through military hardware and more through the dollar."[36]

Yet can one be *that* dissociated from the other in the new forms of affirmation of American power and this *managerial revolution* that Orwell associated with a "cold war," to use the expression he forged in 1945? The argument goes as follows, "it is likelier to put an end to large-scale wars at the cost of prolonging indefinitely a '*peace that is no peace*' [...] by robbing the exploited classes and peoples of all power to revolt, and at the same time putting the possessors of the bomb on a basis of military equality" ... There is a double internal/external dissuasion of which the articulation commands the Cold War as a new global mode of managing the constitutive "conflict" of the "period." The Cold War is not *coextensive* to it; it is *constitutive* of the *globalization of civil war* that tended to take its autonomy (since the exploited classes and the peoples from whom they wanted to take all power revolted throughout the world) and its "management" in an unprecedented form of *military security* produced by a "a tacit agreement never to use the atomic bomb against one another."[37] This ecologistical understanding that controlled the "rise to extremes," where the extremity is no longer a limit (in the Clausewitzian political sense) but the definition of an imperial and planetary playground where the tendency is towards *duels* and the invention of a new type of government of populations (*1984*).[38] The clairvoyance of the analysis (isn't there something very Orwellian in Virilio?) could almost make us forget that the first Soviet atomic bomb (A-bomb) was tested in 1949, or four years *after* the publication of Orwell's article and two years *after* the "Truman doctrine" of *containment* ended up imposing the expression "cold war." This contributed to relativizing the imminence and the *reality* of the Soviet danger (to put it quickly: Stalin had no doubts about American economic-military hegemony; he understood the "message" of Hiroshima and adopted a *defensive* position after the war), at least according to the language used by President Truman in his speech to Congress in March 1947: "I believe that it must be the policy of the United States to support free peoples who are resisting attempted subjugation by armed minorities or by outside pressure." The disconnect ("armed minorities or by out-side pressure," "direct or indirect aggression," etc.) here plays the role of a real *inclusive* synthesis: it does not close on these terms, it announces and states the *unlimited* character of the Cold War strategy as the principle of transformation and *(re-)production of the enemy* by totalizing and *totalitarian* transference. This is the thesis of communism as the new fascism: "totalitarian regimes imposed upon free peoples, by direct or indirect aggression, undermine the foundations of international peace and hence the security of the United States."[39] *Hot Hitler* and *Cold Stalin.*

In a series of articles titled "The Cold War" and published the same year, Walter Lippmann wanted to give another meaning to the policy of containment. He started with surprise at the exclusive reference to "communist revolution" and "Marxist ideology" to explain the supposedly expansionist behavior of the "Soviet government" in the post-war period, even as it respected the spirit of the Yalta Agreement, based on the positions of the Red Army and the importance of its contribution to the defeat of Germany and Japan: "It was the mighty power of the Red Army, not the ideology of Karl Marx, which enabled the Russian government to expand its frontiers." And this, he observes, was in a sense *essentially limited* to restoring the sphere of "tsarist" influence and to "compensation" for the territorial losses of 1917–1921.[40] The USSR behaved like any other major continental power would, while the USA developed such an unorthodox strategy ("a strategic monstrosity") that the diplomatic channels leading to a *pax vera* seemed undermined in advance. Thus, the solution proposed by the "famous American publicist"[41] to return to a more classical balance of power: redirecting "the logic and rhetoric of American power" in the sense of a retreat of *all* non-European armed forces outside Europe to ensure respect of Stalin's commitment to not integrate Eastern countries in the USSR... In short, what Lippmann advances is *breaking out* of the American Cold War strategy if the *only problem* taken into consideration is "Russia abroad." Especially with the dissolution of the Komintern in 1943, the dissolution of the American Communist Party in 1944 (after the members of CP-USA moved from pro-strike positions to anti-strike positions to support the war effort),[42] Stalin's pressure on the Greek and Yugoslavian communists to preserve monarchy, and the protests of English communists against the dissolution of the coalition government immediately after the war, no one could doubt that Stalin had, according to Eric Hobsbawn, "a definitive goodbye to world revolution."[43]

Despite the shared warmongering rhetoric and the apocalyptic tone adopted by the United States alone, the first characteristic of the Cold War, as the British historian notes, was paradoxically defined by the objective absence of imminent danger of world war and the speed of the mutual recognition of a *certain* "balance of power" according, more or less, to the lines of demarcation of 1943–1945. Starting in 1951, the date at which Truman relieved General MacArthur of his functions, after the general, at the risk of resorting to the use of nuclear weapons, expressed the wish to extend the Korean War into Chinese territory (which had become the People's Republic of China in 1949), to the 1970s, including the repression of the worker's insurrection in East Berlin (in 1953, the year when the USSR acquired the hydrogen bomb—nine months after the Americans), and then the Hungarian (1956) and Czechoslovakian (1968) revolts, both defeated by Soviet tanks, the Cold War between the two superpowers increasingly took on the aspect of a *Cold Peace*[44] maintained by the (relative) balance of nuclear terror[45] over populations forced to "choose sides" ("two world camps," bipolarism). One will think here of the Soviet prohibitions against "Titoism" and of the reciprocal advantages taken from all types of repression of "grassroots democracy" in Eastern countries,[46] but also the strategy of the Cold War as a means of imposing American hegemony on his allies through the angle of reorganizing the world-economy towards a *globalization* that could no longer be satisfied with restoring the "classic" political-military forms of the balance of power. After the failure of the "ghost policy" according to which the Soviet Union would fall if strategically surrounded, the race for the most high-tech armaments (H-bomb, Strategic Air Command) was oriented towards a strategy of "massive retaliation" (1953–1960). Supposed to eliminate the possibility of a limited attack with conventional means, it was particularly aimed at limiting the risks involved in *American* neocolonial military expeditions in the hottest zone of the first Cold War: "It is not sound military strategy permanently to commit U.S. land forces to Asia to a degree that leaves us no strategic reserves. [...] Change was imperative to assure the *stamina* needed for *permanent security*. But it was equally imperative that change should be accompanied by understanding of our true purposes."[47] Soviet reterritorialization and American deterritorialization. The American administration claimed here to decide "permanently" between its "nationalist" interests (and components), in other words strictly *geopolitical*, turned towards Asia, and its *global* "internationalist" ambitions directed towards Europe to base the logic of the Cold War on a (exclusively) *strategic* basis. Although the American administration was incapable of keeping with this "choice," the direction was given: it was left to "great-power management" to take charge of the geopolitics of the new imperialism.

In this passage from "Defense," on which the original doctrine of containment could still be based, to "Permanent Security," we reach the change in paradigm found within the Cold War/Peace: the indefinite prorogation of a *peace that is not peace* due to the *strategic threat* of a war so ontologically absolute (*total* destruction, *universal* death) for all civilian populations that the economy of permanent war that it promotes is a synonym (in the West, the playmaker) of the work of *reprogramming* social life as a whole. What Paul Virilio called *endocolonization*,[48] and that should be associated with the obsession with the question of *control* in a historical sequence where American capitalist supremacy is less threatened *abroad* by the risk of a globalization of the Soviet threat than *at home*, at the heart of the "international system of capital," with the explosion of labor struggles and racial war kindled by the tumultuous demobilization in the fall of 1945.[49]

10.3 Cold War Detroit

In 1946, with the first conversions of weapons industries into industries of peace and well-being (from which women were mostly excluded),[50] and with the scuttling of price-control policies (by the Truman administration), labor struggles were capped off in the most worrying way by an impressive crescendo of strikes, wildcat walk-outs (in which more than 8 million American men and women took part), and race riots (Detroit, Harlem, Baltimore, Los Angeles, Saint Louis...) during the "War New Deal." To use Mario Tronti's numbers, although he was not the only one to detect the presence of *Marx in Detroit*: in 1946, 4985 strikes mobilized 4,600,000 workers, or 16.5% of the labor force,[51] which at the time included more than 15 million union members. People started to say (and read) that the phenomenon was "just as disturbing for the world of finance as the rise of Soviet influence abroad." *Life* magazine carried the title: "A Major US Problem: Labor."[52] There was agreement in thinking that it was the most serious industrial crisis in American history (the Great Depression was on an entirely different register) and the wave of strikes in 1946, which also spread across Europe and Japan, was the largest in the history of capitalism. The economic chronicler of an executive newsletter evoked the rise of a "disastrous civil war."[53] The previous year, Schumpeter had predicted the "decline of capitalist society" and its inability to face the vast needs of the post-war period. In this context, General Electric had its first national strike ("For the first time in the history of your company, all of the factories in the country are closed due to a strike"). It ended, after three months of picket lines and occupations, mass meetings, and several solidarity strikes with the support of all the local governments directly or indirectly involved, with the capitulation of the executives on the question of wages that had started the movement. Encouraged on the governmental level, the counter-offensive favored a merciless struggle against unions and their "communist" leaders (it would be called to testify before the House Committee on Un-American Activities)[54] and the "evolution" of the system of collective bargaining towards defending the interests of "free enterprise": this first component was inspired by the Taft-Hartley Act that had just been voted (June 1947)[55] and which General Electric lobbied for effectively, along with an unprecedented public-opinion campaign. Responsibility for discipline was also taken back from the workshops: accompanied by a very effective "Job Marketing" (*Boulwarism*),[56] and it focused on the installation of new machine tools and an ambitious, long-term automation plan (Norbert Wiener was approached by GE in 1949, though he declined the invitation). While automation by itself was the agent of capital's mobility and its decentralization outside labor bastions (according to the strategy of Ford and General Motors to control labor costs and weaken the power of unions), it was more specifically the Numerical Control system (N/C) that was favored by General Electric. More expensive, complex, and difficult to master than the programming technique known as "Record-Playback," it presented the advantage of totally removing mastery of the machine-tool from the hands of the most qualified and most organized workers to return power/control of the production process to management—"and why shouldn't we have control over it?"[57] Constant sponsor of research into machine-tools and tireless promoter of automated factories (the computer-integrated automatic factory) of the "second industrial revolution," the US Air Force used the weight of its contracts with GE to impose the path of computerization. Confronted with class struggle threatening to make social revolution the condition of the welfare state and "full employment" under labor control,[58] the only possible response to its drastic mastery (Taft-Hartley Act), its liberalization (Employment Act),[59] and the threat of its redirection towards the *veterans* (Whites) of the warfare state,[60] techno-managerial control of production, in the name of the free world and free enterprise, became a first end in itself in "General Electric's" anti-communist crusade.

While the year 1946 concluded with the declaration by President Truman that "had it not been for these strikes which we have had, I think we would have been able to issue that order [formal termination of war] now; but under the conditions we can't do it immediately,"[61] it was left to the Cold War to undo the internal enemy (war at home) and to associate the vital forces of the American economy with a virtual-real war (a permanent state of "virtual emergency") that was so materially and strategically profitable. Especially as it did not forbid profiting from and capitalizing on "local conflicts," based on the most classical patterns of the Keynesianism of war. "The Korean War saved us," confided one of the architects of the Cold War who requested (and obtained) a 300% increase in military spending (up to 500 billion dollars annually). He was undoubtedly referring to both the risk of "recession" and the threat of an isolationism that could hinder the rise of American leadership under the auspices of the Bretton Woods Agreement (1944), the United Nations Organization and UNESCO (1945), the Marshall Plan (1947), and the Atlantic Alliance (1949). In his speech on March 12, 1947, President Truman explained: "If we falter in our leadership, we may endanger the peace of the world—and we shall surely endanger the welfare of our own nation." In the name of this "American welfare," Truman proposed an investment opportunity—and a return on investment—to justify to Congress the delivery of financial aid to the Greek and Turkish regimes after Great Britain had withdrawn its support of "anti-communist" forces (facing what this same speech called "terrorist activities"): "The United States contributed $341,000,000,000 toward winning World War II. This is an investment in world freedom and world peace. [...] It is only common sense that we should safeguard this investment and make sure that it was not in vain."[62]

When the military-security and financial institutions of the new world order became as "interdependent as the blades of scissors,"[63] the scissors in question quickly cut away from Roosevelt's vision of a world united by a universal desire for peace supported by "the longing of poor nations for independence and eventual equality with the rich nations."[64] Carried by the ideal of decolonization and development, the United Nations Organization not only imposed a new international law as the concrete institutionalization of the idea of world government—it was imposed on all of its members as the supra-national incarnation of all the American political ideas Roosevelt had redefined in a first "New Deal" for the world in his famous "Four Freedoms Speech" in January 1941, which had prepared the country to enter *war for civil peace and international peace*.[65] The governmentality of the world would thus be unified ("one world") not against the USSR but in a radical surpassing of the English imperialist and colonialist model[66] through an extension of the New Deal which, after bringing *social security* to Americans, would become guarantor of the *political and commercial security* of the peoples of the world. "Aid to Russia and other poor nations would have the same effect as social welfare programs in the United States—it would give them the security to overcome chaos and prevent them from turning into violent revolutionaries. Meanwhile, they would be drawn inextricably into the revived world market system. By being brought into the general system, they would become responsible, just as American unions had during the war."[67] That this was not exactly the case (or that the unions had difficulty maintaining this role of "responsibility" despite their alliance with the Democrats during the war), and that this was not at all the case in 1946, even from Truman's point of view, was an important factor in transforming Roosevelt's reformist globalism into Truman's policy for the "free world." This policy assimilated communism with a global form of "terrorism" to integrate more fully into the Cold War strategy its essential indeterminateness between war and peace, war and politics, interior and exterior, endo-colonization and (control of) decolonization (or neo-colonialism) … The transformation of global civil war into global war for the security of new American imperialism required bringing *domestic policy* to the fore, in other words, the *wars of class, race, and sex*, as observed by Giovanni Arrighi when he wrote "Congress and the American business community were far too 'rational' in their calculations of the pecuniary costs and benefits of US foreign policy to release the means necessary to carry out such an unrealistic plan" like Roosevelt's New Deal for the world.[68]

The first objection was raised by southern Democratic senators of the "Black Belt" who were both the best administrators of segregationist laws (Jim Crow laws) and Roosevelt's supporters in Congress.[69] It could be resumed by this single question kindled by the increase in racist/racial riots in more than 45 American cities (including Detroit, where Roosevelt had to send troops)[70] in 1943 alone, and by their return in the immediate post-war period:[71] "Did black Southerners and Africans deserve 'freedom from fear'?"[72] Published in 1944–1945, the book-interventions of W.E.B Du Bois (*Color and Democracy*), Walter White (*A Rising Wind*), and Rayford W. Logan (*What the Negro Wants*) did not hesitate to emphasize the international aspect of "racial inequality" as both *imperialist and colonialist* to show that the question of domestic/foreign policy that it contained was far from exclusively "Southern." It implied the *dual delegitimization* of the racial construction of American identity and European colonial powers. As an unfortunate confirmation of the African-American argument, the Charter of the United Nations combined the principle of non-discrimination (voted on by a divided American delegation) with respect for national sovereignty, which prohibited the condemnation of colonialism as such and

reserved the application of international law and federal jurisdiction to American domestic policies (in the hands of the
states).[73] Again, according to the facts, racial segregation did not
need "Southern" laws to be practiced throughout the country
(in particular in terms of employment and housing, which had
been the issue for unionized Black workers during the war).
Inversely, "Jim Crow" caused the failure of the Dixie Operation
launched in 1946 by the Congress of Industrial Organization
(CIO) to spread the union victories of the North to the textile
industries in the South. The reality of the "free world's" struggle
against communist "slavery" ("freedom versus slavery" in Truman's speech) took on the accents of propaganda here in the
context of a situation known by all, where the "iron curtain" was
applied to a nation divided North to South by the "color line."
The final report of the president of the Committee on Civil
Rights, submitted in October 1947, based its argument on the
fact that "negligence" in terms of civil rights was a "serious
obstacle" to American leadership in the world. Taking up Truman's arguments, American supremacy over a world on an
accelerated path to decolonization (Asia, Middle East) openly
presided "at home" over redefining the race war as the "last
imperfections" to "correct"[74] in the democracy of capital, *in
order not to give weapons to the communist adversary* by weakening
the *moral position* of the United States. Yet, whatever the cost,
and at the risk of destabilizing the very principle of a liberal and
anti-communist defense of civil rights (an argument borrowed
by many leaders of the African-American movement),[75] the
East-West axis had to *integrate* the North-South axis of the European colonial powers (and their satellites) that were increasingly
closing in on... Africa. There was increasing fear of "premature
independence," especially since American economic interests

were increasingly involved. Among other merits, the Korean War allowed an end to the timid and strategic racial reformism of the American administration[76]—after it prohibited discrimination in the armed forces (July 1948),[77] which had to be remobilized in the name of the ideals of freedom of the Universal Declaration of Human Rights. In the most American sense of the world, it was the "liberal" representation of Cypselus. It was contemporary to the anti-communist turn of the majority of the trade union world and the abandoning of its civil and internationalist agenda in favor of adhesion to the Marshall Plan.[78] In the South, in particular in Alabama, one year after endorsing the Marshall Plan, the CIO took it upon itself to reign in the most radical union branches with the help of elements close to the KKK. The problem was no longer one of racial segregation— but of Black protest movements that became a threat to "national security."[79]

Relayed by constant communication efforts to model *global perception* of the racial question in the United States (Voice of America, the programs of "Cultural Affairs, Psychological Warfare, and Propaganda"), bipolar representation was only interrupted by the growing power and radicalness of the civil rights movement since the mid-1950s (Montgomery Bus Boycott, 1955). Coinciding with the birth of the Non-Aligned Movement (Bandung Conference, 1955) and a new anti-colonialist wave (Ghana, Algeria, Congo, Guinea), it took up the relay of labor struggles by continuing class war on the side of the "underclass," first in the South and then throughout the country.[80] In New York, in 1960, at the time of the plenary session of the United Nations, Castro allied with Malcolm X against "white power" by placing the entire Third World behind the Black-American insurrection. "Black people in the United States have a colonial relationship to the larger society," declared Stokely Carmichael a few years later in the name of the Student Non-Violent Coordinating Committee (SNCC)[81] and as an explanation of the wave of riots that did not stop. Following Martin Luther King, Stokely was taking up the great theme of *internal colonization* started by Frantz Fanon (curiously never quoted by Foucault) and turning it towards Black Power. For the entire baby boom generation, and in particular the student movement, the question of internal colonization was the major instrument of re-historicization and re-politicization of racism which, other than its management in terms of the "police," was only taken into consideration by the "system" in the margins of the analysis of individual competencies of "human capital," before being submitted to a purely economicist approach in terms of "costs and benefits."[82] Developed under the urgency of a political (and electoral) reformatting of this latter approach, the anti-poverty programs of the Kennedy-Johnson years (the "Great Society") only dealt with the most threatening effects of the *war on the poor*.[83] Without touching the mechanisms of ghettoization which fed the ordinary racism inherent in the supposed "moral deficiency" of the Black American community, survival conditions were improved (Aid to Families with Dependent Children [AFDC]) while seeking to neutralize "direct action" and block criticism of the (bio-)political economy of American imperialist power by activists that were "integrated" into the machine of local distribution of social assistance ("community action" aimed at achieving "participation" in society by the poor, of which the overwhelming majority were Black). In the immediate post-war period, weren't the spokespeople of the African-American cause obliged to abandon the critique of capitalism in favor of a more "domesticated," *gradualist* discourse that was more in sync with the crusade of free enterprise? Since one of the accomplishments of the Cold War and McCarthyism was to have overcome the major anti-colonial voices of the 1940s (Du Bois, Robeson, Hunton...). This also explains how the internationalist and anti-colonial revival characteristic of the 1960s coincided with the "return" to the fore of those expelled from welfare (Welfare Rights Movement) and all those left behind by the "American Way of Life." We can think here of Stanley Kubrick's *Dr. Strangelove*, which derailed the White male reality principle of the Cold War by attacking the domestic consensus on its most *gendered* aspect.

Let's summarize by attempting to bridge the *détroit* of the Cold War. The "subject" of the Cold War is none other than globalized capitalism which, in its military-financial constitution, merges with the war machine of capital. This war machine, in the post-war period, made the control of money and of military power the two primordial instruments of United States domination, and inaugurated what would be called the Golden Age of capitalism, starting by "scaring the hell out of the American people" (as Truman's entourage said about the real reason behind his intervention in Korea). The enterprise aimed at a "systematic, deliberate restructuring of *American* civil society"[84] which was itself inseparable from new procedures of (class) regulation, control, and (racial, sexual) division of welfare. In the guise of a "New Deal for the world," its *containment* by the Cold War determined a regime of biopower such that the military-industrial complex would take on a *nuclear* meaning that could be called, literally, "*military-vital*."[85]

This was doubly confirmed by the reality of containment of racial war in the Cold War *at home* ("domestication of anti-colonialism") *and abroad* ("Blacks are Americans")—and by the definitive failure of the enterprise on the horizon of the Vietnam War ("a war on two fronts") which led to a civil insurrection where all the facets of *internal decolonization* would be explored. A few years prior, in the Kennedy era, a march by 50,000 women in front of the Capitol—Women Strike for Peace—broke the *consensus on the reproduction* of the White middle classes by attacking the "tough cold war warrior who was also a warm family man."[86]

Returning to the anti-war perspective and the refusal of family discipline broken down by the first offensives of the Cold War, the reformist position of these women was in sync with Betty Friedan's bestseller, *The Feminine Mystique*, 1963, which gave the name "career" to the "nameless problem" of escaping the inevitability of housework. Yet this demystifying reformism[87] of the housewife's condition was quickly confronted with the feminist re-appropriation of class war in its *Blackest* aspect. The importance of the mobilization of mothers receiving social assistance confirmed the fact that the rise of feminist activism crossed, in the mid-1960s, the Black liberation movements and their struggles on the economic front.[88] In fact, "led by African-American women inspired by the Civil Rights Movement, [welfare mothers] mobilized to demand a wage from the state for the work of raising their children."[89] "Even when women do not work out of their homes, they are *vital producers*," explained Maria Rosa Della Costa and Selma James in their 1972 manifesto. "The commodity they produce, unlike all other commodities, is unique to capitalism: the living human being— 'the laborer himself' (Marx)," of which consumer conditioning reinforces the *social production* of the family and the *social power* of women.[90] In this total reversal of the domestic philosophy of the Cold War, the theme of the "social factory" is singularly displaced to the extent that social relations cannot *effectively* be transformed into relationships of production without inscribing the question of *social reproduction* at the heart of the system, which is thus targeted in its heart… by feminist organizations as Wages for Housework. It is particularly interesting that Selma James insists on the American origins of the movement and its strategy of class war inspired by the struggles of the Blacks *which redefined the very meaning of class by projecting itself into "the most advanced working-class struggle," in and especially outside the factory.* To the detriment, then, of the facile assimilation of the movement with a feminist version of Italian autonomy encouraged by the co-signing of the manifesto with Maria Rosa Della Costa and the start of the international campaign for housework wages in Padua in the summer of 1972.[91]

10.4 The Underside of the American Way of Life

Synonym of democracy *versus* totalitarianism, promotion of the American Way of Life was placed at the heart of the *declaration of Cold War* by President Truman when he explained the world-historical stakes of the new conflict: "At the present moment in world history nearly every nation must choose between alternative ways of life."[92] This would be rather banal (and merely a continuation of total war) if this "life" did not involve the war of subjectivity in a new form of governmentality, inscribing the social engineering of the mass psychology of military-industrial democracy far beyond the cultural containment of "communism" dear to the propaganda war of Voice of America. At home and abroad, psychosocial engineering became the vector of the economy of control by consumption integrated in the permanent technological revolution of the military-industrial, scientific-university complex and the market. They are each guarantors of the political democracy of Capital: "security and challenge in the same breath" of what could only be presented as a "capitalism of the people" (or *People's capitalism*)[93] inevitably opposed to democracies called "popular" (or democracy of the people: People's democracy)[94] because the first production of the Cold War was a *people of capitalism*. Taking aim at "imperialist" and "totalitarian" communism, President Truman could declare in April 1950, on the eve of the Korean War: "This is a struggle, above all else, for the minds of men."[95] The most interesting part of his speech, however, is the moment when he called on the unions at home to bear witness abroad to the reality of wage labor (=free labor) in the United States: "Our labor unions have already done fine work in communicating with labor in Europe, in Latin America, and elsewhere. The story of free American labor, told by American trade unionists, is a better weapon against Communist propaganda among workers in other countries than any number of speeches by Government officials." But for the labor unions to become the best agents of a People's capitalism and for "labor" to no longer be a problem at home, Marx had to be expelled from Detroit. This was in principle accomplished with the signature of the *Treaty of Detroit* (1950) at General Motors that incorporated the "Fordist" relationship between production and mass consumption by tying salary negotiations to increases in productivity—the syndicate thus gave up any ability to question wage distributions (adjusted in function of the cost of living) and profits. "Productivity" became by the same token the "*vitally needed* lubricant to reduce class and group frictions," as voiced as early as 1947 by the director of the Committee for Economic Development.[96] *Fortune* magazine was therefore right to celebrate the agreement as "throwing out all theories of wages as determined by political power and of profits as 'surplus-value.'" The union also accepted management's exclusive control of the workshops (management's control), passing it on in exchange for the company's contributions to welfare (retirement contributions, health insurance) which thus underwent *accelerated privatization* (private welfare plans), albeit not without increasing disparities in the job market.[97] At the same time, the power of syndicates and labor activists was transferred to their national leadership, which had sole power of negotiation with the top management of companies. Negotiations most often concluded with a contractual commitment not to strike (as was the case with General Motors for a five-year period). Locked down by a corporatist productivism where the objective interests of the most "guaranteed" working class tended to blend with management policies (business unionism),[98] and where the unions took up the refrain of "security" in following "commercial" Keynesianism to the detriment of the redistributive aspect that was left to the margins of a compensatory state, social peace (labor peace) became the model of trade unionism at home and abroad. The Marshall Plan took on the task of "selling" the Treaty of Detroit for export as a model of (pacified) social relations and a transitional mode away from the European conflictual austerity threatened by social revolution to a *society of (control through) consumption* in the American style. In short, "what was good for General Motors was now good for the world"[99] in a new world order that made the "reconstruction" of intense development without borders depend on capitalist accumulation using mass consumption as its principle of social regulation.

Once the process of production was placed under the control of productivity, "modernization" through consumption as colonization of daily life was supposed to direct the inflationist social pressure of "full employment" towards the acceleration of production and the circulation of goods (through planning of demand) in the *Americanization of the world*. The "New Deal for the world" is therefore *contained* in the commodification/privatization of "life" that becomes the *subject* of the expansive containment policies of the Cold War, for which the unions (and in particular the AFL-CIO) became the best agents[100] after the Taft-Hartley law did its "work." The Cold War was in fact a "psychological war," the modernity of which was measured in the anti-communism that allowed (the war of) subjectivity to replace the notion of class (struggle). "The importance of the individual," which is the principle of American values and that one of the major documents of the Cold War posited as "*more vital* than the ideology which is the fuel of Soviet dynamism,"[101] was ideologically translated in terms of a propaganda welfare associating "free competitive enterprise, free trade unionism, and limited government intervention" with the "growing classlessness of our society."[102] Through this hyperbole, classless society became the trend for an economy placed at the service, not of the state, but of the people, who took the benefits of capitalism by drawing on the "militant and responsible" forces of *free unions*. "Capitalism in a democracy uses its forces not in a negative way, to depress and exploit the masses, but to expand production, to create new ideas and new wealth."[103] The so-called *communism of capital* here takes on the aspect of *auto-mobile driving* that establishes communication ("Everything communicates!" is the leitmotiv of Jacques Tati's *Mon Oncle*)[104] between the spheres of work, domestic life, and leisure, between factory and suburban home, all connected by the "essential product of the capitalist market" (Debord) known as the automobile. Launched onto a network of highways with no other center than commercial centers, the automobile was not only the flagship product of the Fordist factory-society (6.5 million units were produced in the United States in 1950—or three-fourths of global production). It was also the *vehicle* of consumer society, its machinic-mental apprenticeship, and its training in the commodity mode of socialization. Consumption is the private value *par excellence* that colonizes daily life by Taylorizing domestic space, furnishing it with technological innovations (civil applications of the research and development programs of the "military-industrial complex"), and by privatizing/financializing homes. How can one feel "at home" without owning one's home, without making the *lifetime investment* combining the economic function with a "security-providing (and thus identity-providing) function?"[105]

The mortgage credit of "Mr. and Mrs. America"[106] took up the relay of consumer credit and *corporate welfare* by imposing the entire economy of domestic capitalism as the affective center (focused on the couple, marriage, children, Family Life) of capitalist democracy: *Democracy Begins in the Home, Home Is What You Make It, Building Community Through Family Life...*[107] To the tune of "I'll Buy That Dream,"[108] the nuclear family became the refuge against the anxiety of the Soviet nuclear threat (*The Red Target is Your Home, The Sheltered Honeymoon,*[109] etc.) and the domestic relay of financialization of the economy. Haven't the investment banks that massively invested in the private insurance market, mortgages, and consumption always proven their "vital" role in the real economy and the development of the "welfare" of all?

"Of all" was immediately contradicted by the fact that this welfare was a *welfare of civil war* that can only produce the majority system as motor of its axiomatic by constantly reproducing the system of discrimination that the multiplication of its axioms tries to control and limit in a series of "Fair Deals" and legal-political measures. From there "came a society with a rhetoric of classlessness, but sharply divided along racial lines,"[110] one that was closely linked to a war on the poor that was not enough to end the "war on poverty." It was declared by Lyndon Johnson but quickly "frozen" and then fought by the Nixon Administration due to its perverse effects: "Workfare not Welfare." Incarnated by the Economic Opportunity Act (1964), wasn't the very principle of American Fairness to promote an "equality of opportunity" to the detriment of any equality in *results*?[111] A long history started here on these American shores.

Racial discrimination had long combined employment segregation with housing segregation. And it did so in such an acute way that as early as 1946 it was seen in Detroit as a real "ticking time bomb," one that gained further explosiveness from the great internal migrations (Blacks from the South to the industrial North) and post-war urban development. The principle was that of a *chain reaction of poverty* giving Blacks access to the most difficult and expensive housing in the most ghettoized areas, where the living conditions served as a foil for any policies of integration. Thus more than ten years after the Wagner-Steagall Housing Act (renewed by Truman in 1949), the New Deal of social housing contributed strongly to *racial containment* by focusing its means on movement (new planning developments) or fixing in place the poorest Blacks (in the city centers, according to a principle of concentric urban development that spread from the center according to economic status). Formalized by the Chicago School, the model was encouraged by the privilege given to public assistance for access to property which, on the one hand, combined the criteria of race with the criteria of class ("black transitional neighborhoods" reserved for Black skilled workers and petite bourgeoisie)[112] and which, on the other, became the social condition of access to a White-working-"middle class" founded on a racial segregation of proprietors-consumers. These consumers were encouraged by all the actors of the property market. "THIS IS YOUR PERSONAL WAR TO SAVE YOUR PROPERTY RIGHTS," as one pamphlet explained, combining the "right to private life" with territorial mobilization against the "open housing movement" and federal legislation associated with an insidious form of communist stratification of society.[113] Black migration was described in military terms of *invasion* ("the Negro Invasion") against which owners and neighborhood associations established veritable strategies of "resistance," making residential suburbs the "battlefield" of community and family affairs. Women of the white working class were the first drafted into this defense of the "integrity" of the neighborhood (the home front), associating racial components with the "serenity" of family life for which they were responsible.[114] Control of racial and sexual frontiers fell into line with this war of subjectivity that could only base the new domestic model on the division between interior and exterior by *integrating* the household through the values of the "self-contained home" (Elaine Tyler May) in the great transformation of the working world. The "gendered" privatization of all corporatist values of the factory called in return for the *domestic management* of national subjectivity replacing the notion of class struggle in its spatial logic of racial exclusion and sexual discrimination.[115] This also explains how the United States led the movement that replaced the paradigm-image of the *factory-society* with the *"model home" of suburban society*, where its logic of segregation towards Blacks *and women* ("the comfortable concentration camps of suburbia" highlighted by Betty Friedan) was mixed with the "productive (*and reproductive*) consumption" of capitalist modernization.

In 1954, the year of the Supreme Court decision declaring racial segregation unconstitutional in public schools, Ronald Reagan obtained his first major role as the presenter of the television program *General Electric Theater* (the most popular Saturday evening program) and Goodwill Ambassador of *Boulwarism* in the group's factories.[116] As president, Reagan described his GE years as his "postgraduate course in political science," conceding indirectly that Lemuel Boulware was his real mentor. Coming from a background of advertising and market studies, Boulware was the man who probably changed American Business less than its class consciousness by associating it with that of the American worker, whom he had redefined (in this order) as "investor, customer, employee, supplier, and neighboring or more distant citizen." He provided the reasoning behind his "Job Marketing" in a convocation speech at Harvard Business School on June 11, 1949. After repeating the refrain of the dangers of the "socialist" species, of which communism, fascism, and Nazism were but varieties, he changed focus to the audience of businessmen, whom he addressed in the following terms:

> A really free people can live well materially and spiritually where there is the incentive to work, create, compete, save, invest, and profit. But there must be either force to *drive* men to work. Or there must be incentive to make men *want* to work. [...] What can management do to promote sound economic understanding and resulting sound public action? We have simply to learn, and preach, and practice what's the good

alternative to socialism. [...] [W]e are going to do our part in seeing that a majority of citizens understand the *economic facts of life* [our emphasis]. [...] So let's boldly take—and continue from there on—the leadership that's expected of people like us in this patriot's job.[117]

Teaching these "economic facts of life" would provide material for several economic education programs ("How Our Business System Operates," "In Our Hands," etc.) targeting millions of employees of large (and small) companies. Directly managed by the National Association of Manufacturers and the American Economic Foundation, relayed by the many universities that contributed to forming future participants and supervisors (all managers), the sales policy of *corporate culture* could be seen behind this global enterprise of capitalist subjectivation for which the keyword is "participation." While the desired participation was first that of workers and employees (who were remunerated with participation in company profits), it did not stop at the walls of the factory and the frontiers of the economy in the strict sense. It is the key part of the management theory of "human relations" aiming to redefine each worker and each employee as an "individual" and a "social being in relations with others in a complex social organization" which must be mobilized to increase productivity while relaxing labor pressure on wages and power inside companies. The stakes of what was called in the early 1950s the "second industrial revolution"—the revolution of "human relations in industry"—were to substitute "corporate culture" for class consciousness by dressing the disciplinary lines of economic divisions of power in biopolitical apparatuses (*dispositifs*) of social regulation ("the corporate family together") that could stimulate and direct the consumer change of reproduction into "welfare capitalism." The regimes of social benefits in each company not only compete with the welfare state by emptying it of its political substance and class history: they spread to society as a whole by giving rise to the new industry of "corporate leisure" that came with new relations between workplace, family, and residence (cultural activities for housewives, sports fields for children and teens, childcare, etc.). It was a question of integrating the domestic/affective economy of the family in the factory and to project the company throughout the family "territories" by investing all neighboring communities (towns, schools with a sizable economic education program, churches, associations, and clubs…). For a single goal: to "sell the principles of free enterprise as a real and living force," "promote the business story with the general public."[118] The storytelling of the Cold War made the protecting of individual freedoms from the "communist menace" depend on the defense of American Business, which was built into the ultimate guarantee of the "Empire of Liberty" (to use Thomas Jefferson's expression).

"Job Marketing" and the "Patriot's Job" would thus come to shape the indistinguishably macro- and micro-political contours of the managerial face of the Cold War in its major effect of radically displacing the class war *of the defeated* into the *war of civilization* of the people of capitalism against the slavery of communism.[119] This civilization meant prohibiting any reform of capital other than one brought about by the "participation" of every man and woman in the socialization and individualization of *people* as forces of consumption capable of reproducing the capitalism of total war, which gave the United States an entrepreneurial power of bringing about military-industrial security with an unlimited vocation.

10.5 The Cold War's Business

Against the golden myth of American neoliberalism, which also found its source in Detroit (the "Hayek Project"),[120] American capital engaged in massive and intense redevelopment programs supported by the multiplication of federal agencies coordinating the economy of total war and the incredible logistical effort it involved. (A *logistical war* that made American GIs known as "comfort soldiers.") The total militarization of the economy depended on the logistical revolution (invention of the *container*) made necessary by a war machine running on oil (on P.O.L.: Petroleum, Oil, Lubricants), driving the logistics of capital supported by the geo-economy of war productivism. It was deployed in the post-war period with the Marshall Plan in an integrated geo-politics of production/circulation/distribution ("the whole process of business" becomes an economy of material and information *flows*). It was continued in an unprecedented rearmament in time of "peace" and by European economic integration, which can be considered the major success of "the greatest international propaganda operation ever seen in peacetime" (David Ellwood on the Marshall Plan). Under American influence, it was carried out eagerly as the *outlet* for an imperialism that no longer operated by territorial control but by regulation of the market under its control and by integrated military command (NATO).[121] In Europe, its (political-military and *logistical*) "base" was the new Germany where *Hayek versus Keynes* played to a full house after a monetary reform (June 1948) determined the largest aid package of the Cold War for "social and financial discipline." Per Jacobsen, director of the Bank for International Settlements (and future director of the IMF), could thus observe in 1948 that "neoliberalism is starting to gain ground" in Europe,[122] where the political relationship of forces was in the process of being reversed with help from the European Productivity Agency.[123] The Agency combined transfers of material and social technologies (including the promotion of econometrics as a technology of statistically-assisted economic control),[124] corporate administration, and managerial science promoted by the major industrial groups in the process of transnationalization (multinational networks of production and circulation). Their mode of organization was the source of a new type of capitalist enterprise driving the American cycle of accumulation by vertical integration of all their units and internalization of their transaction costs (from production to consumption: an entire economy of speed). It accelerated the neo-militarization of the economy and the privatization of warfare stemming from the Cold War's economy of war of indeterminate duration. It was the key of "long-term power": Private business must run the Cold War's business.[125] To use the language of the victors who never write history without naming new "sciences": no *business logistics*[126] without the *logistics business*, the intense militarization of society (controlled by) of consumption.[127]

The Cold War is therefore in more than one sense an affair of "just-in-time" (JIT) calculation (of costs and benefits). According to the most general formula, it asserted itself as a *social containerization* of all the civil wars passing through it (wars of class, race, and sex tied to the geometrics of the war on the poor) by the intense socialization of total war that is reproduced and expanded through all of the new means taken on by the war machine of capital in the war of subjectivation. The fantastic operation of semiotization (signifying, a-signifying, and symbolic) which occurred in the domestic training for the consumption of the American way of life as a vector of the Cold War is the best sign of the "centrality" of the question of social reproduction. It was no longer concentrated around the "division of labor in production" (and around class war) but on the "social division of labor" expanded to society as a whole, involving all the components of welfare capitalism. And this is precisely where it cracked, on the front of a war of subjectivation that only passed through the factory (where the labor movement was defeated *as class* with the complicity of the unions)[128] to apply there, in vain, the governmentality of the entire population. *Because it was cracking all over.* The "crack-up" of the 1960s that attacked the big and small narratives of the Cold War by sending its *containers* to the bottom: the nuclear family, marriage and sexuality, housewives, childhood education, consumption, savings and credit, the middle class, the "human factor" and "motivations," corporate culture, factory and office discipline, unions, anti-communism and realized socialism, legal and/or constitutional resolution of social wars, racism, imperialist war in Vietnam, and all the forms of colonialism… The real economy of the Cold War was affected in its global principle of endocolonization and shaken to its core. Only a few short years separated "The answer my friend, is blowin' in the wind" (*The Freewheelin' Bob Dylan*, 1963) and the student's chant at Columbia University in the spring of 1968: "We want a revolution… NOW." Escaping the final scene of Peter Brook's *Marat/Sade*, the riot song of the asylum inmates of Charenton replaced the strike song of the great American revolutionary drama of the 1930s, *Waiting for Lefty*. The New Left was no longer waiting—or was waiting for something else—"to give life a chance." There was only a *political critique of daily life* that could "synthesize" anti-imperialism, anti-militarism, anti-racism, feminism and homosexual struggles, ecology and the underground…

shared by the "prairie power" of campuses, young proletarians in revolt, and the Blacks of the ghettos in the different variants of their common accelerant: "bringing the war home."

"'68" was the cypher of this global revolution for the generation born in the war and brought up during the Cold War. In the name of the Cold War, Silvia Federici could write in the introduction to her collection of articles on the question of "reproduction":

> For after two world wars that in a space of three decades decimated more than seventy million people, the lures of domesticity and the prospect of sacrificing our lives to produce more workers and soldiers for the state had no hold on our imagination. Indeed, even more than the experience of self-reliance that the war bestowed on many women—symbolized in the United States by the iconic image of Rosie the Riveter—what shaped our relation to reproduction in the postwar period, especially in Europe, was the memory of the carnage into which we had been born.[129]

The Marxist feminists of wages for housework/*salario al lavoro domestico* made the destruction of the Second World War the primary reason for their generational break, in other words why "unlike previous feminist critics of the home, family and housework, our attitude could not be that of the reformers."[130] This requires taking the measure of what had to and could happen in the United States and "just in time," the apparatus (*dispositive*) of the Cold War—at home and abroad—to suspend the perspectives of emancipation fed by a half-century of total war. Until the Baby Boom generation rose up against all the sales conditions at the supermarket of the American way of life.

The counter-offensive did not take long. Nixon won the presidential election by standing the "silent majority" of "forgotten Americans" against "minorities," a message in which a large part of the guaranteed White working class recognized itself. Carried by an anti-New Deal populism (the "White backlash") in several industrial cities and former democratic strongholds (including New York, under its fiscal crisis), taking back the capitalist initiative once again passed through money as a response to crisis (with pressure to increase wages) and the civic/civil war that did not stop. The scenario was also critical on the international stage where, because of Vietnam, the Third World gained an autonomy that was less negotiated with the dominant power of the Cold War condominium, which also lost ground in Europe. Abandon of the gold standard for the US dollar and measures to deregulate the movement of capital associated with it imposed the magic formula of "$1=$1." A perfect tautology of the world-money, a formula that had the power to launch the market (freed of fixed exchange rates) into the global financialization of the economy under *American transnational control*, historically associated with neo-liberalism. Reagan could make the United States the debtor nation of the world, financing its stratospheric debt by contributing to the last escalation of the Cold War (into the stars with the Strategic Defense Initiative). The USSR could not follow. Game over.

11

CLAUSEWITZ AND '68 THOUGHT (*LA PENSÉE 68*)*

After the Second World War and erasure of the borders between war time and peace time, revolutionary movements remained dependent on Leninist theorization and practices to grasp the new relationship between "war and capital." Inserting the cycle of struggles that crisscrossed the 1960s into this required grammar, the revolutionary hypothesis failed in the end to think war on the level of the "'68" event, putting all the parts of the world into contact with what has been called a "cold civil war."[1]

Problematizing war and its relationship with capital was a required exercise for all revolutionaries. From Lenin to Mao, from Mao to General Giap and the Vietnam War, the strategic and tactical relationship to war passed through the work of Clausewitz.

---

* With this expression "'68 thought" (*la pensée 68*), our focus is the "core" of contemporary French philosophy as it developed from 1968, in the after-effect of '68, by thinking the "strange" or "impossible revolution of '68"—strange and even impossible in relation to the Marxist-Leninist (i.e. dialectical) codification of "revolution" (centered around the working class as the subject of history). Not overlooking its emergence in the 1960s, we believe the reference to '68 gives its full importance to the concept of the "event" for Deleuze and Guattari, Foucault, Lyotard, Rancière, Badiou... For our Anglo-Saxon readers, we would also note that the "exporting" of '68 thought as "French Theory" is not without connection to the global dimension of '68, which could even be seen as the first appearance of an alter-globalist movement. All of these questions (which also carry the problem of the "limits" of '68 thought) will be at the center of our second volume, *Wars and Revolution*.

In the spring of 1915, Lenin read and carefully annotated the major work of the Prussian major-general, *On War* (*Vom Kriege*), whom he considered to be "one of the greatest military historians." Exaggerating slightly, Carl Schmitt called these notes "one of the greatest documents in world history and the history of ideas."[2]

Lenin found confirmation of Marxist theory in Clausewitz's famous "Formula." "*Proximity with Marxism*," he wrote in the margins of his copy: didn't Marx and Engels see war as "the continuation of the politics of the powers concerned"? However, class struggle still had to become the true motive of war. "Politics" could therefore not be reduced to state policy representing the interests of society as a whole (common interest) as Clausewitz believed (along with those who would be called the social-traitors of the Second International). Yet to the extent that revolution developed inside "imperialist wars," the function and unfolding of these wars could be brought back into the framework drawn up by Clausewitz. The synthesis of Marx and Clausewitz was also present in his works on the *self-determination of peoples*: "A war becomes national, even during a time of imperialism, when a people, small or large, fights for freedom."[3]

Most importantly for Lenin is the idea that in war "the political relationships formed historically between peoples and classes" are not interrupted but are maintained and continued by other means. The war of 1914 was therefore an imperialist war. As for the "irregular war" carried out by the working class, it could be extended and intensified into a movement of insurrection using Clausewitz's theory of the "small war" (partisan war, guerilla) and "means of defense" that are just *types of resistance*. And it is understood that the references to Clausewitz were constant until power was won (and even after, during the civil war).

The "military" writing of Mao Zedong, and in particular *On Protracted War* (1938), which became a classic of "Marxism-Leninism" on the question of war, offered several developments referring to Clausewitz. Mao, however, referred to Lenin's brochures and never quoted *On War* directly. The chapter "War and Politics" opens on point 63 with the Formula "War is the continuation of politics." The Formula is completed in point 64: "War is the continuation of politics by other means." We have only recently been able to confirm, with the publication of Mao's notebooks, that he read the treatise in 1938 and had even organized a seminar around the work for high-ranking officials of the Communist Party.[4] For the most part, however, he followed the Leninist interpretation of Clausewitz, bending it in a more militant direction where there is no separation between political action and military action. War is strictly subordinate to politics (*"In a word, war cannot for a single moment be separated from politics"*), and politics is objectified in revolutionary "class" politics that allows a distinction between "just wars" and "unjust wars." The supreme principle of Maoist strategy relates to the offensive/defensive *dialectic* that favors attack in defense (essentially national and popular defense) to obtain tactical success in "annihilating the enemy."

In his memoirs, General Giap describes how his wife read passages of the treatise to him between the battles of Hanoi and Dien Bien Phu:

> Listening to them, I often had the impression that Clausewitz was sitting before me to discuss current events [...]. In particular, I liked the chapter titled "Arming of the People." [...] His theory corresponded to what our ancestors said: use the means at your disposal to confront an adversary with

superior arms and numbers. Some military authors discuss "small wars" that use small factions that can pass anywhere, find their own provisions, move quickly [...]. Didn't everything we were doing at the time resemble a "small war"?[5]

Buoyed by the Vietnamese victories over colonial France (1954) and the US war machine (1975), the revolutionary movements of the 1960s–1970s were only repeating the achievements of the Soviet and Chinese revolutions when they included struggles for national independence ("*FLN vaincra*") in the revolutionary politics of the "people's war" (*Volkskrieg* was declared: "the people's war is invincible"). War could therefore still be understood in the context of Clauzewitzian thought translated into a class dialectic that was first applied to "imperialist war" as inter-state civil war (Lenin), and was continued on the Yangtse (Mao Zedong's thought: "Imperialism is a paper tiger").

In the 1970s, "professional revolutionaries" were therefore not the ones who engaged in a new problematization of war. As the discourse of "crisis" flourished (in the thermonuclear age, "the hour of truth is crisis, not war") in seeming opposition to the discourse of "protracted war" taking up the Maoist refrain of a "generalized Clauzewitzian strategy,"[6] it was Foucault on the one hand and Deleuze and Guattari on the other who produced a radical break in the conception of war and of its constitutive relationship with capitalism. A unique example in the critical thinking of the time, they took up the confrontation with Clausewitz to reverse the famous Formula: war *is not* the continuation of politics (which determines its ends); politics is on the contrary an element, a strategic modality of the whole constituted by war. The ambition of '68 thought was asserted in the project not to make the reversal a simple permutation of its terms. It wanted to develop a radical critique of the concepts of "war" and "politics" as presupposed by Clausewitz's formula: war *is/is only* the continuation of politics by other means.

According to his genealogical perspective, Foucault sought to base the reasons for this reversal on a strategic reconstruction of what Marx called primitive accumulation and was very hesitant to approach the period of so-called "total" wars. Deleuze and Guattari, on the other hand, directly attacked the relationship between war and capitalism in the twentieth century, and in particular in the period after World War II.

11.1 Distinction and Reversibility of Power and War

'68 thought therefore produced two different but complementary versions of the Formula that radically displaced the Clausewitzian point of view focused on the state. Foucault approached the Formula from a completely new problematization of the question of power, while Deleuze and Guattari carried out the reversal through an analysis of the nature of the movements of capital.

Foucault is undoubtedly the one who went the furthest in his confrontation with Clausewitz, but he is also the one who raised the most doubts by multiplying the versions of this reversal, often in a contradictory manner. Starting in 1971, despite an important absence, war returned more systematically in his work, with differing intensities, until the end of his life. It is the militant and warlike *parresia* of the Cynic—the "philosopher at war"—in his final class in 1984, which Foucault had called *The Courage of Truth*. Yet Foucaldian criticism is almost unanimous in stating that while Michel Foucault "tried" to make war the matrix of relationships of power between 1972 (*The Punitive*

Society) and 1976 ("*Society Must Be Defended*"), this project was definitively "abandoned" in favor of the exercise of power through "governmentality."

Between 1971 and 1976, Foucault problematized the reversal of Clausewitz's formula by reestablishing the reality of "civil war" as condition for the effective intelligibility of power relations. The renewal of the question of power that he carried out when he conceived of politics as a continuation of war was thus undertaken starting from "the most condemned of wars, [...] civil war." It is the matrix of all strategies of power, and thus consequently for all struggles against power.

Reversal of Clausewitz's expression came along with a distance taken from three classic concepts of war. "Not Hobbes, not Clausewitz, not class struggle," wrote Foucault in a 1972 letter.[7] Unlike Hobbes, where it was never a question of real wars,[8] power does not come after civil war, it does not follow a conflict like its pacification; inversely, civil war is not the result of the dissolution of power. Civil war is the "permanent state" of capitalism. Civil war has nothing to do with the Hobbesian fiction of the exacerbated individualism of the "war of all against all" projected into the state of nature. On the contrary, it is always a question of confrontation between qualified collective entities, such as: "the war of rich against poor, of owners against those who have nothing, of bosses against proletarians."[9] Far from being that moment of atomic disintegration requiring the intervention of a constitutive and pacifying mediation (the sovereign as founding principle of the social body), civil war is the very process through which new communities and their institutions are established. It is not limited to being the expression of a temporally limited, constitutive power since it is always at work. Division, conflict, civil war, and *stasis* structure and de-structure power; they form "a matrix within which elements of power come to function, are reactivated, break up."[10]

Absolute monarchy and liberalism come together in the obligation to deny the existence of civil war to assert the juridical subject and/or the economic subject. "The assertion that civil war does not exist, is one of the first axioms of the exercise of power."[11] Political economy is the "science" of this denial. It claims to be a double negation, negation of war and negation of sovereignty: economic interests and individual egotism replace warring passions, while the self-regulation of the invisible hand makes the sovereign useless and superfluous. In liberal ideology, capitalism does not need war or the state.

Foucaldian civil war cannot find a place in Clausewitz's interstate war because it cannot be reduced to war as a pure act of sovereignty and instrument of the balance between European states. It is both the object and the subject of the microphysics of power and the macrophysics of populations: "One should be able to study the daily exercise of power as a civil war: to exercise power is to conduct civil war in a certain way, and it ought to be possible to analyze all these instruments, tactics, alliances that we can identify in terms of civil war."[12] While Clausewitz's point of view is that of the state (leading to the always possible Hegelianization of the Treaty), Foucault proposes to pursue a radical critique of the state in reversing the Formula: the state is not the origin or the vector of relationships of power. Circumventing the state, de-institutionalizing and de-functionalizing relationships of power by substituting strategies and tactics for them constitutes Foucault's method.[13]

This occurs over two moments. Foucault begins by emphasizing the historical limits of the Clausewitzian conceptualization, which finds its source in the European tradition of the "right of the people," and its historical framework in the "war of the state, reason of the state [*raison d'état*]." In producing his formula ("war is the continuation of politics by other means"), "he did no more than observe a mutation that was actually established at the start of the seventeenth century, [with the constitution] of the new diplomatic reason, the new political reason, at the time of the treaty of Westphalia."[14] Clausewitz thus conceptualized in his own way the expropriation and appropriation by the state of the different war machines that raged during the feudal era ("private war") by means of their centralization and professionalization in an army. The state *statifies war*; it takes war outside its borders to increase state power in a context regulated by the constitution of international law at the initiative of European states. "Here again we can see how the Clausewitzian principle that war is the continuation of politics had a support, a precise institutional support, in the institutionalization of the military," in other words the existence of a "permanent, costly, large, and scientific military apparatus within the system of peace."[15] In this peace, however, where the organization of states and the legal structure of power reigned, in this peace where "war was expelled to the limits of the state, or was both centralized in practice and confined to the frontier," one could still hear the sound of a muted war that was the object "at the very moment when this transformation occurs (or perhaps immediately afterward)" of a discourse that was "very different from the philosophico-juridical discourse that had been habitually spoken until then. *And the historico-political discourse* [on society] *that appeared at this moment was [...] a discourse on war, which was understood to be a permanent social relationship, the ineradicable basis of all relations and institutions of power.*"[16] Political power therefore does not begin at the end of the war that it brings to an end; war is the engine of the institutions and political order *and must become (again) the analyzer of relationships of force.* Thus the reversal that takes place in the question of the reversal of Clausewitz's formula: the problem no longer being to reverse Clausewitz's principle that subordinates war to politics but to understand the principle that Clausewitz himself reversed to benefit the state...[17]

While he was, in the mid-1970s, "curiously close" to Marxism in many ways, Foucault could still point out its strategic weakness.[18] In the concept of class struggle, Marxists put the emphasis on class more than struggle. This explains the slippery slope that threatens to send Marxism into a sociology of social classes or into the economism of "production and labor." Class struggle is therefore by no means another name for Foucaldian civil war. The latter is a "generalized civil war" that cannot be reduced to the capital/labor relationship alone. It concerns society as a whole; it involves a multiplicity of "subjects," domains, and knowledge. It is first "wars of subjectivities" in its irreducibility to the dialectical, "historical constitution of a universal subject, a reconciled truth, and a right in which all particularities have their ordained place" according to a logic that is more totalizing than contradictory. "The Hegelian dialectic and all those that came after it must," Foucault concludes, "be understood as philosophy and right's colonization and authoritarian pacification of a historico-political discourse that was both a statement of fact, a proclamation, and a practice of social warfare."[19] The irreducibility of social warfare to the class struggle *that pacifies it* conditions the analysis of political power as war.

If we follow the Foucaldian *doxa*, the 1977–1978 course (*Security, Territory, Population*) marked a major shift in the philosopher's thought; it was characterized by abandoning the hypothesis of war in favor of governmentality. As this shift involved what "I would really like to undertake" and would modify the title of what he wanted to accomplish that year[20] in the direction of a "history of 'governmentality,'" it would be achieved and take on its definitive form in his course at the Collège de France in 1978–1979: *The Birth of Biopolitics*. As proof of this fact, reference is made to a text published two years before Foucault's death, "The Subject and Power" (1982), which retraces the entire path of his work and can be considered his theoretical-political will and testament. The article contains assertions that do not seem to leave room for any other interpretation than a radical change in the "general matrix" of power. "The exercise of power consists in guiding the possibility of conduct and putting in order the possible outcome. Basically power is less a confrontation between two adversaries or the linking of one to the other than a question of government."[21] The famous definition of governmentality as action on an action, as structuring the "field of action of others," continues with the refusal to consider relationships of power through the warring model (of confrontation) or the juridical model (referring to state sovereignty).

In reality, however, Foucault establishes for the first time in this text a distinction between *power* and *war*, one that was suggested in *The Will to Knowledge* (published in 1976) at the conclusion of a strategic analysis of power ("power [...] is the name that one attributes to a complex strategical situation in a particular society") where the question returned of whether there was a need to return to Clausewitz's formula and say that "politics is war pursued by other means." "If we still wish to maintain a separation between war and politics, perhaps we should postulate rather that this multiplicity of force relations can be coded in part but never totally—either in the form of 'war,' or in the form of 'politics,' this would imply two different *strategies (but the one always liable to switch into the other)* for integrating these unbalanced, heterogeneous, unstable, and tense force relations."[22] This is the trail he would return to again when stating what remained interconnected in the courses of 1972–1976 and that he now thought of in terms of a difference in nature between *relationships of power* (disciplinary, security, and governmentality relationships) and *strategic confrontations*. Largely overlooked by Foucaldian critique, the last part of the 1982 article in fact carries the title "Relations of power and relations of strategy." After proposing three different definitions of strategy that tended to show how one can "interpret the mechanisms brought into play in power relations in terms of strategies," Foucault asserts: "But most important is obviously the relationship between power relations and confrontation strategies." Although Foucault did not take it up again, the distinction made in these few pages seems to us to be of the utmost importance. It shows that war and power, while distinct, are in a relationship of continuity and reversibility. Power relationships are of the type *governing/governed* and designate relationships between *partners*, whereas strategic confrontations oppose *adversaries*. "A relationship of confrontation reaches its term, its final moment (and the victory of one of the two adversaries), when stable mechanisms replace the free play of antagonistic reactions. Through such mechanisms one can direct, in a fairly constant manner and with reasonable certainty, the conduct of others."[23]

Establishment of a power relationship is both the objective of strategic confrontation and its suspension, since strategic relationships between adversaries are substituted with relationships of the governing/governed type. Liberals dream of seeing power apparatuses function automatically, on the model of the invisible hand of Adam Smith imposing itself on individuals like a necessity in the play of liberty and power. These "automatisms," however, are first the *results* of war and its continuation by other means, such that war is always latent under disciplinary, governmental, and sovereignty relationships. Once power apparatuses ensure a certain continuity, predictability, and rationality of conduct of the governed, the inverse process can always occur, transforming the governed into adversaries, since there is no power without disobedience that escapes it, without struggles that defy the constraint of power and that once again open the possibility of "civil war." "And in return," emphasizes Foucault, "the strategy of struggle also constitutes a frontier," a threshold that can be crossed towards war. The exercise of power (disciplinary, security, governmental, etc.) presupposes 1/ the freedom of the one on whom power is exercised, and 2/ that this person is "thoroughly recognized and maintained to the very end as a person who acts," in other words as subject of struggle, resistance, insubordination. Such that "every extension of power relations to make [...] submit" freedom, on the one hand, and subjectivity, on the other, can only result in the limits of power. The latter reaches its final term either in a type of action which reduces the other to total impotence (in which case victory over the adversary replaces the exercise of power) or by a confrontation with those whom one governs and their transformation into adversaries. Which is to say that every strategy of confrontation dreams of becoming a relationship of power, and every relationship of power leans toward the idea that, if it follows its own line of development and comes up against direct confrontation, it may become the winning strategy."

It may be most important to understand that power and war, relations of power and strategic relationships should not be seen as successive moments but as relationships that can continuously be reversed and which, in fact, coexist. *"In effect, between a relationship of power and a strategy of struggle there is a reciprocal appeal, a perpetual linking and a perpetual reversal. At every moment the relationship of power may become a confrontation between two adversaries.* Equally, the relationship between adversaries in society may, at every moment, give place to the putting into operation of mechanisms of power."[24]

Whoever is interested today in the "new economy of power relations"—according to the expression advanced by Foucault in his text reworking the Kantian question *"Was heisst Aufklärung?"* into "What is happening in this moment?"—should note that reversibility determines an "instability" that is not foreign to contemporary financial capitalism. "Crisis" does not follow "growth"; they coexist. Peace does not follow war; they are co-present. The economy does not replace war; it institutes another way to conduct it. The "crisis" is infinite and war only knows respite by incorporating the apparatus of power that it *secures*.

It is definitely no longer a question of reversal of the Formula (politics as continuation of war by other means) but an interweaving of war in politics and politics in war that adopts the movements of capitalism. Politics is no longer, as in Clausewitz, the politics of the state but politics of the financialized economy interwoven in the multiplicity of wars that move and hold together the war of destruction in action with wars of class, race, sex and ecological wars that provide the global "environment" of all the others.

In short, in real practice, in its "concrete practices" (as Foucault puts it), *governmentality does not replace war. It organizes, governs, and controls the reversibility of wars and power.*[25] Governmentality is the governmentality of wars, and without it the new concept, placed too hastily at the service of eliminating all the "conducts" of war, inevitably resonates with the all-powerful and very (neo)liberal concept of "governance."

We must recognize, however, that this tendency towards misadventure, as witnessed in most "governmentality studies," has a name—*The Birth of Biopolitics*—and a date—1978–1979—in the Foucaldian corpus. In it, the market recovers its status as enterprise of negation of civil war through a (neo)liberal utopia (announced as such and explicitly borrowed from Hayek by Foucault) "in which there is optimization of systems of difference, in which the field is left open to fluctuating processes, in which minority individuals and practices are tolerated, [...] and finally in which there is an environmental type of intervention instead of the internal subjugation of individuals."[26] Was Foucault tempted by the transporting of Deleuze and Guattari into Hayek's enterprise? Given the "new philosopher"[27] episode and the eruption of the vocabulary of multiplicity and difference in the analysis of neoliberalism, the answer could curiously enough be in the affirmative. Yet this is also what makes "The Subject and Power" more interesting, as it reconnected in 1982 with the most leftist vein of characterization of post-'68 struggles ("transversal" struggles against the effects of power-knowledge, etc.) in the first lesson of "*Society Must Be Defended*," to give them a theoretical outlet in *the analysis of power relations through the confrontation of strategies.*

11.2 The War Machine of Deleuze and Guattari

The reversal of Clausewitz's formula by Deleuze and Guattari is inscribed in the framework of universal history and the world-economy. The strategy they used is therefore very different from Foucault's analysis which, while producing a radical critique of the state, remained paradoxically prisoner of its territoriality (generalized civil war of/in the European nation-state). Deleuze and Guattari developed an absolutely original theory dissociating war and the state from the "war machine."

The war machine does not have the same origin, logic, or goals as the identity apparatus and the form of state sovereignty. An invention of nomads and connected to their "experience of the outside"[28] and their "form of exteriority" in relation to state capture of territories ("land appropriation," state territorialization), the war machine does not have war as its *object*. It is not defined by war unless as *war against the state*. If war ("dispersive," "polymorphous," "centripetal") is there to ward off the formation of a state from the interior, the war machine has always been in warring interaction with the imperial and state formations which it confronts "at the periphery or in poorly controlled areas."[29]

As for the state, it needs bureaucracy and police to establish its sovereignty, and does not include war among its "sovereign" functions. It is obliged to appropriate the war machine of the nomads to turn it against them by transforming it into something very different, passing through the institutionalization of an army, with which the military function and *institution* are exclusively associated. State capture of the war machine makes war its object by subordinating it to the political ends of the state that monopolizes it. The state is Clausewitzian.

The institutionalization of the war machine by the state operates a disciplinarization and professionalization amply described by Foucault as one of the most important sources of disciplinary techniques. This is the importance of the army as *administration of discipline* on productive bodies and, with the labor force territorialized or *sedentarized* by military force, throughout the entire social field. But the process of capture and institutionalization/professionalization of the war machine by the state is far from linear. The military institution is a social reality crossed by always possible tensions and reversals. Capture of the war machine is never once and for all; it can always escape the state apparatus as a foreign body (*a military proletariat*).

The non-linear process of "capture of the war machine" reveals itself to be very useful for historicizing the relationship between war, capital, and state. In fact, while the disjunction that becomes inclusive between state and war machine is the condition of possibility of Nazi subordination of the first to the second in the Party-form feeding the autonomy (and the *ontonomy*) of a war goal without end, the return to the exclusive disjunction between State and war machine opens the possibility of appropriation of the latter by revolutionary forces outside the (Leninist) form of the Party. "Guerrilla warfare, minority warfare, revolutionary and popular war [...] can make war only on the condition that they simultaneously create something else."[30] If more detail is needed: doing something else at the same time does not at all mean ignoring or neglecting real war but creating collectively the means to oppose it, undo it, winning by doing it another way—because "*every creation is brought about by a war machine.*"[31]

In his 1979–1980 courses contemporary to the writing of *A Thousand Plateaus*, Gilles Deleuze undertakes an analysis of the nature of war and its transformation through the dynamic of Capital that strictly conditions the reversal of Clausewitz's formula. The philosopher endeavors to show that the same movement drives capital and war when war is industrial war. The contradictions of capital and the contradictions of war then tend to harmonize. The demonstration unfolds starting from a surprising Marx/Clausewitz relationship. The different moments of this development are not taken up in *A Thousand Plateaus*, which is why it is interesting to reconstruct their logic here.

Deleuze starts by taking up the question of the limits of capital by returning—as he already did in *Anti-Oedipus*—to the chapter on the "tendency of the rate of profit to fall" in Volume III of *Capital*. The thesis is well-known: Capital has limits, but those limits are immanent (*immanenten Schranken*). An immanent limit means it is not encountered as an exteriority, it does not come from outside; capital produces and reproduces limits constantly itself. As capital develops, the part of constant capital (invested in means of production, raw materials, etc.) grows proportionally faster than the past of variable capital (invested in the labor force), which leads to a "tendency of the profit rate to fall" (since surplus value depends on the activity of the labor force). It is a limit (in the mathematical and differential sense) which one approaches but from which one is always separated by some quantity, no matter how "infinitely small" it is. In short, Capital only approaches the limit to push it back.

This movement to the limit that capitalism poses and reposes endlessly is deeply contradictory. Capital is defined as an *unlimited* accumulation ("production for production"), and, at the same time, this endless process must be for profit, for private property ("production for Capital"), such that the *unlimited* movement is subject to a restriction that makes it a *limited* movement. The two movements of capital are inseparable since capital itself launches the deterritorialization of production for production and its reterritorialization on private property and profit. This double movement is the source of periodic "crises." Any attempt to accelerate the unlimited movement in the hope of cutting it from its territorialization in profit is destined to fail (this is the false "revolutionary" solution proposed by accelerationism). How does one account for this contradiction? And is there a capitalist mechanism capable of resolving it?

It is at this precise moment that Deleuze invokes Clausewitz. It allows him both to establish the relationship that ties war to capital and to determine the *historical impasses* against which Clausewitz's theory falters when the war machine is appropriated by Capital. Deleuze then pretends to ask whether it is "by chance" that he feels the need to return to the concepts of Clausewitz's theory of war.

"Let's return to a terminology that we needed for something else altogether, in other words in terms of the problem of war [...]. Like capital, *and this is probably the deepest tie between war and capital*, [...] war has a goal and an objective. And the two are not the same."[32] Clausewitz, he recalls, distinguishes the *political goal* (*Zweck*) and the *military objective* (*Ziel*) of war.[33] The military objective of war is defined by the reversal or annihilation of the adversary. The political goal of war is completely different, since it constitutes the end that a State gives itself when it enters into a war (to produce, as we know, a rebalancing of the "European equilibrium"). Deleuze notes here that Clausewitz is still describing the situation preceding the French Revolution and the Napoleonic Wars.[34] "At that moment, the war machine was captured in the state, in fact, the military objective that relates to the war machine was subordinated to the political goal that relates to the political goal of the state that wages war. What happened when war started to become total?"

At the end of the nineteenth century, capital was no longer limited to passing through the state-form and its war machine for the needs of its own development; it would undertake a process of capture that was indistinguishable from the construction of its own war machine, of which the state and war were only components. This process accelerated with the First World War, which represented a radical break in the history of war in the sense that Capital transmitted to war the infinite, or the unlimited movement that characterizes accumulation, by defining a "type of contradiction" between the objective of war and the goal of the state.

> We can assign a tendency to total war at the moment when capitalism takes hold of the war machine and gives it a development, a fundamental material development [...]. When war tends to become total, the objective and the goal tend to enter into *a type of contradiction*. There is tension between the objective and the goal. Because as war becomes total, the objective, or to use Clausewitz's term, overcoming the adversary, no longer has any limits. The adversary can no longer be identified, assimilated with the fort to be captured, the enemy army to be defeated; it is the entire people and the entire land. In other words, the objective becomes unlimited, and that is total war.

By becoming unlimited, the military objective is no longer subordinated to the political goal of the state and tends to become autonomous. The war machine is no longer under state control, which introduces this "contradiction" that takes form in the Nazi and fascist war machines: they take the line of abolition of the movements without limits of war all the way. "In the development of capital, we find a problem that resonates with the possibility of contradiction between the limited political goal of war and the unlimited objective of total war." The goal of Capital (production for Capital) is limited, while its objective (production for production) is unlimited. The limited goal and unlimited objective are therefore forced to enter into a contradiction for which Marx presents the expression in the chapter on the tendency for the profit rate to fall. "That's part of the beauty of Marx's text to show us that there is, in capitalism, a mechanism that works in such a way that the contradiction between unlimited objective and limited goal, between production for production and production for Capital, finds its resolution thanks to a typically capitalist process. This process is what Marx summarizes in the formula 'periodical depreciation of capital and creation of new capital.'" Through this mechanism, Capital constantly resolves the contradiction at the same time as it proposes it in an expanded manner.

War resolves the contradiction between its limited goal and its objective that has become unlimited in a similar way; and, like Capital, it only resolves it by expanding it. After almost escaping capital between the two world wars (fascisms), the war machine no longer took war as its objective but "peace." The Nazis had made the war machine autonomous from the state, "but they still needed this war machine to operate in wars [...]. *In other words, they kept something of the old formula, that war would be the materialization of the war machine. I do not mean* that today it is not like that, the war machine pursues wars, we see it all the time, *but something nevertheless changed, it also needs war but not in the same way.* The following situation tends to happen, [...] the modern war machine would not even need to be materialized in real wars, since it would be war materialized itself. To put it another way, the war machine would not even need to have war as its object, since it finds its object in a peace of terror. It achieved its ultimate object *suiting its character as total*: peace."

"Peace" resolves the contradiction which it displaces by imposing it in expanded form. But what is this expanded form? The war machine of the state that had carried out the management and organization of all wars coextensive/co-intensive to the entire history of capitalism did not become the war machine of Capital without transforming "war" into what Carl Schmitt and Ernst Jünger, as early as the 1940s (they knew the Reich's war was lost), and then Hannah Arendt and again Carl Schmitt, in the early 1960s, called "world civil war" or "global civil war."[35] A war *for which the political goal is immediately economic and the economic objective immediately political.*

Taking its source in the "threatening peace of nuclear deterrence" and the analysis of it by Paul Virilio, the concept of "total peace" is an ambiguous one today. In fact, while the war machine of total peace is none other than the absolute unlimitedness of capitalist globalization itself, the assertion that war and peace have *become* indistinguishable is still reliant on the Clausewitzian opposition between war and peace as well as the European context that *balances* it. (Although Clausewitz recognizes that signing a peace does not always necessarily mean the end of a conflict, to use his words, "Whatever may take place subsequently, we must always look upon the object as attained, and the business of war as ended, by a peace.")[36] Reversal of the Formula should on the contrary affirm the *continuity* between war and politics, war and economy, war and *welfare in the constitutive multiplicity of war and wars* that mobilizes the entire planetary social environment by submitting it to a *total civil war in action*. All the modalities of war machines that the state appropriated for itself starting with primitive accumulation, and that it capitalized in its army and administration, in the post-war era, they carried out this "global civil war" waged directly by capital, leading to the explosion of 1968.

"Peace" is not limited therefore to "peace that technologically frees the unlimited material process of total war"[37] (the unbridled arms race, the military-scientific-industrial complex), it takes charge of integration policies on the global level, in other words the war of labor, the war of welfare, the war of internal colonization and external neo-colonization, etc. Peace becomes the *means* by which the war machine of capital "takes over a maximum of civil functions"[38]—to such an extent that war "disappears." But it only "disappears" because there was an "extension of its domain" by establishing a continuity between "financial, industrial, and military technological complexes."[39]

Reversal of Clausewitz's formula only appears at this moment, according to Deleuze and Guattari (who curiously enough use the same expression in French as the one used by Foucault above: "*apparaît seulement à ce moment*"). It is only uttered from the perspective of power and the political state, of those states *that no longer appropriate the war machine, that reconstitute a war machine of which they themselves are only technical parts.*[40] From the perspective of the "exploited," however, the reversal of the formula has always already occurred in a manner of "historico-transcendental doublet" (Foucault) that defines and subjects them as such.

The double reversal of the Formula operated by Foucault and Deleuze-Guattari appeared in a context of changing circumstances that marked the beginning of a new political sequence, where the war machine of Capital alone dominated the period through its "creativity." At the same time, the new theory of war and power was not able to confront and draw on real political experiments, since between the end of the 1970s and the early 1980s, the radicalization that resulted from '68 ("Rampant May") faded, weakened, and finally collapsed in the repetition of the modalities of civil war codified by the revolutions of the first half of the century around the October Revolution of the Bolsheviks. After the failure of insurrection movements, the "Winter Years" began, and have yet to end. The impetus of these formidable intuitions and the "insurrection of knowledge" in which they participated was cut short and fell into the political void of the period.

Since this implosion (*implosion of the social, in the shadow of the silent majorities*, etc.), the initiative of capital has only grown by defying every limit in a destructionism without exception on which the iron law of productivism is based. Emerging victorious from the confrontation with the movement and thought of '68, the neoliberal war machine has continued to win victory after victory. These victories come with an erasure of the memory of wars, of civil wars, of the wars of class, race, gender, and subjectivity from which the victors gain their domination. *The neoliberal eraser.* Walter Benjamin reminds us that reactivating the memory and reality of wars and civil wars can only come from the "defeated." The fact that the "defeated" of the strange revolution of '68 were unable to see, describe, and counter-act the transformation of the war and social wars imposed by the enemy demonstrates the weakness of critical theory and represents one of the reasons for the disappearance of revolutionary political war into its inability to *divide war and multiply confrontations that could create new war machines.*

'68 thought did not show itself capable of producing a strategic knowledge adequate to the civil wars Capital was able to restart as an overall response to its global destabilization, which reached its climax in 1968. As proof, if needed, it is not enough to state that micropolitics has to pass into macropolitics to transform it (even though this is often forgotten): both micro- and macropolitics have to be included in the multiplicity of wars that take place there, without which both micro- and macropolitics collapse and the struggles occurring there lose their consistency in a "becoming-minor" of not many people. "Make the one you are fleeing flee," said Deleuze and Guattari when distinguishing between the schizo and the revolutionary.

12

THE FRACTAL WARS OF CAPITAL

> Nations make war the same way they make wealth.
> —Vice-Admiral Arthur K. Cebrowski and John J. Gartska (1998)

After the attacks on November 13, 2015, the President of the French Republic declared a state of emergency and it was immediately passed by Parliament. How should we understand the "extraordinary powers" conferred on "administrative power," with the restrictions on public freedoms that ensue and the suspension of the separation of powers between the executive, legislative, and judicial branches in favor of the executive?

Following the path of the "state of exception" and examining its relationship with law[1]—as Giorgio Agamben has done— seems to us to be a somewhat sterile (and vaguely academic) exercise where the *tree* (of law) *hides the forest* (of power). Must we think the permanent state of emergency on the exclusive level of its relation to the law, of its reduction ("crisis" law), or its founding suspension of a new juridical order, if it is no longer a *government act*—given the "exceptional circumstances," decreeing when it is time to exercise the law of "full powers," *not governed by the Constitution*—but a *constitutive principle of governmentality*? We do not disagree that the state of emergency can (and should) cause its juridical form to evolve to institute an intermediate state allowing "a framework for taking exceptional measures for a certain period *without recourse to the state of emergency* and without compromising public freedoms."[2] This return of the state of emergency to the constitutional order (which could *even* bring an end to it),[3] still shows, in our eyes, something else altogether: that *the time of full-powers is replaced by a space full of powers* that must be questioned as such. The "juridical void" may be unthinkable for the law (as Agamben asserts),[4] but not for a practice of power that, according to Foucault's teaching, constantly circumvents it and passes outside the form of juridical-political sovereignty of power and the state.

What operates "almost without interruption from World War One, through fascism and National Socialism up to our own era"[5] is thus less the state of exception than the affirmation of the *war machine of capital,* for which the state of emergency is only an apparatus (*dispositif*). Starting with the First World/Total War, state and war become components of the capitalist machine that imposes a radical transformation on their functions and their relations. The models of scientific organization of labor, the military model of organization and conduct of war deeply penetrate the political functioning of the state by reconfiguring the liberal separation of powers, while, inversely, the politics, not of the state but of Capital, is imposed on the organization, conduct, and finalities of war.

The new war machine of Capital implies an intertwining of civil power and military power, of war and politics, that tends to make them indistinguishable. In terms of the state, it is a reconfiguration of the separation of powers that progressively tends to privilege executive power to the detriment of legislative and judicial power, and of an in-depth transformation of its administrative and governmental functions being translated by an almost daily production of laws, decrees, and directives that is impressively more effective than the one-off interventions of the state of exception. The state of exception is only one of the expressions of reinforcement of executive power under the impulse of its capitalist control which, in the new dimensions of the world-economy determined by and in World War I, represents the necessary condition for "government" to intervene effectively in the two strategic fluxes of Capital that are *money* and *war*.

The speed of interventions and the efficacy of decisions required by the *fluxes of financial money* and the *fluxes of war* prescribe a new material constitution where executive power adopts, to absorb a large part of judicial and legislative power, a dual model of organization and command: *the army* and *the scientific organization of labor*, such that the government is configured as a "political-military" power alongside the "military-industrial complex."

Capital appropriates war, starting by transforming it into "industrial war," then into "war amongst the people," or as we rephrase it (following the standard French expression "guerre au sein de la population") "war amongst the population."* It is defined by its strategists-theorists as an "antithesis" of the "industrial war" that endured throughout the twentieth century (at least in part: the "arms race" aspect of the Cold War), despite its lack of adaptation to the new conditions of conflict ("other types of enemies in conflicts of a different type"). These new conditions and these "new threats" define "war amongst the population" as the apparatus (*dispositif*) of control and governmentality suited to the new composition of the world labor force tied to the internalization/externalization of the world-market (the globalization of human capital, the global assembly line).

---

* See Translator's Note, p. 441.

This new paradigm implies the integration of politics into war in a very specific way that could be defined, to borrow Foucault's expression, as *governmentality of the population* (*gouvernementalité de la population*), on two conditions: 1/ contrary to what is said by Foucauldian critics, war is not removed from power relations but, on the contrary, informs them; 2/ war governmentality is exercised not on "the" population but "on" and "through" its division. The object of war is the production and expanded reproduction of the class, sex, race, and subjectivity divisions of the population. The paradigm of "*war amongst the population*" therefore expresses, from the point of view of new forms of militarization/concentration of power, the concept and organization of *wars within populations* on which capital depends to secure productivity. Or to put it another way: the multiplicity of *wars against populations* is what we are not supposed to see in "war amongst the population," of which the first theorization—in the French context of anti-colonial struggles and revolutionary wars during the Cold War—was thought of as "*war in the social milieu.*" In an article with this title, General Jean Nemo explains that "islands of combat over the entire territory" can emerge "since the front is in fact less determined by a frontier than by the horizontal plane that separates opinions and traces their contours." Thus war amongst the population should be prepared at every level, even at the most modest levels, since "we are working directly on 'human clay.'"[6]

The result of the process of concentration of powers is found in neoliberalism, where "government" and its administrations *execute* the strategies of financial capital. The process of absolute subordination of the state and war to capital is due to the intensification of the domination of finance, as it is capable of exploding all the political-economic mediations/regulations to which it has been subjected since the Bretton Woods Agreement. (This 1971–1973 sequence was marked by the end of international convertibility of the dollar to gold and the adoption of the regime of "floating exchange rates" in function of *market forces alone*.) True executive power does not come from the will of the people, the nation, or the state; it is the power that financial institutions have progressively rebuilt for their own benefit. Remember Foucault's admonition: neoliberalism can be identified "with permanent vigilance, activity, and intervention"[7] that should be bent in the direction of the instrumentalization of a strong state (what Philip Mirowski calls the "double truth doctrine" of neoliberalism). In the same way, the complete subordination of war to the objectives of capital takes its definitive form at the end of the twentieth century, when the exhaustion of inter-state war left room for the exclusive and inclusive paradigm of war—or more precisely, *wars*—*amongst the population* by creating a *virtual-real continuum* between economic-financial operations and a new type of military operations that were no longer limited to the "periphery."

We propose to analyze and combine these two different and complementary processes that do not receive their logic from the state of exception but from the organization of the war machine of capital, which we understand as the "organizational revolution" of the *governmentality of capital*.

12.1 The Executive as "Political-Military" Apparatus

We will focus on France in analyzing the reconfiguration of executive action and its administrations. While participating in a general process, it is carried by the very French illusion as to the re-establishment of the autonomy and grandeur of the state, the values of the Republic and the Nation, which reached their apex in the Fifth Republic. Like everywhere else, however, the loss of sovereignty of the nation-state, its full subordination to economic and financial policies, the reduction of Parliament and "national representation" to the level of simple foils of executive power, and the war governmentality of the population that institutions exercise on its divisions come from mechanisms that existed long before the 1970s. To understand the origin of these changes, we must return to the First World War and the strategy of appropriation of the state and war by Capital that started to take shape at that time.

The juridical-political context does not allow us to grasp the way in which the war machine of Capital reconfigured the modalities of organization, command, and decision-making of the government and administration of the state. Its model is in fact the chain of command of the new management of companies (Taylorism) and of war. Only the parallel evolution of the *company*, *army*, and *government* could account for a process that could be summarized as follows: industrial war affirms the role of civil power in the military universe; once war is over, this experience of hybridization between civilian and military "returned" to the ways of thinking and acting of the functions of government power.

We have analyzed industrial or total war in great detail. We will limit ourselves here to a few remarks on its management by calling on the recent work of Nicolas Roussellier. It not only concerns the conduct of military operations but first and foremost the "conduct of war in all its dimensions: economic, financial, communication, and management of the population. Governments and not army leadership are best able to mobilize the nation and its population." It is a "war of government" more than a "war of armies," since the knowledge and management of resources that need to be mobilized belongs to civil power. "War is now 'in-depth war' of the population, labor, industry, and opinion more than the projection of an armed detachment of a nation." Industrial war is accompanied by a reconfiguration of executive power that does not end with the end of hostilities. "By learning to lead a Nation in war, the Executive opened the way to a 'return' of the military in the very definition of the nature and functions of political power." The feedback of the conduct of war on the manner to conceive of and organize executive power opens the way to thinking and organizing an "Executive that is political-military in nature"[8]—or political-military-industrial.

The conduct of war integrates disciplinary techniques and security techniques. A hierarchical and *disciplinary* model of organization and management of people, a *security* model for the management of war as a series of unpredictable events (Clausewitz's "fog of war"). Thus the model of *industrial management*, since war represents a vast "labor process" (Jünger) of which the logistics concerns society as a whole, must be joined with the model of *security intervention* which, unlike industrial planning, has to account for the fact that war is "action," risk, unpredictability, and therefore needs to produce inventive strategies of attack/response that are always disposed to adaptation (war is properly "action on an action," reciprocal action, which leads to its always random programming).

With the end of hostilities, reconstruction is most urgent and becomes economic-financial. Management of money, in particular, requires, like the governing of total war, centralized powers making quick and efficient decisions. Like at the very beginning of the history of capitalism, we find exactly the same deterritorialized fluxes: army and war on one side, money and credit on the other as the constitutive forces of a new phase of its development.

The post-war period does not lead to an inversion of the process of concentration of executive power to the detriment of the legislative and the judiciary but, on the contrary, to an acceleration of this process under economic (and notably financial) pressure.

Reorganization of the functioning of the government, with the organization of the army, has another model to follow in restructuring itself: the scientific organization of labor introduced by Taylorism. The homogeneity between the organization of the army and the organization of production was indicated by Marx and is confirmed at each new turn in the strategy of Capital. Government and administration have to be subject to the laws and rules governing the capitalist enterprise. "Government, considered as a machine, now has to respond for its 'output.' It is placed at the head of a 'production' for which it ensures the 'cadence' [...] and as Alexandre Millerand said after the war, 'it behooves the government to be organized on the plan and mode of industry.' [...] Government becomes a factory of laws, decrees, and regulations."[9]

To account for the functioning of the "machine to produce laws" that executive power has become under the hold of finance and war, Carl Schmitt takes up the expressions—that were in vogue under the Weimar Republic—"motorized legislator" and "growing motorization of the legislative machinery." After World War One, he explains, "the passing of new legislation became faster and more streamlined, the road to legal regulation shorter, and the role of jurisprudence accordingly smaller."[10]

While war imposes a change in the separation of powers by privileging the executive since it needs an efficiency that parliament does not allow, economic crisis, and in particular financial crisis, is for its part synonymous with a speed of initiative and reaction that leads the government to replace laws, which are subject to parliamentary examination, with decrees. "But the motorization of law into mere decree was not yet the culmination of simplifications and accelerations. New accelerations were produced by market regulations and state control of the economy—with their numerous and transferable authorizations and subauthorizations to various offices, associations, and commissions concerned with economic decisions." After decrees, directives best express the next stage in centralizing and evacuating parliamentary representation. "Whereas the decree was called a 'motorized law,' the directive became a 'motorized decree.'"[11] Schmitt and Weber share the idea that the modern state has become, in many ways, a big factory.

The First World War was also global in that it produced the same effects everywhere. The need for quicker and more effective methods of political action was felt by all the countries involved in the conflict. In Italy, state intervention in the war, "desired and called for by the major bankers and industrialists," also underwent a marginalization of legislative power, centralization of the executive, and reinforcement of the war machine of Capital. As the state extended its involvement in the war economy, the relationship between state and finance became closer. Finance ensured itself "a direct, immediate control of the government apparatus that would thus be removed from parliamentary control. The neutralization of democratic institutions took hold: the need for a profound change in political regime began to be raised."[12] The evacuation of national representation was accomplished through administrative and political means well before the liquidation of democratic freedoms by fascism.

The model of organization for "motorized" action of the government and administration was provided by Taylorism and should not be seen as an extension and refinement of the methods of production of Adam Smith's cherished pin factory. Taylorism *is* a new mode of command. "The true impact of Taylorism is therefore not the technique but the *organization of power*."[13]

The political debate and battle were no longer over the alternative between monarchy and republic; they were carried and carried away by "scientific analysis of the governmental *fact*." This process was inscribed in the *language of technology* much more than any other constitutional domain because management allows a circumvention of the juridical-political framework that is still the framework of the state of exception for Schmitt and Agamben: "If 'government reform' placed itself under the auspices of technology, it was also because it was influenced by the new theory of 'scientific management' of labor."[14]

In France, the debate took place under the dual influence of Taylor (first translated in 1907) and Fayol. For Fayol, the problem was less that of making the organization of labor scientific than the activity of direction and management that brought together different functions: programming, organization, command, coordination, and control. It was openly discussed that the industrial factory had undergone growth that required reinforcement of the administrative functions of command. These functions were distinct and *projected under* the classical functions of production, commercialization, and accounts management by producing a new type of personnel: managers, who were "specially charged with coordinating and systematizing all of the techniques implemented in a company."[15] *Industrial and General Administration* is the title of this mining engineer's most popular book, the main contribution of which was to extend the principles of factory management to other types of organizations, in particular state administrations. At the time, "his model was deliberately presented as capable of being transposed to the framework of state administration and the very organization of a political government."[16]

We know that Paul Virilio establishes a strong relationship, which he calls "techno-logical," between the army, the factory, and its managers. He does not limit the "military class" to army officers alone. His definition is broader and covers all types of managers. "The so-called 'technocrats' are very simply the military class. They are the ones who consider rationality only in terms of its efficiency, whatever its horizon. The negative horizon's apocalyptic dimension doesn't strike them. It is not their problem."[17]

A new "class" of technocrats works transversally at different state or private institutions according to corporate methods that contribute to increasing their bureaucratization. Contrary to a widely-held assumption, bureaucratization is not a characteristic of state administration but is first the "product" of large companies, especially American ones, and their management. "Scientific managers were asked to change the organization of labor from top to bottom like the new government leaders were led to rethink the entire concept of executive power."[18] The managerial revolution that started with the government later spread to the administration as a whole. It is this techno-logic that is deployed by neoliberalism by subjecting all the apparatuses (*dispositifs*) of welfare to the accountability and rules of operation of the financialized company. It thus contributed to redefining the form and functions of the state by feeding a new bureaucratization, the denunciation of which would allow privatization of new sectors, "which only leads to more spending and a more intrusive infrastructure of government operations."[19]

This reform of the executive was achieved and inscribed in the Constitution of the Fifth Republic of France by a general, de Gaulle, who, "starting from a preoccupation with reestablishing the art of war, [...] ended up reestablishing the art of governing."[20] Military reform "was presented as a reform of politics as a whole."[21]

While World War I (in which de Gaulle participated as a captain) revealed the crisis of a mode of command based on the separation between decisions made at headquarters and execution on the battlefield, "in the sphere of constitutional politics, the separation between legislation and execution was [also] called into question."[22]

The reform of governmentality determined a new process of legitimization of *decision-making*, and we can see here the extent to which it is neither (in the Schmittian sense) "a specifically juridical formal element,"[23] nor (in Agamben's use of Schmitt) the "empty space" of the state of exception (becoming permanent and "mobile") as constitutive dimension of law.[24]

The directives that constituted "motorized legislation" under the Weimar Republic were taken up by de Gaulle as early as the Free France period. Instead of being strictly limited by the legislative, the executive moved it aside. "The Assembly brings 'the support of qualified opinion' but does not participate in the decision-making process."[25] Politicians do not have to answer "to the people" through the intermediary of the *Assemblée*, as the republican tradition would have it, but to the state. The passage towards the moment where they would only answer to the war machine of Capital has already been prepared.

The same process occurred with non-presidential political systems like the Italian one, where statutory directives became the primary approach of the government after the Second World War, circumventing in this way the principles of the Constitution.

The Italian Republic, like every other contemporary democracy, is no longer "parliamentary"—it is, to borrow Roussellier's term, "an *executive* democracy."

Nevertheless, the Fifth Republic, while representing one of the constitutional systems that took the process of concentrating power the furthest, remained within the history of the nation-state and its sovereignty. This was no longer the case with the liberal counter-revolution of the 1970s, which organized a new model of power where the executive, resolutely passing beyond the limits of the state, represented a simple, albeit essential, cog of financialization. It did not restrict itself to accelerating the "motorization of the legislative machinery" and reducing parliament to serving a consultative and legitimizing function: it finished building the war machine of Capital. This is the key element of neoliberal *constructivism*, which takes it well beyond the "uncoupling of the market economy and laissez-faire" that Foucault analyzed.[26]

12.2 Realization of the War Machine of Capital

True executive power is no longer a state apparatus but an ensemble of transnational institutions including states as one of their articulations dominated by financial capital. While being "laissez-faire" with financial fluxes, this "shadow" government decides and sets the level of employment, salaries, public spending, retirement age and benefits, tax rates, and more for different categories of the population. National executive powers are limited to executing and implementing the directives and decision of this center of globalized command. Shorn of its classical form of "sovereignty," the nation-state is reduced to reterritorializing the *world-economy of debt* (which it actively administers and manages). It goes without saying that the American government is the exception, as it is not a nation-state (in the classic sense) but an imperial state that redefined its "national interest" in terms of the defense and extension of "global capitalism," since it governs the axiomatic of the world-economy of debt by dominating the transnational institutions that it largely established.

A first approach to the new nature and new functions of war and the executive (*executive war*?) combined as components of the war machine of financial Capital can be found in the book published in 1999 by two colonels of the Chinese Air Force, Qiao Liang and Wang Xiangsui: *Unrestricted Warfare*. In the post-Cold War context of a reheated rivalry between China and the United States, they see financial activity as a "bloodless war" that can have effects comparable to a "bloody war." Finance is therefore integral to a strategy of *non-conventional war* renouncing both "people's war" and "technological war" to confront US supremacy. In an interview given a year after publication of their work, Qiao Liang gave a more diplomatic summary of the main thesis of the book that emphasized the importance of "non-military operations" which include "trade wars, financial wars, etc."

Today, as they observe, the factors threatening "national" security are less the military forces of an enemy state than "grabbing resources, contending for markets, controlling capital, trade sanctions, and other economic factors."[27] With this change in paradigm, it is time to recognize that damage from new "non-military weapons" can be just as dangerous as the damage from "military weapons." The authors place particular emphasis on finance, since it is the most effective way to produce threats on the level of a country or the entire planet. "In terms of the extent of the drop in the national security index, when we compare

Thailand and Indonesia, which for several months had currency devaluations of several tens of percentage points and economies near bankruptcy, with Iraq, which suffered the double containment of military attacks and economic boycott, I fear there was not much difference."[28] This is also the reason why redefinitions of the conflict between Greece and transnational financial institutions in terms of "war," "colonial war," "occupation," and "colonial mandate," among others, were more than just metaphors.

States lose the monopoly on violence and on the use of violence as the means of constraint become diversified: they have become economic, diplomatic, social, cultural... The effects of war can therefore be pursued and realized by a multiplicity of apparatuses (*dispositifs*), of which financial violence is surely the most effective since its effects destabilize society as a whole while differentiating its effects. Waging war is therefore no longer the exclusive domain of the military: "Obviously, warfare is in the process of transcending the domains of soldiers, military units, and military affairs, and is increasingly becoming a matter for politicians, scientists, and even bankers. How to conduct war is obviously no longer a question for the consideration of military people alone. The economy and especially the financial economy can replace military means and lead to 'bloodless war.'"[29] (A few years later, General Rupert Smith was careful to avoid this terrain. Yet he confirmed that the new identity of governmentality and war led to the reversibility of economic, political, military, *and humanitarian* interventions: "In the new paradigm [of war] military operations are but another activity of the state.")[30]

When they focus more directly on the functioning of *financial strategy* to include what they do not hesitate to call "*financial terrorism*," our two Chinese officers arrive at a model of the war machine of Capital that is particularly useful for understanding the nature of transnational executive power and the new reality of war. They explain that the model of government of the world-economy has become "vertical, horizontal, and interlocking supra-national, trans-national, and non-state combinations. [...] The brand-new model of "state + supranational + trans-national + non-state [levels]" will bring about fundamental changes."[31] The example of the Asian crisis in 1997, with its speculation attacks that first targeted Thailand and then spread throughout Southeast Asia along with its round of "structural reforms," revealed the list of actors involved: the United States, or the only state that can be "represented" by its omnipresent financial institution (the Federal Reserve); the IMF and the World Bank (transnational institutions); investment funds (private multinational companies); Standard & Poor's, Moody's, and others (non-state ratings agencies). *Real* executive power represents the *realized* identity between economy, politics, and the military that fundamentally transforms "the face and final outcome of warfare, even changing the essential military nature of warfare which has been an unquestionable truth since ancient times,"[32] to satisfy the "hyperstrategic" weapon of financial war. The resulting war machine is *by definition* not a regulatory institution but a power for planning and executing the new civil war that some military officials (including Sir Rupert Smith) analyze as "war amongst the people." This new type of executive power and war machine was at work in its "non-military" version during the Greek debt crisis. European institutions, the IMF and the ECB do not have to respond to the people or to states for the violence and arbitrariness of the *decisions* taken; they only have to respond to the transnational financial institutions that are now the main vector of multiplying *"civil" wars against populations.*

While the process of subordination of the judiciary and the legislative branches to executive power continued to grow throughout the twentieth century, now all state powers are subordinated to a new transnational executive power. According to Qiao Liang and Wang Xiangsui once again, as the result of capitalist globalization, "while constricting the battlespace in the narrow sense, at the same time we have turned the entire world into a battlefield in the broad sense. [...] [T]he weapons are more advanced and the means more sophisticated, so while it is somewhat less bloody, it is still just as brutal."[33] The *extension of the domain of war*, which establishes a continuum between war, economy, and politics, combines the strategies of horizontality (multiplication and diffusion of centers of power and decision-making) and verticality (centralization and strict subordination of these centers and power and decision-making apparatuses (*dispositifs*) to the logic of "maximizing value for shareholders").

Before closing this new treatise on war, we would add two thoughts. First, a verification of our original hypothesis: the two fluxes through which we defined the force of deterritorialization of capital at work since primitive accumulation, money and war, *perfectly overlap* in contemporary capitalist globalization. Finance has become a non-military weapon with which "bloodless wars" are waged, producing effects just as devastating as "bloody wars." War is no longer the continuation of politics by bloody means; the politics of Capital is war continued *by every means made available by its war machine*. Second, the epitome of "crises," financial crisis, from which crises of production and trade crises emerge and follow in the classic economic cycle, seals its identification with "war." War takes the relay of the "crisis" it subsumes. In the Marxian cycle, the contradiction between "production for production," that serves as impetus for the absolute development of productive forces, and "production for Capital," or for profit and private property, determines violent crises that *can* lead to wars. Under the current situation, *crisis is indistinguishable from development, and crisis is indistinguishable from war.* In short: *crisis is indistinguishable from the development of war.* For this to happen, the phenomenology of the concept of war can no longer refer to interstate war, but to a new form of transnational war that is inseparable from the development of Capital and is no longer separate from its economic, humanitarian, ecological, and other policies.

This definition of finance as "bloodless war using non-military means" seems to us to be far more realistic and politically effective than the theory of heterodoxical economy that understands finance as a "new convention." No convention in the form of a new avatar of the old "contract," but a strategy where economy, politics, and war are strictly integrated in the same project of *enforcing* global capitalism. As a result, and without developing again the difference established by Foucault between (executive) government action and the apparatuses (*dispositifs*) of governmentality, the question of the relationship between these two types of institution cannot be ignored. The American administration started by paving the "anti-inflationist" way of monetarism by inventing new apparatuses (*dispositifs*) of power aimed at containing the political effects of full employment, but the modalities of neoliberal government proclaiming itself neoliberal ("the Neoliberal Thought Collective," to use Philip Mirowski's expression) were sustained, developed, and imposed by the Thatcher and Reagan "governments," and before them by the fascist government of Pinochet, which immediately engaged in the denationalization/privatization/deregulation of the economy.[34] Without this "government" intervention, there would be no effective capitalist counter-revolution as a political-disciplinary response to the social crisis of "human capital" using these new forms of governmentality (of war and through civil war) commanded by the explosion of finance.

The contemporary war machine of financial capital continues the "colonization" of the state, which it makes conform to its functioning not only through companies but through the administration. Simultaneously, "governments" have quickly become agents of this colonization of the administration as place of development, control, and imposition of a large part of the techniques of "governmentality."

The management of contemporary administration finds its model in the economy but unlike the period between the two World Wars, it is directly informed by finance and no longer by the scientific organization of labor by industrial capitalism. Both companies and administration are restructured to maximize value for shareholders to the detriment of any other economic subject (worker, consumer, public services user, taxpayer, etc.).

A powerful catalyst for state reform, the *Loi organique relative aux lois de finances* (LOLF) triggered a process of radical transformation of state budget and accounting rules in function of financialization. Financialization thus achieved the elimination of any trace of democracy from state institutions. What has been hypocritically called the "crisis of the model of representative democracy" has the same genealogy and follows the same timeline as the process of concentration of executive power that began in the First World War. With the imperatives of total war, national representation and the "democratic debate" between representatives of the people were progressively marginalized, with no further role to play other than the televised staging of the age of the financial executive.

We should emphasize that the generalization of universal suffrage coincided with its neutralization by a process that tended to reduce elected parliaments to simple institutions of legitimization of a "motorized" executive. Jacques Rancière describes this democratic-liberal system as a compromise between an oligarchical principle (the people delegates its power to representatives of economic, financial, etc. forces) and a democratic principle (with the power of all reduced to the exercise of voting). Nicolas Roussellier proposes a definition of democracy that seems just as pertinent since it appears to correspond to its most real functioning: "executive democracy"—which we understand as the institutional articulation of the war machine of Capital. Nevertheless, as the expression of policies of national modernization, "executive democracy" is still completely surpassed by the new war institutions of globalization to which it is completely subordinate. In France, it has been the recipe for François Hollande's *sauce hollandaise*, which Emmanuel Macron has now placed in the juicer.

12.3 Wars Amongst the People, or Against the Population[35]

The war machine of Capital thus introduced its politics (financial order and governmentality of this order) into the conduct of war in two different ways: industrial war and "war amongst the people," i.e. the *population*.

The process of integrating war into strategies that are no longer of the state but of Capital modifies the nature and functions of war. The Chinese strategists advanced this thesis of a lack of distinction between economy and war in their analysis of the "Asian financial crisis" in 1997. A new turn was taken by reflecting on the reasons for the failures faced by the American military superpower in the conflicts of the early twenty-first century. The systemic vision of the functioning of war developed by the Chinese officers gave way to the imperatives of "war amongst the people/population," which had to grasp the new nature of war by making room for the *war of subjectivity*. It is the question of the "essential role of the human factor" (or the "human terrain," in good English) in an "irregular war" that becomes the regular form of war[36]—and the war of division of/among the people. The first modelling was done by Gregory Bateson under the name of "schismogenesis." Developed in a colonial context in which Bateson participated very actively, fed by the "denial of Empire" of the post-colonial era, accelerated by the rise of guerillas and operations in urban areas, which are *populo-centric* by essence, "schismogenesis" borrows the figure of "protection of the people" to impose the doctrinal revision of military action by spreading the domain of counter-insurrection to the entire external and internal front. The strategic environment is that of the recognition of an "era of persistent conflicts" leading to privileging "stabilization operations" to intensify the enterprise of systematic colonization by continuing the war of primitive accumulation as an operation of transnational police. In this sense as well, the war machine of Capital provides the transhistorical truth of its entire process: capital identified with a liberal imperialism that can only take its authority from "international law" by militarizing all of its "policing" operations as wars of "pacification" amongst populations.

The end of the Cold War was accompanied by exhaustion of the "industrial war" that had largely dominated the twentieth century and its replacement with a new paradigm presented as its "antithesis." In Europe, it was defined by two generals, one English, Sir Rupert Smith, with an impressive service record,[37] and the other French, Vincent Desportes, as "war amongst the people" and *"guerre au sein de la population."*[38]

The conditions of possibility of industrial war were *in fact* neutralized by the atomic bomb, which contributed to a first *strategic demassification* of armies. However, it was not until the failures of the neocolonial wars waged by the USA after the fall of the Berlin Wall that definitive proof of the impotence of "industrial war" was provided in the face of the new modalities of conflict in the socioeconomic conditions of globalization.

The different restructurings of the American army—RMA (*Revolution in Military Affairs*), *transformation* favoring innovation in every domain and throughout the spectrum of operations, Information Dominance and Network-Centric Warfare, establishment of the O³ concept (pronounced "O-cubed") for *omniscient, omnipresent, omnipotent*—that had given the USA the illusion of an automatic translation of technological supremacy into strategic supremacy were all conceived using the paradigm of "industrial war" and its managerial digitization (the Wal-Mart model).[39] The digital adaptation of the American doctrine in place since 1945 was perfectly summarized by Henry Kissinger: *"technology plus managerial skills* gave us the ability to reshape the international system and to bring about domestic transformations in 'emerging countries.'"[40] The organizational changes that it faced to win the battle of time on the cyber-front of instantaneousness only displaced the Vietnam "question" by revealing themselves just as powerless in the face of the new "enemies" that emerged from capitalist, post-communist/colonial globalization: they are there *to endure* and establish war *in their duration.* In Afghanistan (2001) and Iraq (2003), the "victory" all-too-easily achieved by large-scale kinetic activity (following the "adapted" model of the first Gulf War) and the massive application of "intelligent" lethal force (or the supreme stage of industrial war as *manifestation* of American superpower) did not decide the end of hostilities but on the contrary their continuation and mutation. And, in the end, the departure of the American army, leaving behind the disaster of a country in the throes of the "bloodiest" chaos and civil war.

As early as 1997, however, an official historian like Williamson Murray could write a critical article in *The National Interest* with the unambiguous title: "Clausewitz Out, Computer In." He returned to his critique two years later in *Orbis*, published by the Foreign Policy Research Institute:

> Indeed, what appears to be occurring—especially in the air force—is a reprise of the sort of mechanistic, engineering, systems-analysis approach that contributed so much to failure in Vietnam. [...] Two years ago a senior army general announced to the students of the Marine War College that "the digitization of the battlefield means the end of Clausewitz"—in other words, computer technology and modem communications will remove fog and friction from the future battlefield, at least for American military forces.[41]

With the impasses of hypermodernism for the American armed forces, debate began over the new strategic conditions of war against increasingly less conventional adversaries in theaters of operations that could no longer be separated from the geopolitical consequences of techno-financial globalization ("This enemy is better networked than we are").[42] The new paradigm of "war amongst the people/population" asserts the *interconnectedness* of civilian and military, its *integration* in the capitalist machine of globalization that imposes its political governance in a continuum of which the components are nothing other than all forms and all varieties of war—except one: waging "high-tech" battle against a conventional enemy. John Nagl, the protégé of General David Petraeus and closely associated with "his" counter-insurgency manual (published late 2006), explains this situation well: "The real problem with network-centric warfare is that it helps us only destroy. But in the 21st century, that's just a sliver of what we're trying to do. It solves a problem I don't have—fighting some conventional enemy—and helps only a little with a problem I do have: *how to build a society in the face of technology-enabled, super-empowered individuals.*"[43] There is no better way to emphasize that there is no renunciation of the Information Technology (IT) that feeds network-centric warfare (it is the unavoidable, irreversible "machinic phylum"). It is more a question of breaking with its "off the ground"[44] mythology and mastering the *social* feedback loops by integrating, adapting, and reterritorializing it in the modalities of engagement of an *endless war* amongst the "people." Here is the breaking point with the "revolution in military affairs" that claimed to conclude war as fast as possible. The high-speed continuum's payoff—to use the business vocabulary of American military-revolutionaries—was to *stop wars*—"which is what network-centric warfare is all about."[45]

Lacking sensitivity to the juridical and political arcana of the state of exception, could members of the military define the nature of the capitalist initiative better than academics (philosophers, political scientists, sociologists, economists), given their objective necessity to rethink war in order to *maintain world security*[46] in the age of advanced neoliberalism?

Replacing industrial war with war amongst the people is a strategic necessity of Capital. As long as major globalization was territorialized in the nation-state, war had to take the imperialist form of interstate war. In contemporary globalization, the space of accumulation is transnational. The modalities of engagement and continuing conflict are therefore redefined less in function of states than in relation to the globalized populations to be subjected to its logic. "War amongst the population" does not only address "terrorists and insurgents." In its plural form of *wars against populations*, it is the main instrument of control, normalization, and disciplinarization of the globalized labor force. The aphorism painfully rediscovered by the American army in Iraq must therefore be *generalized*: "*Money is a weapon.*" With neoliberalism, the *Reason of Capital* was able to incorporate like never before the motto of American senators: "Think globally, act locally" (ATTAC took it up as well, with varying success).

"We fight amongst the people, not on the battlefield,"[47] claims General Rupert Smith decisively. War amongst the population should therefore be distinguished from asymmetrical war. Asymmetry is caught up in a definition of war that is too conventionally general and generic.

> It is the reality in which the people in the streets and houses and fields—all the people, anywhere—are the battlefield. Military engagements can take place anywhere: in the presence of civilians, against civilians, in defense of civilians. Civilians are the targets, objectives to be won, as much as an opposing force. However, it is also not asymmetric warfare since it is also a classic example of disinterest in the change of paradigms. The practice of war, indeed its "art," is to achieve an asymmetry over the opponent.[48]

The "limitlessness" of industrial war, the unlimitedness of destruction, is transformed in the new paradigm into the limitlessness of intervention amongst and against populations carried out in the name of "stabilization operations" participating in a system of global pacification where war can no longer be "won." "Population-centric counterinsurgency" is a synonym for *infinite pacification*.

The enemy is less a foreign state than the "undetectable enemy," the "hidden enemy," the "nondescript enemy" (*ennemi quelconque*) produced and reproduced within the population. This new definition of the diffuse, dispersed, *swarming* (in other words *minor*) enemy emerges in military literature after 1968. In the Cold War, the designated enemy was the USSR and communism. Well before the fall of the Berlin Wall, with the challenging of the party-form and the emergence of new political forces, new modalities of organization ("segmented," "polycentric," and "reticulated"),[49] and strategies of struggle and "secession," reference starts to be made to the "ordinary enemy," by taking up a term that appeared in the literature on nuclear security. The population is the fertile ground from which this not clearly identifiable enemy could emerge at any moment. "He needs the people in their collective form to sustain himself. Like a parasite he depends on his host for transport, heat, light, revenue, information and communications. The Russians understood this and before attacking the Chechen capital of Grozny in 1994–1995, in an attempt to bring the Chechens to a decisive battle, they removed the people before levelling the city."[50]

General Vincent Desportes calls contemporary war "probable war" (*guerre probable*) but arrives at the same conclusions. In its difference with industrial war waged by the state, probable war has no "front" and coincides with the population, from which the "*probable adversary*" is never clearly distinguished. "Probable war does not occur 'between' societies; it takes place 'in' societies.

The population now becomes an actor and major concern [..]. Moving from a mode where the population represented the 'rear'— as opposed to the front, the essential military zone—armed forces now act in populations and in reference to them. Military forces have entered the era of war amongst the population."[51]

The expression "*guerre probable*," or probable war, is the perfect statement of the functioning of a war machine that does not have "War" as its goal, to the extent that *it transforms peace into a form of war for all*. War (no longer in a Clausewitzian sense) is one means among others for the war machine. The unity and purpose of the war machine are not given by the politics of the nation-state but by the politics of Capital, for which the strategic axis is constituted by credit/debt. The war machine continues to produce *wars*—including, in a limited way and most often indirectly, interstate wars—but they are subordinate to its real "objective" which "is human society, its governance, its social contract, and its institutions and no longer one province or another, this river or that border; there are no longer lines or land to conquer or protect. The only front the forces involved have to hold is the people."[52]

The people (*population*) became a military objective in a new (and renewed) sense during World War II when European and Japanese cities were heavily bombed, sometimes to the point of annihilation. But it was a question of the population of an enemy state. In the new paradigm, "the two parties fight amongst the people"[53] which is the only "theater of operations" for a multitude of actions of very different nature where "communications" (to gain the support of a differentiated population) and the "subordinate level" are favored. "Operations will therefore all be minor and only their connection will provide a global effect; they will be local and more often than not tactically disconnected, since the structure of the new adversary makes it very unlikely to see the systematic effect established in the past as the touchstone of war."[54]

For these generals, the concept of population does not present the totalizing and generic aspect that it has in political economy and that Foucault still used. We could even suggest that the concept unknowingly integrates Marx's critique of a "population" that only embodies itself in classes, interests, and struggles. In the new paradigm of war, the population is not "a monolithic block. It is made up of entities based on family, tribe, nation, race, religion, ideology, state, profession, capability, trade, and various interests." The nature of the population is not "naturally" economic since the diversity of opinions and interests can converge and find their "unity" in a political direction that is not the direction of "civil society." And if the population of the new paradigm achieves the conditions of the Foucaldian relationship of power, it is not as an alternative to war but as its always possible involvement in civil war and what are now being called "degenerate guerillas." The people can "always rebel" and with this act they can be seen as "free." The people want "things that can be classified between 'liberation from' and 'freedom to.' They want to be liberated from fear, hunger, cold, and uncertainty. They also want the freedom to prosper and act." This lesson is of course colonial and rejoins the long history of *endocolonization* closely associated with it—even in its global crisis.

Military strategists recognize freedom in the adversary who lives, hides, and prospers in the people, but also an active, inventive, *creative* disposition, since "refusing to respect the existence and use of their creative will [...] predisposes you to defeat."[55] It verifies that war amongst the population is the late conceptualization of the dynamic of global civil war that started in '68 and all of the (anti-colonial, anti-racist, labor, feminist, ecological) struggles of the 1960s that crystallized at that time. It refers to the deployment of wars of the sexes, races, classes, subjectivities, in other words the wars that have formed the thread of the power of capitalism since primitive accumulation. These wars of accumulation that always accompanied its development are reconfigured by their passage through the vast socialization of production and domination represented by the two total wars and Fordism. Starting in '68, we entered what these generals call "the era of real, hard, *and permanent* conflict."[56] It is not new in itself but *for them and for us* in the new forms it takes.

The population is not a homogenous block because a multiplicity of fractures traverses it; these fractures are confirmed by the offensives launched by the neoliberal counterrevolution against the labor class of the post-war boom, starting in fact from the divisions that they operated along racial lines (reactivation of state racism), gender lines (feminization of poverty and its exploitation—almost slavery in "Third World" countries, off-the-books work, domestic work abroad in "developed" and "less developed" countries, prostitution everywhere—coinciding ironically with UN campaigns for women's liberation), and class lines (displacing the terrain of confrontation of industrial capitalism to financial capitalism).

Renouncing the concept of war for that of governmentality, Foucaldian critique is in an awkward situation in relation to these strategic debates which confirm the most contemporary reality of capitalism in the perfect reversibility of *governmentality* of the population with *governance* of war. Reading these military strategists, Foucault's text "The Subject and Power" (1982), which distinguishes between war and power while examining their coexistence, is indisputably relevant today. Governmentality is governmentality of war that has become *hybrid* in the hybridization of "defense culture" and "security," indistinguishably local and global. The "security" aspect of Foucaldian governmentality is omnipresent in the strategists of the new war, who, by definition, are unable to renounce the use of force.

Since the adversary can only be "irregular," "the only way to intervene is to 'control the milieu,' to intervene to 'control the environment'" in which the people live and in which the irregulars live. The modalities of control and intervention of (temporal and factual) security techniques on the *homo œconomicus* described by Foucault are homogenous to the techniques of control and intervention against the irregular enemy undetectable by capitalist globalization. Think here of the "nebula of transversal threats" and the existence of "gray zones" (where capitalism concentrated the poorest classes), regularly denounced in France since the 1970s.

The action of the army must consist less in the identification and destruction of targets than in the control of territory and in particular cities, since cities represent the milieu or the environment of the people and globalized poverty. While the city replaces the countryside as the place of war in the new paradigm, it is not in the sense where "it is a question of [...] winning [...] the war of the city but the war amongst the peoples in the city."[57]

Virilio brings an important change in focus to the definition of confrontation when he asserts that its terrain is no longer the city but the "suburbs" and the "housing projects" of the periphery that form *sub-cities*. Because the classic city no longer corresponds to the development of capitalist initiative and war amongst the population, "cities have to die," proclaims Virilio (the "gentrification" of increasingly museum-like cities is a perfect illustration). The future, he explains, will be the age of the end of cities and the indefinite extension of "suburbs": "the defeat of urban integration in favor of the megasuburb. Not the megalopolis, the megasuburb."[58] It is the last stage of the *peri-urban* as domain of intervention of urban war against the segregated people "dominated" by the postcolonial internal enemy.

In the art book *Dead Cities*, Jean-Christophe Bailly penned a short text titled "The Neutralized City." He highlights two observations he made from studying the photos taken by Guillaume Greff of the *Centre d'entraînement aux actions en zone urbaine* (CENZUB) set up for urban warfare training by the French army (94th infantry regiment) in the vast military camp of Sissone (Aisne): "The first is that the typology of the décor designates just as much if not more an internal enemy (riot) as an enemy from abroad and the landscape produced is more one of repression than war as such. The second is that the resulting décor, with its extreme poverty and with the negation of any style or accent, sometimes strikingly resembles certain peri-urban fragments." In the "neutralized city of the theater of neutralization," *the cut-rate city becomes the norm of knocked-down life.*[59]

However, the definition of war as governmentality would remain abstract without its reality as instrument of production of subjectivity and means of control of conduct. "Destruction has now reached its limits"[60]: they are the limits of the quantitative approach, which privileges destruction and disregards "immaterial dimensions." Before aiming for "destruction," the objective of war is the actions, behavior, and subjectivity of the adversary. To reach its objective, it must invest "psychological fields as much as material ones" to the extent that the universe of the people is not "military and rational" but more "civilian and emotional." "It is no longer a question of spotting masses of tanks and locating potential targets but of understanding social milieus and psychological behaviors."[61]

The question is not whether to *take along* the social sciences (embedded social science implicated in the failure of the American Human Terrain System (HTS)),[62] as they have long been present (from the colonial birth of anthropology to (direct or indirect) military financing of university research), but to regulate the use of force according to a "global approach" recognizing the predominance of the social and political over the purely military approach, which must actively integrate the dimension of war of subjectivity into its apparatus (*dispositif*). On the American side, it means "human-centric warfare" aimed at *returning utility to force* after learning at one's own expense that "we will not win simply by killing insurgents" (General McChrystal, commander of the ISAF).[63] The last Secretary of Defense of the Bush Administration, kept by Barack Obama as the strong man of the Pentagon, Robert Gates explains that knowing how to wage "small wars" is needed, where 90% of the actions are non-military, like a communications operation where battle is only one of the *arguments*. Ethnocentric concepts, he explains, have to be strategically condemned along with the *technocentrism* they engendered (the doctrine of "full-spectrum dominance").[64] More realistically, since the war of communications on the internal front is not irrelevant to the chain of statements that contribute to the democratic mythologizing of the *Surge*,[65] we can posit that maintaining American domination ("dominance's persistence" according to the same Robert Gates) should *also* include other means including the study of the "human terrain" to wage social and cultural war there. But shouldn't we then speak of *social-centric network warfare*? Without which, as has been said, this could be seen as only "a clever retranslation of T.H. Lawrence's '27 Principles' published a century earlier in the *Arab Bulletin*." Principles that themselves were not far from the "ethnographic" priorities put into practice by Lyautey (in Morocco) and Gallieni (in Tonkin and in Madagascar).[66]

The action of the army must "face the adversary on his or her own terrain, by 'sticking' as close as possible to its fluctuating reality" using a method that is the reverse of the one practiced by the army of industrial war. "The traditional 'top-down' approach of interstate conflicts is supplanted by a 'bottom-up' approach" because, more often than not, there is a need to rebuild the state[67] from the ground and the people or to change the regime or government. War also has its dual macropolitical and micropolitical dimension. "In the past, most military action involved destruction and information, and first information on the objectives, while now, the essential aspects are understanding and situational intelligence, seeing micro-situations and micro-objects."[68] We can measure the distance from the *infowar* of network warfare where "affecting an adversary's will, perception and understanding" led to "total control of the environment."[69] This rapid domination (*Achieving Rapid Dominance* is the sub-title of the "Shock and Awe" doctrine favored by Bush Jr. and his administration of neo-cons led by Donald Rumsfeld) must be abandoned to reach the absolute processual proximity with war at the microscale of everyday civilian life.[70] Maxwell's demon discovers the paradoxes that the physicists of relativity imposed on it.

To remain in the path traced by Foucault, governmentality must be understood as both action on the population and the public, since "the public [...] is the population seen under the aspect of its opinions [...]. The population is therefore everything that extends from biological rootedness through the species up to the surface that gives one a hold provided by the public." Economy and opinion, Foucault concludes, are "the two major elements of reality that government will have to handle."[71] War is a *global war of perception(s)*.

The new war is brought into the population but also into the public which, "thanks to the media," has become global. This "world public" functions as a constraint and an opportunity. The media, "to a large extent [...] shared by all actors in the conflict," is a *weapon* for the simple and good reason that its use depends on the war machine using them. Once again, it is impossible to speak of autonomy or automatism of techniques like the critical theorists obsessed with media and technology. The technical machine depends on the war machine. Reflecting on the Vietnam War ("our first television war"), Marshall McLuhan asserted with reason in 1968 in *War and Peace in the Global Village*: "Television war has meant the end of the dichotomy between civilian and military." And he went on to explain: "The public is now participant in every phase of the war, and the main actions of the war are now being fought in the American home itself."[72] Three years later, Hannah Arendt wrote in her "Reflections on the Pentagon Papers," which revealed to the public the secret defense planning of the Vietnam War: "Image-making as global policy—not world conquest, but victory in the battle 'to win people's minds'—is indeed something new in the huge arsenal of human follies recorded in history."[73] It would therefore not be overly surprising to learn that the impact of world media is fully integrated into "culture-centric warfare," according to the nomenclature used by General Scales in the context of the "Surge" (which General Desportes translates as "*surtension électrique*" or "power surge"): the creation of "special media forces" is encouraged in the theater of operations, which definitively becomes a *theater of cultural intervention*. On the British side, the "televisual" dimension was not left out of the characteristics of war amongst the population: "we fight in every living room in the world as well as on the streets and fields of a conflict zone."[74] That this *globalization of perception* falls under the "information revolution" shows how this revolution helps send cyberwar towards a netwar that does not distinguish between social and military. "More than ever before," as summarized by the reporters on a research project supported and financed by the RAND National Defense Research Institute called *Networks and Netwars*, "conflicts revolve around 'knowledge' and the use of 'soft power.' Adversaries are learning to emphasize 'information operations' and 'perception management'—that is, media-oriented measures that aim to attract or disorient rather than coerce, and that affect how secure a society, a military, or other actor feels about its knowledge of itself and of its adversaries. Psychological disruption may become as important a goal as physical destruction."[75] It will be noted that one does not replace the other from the perspective of the "challenges for counter-netwar," including, in no particular order, Al-Qaeda, "transnational criminal networks," "gangs, hooligans, anarchists," the Zapatista revolt, and the "Battle for Seattle." The new theater of war is a theater differentiating the functions of war, police, information, and their inclusion in a media-security whole.

The "peace-crisis-war-solution" sequence of the paradigm of industrial war, where military action was the decisive factor, emerges completely modified. In war amongst the population, "there is no predefined sequence, but rather a continuous crisscrossing"[76] from one moment to the other. If, according to our hypothesis, the evolution of war follows and continues the evolution of capitalism, then the disruption of the classic sequence of war follows directly from the disruption of the classic sequence of the economic cycle: "growth-crisis-recession-new growth." From there, war amongst and against the population is, unlike industrial war, *un-de-fined*. As the Americans learned after Afghanistan and Iraq, military victory does not mean the end of military operations, and therefore "peace" (as precarious and unstable as the reality covered by this term is), but the un-de-fined continuation of war among the people.

In industrial war, "the whole of society and the state were subjugated" to victory. "All the machinery of state focused on this undertaking, whilst society and the economy completely halted their natural flow and productivity [...]. War therefore had to be completed as soon as possible in order to allow for normal life and commerce to resume." While we cannot accept this conclusion, with its touch of British "nostalgia" that is incompatible with the principle of long-term rupture of total wars, we understand the difference with the new paradigm where war operations among the people "can be sustained nearly endlessly: they are timeless."[77] For his part, the French general explains that "final victory—but this term is hardly appropriate now since the concept of victory belongs to strategy, not politics, and our probable wars are fundamentally political—is not a military result."[78]

In Industrial war, victory was supposed to impose peace for a few decades; in probable war, for a few hours, days, or weeks. Axiom: the enemy refuses the battle-form; corollary: if forced to accept battle, it is defeated but refuses to accept the "verdict of arms," and continues war by all means at its disposal. Or, to win, it does not have to win (to win by winning), it is enough not to lose (to win by not losing) a war in which no party can win anymore. There must therefore be a "reasoned" use of military force to avoid alienating the population while constraining it to what is presented (and announced) as a *long war* (*The Long War*, according to the title of the Quadrennial Defense Review by the

Pentagon in 2006). The *long war* becomes the strategic truth of the hybrid war on terror started by Bush five years earlier (Global War on Terror).[79] In what was established as overcoming the metaphysics of war, Heidegger inserted a paragraph in 1951 that gave an entirely different resonance to the ideas developed by Jünger in the 1930s: "This long war in its length slowly eventuated not in a peace of the traditional kind, but rather in a condition in which warlike characteristics are no longer experienced as such at all and peaceful characteristics have become meaningless and without content."[80]

This change in method in the conduct of war that can no longer end in *a* peace is often reduced to simple "policing" functions. Yet reduction of the military to the police risks missing the constitutive role of war in power relations among the population. It remains to be clarified that if the goal of "future wars" is "political," to borrow the words of General Desportes, it is not, as he would believe, in the Clausewitzian sense of pursuing a "classic" political project such as the establishment or reestablishment of the "social compact," the Constitution, or the sovereignty of the state. It is in fact a new transnational state of biopolitics that determines and drives peacemaking, state-building, and peace enforcement, in a logical continuum that no longer makes the distinction *in law* between time of peace and time of war (as emerges from the UN *Agenda for Peace* [1992],[81] of which our two generals are the inheritors, in different ways). Counter-insurrectional war thus has the latitude to take its "humanitarian" turn. Is there still need to recall that before being put forward as motives for military intervention, government legitimacy and "good governmentality" were long considered to be the *best arguments* of counter-insurrection, which always saw itself as invariably politically Clausewitzian?[82] Under the conditions of the "social compact" of neoliberalism, the constitutive function seems to turn more towards maintaining and controlling a situation of general insecurity, spreading fear, and progressively degrading the socio-economic conditions of the population. Its consequence is a generalization of governmentality through fractal civil war maintained by constant securocratic campaigns. The Clausewitzian "misunderstanding" comes from the fact that the "goals" of war are no longer the goals of the states but those of Capital, which cannot be identified in any way with something that might resemble, from near or far, the "general interest."

When British and French military strategists evoke the principle of a war amongst the population on the strength of their colonial past, they obviously have in mind the people of the "South" of the world who were the first target of the civil wars of the time (there were no less than 73 between 1965 and 1999, mostly for control of natural resources). They and their American counterparts, however, after undergoing a required rereading of the theorists of counter-insurrection and small wars, and in speaking more of *hybrid conflict* (or *hybrid war*), are not ignorant of the fact that since the end of World War II and the acceleration of the 1970s, internal and external colonizations are no longer distributed only geographically—they fracture all territories. The North has its *Souths* (immigrants, descendants of colonized peoples who inhabit colonizing countries, workers, unemployed and at risk, poor, etc.) just as the South has its *Norths* on the inside (zones of high-tech production and consumer zones for those who enrich themselves: *comprador elite*). Such that we could define war as "fractal": it (re-)produces itself indefinitely, following the same model but under different modalities, on different scales of reality. The abandon of the "weak" reformism of the post-war boom by capitalist elites opens onto a generalized civil war, *a fractal, transversal civil war in the North(s) and South(s)*. What changes between the North(s) and South(s) is only the intensity of war amongst the *divided* population (and that is divided), not its *communicating* nature. In the global axiomatic of neoliberal capitalism, it is war *amongst and against the population* that allows communication between the different levels formalized by Jeff Halper in terms of hegemony: 1. "Maintaining Overall Core Hegemony"; 2. "Maintaining Core Hegemony Over the Peripheries"; 3. "Ensuring the Control of Transnational Elites of the Core and Semi-Periphery Over Their Own Societies."[83]

In the countries once known as the "Third World," wars amongst the population are practiced by a war machine that uses both military and non-military weapons to engage in hybrid war of neocolonial globalization. The violence that takes place there is a *composite* of bloody and bloodless wars that confront the population with external interventions and affiliated operations,[84] military assistance to regimes or subordinate factions, warlords and traffickers, structural adjustment programs favoring the liberalization of trade, financial deregulation, land privatization, and the "rationalization" of agriculture turned towards exports, without forgetting the NGOs operated as subcontractors of the World Bank, the United Nations, or rich donors (mainly American) in their management of food aid… *Food aid as furtive war economy*: by stimulating the dependence of poor countries on imported food, "food aid has become a major component of the contemporary neocolonial war-machine, and the war-economy generated by it" as Sylvia Federici reminds us. This is because "[w]ar has not only been a consequence of economic change; it has also been a means to produce it. […] It is through this combination of financial and military warfare that the

African people's resistance against globalization has so far been held in check, in the same way as it has in Central America (El Salvador, Nicaragua, Guatemala, Panama) where throughout the 1980s open US military intervention has been the rule."[85] As the centerpiece of this entire apparatus (*dispositif*), *structural adjustment is war continued by other means.* In India, in the "world's largest democracy," the reforms imposed by the International Monetary Fund defined the same war on the poor, peasants, and women of which the result is a middle class of 300 million people living alongside "the ghosts of 250,000 debt-ridden farmers who have killed themselves" and "800 million impoverished and dispossessed" of everything, surviving on "less than 20 Indian rupees a day." The Indian army was restructured to ensure these divisions of the population from which it must learn to protect itself. "One of the biggest armies in the world is now preparing its Terms of Engagement to 'defend' itself against the poorest, hungriest, most malnourished people in the world."[86] This is the importance of the "psychological operations" of perception management in the direction of the middle class for which it was recently developed.

The two deterritorializing fluxes of war and money can be found everywhere, in the North and South. Money acts not only through the macroeconomic action of stock and currency markets but also at the most "micro" level of direct contact with the people. Gilles Deleuze would be forced to revise his opinion of the use of the non-military weapon of debt, which he had thought was reserved for wealthy countries when he stated: "One thing, it's true, hasn't changed: capitalism still keeps three-quarters of humanity in extreme poverty, too poor to have debts."[87] In the name of the fight against poverty (Finance against Poverty), policies of "microcredit" (or "microfinance") introduced in India by the Grameen Bank and its Nobel Prize winner Mohammed Yunus, *corporatize* the extorsion of farmers and women (primarily the two target publics). "The poor of the subcontinent have always lived in debt, in the merciless grip of the local village usurer—the Baniya. But microfinance has corporatized that too. Microfinance companies in India are responsible for hundreds of suicides—two hundred people in Andhra Pradesh in 2010 alone."[88] All of which contributed to the resurgence of armed resistance by farmers in the context of Naxalite renewal.[89]

War amongst the population draws its genealogy from the "small wars" that "irregulars" waged against the primitive accumulation of capital and in the revolutionary wars of the nineteenth and twentieth centuries. Its origins can be found in the counterrevolutionary and counter-insurrectional techniques that make it, in many ways, the inheritor of the "unconventional" war waged in the colonies (or former colonies) in the twentieth century: isn't it based more on (geographical, anthropological, and sociological) knowledge of the daily life of civilian populations than on tactical knowledge of the movements of combatants?[90] And isn't the conjunction of anticolonial struggles with revolutionary war at the heart of the most "modern" and most "political" form of guerilla to which counter-insurrection had to learn to adapt? We find here the meaning of General Petraeus' homage to the work and career of David Galula, the author, in Petraeus' eyes, of the "most important piece of military writing of the last century": *Contre-Insurrection. Théorie et pratique* (1964), which opens with a quote from Mao Zedong on the strategy of Chinese revolutionary war and that he prefaces by highlighting the importance of the conflict in Algeria, from which Galula had drawn a previous book in 1963: *Pacification en Algérie, 1956–1958*. We know how the "Battle of Algiers" was a model for the French army, which exported it, with help from the American army, to Latin America (in particular, Chile and Argentina).

Unlike his predecessors in the Vietnam conflict, however, the commander of the "Surge" did not favor the exclusively coercive model (combining the generalized use of torture with "offices of psychological action") or the enemy-centric model of the Battle of Algiers. He favored the model of the informed observer of civil wars (in China, Greece, and Indochina) and of the great reader of revolutionary war theorists that would be used in the "successful" pacification operation in part of Great Kabylia, in which Galula participated as captain of an infantry company. "By firmly applying original methods,"[91] he placed the population at the center of the conflict in a way that could not be reduced to the "Urban Protection System" (*Dispositif de protection urbaine*, DPU) and the "winning strategy" of Colonel Trinquier. After first "crushing or eliminating" rebellion in the selected regions, it was a question of regaining political control over the population by conducting the conflict as a type of *argument*. It was less a question of "rallying" the population (or part of it, while terrorizing the other part) than of *convincing* it of the "no future" aspect of insurrection to *defeat* this insurrection... The use of force therefore has to be measured against the political-military yardstick of this war of subjectivity that associates the closest disciplinary network over the territory (control of the population) with a biopolitical project investing "the economic, social, cultural, and medical fields" to show the population that its security and prosperity will be better ensured by the market economy than by "collectivism" ("winning the support of the population").[92] The demonstration is still unavoidably *Foucaldian* during the phase where the question is to "build (or rebuild) a political machine from the population upward" by using "propaganda directed toward the population" on three points: "the importance of the elections, complete freedom for the voters, the necessity of voting." In his conclusion, the man who was a Visiting Fellow at the Harvard Center for International Affairs does not hide that the "idea" of counterinsurgency that he proposes is "simple" but "difficult" to implement. He refers here to "a context utterly alien to a revolutionary situation, in a peaceful and well-developed country." Which country? The United States, where the public's indifference towards politics, especially among the poor ("We never vote"), is a serious cause for concern.[93]

General Petraeus, who emphasized the debt of the new American counterinsurgency thinking towards Galula's work, would not be unaware of the way techniques of control of minorities (the *dangerous poor*) in the US benefitted from the lessons learned in the Vietnam War. Under the influence of guerilla techniques perfected by the American army in a war defined by McNamara as a "pacification security job," the race riots in Watts (1965) led to the first big wave of militarization of American police with the creation of its "elite units" (SWAT, for "Special Weapons Attack Team," then "Special Weapons and Tactics").[94] "High intensity" police operations would become indistinguishable from the "low intensity" wars that they join in the securocratic battlefield of the aptly named Integrated World Capitalism (to use Guattari's expression).

Emerging in the United States at the end of the 1960s in an especially troubled political context, the security militarization of "civil peace" became a powerful *attractor* for the aggressive global pacification that occurred post–September 11. It was able to operate on an entirely different scale, both internally and transnationally, under the principle of equivalency between counterinsurgency and anti-terrorist war. Judging by the Law

Enforcement Exchange Program (LEEP) signed in 2002, the model became *Israeli*. "[W]ho better to turn to for training and inspiration than the most militarized and admired police and security forces in the Western world: Israel."[95] The old integration of American and Israeli military-industrial complexes could thus find its basis in a security principle of militarization of urban space that normalizes, with the idea of the permanent state of emergency, the paramilitary treatment of the Palestinian question, and allowed it to be exported to the neighborhoods of the dangerous classes. And, if it needed to be said, at a level far beyond the fiasco of the Iraq War and its Israeli matrix (peace with high-tech strength)—which was itself inherited, in a "deterritorialized" manner, from English colonial practices.

Because it is precisely waged in the name of a *humanization* of so-called asymmetric war, the critique by "liberal" military figures (Petraeus, Smith, Desportes) of the "Shock and Awe" tactics of cyberwar, with its intention to remove the old model of "boots on the ground" territorial domination reminds us here of the existence of this war amongst the population that is combined with the very history of liberalism, and that carries with it the Clausewitzian legitimization of war *as political intervention*.[96] In this *liberal* sense—which is definitely not that of Spanish guerilla!—General Petraeus can call David Galula "the Clausewitz of counterinsurgency" and make him the reference point for his politics of social engineering.

Conversely, Lenin recognizes in Clausewitz's formula a dialectical thesis of which the truth leads to, in the revolutionary era, Spanish "guerilla" against Napoleon's army to the organization of the "people's war" that wins the civil war by asserting its absolute hostility to the class enemy. Yet after theorizing and practicing revolutionary war by denouncing the danger of a

European-style revolution, "the antithesis of industrial war waged by victorious revolutionaries is developed to the point that it fuses with the conventional paradigm."[97] Revolutionaries adapt capitalist forms, conventions, and institutions not only on the military level (transformation of guerilla into a regular army) but also as concerns the state, the organization of labor, industry, technology, and science. Nevertheless, still according to General Desportes, "at the end of World War II, the precise characteristics of the antithesis of industrial war had been set as a combination of guerilla and revolutionary war."[98] While the two sworn enemies (USA versus USSR) waged what remained an industrial war at this level, the lateral conflicts of the Cold War began to show some aspects of the new paradigm.

The arms industry, of which the economic-strategic functions still played a determinant role in capitalism, is equally caught up in the evolution of war amongst the population. The *military-industrial* complex of the Cold War was supplemented by an *industrial-security* complex that extended war to all types of control in a continuum connecting urban policies of social segregation at the local, national, and global levels of the state of emergency, while its soft power version took care of adapting commercial practices to the cultures of mobility and new ways of life while refining control of the *habitele* by plugging the arborescence of police information on the rhizome of daily life (datamining, smart intelligence).[99] "[A]s the everyday spaces and systems of urban everyday life are colonized by militarized control technologies, and as notions of policing and war, domestic and foreign, peace and war become less distinct, there emerges a massive boom in a convergent industrial complex encompassing security, surveillance, military technology, corrections, and electronic entertainment."[100] There is no surprise that the perpetual war of securocratic pacification quickly became the leading industry of neoliberalism in post-September 11 America.[101] Exactly eleven years earlier, on September 11, 1990, Bush Senior had announced his decision to go to war against Iraq.

A few days after the attacks on the World Trade Center and the Pentagon that connected and combined into a single target the center of military command and the financial capital of the world, John Arquilla and David Ronfeldt hastily added a postscript to their research for the RAND Corporation. In this dramatic context, to which they reacted with curious reserve ("if this [al-Qaeda] is indeed the key adversary, or one of them"), they lay out what they see as the real procedural stakes of the change from counterinsurgency to counter-netwar: "A particular challenge for the cumbersome American bureaucracy will be to encourage deep, all-channel networking among the military, law enforcement, and intelligence elements whose collaboration is crucial for achieving success." They conclude, with a certain degree of foresight in regards to the coming disaster in Iraq: "at its heart, netwar is far more about organization and doctrine than it is about technology. The outcomes of current and future netwars are bound to confirm this."[102]

While its nature changes under the action of contemporary financial capitalism, war in its different aspects remains more than ever the effective action of social relations. Reversal of Clausewitz's formula finds its definitive form when war, beyond its simple permutation with politics, of which it reverses the foundation, is diversified into wars amongst the population as politics of Capital by involving in its enterprise of fear, pacification, and counter-subversion all the networks of power of the economy through which the new order of world security capitalism is deployed. Nevertheless, "the extension of the political and economic markets of fear is not infinite: domination is never limited except by the resistance opposing it and the implementation of this new security order only occupies the space that the oppressed are willing to leave it."[103]

There is therefore a need to produce a critical concept of pacification, one that can relaunch the Foucaldian critique of class struggle. Marxism asserts that capital is a social relationship, but its definition is limited, both too narrowly and too broadly qualified, and especially largely *pacified* in a dialectic that fails to articulate the relationships of social domination and exploitation in a set of strategic confrontations. These confrontations are not only a question of "struggle" but of war and *wars*, the multiplicity of which overflows the two classes of bourgeoisie and proletariat alone by exceeding the notion of class consciousness and its Marxist-Leninist articulation with the attempt by the labor movement to become a state. Becoming-state was the function of the "organized party of the working class." Yet the working class was unable to make itself a *governing class* and "this great Leninist break did not prevent the resurrection of a state capitalism inside socialism itself."[104] It is hard to contradict Foucault here: there is no *socialist governmentality*.

12.4 Heterodox Marxism and War

Mario Tronti, one of the few authors to have thought with and beyond Marx about the "organic" ties between capitalism and war, reproached the movements of 1968 of having in a way *rinsed out* politics by interrupting the program of reconverting war into politics accomplished by the centrality of class struggle;[105] and from there of opening the *small twentieth century* by bringing an end to the "era of big politics": solidly entrenched in the second nineteenth century, it "truly goes from 1914 to 1945" and concludes in the 1960s.[106]

Let us be clear: we are not trying to deny the "historical greatness" of the working class that culminated in the struggles of the Fordist phase (through which operaismo redefined the "class struggling" in the antagonism of working class struggle against labor), but of thinking *with and after* the no less historical failure of that which Tronti still wants to consider, in the present of a Hegelianism to which he alone holds the key, as its "destiny."[107] Tronti refuses to see that "'68" coincides with the exhaustion of a certain way of understanding and *doing politics* from the Capital/Labor relationship of which the truth is the party-form, and that this end of the race is not without relation with the impossibility of continuing to think and to *do war* from the state-form of the Nation. On the workers' side, the "great initiative" that was already *late by one war* since it continued to wage politically a war "formed, civilized, and fought on the model of the *Jus publicum Europaeum.*" The argument is irrefutable: "Regulation of the conflict, abandoned at the level of international politics, was maintained on the level of national policies [...] when formless civil wars were raging."[108] Yet these strategies of the "working-class subject" (how different from the reality of labor struggles in the factory of the "Hot Autumn")[109] turned towards the "great mediation" which, on the one hand, explains their historical defeat (the world wars served "to produce the definitive globalization of the economy" through which "capitalism definitively won")[110] and on the other, made '68 incomprehensible because the intention was to maintain at all cost the political project of the "working-class subject." '68 was accused of injecting "the poison of anti-politics" in the veins of society by its anti-authoritarian revolution that was profitable above all to the modernization of capitalism, when "it had to project, invest, a new politics from on high into the movements below."[111] The thesis on "the autonomy of politics" (developed in the 1970s) came to finalize the counter-movement by finishing to show that politics and war *after '68* had become, for Tronti, as opaque on the route that had led "the flower children to years of lead." The demonstration passes through this "observance of fact," "without the least value judgment," to which Tronti gives great importance: "a truth that cannot be said and therefore must be written"; he then writes: "with the end of the era of wars, the decadence of politics begins."[112] He continues with what appears to be his post-communist version of the *end of History* and the *end of politics* following the "deep coma" into which politics fell in the 1970s-1980s: "The collapse of the Soviet Union and world reunification under the hegemony of a single power, as illustrated by the Gulf War that followed, offered the scenario of a new *possible hundred-year peace*. The twentieth century is retracted. Return to the nineteenth."[113] Tronti confuses the "new possible hundred-year peace" with the enterprise of global pacification undertaken, during the period (of counter-revolution) in question, by the war machine of Capital. It is the new *paradigm* of war amongst the population, which reaches its axiomatic power of multiplication of war when capital recapitalizes its entire history by short-circuiting any mediation between *Weltpolitik* and *Weltöconomie*.

War amongst the population, as General Desportes insists, "is not a degraded form of war: it is war, period. And if we look back, the war that, throughout time, has been the most frequent."[114] On the other side of the mirror, the same happened with the struggles that erupted in and after '68: they are not degraded forms of class struggle but new modalities of these struggles, these conflicts, these wars that have adorned the entire history of capitalism and so well preceded the Fordist Capital/Labor class struggle that counter to what Tronti thinks (who relegates them to their "subaltern" level), they made possible the radicalness of *working class struggle against labor*.

At this level, all too often reduced to a "subaltern" function by the Marxism of the 1960s, Tronti does not have a sufficiently *global* vision of the history of capitalism and its conflicts. Even when he turns to the United States, even when he tries to give feminism its place, even when he tries to get away from a linear vision of history and critiques the "accelerationist" tendency of his frenemy Negri,[115] or when he asserts the primacy of struggle over organization, his point of view is still enclosed in "European civilization" and participates in what Foucault denounces as "economism" in the theory of power. It bears repeating: revolutionary wars, insurrectional movements, sabotage, and wildcat strikes of the nineteenth and twentieth centuries are raised to the pedestal of resistance and wars of class, race, sex, and subjectivity waged in the world-economy long before the "centrality of the working class" was forged.

'68 not only confirms the "new class" *within and against* Fordist-Taylorist-Keynesian capitalism that commands its emergence. While '68 reconnects below and beyond the historical-global sequence leading to it (major strikes of the Liberation, unaligned movement, Chinese Revolution, Yugoslavian self-rule, Hungarian workers' uprising in 1956, FLN networks…), with the multiplicity of wars of primitive accumulation, it repeated a singular event that played a fundamental role in the formation and the imaginary of the labor movement: the Paris Commune. In the conditions of a capitalism "developed" by the cold totalization of different war economies and the colonial conquests that started to blossom in 1870 to enter into a definitive crisis in the post-war period (hot decolonization), '68 poses the social question anew in the terms of the Commune: 1/ there is no "people acting for itself by itself"[116] without displacing and resituating politics into life (critique of socialism "from above"); 2/ communism is de-subjection of life in relation to the machine of the state, the "huge governmental parasite, entoiling like a boa constrictor the real social body in the ubiquitous meshes of a standing army, hierarchical bureaucracy, an obedient police"[117] (de-statification of life). A question, an affirmation ("The political instrument of their enslavement cannot serve as the political instrument of their emancipation")[118] quickly closed by the communist tradition that, unlike Marx, was not concerned with problematizing its urgent need or with drawing all the consequences of the strategies required by entry into the era of the major European and global civil wars.

Kristin Ross: "The insurgents' brief mastery of their own history is perceptible, in other words, not so much on the level of governmental politics as on the level of their daily life: in concrete problems of work, leisure, housing, sexuality, and family and neighborhood relations."[119] Revolutionary struggle, instead of enclosing itself "in a strict and binary opposition between Capital and Labor," invested all power relations as relationships of force verifying the lack of distinction between economy and politics in the urgency of civil war and the new internationalism that accompanies it (it is Élisée Reclus' famous "the whole world is our homeland").

The "existence in action" of the Commune (Marx) relates directly to what '68 brought back to a *transhistorical present*: the process of emancipation takes place "here and now," it is not affected by any lack or delay and is therefore not dependent on any development of labor and production, any acceleration of science and technology. Marx again: "The Paris Commune may fall, but the Social Revolution it has initiated, will triumph. *Its birth-stead is everywhere.*"[120]

Lenin, however, focuses on thinking about the Commune from the perspective of the massacre of 30,000 Communards bringing an end to "an event unprecedented in history," that "[n]o one consciously prepared [...] in an organized way" and that served as an act of re-founding the (Third) Republic and its "democracy" sanctioning the imbalance of forces manifested in the war in "civil peace." The conclusion he draws in an April 1911 article, "In Memory of the Commune," pulls all Marxism in the direction of the development and class consciousness of the labor party that alone could confront the opposite party *power to power.*[121] In Lenin's text: "For the victory of the social revolution, at least two conditions are necessary: a high development of productive forces and the preparedness of the proletariat. But in 1871 neither of these conditions was present."[122] One could comment on the immortality of the Commune, but what would be lost is what Lenin himself calls the *cause of the Commune* and that he associates with a "social revolution" defined by "the complete political and economic emancipation" of workers. What other meaning could it have if not that "revolution consists not in changing the juridical form that allots space/time [...] but rather in completely transforming the nature of space/time."[123]

Not recognizing this radicalness, not making it live in and alongside the struggles of the working class (the "artisans, farmers, shop owners, etc." of yesterday and the "micro-entrepreneurs" of the *gray market* that followed them), not subjecting political thought to the cultural revolution of this explosion of subjectivity could only lead to the political dissolution of the working class and its party. It must be stated and restated: the Party is fully responsible for the "small century" of post-'68, the Party that historically disappeared due to the intensification of the new conditions of a conflict that is *less dialectical than ever.* The working class not only politically evaporated under the attacks of the global civil war launched by Capital in the immediate post-'68, it also and especially evaporated under the *progressivism* that maintained a "workerist" and "Eurocentric" point of view making it incapable of connecting its strategy with the global socialization of production and the subjective modalities of struggles born, in the West, of the pseudo-peace that operates a continuous war *amongst all the populations of the world.*

In terms of this global war, Mario Tronti and Carl Schmitt share a common nostalgia for the time coinciding with each one's "big twentieth century," albeit not the same one, where the state monopolized and centralized force as the sign of distinctive legitimization (Schmitt) and where class struggle centralized and monopolized the multiplicity of the subjects exploited and dominated into a single worker-subject carrying politics (Tronti). This does not prevent Schmitt and Tronti from sharing the idea, which would be enough to make us avid readers of both, that while "[f]rom the beginning, liberal thinking raised the accusation of 'violence' against the state and politics,"[124] it was to produce an even more terrifying pacification where peace loses all meaning, and any meaning other than that of the continuation of war amongst the population. We are now reaching the blind spot of our generals, with their diplomas in the liberal sciences, who could not *popularize* the expression except by declaring the conditions of life and reality of the *probable absolute enemy* who, in the end, is defined by its break with the hypothesis of *liberal peace.* Mark Neocleous has perfectly summarized the mytheme: "peace is the focal dynamic of civil society, that the state exists in order to realize this 'liberal peace' within civil society, and that international law exists to ensure peace between states. On this view, war is an exception to peace. As a myth, this has served to gloss over liberalism's own tendency to carry out systematic violence *of* the liberal peace."[125] Inversely, however, and this time *outside and against* Tronti and Schmitt, 68 is the number of the globalization of conflicts that can no longer be centralized and controlled by the state (and its conventional army) or by class struggle as codified by the communist tradition. In this sense, the contemporary situation is much closer to the anti-dialectic of continued primitive accumulation than the bildungsroman of politics in the "big twentieth century."

12.5 The Anthropocene War Has Not (Yet) Happened

Giving us a sense of the crucial meaning of the work of climate change scientists and the definitive change in the relationship with the world it and they imply under the name of the Anthropocene, Bruno Latour asserts from the start that "no postmodern philosopher, no anthropologist, no liberal theologian, no political thinker would have dared measure the influence of humans *on the same scale* as rivers, volcanos, erosion, and biochemistry."[126]

Among the many "exceptions" that could be raised and that argue against the thesis of a war declared against the "Earth system" without our full knowledge (or "unknowingly" as James Lovelock famously put it),[127] we will take one by an old communist revolutionary known as Karl Marx, who is credited with a first *denaturalization* of the energy feeding the Industrial Revolution (*under steam, sweat, and blood*). He described the new nature of the productive forces mobilized by capitalism in this way: "Bourgeois industry and commerce create these material conditions of a new world in the same way as geological revolutions have created the surface of the earth."[128] The fact that this metaphor was not simply for journalistic use is confirmed by the fact that attribution of a telluric force to the powers mobilized by capitalism was deeply rooted in the ontology of "production" which Marx was the first to endorse. Deleuze and Guattari summarized it very efficiently in a two-step formula: it is the identity "wherein Nature = Industry, Nature = History."[129] There is no distinction between nature and production, no division between Human and Nature: "man and nature are not like two opposite terms confronting each other [...]; rather, they are one and the same essential reality, the producer-product. [...] [T]he human essence of nature and the natural essence of man become one within nature in the form of production or industry." History, and the history of the distinction follow. The distinction, as the two authors previously recalled, considered "from the point of view of its formal developed structures, presupposes (as Marx has demonstrated) not only the existence of capital and the division of labor, but also the false consciousness that the capitalist being necessarily acquires, both of itself and of the supposedly fixed elements within an over-all process."

What should we think, then, of the supposedly radical break brought about by the Anthropocene by taking away from the "Moderns" the distinction they established between Nature and Society, and the "front of modernization" that it would have opened, if the critique of the modern distinction is not unrelated to the Marxist concept of "production"? Knowing that this very same critique would be taken up by Deleuze and Guattari, even in the affirmation of the *unsustainable* aspect of the capitalist metabolism, and that its perspective concerned "[n]ot man as the king of creation, but rather as the being who is in intimate contact with the profound life of all forms or all types of beings, who is responsible for even the stars and animal life,"[130] could the Anthropocene be the name of something other than the revelation of the "geological force" of "humanity" in a war that has already happened and that *we* have lost for *living through it without living it*? Isn't this last phrase a possible definition of the "false consciousness" of capitalist being, to which the *depoliticized* "nature" of the Modernity of the Great Bifurcation (Nature/Culture, Subject/Object, etc.) should be referred?

Scientific debate has not yet made it possible to determine the official date of entry into the new geological era,[131] nor is there a definitive decision on this beginning. Several dates have been proposed that could just as well serve as "phases" of the Anthropocene.

A possible first stage of full entry into geohistory through the *geopower* behind it occurred in 1610. Following the analysis of ice from the poles, scientists have determined that at that date, the quantity of CO_2 in the atmosphere reached an abnormally low level. The reasons for this phenomenon are most instructive since they place objective values on the genocide carried out by European colonial powers on Amerindian tribes: a fifth of the planet's population disappeared when the indigenous population of the planet plunged from 55 million to 6 million. We then have a better understanding that the *greatest demographic disaster in the history of the world* led to reforestation of the continent and increased CO_2 storage so much that climatologists can use it as a minimum benchmark from which they can measure its subsequent increase. According to this hypothesis, the Anthropocene began in 1492 with the *end of the world* for the people of the Americas.[132] The Anthropocene is a Necrocene. 1492–1610: genocide precedes and leads to the ecocide *to come* and that we can *calculate* using it (accumulation through extinction). The "destruction of space by time" (according to the Marxist formula describing the capitalist philosophy of the "speed of circulation") is measured from the destruction of *their* time and by the space that it freed for the colonialist exploitation of "nature"—always already composed of humans and non-humans. An indigenous person or an African slave (like the men of every color living in semi-colonial regions, like the majority of women) was not of Society but of Nature. *Cheap Nature, Cheap Labor*. Marx again, in *The Poverty of Philosophy*: "Without slavery you have no cotton; without cotton you have no modern industry." The world-ecology *of capital* establishes the "law of value" in this environment of death destined for its "industrialization."[133]

The second proposed date, 1784, coincides with the start of the Industrial Revolution and the invention of the steam engine at the end of the eighteenth century. By choosing the date of James Watt's patent, the Anthropocene affirms itself as a Thermocene and an Anglocene, where the hegemonic power of the nineteenth century fueled by coal (Great Britain) was followed by the United States, whose power also relied on carbon, in the form of petroleum. What Timothy Mitchell has called "carbon democracy"[134] was on the horizon.

Others—most, in fact—start the Anthropocene in 1945 due to the clear radioactive signal and the message it sent. The two atomic bombs dropped on Japan after the Manhattan Project and the multiplication of nuclear tests that followed are held up as the first sediment of the "Great Acceleration." Yet before fueling the post-war boom of the *Trente Glorieuses*, the petrolization of Western Europe, and "atoms for peace," there was the productive and destructive acceleration of two total wars. The Anthropocene is a Thanatocene used indistinguishably for military and civilian purposes.[135]

These three dates represent possible alternatives for scientists but not for common mortals. By designating three stages of the development of capitalism, they express the *inner nature* of the Anthropocene: the Anthropocene is a Capitalocene.

Bruno Latour, whose long-term project is to *re-politicize* Science (by means of the sociology *of the sciences*) and "Nature" (the quotation marks indicate the radical contestation of its object),[136] has nonetheless succeeded in writing a book on the Anthropocene (*Facing Gaia*) that attributes entry into the new geological era with the same importance for "humanity" as the conquest of the Americas (which it closes on the surface and condemns under the surface of the Earth) without ever (or almost never) using the word "capitalism." The causes for climate imbalance are connected to "Moderns," "Westerners," and "Humans." The same is true of a major player in *subaltern studies*, the historian Dipesh Chakrabarty, who, after critiquing Marx's Eurocentrism and the historicism of the continental philosophical tradition in *Provincializing Europe*,[137] finally succumbs to the epochal vertigo of the Anthropocene by reinventing the universalism of the "species" (51 occurrences counted by Bonneuil and Fressoz in his pioneering article!) in the adjectival mode of humans as "geological agent on the planet," of which the *scale* exceeds any possible history of capitalism...[138] Using agents as undifferentiated as humanity or the species and as generic and abstract as Westerners or Moderns glosses over any specific and *situated* analysis of the modalities of exploitation, domination, and division involved in the multiplicity of wars that led to both political and technological decisions following victory or defeat that one portion of humans made against other humans (and non-humans). A return to linear and empty time in the form of a bio-historicism for an historian as knowledgeable as

Chakrabarty, to totalization and to an "overarching view" for a philosopher as innovative as Latour, who may push a bit too far his denunciation of "constructivism inherited from the critical tradition" by confiding the composition of a "common world" to diplomats alone... Or to a "diplomatic enterprise" charged, at first, with *heightening conflicts* the better to define the conditions for arbitrating *peace*.[139]

Chakrabarty's explanation of the limits of the critique of capitalism in understanding the Anthropocene is fascinating: because the "rich and privileged" cannot escape disaster as skillfully as they can economic crises (no "lifeboats" available to leave the planet!), the problem is a problem for humanity, the species, humankind. He gives an unprecedented meaning to the humanism that was so ardently fought by the thought of the 1960s. For Latour, the objective is "to restore meaning to the notion of limit," to maintain "our activity within limits agreed on deliberately and politically"[140] and thereby confront "an entirely new situation: the Earth is not nature or culture but a mode of existence *sui generis*."[141]

One only needs some knowledge of the real functioning of capitalism to understand that the concepts of "limit" and "disaster" sound very different to the ears of a capitalist and to those of the organic intellectuals of the Anthropocene. The *sui generis* politics that follow are unfortunately radically heterogeneous. Unless it is in the most strategic sense, no disaster can threaten or properly serve as an alert for a capitalist, just as no limit can *truly* worry the capitalist, since disasters are normal modalities of its functioning and limits represent the means of production of its development. A disaster involving the entire species does not bother capitalists at all: they long ago incorporated the most immaterial philosophy of the *banality of evil* (Donna Haraway).

On the contrary, disaster represents an *opportunity* that allows capitalists to move from one mode of valuation to another (the most basic Marxist analysis suffices here). As for limits, capitalism knows none other than immanent limits. "It would like for us to believe that it confronts the limits of the Universe, the extreme limit of resources and energy. But all it confronts are its own limits (the periodic depreciation of existing capital); all it repels or displaces are its own limits (the formation of new capital, in new industries with a high profit rate). This is the history of oil and nuclear power. And it does both at once: capitalism confronts its own limits and simultaneously displaces them, setting them down again farther along."[142]

Confronting limits and displacing limits, as Deleuze and Guattari say. Capitalism behaves in the same way with ecological limits as it does with every other limit it generates. (Hasn't it in more than one way *constructed* "nature" as a *whole*?) It makes them the condition and the source of a new valuation while displacing and worsening the ecological degradation of the planet. André Gorz asserted as early as 1974 that, since the ecological impasse was unavoidable (confronting limits), capitalism would be able to incorporate the constraints, no matter what the cost to the people, as it had for all the others it had faced (displacing limits).[143] Disaster represents an essential element of the strategy of integrating ecology into a new valuation. By spreading fear, the anxiety of imminent danger, and the guilt of shared mistakes, the most "enlightened" capitalism pushes for "change" and "reforms"—exactly as it did for the debt "crisis."

Sustainable development, green economy, and renewable energy are a displacing of limits for a new regime of *destructive creation* made politically more palatable by the multiplication of diplomatic mediations and negotiations that are not put into *anthropo-scene* without calling on the most qualified analyzers of climate imbalance. Scientific actors who have become anthropocenologues are called on to take charge, in a negotiated way, of the "planetary stewardship" of environmental management to "optimize the climate." With the non-negligible advantage of being in a situation to "pass as contraband the countless alliances between the sciences and financial, political, industrial, or military powers that, for a quarter century, have led to the major contemporary ecological upheavals."[144] Yet it is not only "scientists" who would like to forget that capitalism is not a "mode of production" without being at the same time a *mode of destruction*—in which they could only participate—and of which the Anthropocene is less the end point than the "cosmogram" and the cosmodrama. The philosophers of the Anthropocene also draw back from the strictly capitalistic nature of the *infinite* that they denounce. Thus, Bruno Latour only tackles its *modernist concept* (would we have been modern?) and in such a *metaphysical*[145] way that the ecosocial physics of the introduction of the infinite into production can only escape the simultaneous introduction of the infinite into the *creative destruction of capitalism*. 1492–1945: accumulation without limit and destruction without limit, didn't they celebrate their nuptials of iron and fire during the first half of the twentieth century through feedback of their most genocidal dimension?[146] It was there, in the total wars of capitalism (or of "imperialism as supreme stage of capitalism") that "the apocalyptic dimension of which we are the descendants"[147] was crystallized (a "situated knowledge," in fact). As Lewis Mumford wrote: "war has taken on an infinitely more destructive form: breaking through all physical barriers and moral restraints, it has turned in our day into unrestricted genocide, which now threatens all life on this planet"[148]

Is there any need to recall the particularly acute perception of capitalism as "mode of destruction" at the end of World War II? The nuclear apocalypse that concluded an already-won war became the vector of apocalyptic thought attached to the "ontological" reversal of the "emancipatory" functions of productive forces. The "destruction" is now deeply inscribed in Labor, Technology, Science and accompanies "production" as its double. The "power of annihilation" replaces "creation" *ex nihilo* and the promethean power of humans. Capitalism thus introduced something remarkably new to the history of humanity: up to the advent of the atomic bomb, only individuals were mortal, while the species was immortal. With total wars, "the venerable expression 'All men are mortal' lost all meaning," since the atomic bomb brought with it the possibility that "humanity as a whole could be killed and not only all men."[149] Whether the bomb is used again or not, we will always live in "the shadow of this unavoidable companion." The threat of disaster will always be present and will lead us into the time of survival of those *under a suspended death sentence.*[150] The bomb, as Günther Anders explains, "succeeded where religions and philosophies, empires and revolutions had failed: it was truly able to make us a humanity [...]. Now we are in fact under a suspended death sentence. Let us prove that we can be without being resigned to it."[151] The powers of emancipation that the "people of the new world" had elicited in the nineteenth century were tragically reversed "like the fable of the sorcerer's apprentice." "Mankind now lives under the threat of self-destruction, on a scale hitherto unthinkable by methods heretofore unimaginable."[152] For this reason, the total wars were a radical break with "progressive" ideas of development. By "passing from a limited order of destruction and violence, directed towards limited ends, into systematic and unrestricted extermination,"[153] war transmits its *unlimitedness* to technology, work, and the new realities of a Cold War taking charge of the peace: *total peace*, the "absolute peace of survival." With it, "it *is peace that technologically frees the unlimited material process of total war*."[154] The reversal of Clausewitz's formula here means that the destruction *produced* by the total wars was not temporary but *ontological*—such that capitalism can no longer be, if it ever was, dialectical and that the reformist illusion of the thirty-year post-war boom associating the bomb with prosperity was beaten back before the cosmogony of progress ever took hold.[155] This "apocalyptic" critique of modernization was lost in the euphoria of the Sixties before returning in "ecological awareness." While it has not lost its anti-capitalist character, the relationship with the total war of Capital and its civil wars has regrettably been left behind.

The explosive destruction of the total wars and their nuclear concentration in the atomic bomb have, however, pursued uncontested their capitalization through consumption producing daily destruction (global warming, pollution, deforestation, privatization of "natural" common spaces, etc.) by *developing* the most imbalanced "ecological exchange" ever seen. Not only between North and South, but between the Norths and Souths of each city and their periphery, verifying that all environmental questions are also questions of social reproduction. As we know, this is the strength of ecofeminism, bringing environmental questions back to the home, and in particular to areas suffering the *multiscalar* physical reality of "environmental racism."[156] We could discuss the complex relationship between the *environmental history of the race* with gender as *matrix of race*.[157] But there is no denying the reality of the social ecology of conflicts that pits "humanity" against itself, ever more divided by heterogenous interests that are far from being only economic in capitalism, which must decidedly be situated as the sole "power of historicization" of Gaia.[158] It is therefore necessary to go farther in deconstructing the official description of the Anthropocene. In many ways, doesn't it take the historical relay of the Great Narrative of the Cold War by substituting a new, supposedly more sustainable, cybernetic governance of the Earth-Humanity system for the nuclear defense of the free world, relayed by an entirely virtual universality? Following this loop, the climate-sceptics (or *climate-deniers*) would be the only obstacles to the march towards a new spirit of capitalism recognizing the portion of (individual and collective) responsibility of mobilized eco-citizens, under the authority of Science and/or the geosciences, to push back the "end times."[159]

The Anthropocene is not only a universalism that distributes responsibilities indiscriminately even though "we know who is responsible"; it is also a theory that evacuates conflict, struggle, and war by transferring them to a *diplomatic obligation* for results strangely posed by its most advanced fringe as the key to *re-politicizing* ecology.

The first function of power, which consists in denying the existence of the ongoing civil war, is perfectly ensured by the Anthropocene in its appeal to a generic humanity raised to the rank of new subject of a *natural history* that it has dangerously "hystericized." It is against this yardstick that we must seek to understand the irruption of war for the later Latour in its dialogue with Gaia. After promoting, as a good sociologist would, his own solution to the problem of how to "live together" through a "new natural contract" and the intermediary of cosmopolitical politics of reconciliation between humans and non-humans, he declares that the Anthropocene is an introduction to a "state of war," a "war of the worlds," and a "state of *generalized war*." This is where Latour begins by recognizing the fact that "humans are divided into so many war parties"[160] against the idea of a humanity too quickly unified (or globalized)[161] according to a symmetrical copy of the Hobbesian strategy gathering the Moderns into a civil peace "guaranteed" by an unlimited (never declared) war on Nature. Which is all the more impossible *and dangerous* since the situation is absolutely reversed: the Earth projects us into a "new state of war" *with itself* by retroactively acting on "human actions." Humanity cannot change its spots and reveals itself through its harmful acts. As Latour summarizes it: "Our situation is thus at once the same as and the opposite of that of Hobbes: the same because it is imperative to seek peace; the opposite because we cannot go from the state of nature to the State; we can only go from the State of Nature to the recognition of a state of war."[162]

Isn't it possible to redirect Foucault's critique of Hobbes against Latour's discovery of war? In other words, the transposition of the war of all against all in the Anthropocene would be a *fiction squared*, fiction within a fiction commanding pacification between "collectives" and peoples" as "multiple and dispers[ed]" that they end up passing inside each one of us… Isn't this the indication of a war without a front or subjective break other than the most generic opposition between the "Old Climate Regime" and the "New Climate Regime" calling for a true revolution in our "relationship with the world"? QED: "Give peace a chance"? But is the task so impossible, or useless, to "designate by their names some of the representatives of the 'Human' army on the front lines, those who are the most directly responsible for the growing aggravation of the anthropocenic disaster"? "After all, to start—continue Danowski and Viveiros de Castro—there are only 90 major companies responsible for two-thirds of the greenhouse gases in the earth's atmosphere."[163]

Without a principle of response where the geopolitics of the "territories involved in the struggle" take a decisively *anti-capitalist* turn, the question returns: if humanity can have no enemy, who *in fact* are the enemies in Latourian war? "Humans" and "Earthbound." The first are the master modernizers and owners of nature; the second, the creatures of Gaia reterritorialized or *reterrestrialized* by the Anthropocene! We are not far here from another film in the *Lord of the Rings* series. And Latour recognizes it in passing: "To put it in the style of a geohistorical fiction, the Humans living in the epoch of the Holocene are in conflict with the *Earthbound* of the *Anthropocene*."[164]

Latour's political project, consisting of declaring that war—what he now calls the "declared ecological state of war"[165] to establish a negotiated peace through "diplomacy," or the principle of *a war that leads to diplomatic peace*—can only rely on Clausewitz's concept of war as the continuation of politics ("through other means"). Yet how, then, does this "cosmopolitics" avoid becoming prisoner of the *delay* in Clausewitz's formula in relation to the real politics of "modernization" that are just forms of civil wars continued in and through capitalism? A capitalism which itself is never "limited" to *land appropriation* (to use Schmitt's expression). Such that it is not enough to extend and *reverse the land appropriation* exercised by Humans *appropriated by the Earth* defining the Earthbound for everything to change.[166] Latour's invention of a new form of war is a "diplomatic" construction projected to resolve *in theory*—giving it its frankly *extraterrestrial* character!—all of these "problems," *which are all part of the anti-capitalist perspective he wants to avoid at all costs.* But at what cost? The cost of the operation of "radical inversion of the direction of appropriation" is measured by its *diluting effects* on the ecological battlefield: on the Human side, "it is impossible to draw a precise map of their geopolitical conflicts"; on the Earthbound side, the map of their territories is "made up not of nation-states enclosed within their borders [...] but, rather, of networks that intermingle, oppose one another, become mutually entangled, contradict one another, and that no harmony, no system, no 'third party,' no supreme Providence can unify in advance."[167] Literally, this is not wrong, as long as ecological war is included as the *constitutive dimension* of the multiplicity of wars of class, race, gender, and subjectivity that transform in return the very notion of ecology in the sense of a transversal, generalized ecology with "interactions between ecosystems, the mechanosphere, and the social and individual Universes of reference."[168]

Without a *theory of the evolution* of capitalism and its *divisions of wars*, it is impossible to produce a theory of war at the time of the Anthropocene. If "ecological" ravages are the results of the victories of the capitalists in all the wars they have waged *against us*, we may be the only ones capable of saying one day: *it was the end of Nature and the rebirth of ecology.*

Human, all too human, capitalists seized on the Club of Rome document on "the limits of development" ordered in 1970 and published in 1972 as an imperative to transform the "ecological" limits created by Capital itself into new sources of profit. True to its dynamic, they have since only succeeded in amplifying the ecological disaster. Based on an old story that begins with the "enclosures" of the most primitive Anglocene, the idea was a good one and was argued with the brio and bravado of the neoliberals: to guarantee the longevity of "common spaces," of land, sea, and air, they have to be withdrawn from use by all and privatized, in other words subject to a cost/benefit logic regulated by the market. As the commodification of nature was a particularly promising market, and regulation an affair of market economies, the idea of markets for pollution rights ("carbon markets") soon followed. The European Community made it one of its specialties (European Union Emission Trading System, EU ETS); it is the largest one in the world.

Finance invested and soon developed these new domains of value creation by becoming "environmental." Beyond the insurance operations that had been around for some time in the US, finance became completely "green" by emitting "cat bonds" ("catastrophe bonds") and "green bonds," "climate derivatives," "environmental loans," etc. They share the fact that they insure the "new risks" through "securitization" (since security *also* has a financial meaning) by participating, through intermediary agencies, in *disaster modeling*,[169] to the point that people speak today of "marketization through modeling." A shared culture of speculation has been created on the green markets and exchanges, "aligning nature with the new spirit of capitalism and the logic of finance. [...] A multitude of new financial instruments have been developed in recent years to profit from 'natural capital' and its 'services.'"[170]

The patentability of living things (sold to the public as a tool to preserve biodiversity) and biodiversity markets provide the definitive philosophy of neoliberal biopower that feeds the geopower of capital as the final figure of globalization.

Is anyone surprised that the marketization and financialization of nature brought into the time of the Anthropocene in the *capitalization on chaos* come with "the growing interconnection between war and ecology"[171] and that they turn armies into *specialists in chaos?*[172] Pacification for security and the "new military humanism" are proliferating at the speed of natural disasters and the management of the social risks they amplify. The latter are fully integrated in the functioning of ecological "crises" as "threat multipliers." Think of Hurricane Katrina in New Orleans in 2005, which served to reveal environmental racism and accelerate the gentrification of the city by making it a case for applying a "shock strategy" with the National Guard.[173] There are also the greenwashing operations of armies equipped with "ecological intervention units" that relate the "preservation of nature" with its militarization, duly programmed at "the intersection of climate change and national security." Thus came the idea of creating *Green Helmets* to control the multiple *green wars* that involve all the components of the most political history of postcolonial nature.

Yet "greenwashing" is especially a reminder of the "constitutive" role of the military complex in the Anthropocene. Outside the colossal processes of ecological destruction produced by the industrialization of wars subjected to the unlimited logic of capital, the war economy, beyond the increasingly energy-hungry theater of operations and handling of armies, has continued to innervate the "progress" of "development." "The military apparatus, war, and the logic of power, with their unsustainable technological choices that are then imposed on the civilian world, carry a heavy responsibility in the disruption of local environments and the entire Earth system."[174] An exemplary case if ever there was one, the transfer of nuclear power from the military to civilians threatens the entire system twice. It entails both the *possibility* of the hot extinction of the human species and the *reality* of the "great acceleration" in the Cold War,[175] which was able to launch the socialization and capitalization of all productive/destructive forces of total war into a race to "made in the USA" civilization.[176]

In its major narrative unifying the species, the Anthropocene is not only a universalism and a humanism, but it is also a "physicalist" reductionism maintaining the diplomatic-scientific illusion of a "spatial fix." However, while the climate threat comes from a geohistory that made an event from the break in the balance of the Earth, this event is itself less politically global than *locally and globally political*: it imposes the abandon *everywhere* of the negotiated hope of an "exit from the crisis" and the reversal of Chakrabarty's thesis by agreeing with Benjamin that *only capitalism will not die of natural causes.*

For this reason, in coherence with the ontology of Nature = Industry = History, Félix Guattari invites us *never* to separate what capitalism has held and exploited since its birth. Which leads us to revisit the thesis of the Great Divide of which Modernity was the milieu and the Moderns, the deceptive and deceived instruments of a representation of the world based on the division of Nature and Culture. For it is capitalism that does the work of *irreduction* and appears *irreducible* in relation to the abstract concept of modernity and its regime of distribution, which "disanimated" objects by "animating" subjects alone according to the principle of a "naturalism" (Descola) positioning humans outside nature.

"Nature" has never been a mere "backdrop for human action" (as Latour puts it, to emphasize the difference between the Anthropocene and the Holocene) since it is *caught* (*prise*) in the assembly of Capital. To take our turn with Carl Schmitt: Nature is the *land appropriation* (*prise de terre*) of Capital. The simplest definition of Capital involves "constant capital" (raw materials, machines, etc.) and "variable capital" (labor force), in other words a "hybridization" of humans and non-humans that does not refer to Modernity (with a capital M) but to the capitalist organization of exploitation. No possible exteriority, since "nature" is invested *extensively* (colonization going to the limits of the earth) and *intensively* (colonization to the limits of "matter").

The functioning of Capital is not bothered by the "modern" dualisms of subject and object, words and things, Nature and Culture or Society. The subject/object, human/machine, agent/matter relationship fades to leave room for a global configuration where there is the encounter and assemblage of forces that are not divided between "dead" and "living," subjective and objective to the extent that they are all diversely "animated" (physical and sub-physical forces of matter, human and subhuman forces of "body" and "mind," machine forces, powers of signs, etc.). In this "production," there are relationships, agents and signs, but relationships are not intersubjective, agents are not people and semiotics are not representatives. Human agents and non-human agents function as points of "connection, conjunction, and disjunction" of fluxes and networks that constitute the capitalist agency exploiting all these relationships.[177]

We will take the liberty of making Guattari-Deleuze speak here: "Without production of subjectivity, no long march towards the Anthropocene and no Anthropocene *at all!*" Not only is human action inseparable from that of non-humans, humans are, moreover, subject to processes of formatting of subjectivity that, historically, have been profoundly different: the "humans" of primitive accumulation, industrial capitalism, and financial capital are not all the same. Their subjectivity must be *produced* in a specific way each time to respond to the demands of *production*. One day it will have to be explained to us how anthropologists, who are so present on the new scene of the

Anthropocene, can have such little interest in grasping the "differences" in colonizing societies after revealing the finest "differences" in colonized societies.

The discussion raised by the Anthropocene seems to represent a perfect example of "one step forward, three steps back" in relation to the proposition made by Félix Guattari in 1989 to construct a general political ecology that could wage war on triple ravages: ravage of "nature," ravage of the "socius," and ravage of "subjectivity." What other meaning could Latour's "state of generalized war" have?

Polarized by only one of these ravages ("nature") to the detriment of the two others, the grand unifying and pacifying narrative of the Anthropocene, in its official version, is a barely-disguised hymn to the redemptive function of science. Real solutions will come from science, technological innovations, or geo-engineering, reminding us that the R&D of the Cold War has found an outlet worthy of its cybernetic ambitions. It could even call on certain antecedents, with its retroactive loops caught in "human-machine systems." "In fact, post-war cybernetics and the science of cyborgs did not wait for Latour, Haraway, or Descola to celebrate the disappearance of the nature/culture frontier, since their precise aim was to optimize systems connecting the human and non-human."[178] Cybernetics is not for nothing the capitalist science of the Cold War... which is itself the closest threshold for entry into the Anthropocene.

At the time of the greatest dangers, everything depends on the diagnosis of the situation. If those responsible are Humanity, Moderns, and Westerners, then only experts can find the right solutions. This is the ecomodernist version of the politics of "experts," which is upheld by the contemporary neoliberal ideology that has already put in place so many "governments of experts."

If, however, as we believe, the most pertinent diagnosis of the continued causes and origins of the Anthropocene is strategic,[179] then the politics of "territories of struggle" must resolutely engage in the very real "ecological war" now underway and that, like many others and at the intersection of all others (wars of class, race, sex, and subjectivity), we are probably losing.

12.6 War Machines

When financial capital becomes hegemonic, and makes the war and state it has appropriated into the direct instruments of its strategy, what dynamic, what energy does it breathe into the war machine?

In Book III of *Capital*, Marx defines the credit system as the institution that allows someone to "transform [money] into capital without having to become an industrial capitalist."[180] It is that class of capitalists who, as "agents of capital" (a capital that, no matter what Marx says, is not all "fictive" but as real as capital can be!), introduce a structural instability into the economy and society through which the "development" of capital *itself* passes. The mode of value-creation of industrial capital advances through *periodic crises* due to the fact that the "absolute" or "unconditional" development of productive forces would be in contradiction with its subordination to the logic of profit and private property. Yet under the impetus of financial capital, crises quickly come so close together that the very notion of "crisis" ends up losing all its structural meaning and is replaced by a state of permanent instability. The very idea of crisis as "means immanent to the mode of capitalist production" seems oddly *old hat* here, including the general principle according to which things only work (well?) if they break down.

The depreciation of existing capital and the formation of new capital (crisis) to soften the fall in the profit rate is now produced *continuously* under the pressure of the "competitiveness"[181] that is so dear to financial capitalists and other "institutional investors." Under this last category: pension funds, collective investment funds based on private retirement plans by capitalization and employee savings, insurance companies, investment companies, corporate and investment banks, and the "investment" sectors of banks that have become *universal*. It is less *finance for all* (the hazy "democratization of finance") than the forced financialization of all to benefit the "few." Yet it is above all the definitive financialization of industrial capital of which they are the system, and *world-system*. "Finance" governs the globalization of production and the new *transnational* division of labor (global production networks) which are subject to the erasing of borders between financial activities and productive activities while "finance" escapes any perspective of effective regulation.

The number of large or small financial crises that have occurred successively since the years 1974–1975 (marked by a first form of financial crash with banks at the epicenter) and the "1979 coup" (liberalization of public debt securities markets, increase in American interest rates and the dollar, anti-inflationist configuration of monetary policy) is frightening.[182] And for good reason: the phenomenon reveals the number numbering the total deterritorialization of capitalism as it is totalized in the system of the three "Ds" of financialization: "*deregulation* or monetary and financial liberalization, *departitioning* of national financial markets, and *deintermediation*, or the opening of lending operations previously reserved for banks to all types of institutional investors."[183] These three engines are at work behind the "exuberance" of financial markets and the *explicans* of "volatility" unleashed immediately after the Asian crisis in 1997 (didn't it have the merit of placing Korea under direct control of the American Treasury?). As a reminder: the Asian crisis followed the Mexican financial crisis (1994–1995) which was considered at the time to be the "first crisis of the twenty-first century,"[184] and that was only "contained" by improvising a "Powell financial doctrine"—under the name of the architect of the first Iraq War, which was associated with tens of billions poured into the banks of a country facing the Chiapas Rebellion ("the largest nonmilitary commitment since the Marshall Plan").[185]

That 3D Capital can regulate itself under these conditions is the pious wish of the liberals (or the most naïve of them), even though it can be found in Foucault. *Global insecurity* is the condition of the security governmentality of contemporary capitalism. The "norming" and normality of the state of emergency feed fear and insecurity instead of protecting the people from them (according to its stated motive), and their source is not found in some legal-political dimension but in Capital and its military-financial war machine operating through *structural adjustments*. This term was coined by Robert McNamara in 1972. President of the World Bank from 1968 to 1981, he had been the Secretary of Defense from 1961 to 1968 under Presidents Kennedy and Johnson and during the Vietnam War.

Analyzing the "tendency of the rate of profit to drop" as presented in Book III of *Capital*, Deleuze observes that the moment of passing from the depreciation of capital (crisis) to the formation of a new capital creates the conditions for a "possible" emergence of revolutionary forces.[186] Given the nature of the movements of financial capital and the accompanying accelerationism imprinted by it, the emergence of subjects in political rupture must always be considered possible (even if there is no "current" alternative) in the form of a possibility that is *always present* in reality. Contributing to "systemic instability," the multiplication of these *probable enemies* reinforces the necessary aspect of developing a military-security system of social control at the domestic and international level. As instability becomes permanent with the saturation of the system, the "militarization of the government" responds to the fundamental task of predicting, anticipating, and preventing, in other words to *break down in advance* the countless possibilities of rupture that are always virtual-real, since they are inscribed within the dynamic of absolute domination of financial capital and its war logic that tends to make the enemy (to use Clausewitz again here) "incapable of further resistance." An *infinite* process…

The order of financial capital is a *postcritical* dis-order that is highly unstable and perfectly insatiable, a state "far from equilibrium," in constant change, perpetual evolution, and always seeking to re-produce new possibilities of value creation by displacing every limit it encounters. Contemporary financial Capital flees equilibrium like the plague, since balance is equal to zero profits from the point of view of maximizing "shareholder value," which has no concern for world development indicators (the record of neoliberalism in this matter is disastrous).

State and war, which represent respectively the strategic component and element of the war machine of Capital, have had to adapt to this evolution.

Despite being pursued since the First World War, the restructuring of the separation of powers that gave exorbitant power to the executive and the administration is still insufficient to control such a *fundamental* instability. Control of executive power has to be directly in the hands of Capital and its financial institutions that exercise their "power to act" at the level of the world-economy which states will be made to serve (by financing budget deficits and "securitization" of public debt on the one hand, and the independence of central banks[187] on the other). In the context of the nation-state, the state and its executive are led to declare a set of measures that seem to be in full contradiction with the aberrant movements of capital: "financial stability" laws and strictly "balanced accounts" that some in Europe wanted to put in constitutions. In reality, there is no contradiction since stability and balance only concern the budgets and spending of a portion of the population thus placed under tighter "surveillance" on the national and international level. It is the principle of the rules of "conditionality" adopted and codified by the International Monetary Fund starting in 1979. This same IMF can also, when needed, be held as solely responsible for budget austerity measures, even if they are negotiated with *friendly* governments, which potentially know how to benefit from the opportunity to tighten the program. As a result, the IMF also has *enemies*. In each case, Dominique Strauss-Kahn was right when he summed up the point of view of the institution he led in a brief phrase: "Crisis is an opportunity."

Without waiting to be supported by a "dual"[188] platform encouraged by the financial restructuring of its industry in the 1990s, or to become officially "preventative" (in 2001) to be able to respond on all fronts, both internal and external, war has also adapted to the new conditions of accumulation by combining them with its spatial or temporal development "without limits" (Reagan's second Cold War as a continuation of Nixon's Kitchen Debate). According to the neoliberal model of *internal security of capitalism* identified with the reaffirmation of all forms of its class power, its first function is domestic: it consists of intervening among the population and on division by declaring *in fact* civil war for the control of salaries and social spending. It is the political-military principle of the "conservative revolution": to be able to get off on a "Keynesianism" of *war profiteers* (from "star wars"), the structural imbalances of capital have to be "balanced" by acting on salaries, revenues, employment, and "job seekers," the systems of social protection for part of the population (a sub-section of which relies on welfare for its most basic survival). In other words, *a counter-Keynesianism of war.*

The financialization of the end of the nineteenth and beginning of the twentieth centuries led to the two total wars, with the 1929 crisis in between, and to the European civil wars. A century later, contemporary financialization is hastening us into the polarization of the civil wars of "ultimodernity" (to borrow from Jacques Bidet). Starting with the "crisis" of 2008 (we will describe it in more detail later), we are entering the era of the subjectivation of civil wars and its circulation by successive lateral pushes across the planet.

These wars that we have analyzed starting with primitive accumulation as the economic, political, and subjective condition of Capital are the strategic axes on which the constitution of contemporary war machines is decided.

There are several possible scenarios involving the unfolding and the result of these wars. History has raced ahead since 2008 (total crisis)-2011 (Arab Spring) but, as we know all too well, not always in the right direction: the relationships of force are too imbalanced in favor of the war machine of Capital and the new fascisms that reinforce and feed on one another. Our only certainty: the connections and breaks will be decided on the terrain of civil wars and their total immanentization. We can only affirm some "trends" of which the main characteristic is less to be dis-proven by what "happens" than to connect in an a priori improbable way.

The "Greek scenario," where the direction of the war remains in the hands of the financial machine, is the "capitalist" hypothesis. Governing/governed "relations of power" and "strategic relations" coexist to the benefit of those who govern: all apparatuses (*dispositifs*) of governmentality function as weapons aimed at controlling the people and reproducing the power of lenders. This is what happened and is happening—with less cynicism, violence, and deadly determination than in Greece, while infant mortality and general mortality have doubled since 2010—in every European country. The war machine of Capital doggedly pursues its intention of making the people pay from its "financial innovations" by declaring an economic and political "state of emergency."

The formidable novelty of the sequence opened by the "cri-sis" of 2008 is exemplified not only by the intensification of the governmentality of wars amongst the population ("austerity poli-cies") but also in the relationships that the war machine of Capital will be led to maintain with the expansion of post-fascist war machines. New fascisms are deeply implicated in this political sequence since they subordinate the governing/governed rela-tionships of power to the perspective of "war" (friend/enemy). The scenario of the new fascisms is explicitly established in the area of civil wars. It clearly designates the foreigner, immigrant, refugee, Muslim as an internal and external enemy, at the same time as it reaffirms the "naturalness" of heterosexuality, which has been seriously shaken as an apparatus (*dispositif*) of power since the 1960s. "Race" is not limited to defining the enemy but, with patriarchy and heterosexuality, represents the terrain of fascist and identitarian subjectivation (in France, the Front national and the "Manif pour tous" against "gay marriage" are its dual political expression).

"Race" and patriarchal "heterosexuality" represent a different perspective on globalization than the one found in financialization, but they are just as formidably powerful. Race and gender wars are two key apparatuses (*dispositifs*) of "biopolitical" control of the population that constitutes the international division of labor and sexual division. Before decolonization, race wars established divisions between people of the North and South of the world. They now run through "developed" countries by discriminating the populations of "internal colonies," like the migrants and refugees whose movements have become, with land and raw material predation, "structural." What the war machine of Capital, and along with it the new fascisms, is *reacting to* is the turn taken by the collapse of the distinction between "interior" and "exterior" that is largely its own doing. Internal wars of the "civilized" against the "non-civilized" can no longer be unleashed without an immediate response. All the predation, wars, expropriations, massacres, and swindling inflicted on the "exterior" or through "externalization" are turning back on the West with a speed that seems to equal the acceleration of history. If, with September 11, the "war on terror" took time to come home to those that declared it, the "refugee crisis" is this now instantaneous return. Caught in a barely-disguised panic, power constantly raises walls of all types, and the most formidable walls are not always the ones it builds or wants to build on its borders! And haven't these borders, with the institutional practices associated with them in terms of differential exclusion/inclusion long been displaced to occupy *everywhere* the "center of the political community"?[189]

Wars on women have the same strategic scope as race wars. The most reactionary leaders expose the order of reasons that govern the eternal return of "biopolitics" in its *history channel* version. The Turkish "sultan" Erdogan states them bluntly: making contraception illegal to retake *control of women's bodies* to produce more men for the state and its army. Sexism has a precise class connotation: fighting the "refusal to do the work of procreation" by retaking control of the production and reproduction of the population, in other words of the strategic "merchandise," the labor force. Not just in Turkey but throughout North Africa, control over women's bodies has escaped authorities as fertility has dropped to the European level.[190] The hatred shown by Islamists towards women has no other real cause than this: patriarchal power is threatened with collapse. It is perfectly in tune with the lessons of freedom and emancipation granted by the secular and natalist Republic to Muslim women in the name of the "modernity of progress" that instrumentalizes feminism by placing it at the service of a neocolonial civilizing mission that has kept all its symbolic *markers* (*re-pères*).[191] Brought back by French socialists, "unveiling" harkens back to the worst hours of the Algerian War and the "colonial feminism" embodied by associations of "female solidarity" created by the spouses of putsch generals Salan and Massu: among their initiatives was the organization of a public removal of veils from women in Algiers in May 1958.[192]

By making them reappear as terrain of subjectivation, the post-fascist project refers to the secular modes of exercising power over the population. In this sense, it is essentially reactionary but it is a reaction that takes hold of contemporary political confrontation at its most untimely point. In post- or neo-fascist projects, the economy and governing/governed relationships no longer assign us a place in production, a nationality, an identity, a gender, it is the logic of wars of race and sex ("national preference," "anti-gender" crusade). The "economy" is subordinate to the logic of civil wars as soon as it is impossible for liberal territorialization (of "enrich yourself," of the self-entrepreneur, of human capital, etc.) to realize what it promised in the 1980s-1990s. Fundamentally protectionist, the neo-fascist project encounters and feeds the resentment, frustration, and fears of White workers to reestablish, through maintaining sexual hierarchies and guaranteeing identities, the nationalization of work and wages, power over non-salaried workers, and control of the unemployed.

The new fascisms play on a dimension of the world-economy, colonialism, which far from disappearing, has "colonized" the colonizers. Recently taken up again by researchers working on "internal colonization" on both sides of the Atlantic, the concept of endocolonization, which Paul Virilio used to define the change in the army and war after 1945 into *war amongst and against the population*,[193] can be useful in several ways. It immediately configures governmentality as a set of civil war apparatuses (*dispositifs*). It politically identifies the concept of "biopolitics" to the extent that colonization, which holds together, since primitive accumulation, race war and the war on women for control of bodies, is now applied directly to class conflicts. Greece was very naturally spoken of as a "colonized" country, a population placed under a colonial "mandate" to the extent that all the apparatuses (*dispositifs*) of the war machine of Capital are mobilized to organize an endocolonization of all social relations. And finally, the concept presents in a new light the reality of contemporary civil wars: 1/ because endocolonization establishes an immediate continuity between the Norths and

Souths of the world-economy and reveals the way the Souths are lodged in the Norths; 2/ because all the wars of which we have described the nature and development since primitive accumulation converge on the endocolonized; 3/ because the techniques of colonial wars, first applied to the populations of the "colonies of the interior," are then generalized to the entire population, and notably to protest movements (during the protests against the "labor law" in France, the techniques of controlling the protests and the use of police violence in all evidence crossed a threshold in relation to the security state).

Relating the true nature of the conflicts underway to the "division between rich and poor," Alain Joxe defines war as "fractal," in the sense of a "'suburban war' at every scale."[194] Which again refers to the "endo-colonial segregation" characterized by a set of "forms of warlike violence: tested in the colonies [...], reformulated to be applied to the control of the colonized in the homeland, [they] influence the transformation of the management of the popular classes in general."[195]

All the wars of which we have described the nature and development converge first in the endocolonization of originally colonial populations who suffer what French Prime Minister Manuel Valls called, in a rare moment of lucidity, "a geographical, social, ethnic apartheid." The wars of race, sex, and class pass through and mark these populations by inflicting social violence combined with an extreme "molecular violence" (Achille Mbembe) by bringing the colonial relationship into the conditions of the most contemporary capitalism. This interconnexion of wars is mobilized to control them and repress them by acting as a powerful means of division inside them, before being spread to other dominated social layers to be turned against them. "Endo-colonial segregation is not structured only by race and class [...]

it is carried by an ideological system based on the reproduction of a patriarchal power where the authority and force of the state take precedent as 'father' and 'master' [...]. The manner in which police segregation discriminates between men and women, Whites and non-Whites, produces a space of structured conflict by and for the reproduction of sexist separations and virile oppressions inside communities *damned* by race and class."[196]

The endocolonized are thus at the heart of the *war of subjectivity*, which is the real *milieu* of war amongst the population. It involves in fact the population as a whole that it divides through recourse to the machinations of "race" and the "freedom" of women. The major operations of identity and neo-fascist subjectivations take place at the expense of the endocolonized population (Muslims, foreigners, migrants, refugees, women wearing the veil). Once the danger of communism had disappeared, and the antisemitism that had ravaged Europe before and after the two world wars was swept under the carpet, the enemies, starting in the 1970s, were slowly but surely identified as immigrants, then terrorism (the "Years of Lead"), with a final convergence on Islam (as an abbreviation for Islamist terrorism). The transformation of political stakes into religious conflicts and wars of civilization against the backdrop of the "racial question" was knowingly pursued by all the apparatuses (*dispositifs*) of power.

The threats pertaining to the "crisis of politics" fed by Capital's politics of total war (financialization "without limits") leave no other strategy than the intensification of the "structural adjustment" policies implemented by the IMF since the 1980s. Once again, it is not the dynamics of biopower that determines "racism" (the "struggle of the races") but the need to produce and reproduce class division in a "population" that is not in itself a "subject" (the "subject-population," as Foucault says) without being "split," in other words *biopolitically differentiated* in and through the strategies of capital of which "the [class] domination is always-already racializing."[197] To the fundamental instability coextensive with financialization (*the age of turbulence*)[198] which had already, at the end of the 1990s, moved the system from "failure prevention" to "failure containment," another whole level of destabilization was added with the not situational but structural failure of the new strategy of *containment* in the face of the "derivative products" of the *debt economy*: they crystallized in fact and over many years the innovative capacity of the world of finance (speculative hyperrealism?) creating for itself a made to (excess) measure shadow banking system (in which, if we need reminding, European banks actively participated). To avoid the collapse of the system carried, from the United States (equipped with "special investment vehicles" (SIV)) through "securitization" of the *democratization of finance*[199] and to manage the long-term effect of the "worst financial crisis in Global History" (the global crisis of 2008) by making people accept the management of the financial breakdown by transferring the debts of capital to the taxpayers, the transnational war machine of Capital could only precipitate a new wave of *internal* and *external colonization*. Racist policies (institutional racism) were part of it and represented the subjective aspect of the strategies to "exit the crisis," particularly in the Eurozone. The global point of political annihilation was reached with the transatlantic combination of class struggle and race war in the dominant subjectivation of the "global civil war."

The circle is complete, in a way, if we remember that the African-American "question" was the "Achilles heel of working-class integration into the American Dream."[200] It is still the case and has even become more pressing (close to 500 Black Americans killed by the most militarized police in the world in the first half of 2016 alone), but it took Dallas (and five police officers killed by a Black veteran of Afghanistan, or the worst "damage" to American police since September 11, 2001) for the media to print the words "race war" in their coverage (of the event). Only one journalist had the immediate reaction to note that the United States has *also* been in an "uninterrupted war" since 1990.[201] The relationship is nonetheless obvious with the risk of autonomization of a neo-fascist and neo-racist war machine that would send the entire neoliberal apparatus (*dispositif*) into the wall that its system of planetary domination built brick by brick. Thus the fear of the American establishment, which has already lost the war of subjectivity it started during the Bush years.

In Europe, the neoliberal counter-revolution was accompanied by a vast enterprise of mass subjectivation mobilizing the state, media, politicians, and experts of all sorts to stir up resentment, frustration, fear, and guilt before raising racism to the level of *state strategy* after the 2008 crisis. It took nothing less to produce the largest conversion of subjectivity in post-communist European societies. The Brexit episode is the most important signal so far. The first European country to adopt neoliberal policies conducted as class war voted for national preference ("Britain First") "to Take Back Control" and was propelled by voters into a *war to defend the White race*, drawing all the consequences of the Labor slogan in 2007 ("British jobs for British workers"). "National preference" cannot be part of the functioning of welfare as apparatus (*dispositif*) of control of the population on the interior without having the fear of refugees, immigrants, and Muslims mobilized and placed at the service of controlling the mobility of populations from the

South of the globe. The contradiction between the complete freedom of flows of capital and the restricted mobility of flows of people thus finds a necessary apparatus of "regulation" in the new fascisms. And these fascisms can escape control (a real *trumpery!*) since the war machine of Capital has to be *openly* situated on the field of civil wars. The Greek scenario was subjected to the ordoliberal White mythology of Wolfgang Schäuble, but here an entirely different WASP hypothesis appeared: transmitted by what Akwugo Emejulu has called "the hideous whiteness of Brexit,"[202] it reminds us that war of subjectivation is the very principle of these mass movements where the fascists have always been the strategic avant-garde.

Under these conditions, the strategic space-time where the problems of financial accumulation and its governmentality are combined can only be the continuum of bloody and bloodless civil wars that are spreading from Europe to the Far and Middle East, Turkey, and Afghanistan. Greece is the point of passage between these different types of wars and is the focus of a dual experiment: one of the *political* governmentality of civil wars fed by the "debt crisis" and one of the *humanitarian* government of refugees, a consequence of the predations of the Souths of the planet (including *all* of Africa). The "subject"—that must be taken as *political* since they are homogenous with the integrated global market and actors in struggles over the "proliferation of borders"—who are closest to expressing the truth of this continuum are the refugees and migrants who risk their lives traveling it. The *sea cemetery* of Mare Nostrum.

They land in Greece: "the cradle of democracy and of Europe." After the ordeal of austerity policies imposed by the European Union to "clean up" its public finance—which also led to a serious "ecological crisis" (with warnings from the

Directorate-General for the Environment of the European Union) making Greece a "textbook example of energy poverty"[203]—the "land of the Gods" combined an economic war, presenting the "material" and "subjective" ravaging of the population as a medicalized policy, with the migrant "crisis." This "crisis" was none other than the reversal or return of colonialist technology for the regulation of migratory movements into Europe by *over-flowing* the selective filtering of labor mobility.

The transversality of wars amongst the population spread to the other side of the Mediterranean in the former colonies and mandates. In the Middle East, fractal wars are a series of civil wars that overlap in a *blocked decolonization*. This aspect was highlighted again by the "Arab Springs," as their appearance immediately shut down the rumor that oil states were going to abandon the dollar as currency of exchange. To their great relief, the Islamist obsession of the political-media complex in the West obliterated the class, gender, race, and subjectivity nature of the struggles that had erupted in 2011, in particular in Egypt, where the mobilization of workers preceded and accompanied the protests in Tahir Square. The states in the North were constantly maneuvering to lead the Arab insurrections into "authoritarian" regimes hastily (re)established or rushed into "jihadism." The democratic experiments that did take place on the horizon of these civil wars[204] were violently repressed by both the regimes in place and their Western allies.

The "small wars" that have broken out in these ex-colonies with effects as catastrophic and destructive as a "big" war have the objective of leading the "objective" breaks produced by the most predatory globalization and the "subjective" breaks operated by the "Arab Springs" back to the war machine of states or to those of Islamic fundamentalism.

Fractal war amongst the population and the small wars that serve as its model and lines of flight bring the "creative destruction" of capitalism up-to-date by adjusting the power—and the power to act—of Capital's mode of destruction to the post-democratic times of the planet's major financiers. To the extent that the "economy" is the politics of Capital, it applies to the continuous war referring any possibility of economic "change" to the mutation of those "subject" to these wars into strategic subjects *of* these wars. The intensification of the permanent "crisis" that appeared in 2007–2008 will not see any remission since the war machine of Capital cannot bring down the power relations and strategic relations on which it is based and that have led, after forty years of unadulterated neoliberalism, to our *post-critical* situation.[205]

No "New Deal," no "social pact," no "new regulation" is to be expected *because* the relationship of force is too imbalanced in the long duration of global counter-revolution that is our only habitat. No glimmer of hope either from the monetary policies known as "quantitative easing" and their potential service to a "neo-Keynesianism" of demand supported by a strong state (*Aren't We All Socialists Now?*).[206] Strictly placed under American control (the Fed is confirmed as the world bank of last resort),[207] they were projected to "save the banks" and accompany, with the help of "conditionality," new programs of *flexitarian* "structural adjustment" combining the "open space" forms of control with the most disciplinary forms of labor exploitation and security management of society. This is the real meaning of "flexisecurity": while it is the sign of a "postmodernity," the Anglobalization of which it is a synonym exacerbates wars of class, race, sex, and subjectivity encompassed *since the nineteenth century and its return* in financial "crises."

The indefinitely expanded and increased reproduction of strategic and power relations contributes to the formation of what is called "bubbles" in the language of economists. Their main property is that sooner or later they burst. However, it is not only the new bond bubble that risks bursting (their number and value have grown vertiginously since 2010). More explosively, these same power and strategic relations supported by monetary policies rely ever more exclusively on the governance of wars amongst the population to ensure the survival of the "world-system" of capitalism.

Yet no historical necessity, no contradiction "in the final analysis" will guide—or resolve "on the edge of the abyss"—this process. Capitalism will not die a "natural" death because its "economy," unlike what Marxist orthodoxy states, is inseparable from war and the *new war economy* of which neoliberalism is the name and the necessary reality. The *unsustainability* of its process, the limits of which are always being moved, accentuates the scope of the global civil wars, from the micromanagement of "permanent molecular insecurity"[208] to their "fractal" echoing across the whole planet through the Mediterranean (where a "low-intensity war" is being waged against migrants[209] that is taking place in the heart of Paris as well).

There are no other forms of "sovereignty" behind contemporary capitalism than the categories through which we began this work: money and war, the codetermination of their power of destruction and deterritorialization always functions together. What changes and brings about changes in the form of new technologies of power is that money and war are codetermined and feed *directly* on the dynamic of unlimitedness that belongs to Capital.

The two forces of deterritorialization unleashed by neoliberalism do not pursue any political "goal" in Clausewitz's sense. They seem to be more attached to perpetuating a global "chaos" while attempting to control its forces so that it can always reproduce the limitlessness of financial exploitation for which the continued intensification (Capitalizing on Chaos) applies to the extension of the domain of fractal war amongst the population. Without any other mediation than ones that lead to defeating the adversary. *Graecia docet*. And *docet omnia* (duly corrected here as *she* "teaches everything") according to the proud motto inscribed on the frontispiece of the Collège de France where Foucault once taught politics as continued war.

Or more precisely, to use the philosopher's own terms, it is a question of *war as analyzer of the relations of power and of the operators of domination*. Because it is through this means that civil wars are imposed as the strategic terrain for building revolutionary war machines, even though these are the weakest and most embryonic political projects today. Anti-capitalist movements are still incapable of waging "class war without the working class." Since the political defeat of the working class in the longest duration of the Cold War, no collective "theoretical practice" has been elaborated or tested at the scale of the civil wars launched by Capital.

The labor movement formed by reducing the colonial division and the sexual division of labor to "secondary contradictions." This operation of subordinating "minorities" is no longer tenable given that throughout the twentieth century, the colonized and women asserted themselves as subjects and political perceptions carrying social perspectives, economic demands, and modes of subjectivation that did not coincide with those of the "working class" and the unifying process of "awareness." '68 marked at the same time the defeat of the communism of the nineteenth century and the Leninist revolution, the failure of its institutional translation into the parties and unions of the "working class," and the crystallization of an irreversible change in the relationship of forces within a multiple global proletariat that was unable to create a war machine capable of expressing all its powers. Nevertheless, the struggles for decolonization and feminist movements greatly undermined the power of salaried workers over "minorities."

The same problem is the object of experiments in contemporary movements. Not a new, generic democracy but the invention of anti-capitalist, democratic war machines capable of taking as their strategic tasks civil wars and the struggle on the front of subjectivation.

The fight against the "labor law" and the occupation of the Place de la République in France by *Nuit debout* sum up the difficulties of gathering the conditions of reality for this process and organizing these machines. It is not a lack of *techne* or difficulty in projecting *in abstracto* an effective strategy against the power of financial capitalism that is preventing the effective practice of a force capable, if not of breaking the long series of victories of Capital, at least to fight it by including war when posing the problem. As for the new technologies, far from announcing the autonomous subject of a *Commonfare*, they are not foreign to the mode of functioning of financial capital and act inside a social division of labor that they contribute to reproducing according to the functionality of "capitalism 24/7"[210] that can always, up to a certain point, turn towards a cooperative use of knowledge. In two days with *Nuit Debout*, a "Debout" radio and television were developed using social networks and their "algorithms." But after two months of struggle against the "labor law," the French spring movements had trouble overcoming class divisions between full-time and temporary workers, between employees and the unemployed. The long temporality of the sexual divisions of the world and the colonial gap were also reproduced by separating the non-Whites of working-class suburbs from the young urban Whites of hip neighborhoods.

The very real "convergences" that are produced and tested at the base between salaried workers, temporary workers, students, and new subjectivities are contextual, not strategic. They do not define a new politics allied with new forms of organization *and disorganization*. The positioning of a union like the CGT is emblematic of the impasses and limits of these convergences. At its last congress, the CGT rediscovered its "class" nature but its "radicalization" still remains buttressed to full-time salaries, the national framework of its action, and the respect of forms of legitimacy of governmentality. During this time, the financial machine works transversally to the apparatuses (*dispositifs*) of power (salary, precarity, welfare, consumption, communication, etc.) to intervene in all wars of class, race, and sex that it passes inside individuals as much as in the socius by constantly articulating the national context (that it absorbed) to the world level (which is its own: that of the "world market" Marx included in the *concept* of capital).

However, while active alterglobalization movements are still looking for the methods of organization and use of "force" capable of threatening the power of Capital,[211] they have indisputably produced a conversion of subjectivity and opened a new space-time of political experimentation symbolized by the "occupation of places." What kind of experimentation is it? Evidence shows that the democratic speech of some and the institutional outlets of others are only a small part of what these struggles express.

What was tested in Greece, Spain, France, in the countries of the Near and Middle East, in the USA and elsewhere is a *very first attempt* to break with the governmentality of wars amongst the population that assign us a place and a productive function, define our gender, identity, nationality, and a national history that is quickly revealed to be postcolonial. The equivocal multiplicity of desires that has been asserted in these protests seeking a new path between *molecular revolution and class struggle* (to use the very first question by Félix Guattari) was motivated above all by the univocal refusal to be governed, by the will/need to be liberated from the power relation governing/governed, from its apparatuses (*dispositifs*) (salary, consumption, welfare, heterosexuality, etc.), and its axioms (competitiveness, parliamentary democracy, participation, etc.). Everything happening as if there was no longer any other object/subject of collective experimentation than the refusal of submitting to governmentality *as such*. But this governmentality has never been "social division of labor" (Marx) or "distribution of the sensible" (Rancière) without also, and more fundamentally again today, being the organization of wars of class, sex, race, and subjectivity.

If struggles can only be engaged in from the condition of the governed, they must imperatively free themselves from the axioms of governmentality to reach their own strategic terrain of affirmation. Which not only implies designating an enemy that will always be both local and global but also to risk a form of rupture involving a subjective conversation, a process of critical and clinical breaking with our condition as salaried workers, consumers, and users—in short, as "normopaths"—since, with these subjections where the "off-the-subject" is forbidden, we are all, in one way or another, "pieces" of the megamachine of Capital. These wars that we call fractal, waged amongst the people, are characterized by an asymmetry that is not questioned as long as war is not problematized.

The war machine of Capital has constructed and used a continuum between bloody war and bloodless war where the field of action is the population. It organizes and carries out global civil wars and it must imperatively deny that they exist. The continuum is this way only so that Capital and the block of social and political forces that attach to its power and that pass, depending on the terrain, from the use of military weapons (with which the police are increasingly armed) to the use of non-military weapons to fight an *enemy* whose hotbed of development is known (the population), but not its identity (it remains undetectable, probable, and rightly unknowable) even though its place of birth is overdetermined by a global postcolonial logic.

For the exploited and the dominated, this continuum only exists if it is *pro-duced*—and *actively* constructed. Nothing is less *given* than this subjective continuum of collective rupture that has to invent itself in an autonomous temporality to oppose the continuity between the bloody wars and bloodless wars of Capital. If there is a political asymmetry, it is verified and announced here in the most brutal terms: since the 1970s, Capital has had a strategy and a war machine; proletarians and their affiliates have had no strategies or war machines. For almost *more than fifty years*, they have suffered, powerless, the initiative of financial Capital, which has not buried the war hatchet but any political perspective that could contribute to reforming capital in the short, medium, or long term.

Let's start from the most advanced point of '68 thought on war to expand this asymmetry, which is by no means an "asymmetrical war." To do so, we will return one last time to the distinction Foucault established between *power* (relations between governing and governed) and *war* (relations between adversaries) with their "indefinite succession and perpetual reversal" that, for us, relates directly to the instability of the *aberrant movements* of Capital. We will also use Deleuze and Guattari's concept of the "war machine." As distinct from war and the state, and in relation to social war, it allows us to posit that *power and war* (in other words the relations between governing and governed and the relations between adversaries) represent the *double articulation* of the war machine of Capital.

Going back to Greece where a financial war took place that is, as our two Chinese officers said about the Asian "crisis," a "real war" characterized by the asymmetry with which we are trying to come to grips. And let us transpose the major indication of our analysis there: while the institutions of financial capital have a strategy (debt), a clear definition of the adversary (part of the population), and non-military weapons of mass destruction (austerity policies) to achieve it, those who are subject to the initiative and offensive of the economy of debt fight *in the position of the "governed" without strategy or war machine*. Everything is visible, nothing is hidden in the strategy of Capital. In Greece, in July 2015, a passage manifestly occurred towards a *politics of governmentality of civil wars*. Greek movements, which were terribly isolated, were unable to follow the enemy onto this new field of confrontation. The refusal of governmentality can only consist in the refusal of the "freedoms" implied by the governing/governed relationship. This process is particularly difficult, since the labor, communist, or revolutionary movement has not been able to produce a concept of freedom to oppose liberal "freedom."

For the war machine of capital, debt is both a relatively stable *relationship of power* where governing and governed are opposed and a *terrain of strategic confrontation* where adversaries are opposed. Through debt, the governing lead the behavior of the governed in a relatively predictable way. Relatively, since the governed, using their "freedom," resist, oppose, and divert the economic constraints, push the war machine of capital to extend the apparatuses (*dispositifs*) of financialization and intensify austerity policies to overcome this resistance, opposition, and diversion.

Foucault asserts that the governing/governed relationship is neither legal nor warlike, since it represents an "action on possible actions" performed by "free subjects." Yet the possibilities, freedom, action, and the behaviors supposed by the *relationship of power* are still defined in the context of governmentality. The freedom of the governed is the *liberal freedom* of human capital or the self-entrepreneur or the consumer, in other words the "fabricated" freedom solicited and incited by the apparatuses (*dispositifs*) of power to respond to the new demands of accumulation of Capital. They can fight "within and against" but (within and against Foucault?) always caught in the social division of labor and in its subjective assignments.

Something else altogether is the freedom that creates its own possibilities, that structures its field of action and subjectivizes itself in this creation by becoming *autonomous* and *independent* of the "governing," in other words *undecidable* in relation to the level of governmentality. The governed are only "free" if they are able to cross the threshold that separates them from strategic confrontation *by investing* with their own war machine the wars amongst the population that Capital wages endlessly. As we have seen, Foucault did not explain how the passage from *governed* to *adversary* works. He did not thematize the break as condition for the subjectivation needed to exit this "minority state" (Kant) with which he was obsessed in the last years of his life *because he did not problematize the construction of the war machine*. This, however, is the necessary condition of a process of collective subjectivation operating by transversal connections, in rupture with the semiology of capital and all of the apparatuses (*dispositifs*) of governance of divisions.

Since 2011, anti-capitalist movements have multiplied the modalities of subjective rupture. But they have quickly found themselves faced with an unavoidable alternative. Either "disappear" and dissolve as organized forces or establish themselves in new forms of representation by resuscitating the modalities of modern political action that are in the process of dying off. Extraction from the relation of governmentality requires using both sides of the relation. Not only to exit the state of subordination (of the "governed") but also to refuse to become the new "governing," new pretenders to a better *representation* of the "interests" of the dominated than the one performed by the "elites." The "new parties" born of these movements plaster over parliamentary representation by reproducing the illusion that this "politics" can change something, when "another politics" within governmentality is impossible. The recent electoral misadventure of Podemos in Spain is further example (it failed at the threshold of "power"). Less than a year after the fiasco of Syriza (which, in principle, still holds this same "power").

In this book, we have continued to *practice* the Foucault of the first half of the 1970s, in no small part because the current situation encourages us to look "beneath the problem of the production of wealth so as to demonstrate that it was ruination, debt, and abusive accumulations that created a certain state of wealth."[212] What we need is less a new economic theory of value and an alternative approach to governmentality than to ask the political question par excellence in the age of the global civil war of the "Capitalocene."

The struggle that took place in Greece put in the presence of a "population" that did not have ambiguities attached to its concept, both in political economy and in the concept of biopolitics (it is suspected that one may have influenced the other). The population, like any social reality in capitalism, is divided, and divided according to the logic of hostility. War is conducted by one part of the population against another. The results of the referendum of July 2015, 60% and 40%, give a closer idea of the reality of the division that divides society than the slogan of the 1% opposed to the 99% in the Occupy Wall Street movement. These numbers may be "true" at the level of the distribution of revenues and assets (which could be the limit at which economic power becomes financial power), but it does not account for the blocks of force that are formed as lines of subjectivation from "economic" divisions differentiated and arranged differently by the line of financial fracture. It also contributed to keeping the Occupy movement of 2011–2012 in a counterculture of "social networks," which put it in an awkward position in relation to the call for a general strike in May 2012, a general strike that was itself poorly compatible with some of the proposals inherited from the 1980s (Tobin tax, campaign finance reform, etc.). It is hard to say that Philip Marowski was completely wrong with his vitriolic statement: "Know your Enemy before you start day-dreaming of a better world." And he concluded: "In this one particular respect, Carl Schmitt was right."[213]

In the United States, like in Greece and Spain, the forces in opposition to the debt economy have not yet been able to produce the move from the subjected figure of the "governed" to the strategically independent figure of the *autonomous enemy* taking its autonomy in relation to all forms of governmental constraint to take political form in a process of subjectivation of civil war that imposed on it and to which it exposes the adversary, in the modification it has imposed on it.

In making this move and operating this break, the struggles that have multiplied since 2011 have met with major difficulties. First, Capital in its financial form presents itself as a set of anonymous and impersonal apparatuses (*dispositifs*) that are difficult to pin down in the figure of the adversary: the form of exploitation and domination and the subjects of command are more abstract and *immanent* than the industrial "executives" and the nation-state. Next, the fractal war that is being produced indefinitely on every level of reality (its multiscalar reality) does not have the form of inter-state war or the form of civil war that the nineteenth and twentieth centuries handed down to us. It is hard to fight in a situation that escapes the alternative between war time and peace time, and where the social pacification targeted by the strategy of financial capital first passes through the security control of the population delegated to the "soft power" of the markets. The third obstacle is represented by the wars of class, gender, and race that produce deep divisions within the proletariat. The passage from power relations to strategic relation, the capability for resistance and attack, the accumulation and exercise of force, and processes of subjectivation have as their condition the neutralization of these divisions and the construction of revolutionary connections between "minorities" which are only minorities in the most philosophical sense (the "formula for multiplicities" of Deleuze and Guattari). Finally, thinking in terms of the war machine means confronting what we see as the essential limit of '68 thought: its inability to think of war in all its components as total form of value creation of capital relegating its reformist "moments" to strategic parentheses in the grand capitalist utopia of the free market.

The counter-history we have engaged in had no other function than to recover the reality of the wars inflicted on us and denied to us: not the ideal *war* of the philosophers but the *wars* being waged "inside the mechanisms of power" that constitute "the secret motor of institutions." This war of wars, if we were to continue where Foucault stopped, or deconstruct the subject speaking in this discourse, *it is not enough to rediscover it as a principle of explanation; it must be reactivated, removed from the larval and blind forms where it is pursued without our awareness and lead it into the decisive battles for which we must prepare ourselves if we want to avoid constant defeat.*

NOTES

Introduction: To Our Enemies

1. We are using "war against women," "war of the sexes," and "gender war" interchangeably. Without entering into the debates that overlap feminism, the concepts of "woman," "sex," and "gender" (like that of "race") do not refer to any essentialism but to the political construction of heterosexuality and the patriarchy as social norms of procreation, sexuality, and reproduction of the population, of which the nuclear family is the foundation. It is a continuous war waged against women to submit them to these processes of subjection, domination, and exploitation.

1. State, War Machine, Money

1. Michel Foucault, "Nietzsche, Genealogy, History," *The Foucault Reader*, edited by Paul Rabinow (New York: Pantheon Books, 1984), p. 90.

2. Aristophanes, *The Wasps* (https://ebooks.adelaide.edu.au/a/aristophanes/wasps/)

3. In one of his courses on Foucault (January 28, 1986), Deleuze analyzes the importance of the buckler with a double internal handle (*antilabe*) that "welds" a soldier to another in a basic military unit where technique is internal to the social and mental. Deleuze refers to the pioneering text by Marcel Détienne, "La phalange: problèmes et controverses," in Jean-Pierre Vernant, *Problèmes de la guerre en Grèce antique* (Paris: Mouton-École Pratique des Hautes Études, 1968). This collection of studies was also particularly important for Foucault's thinking.

4. Michel Foucault, *Lectures on the Will to Know: Lectures at the Collège de France (1970–1971)* (New York: Palgrave Macmillan, 2013), p. 124 (lecture of February 17, 1971).

5. *Ibid.*, p. 123–130.

6. *Ibid.*, p. 139 (lecture of February 24, 1971).

7. Édouard Will, *Korinthiaka: recherches sur l'histoire et la civilisation de Corinthe des origines aux guerres médiques* (Paris: Éditions de Boccard, 1955), p. 470 et seq.

8. Given the lack of silver mines in Corinth, Will surmises that the first stock of metal consisted of smelting the valuables of dispossessed aristocratic families.

9. Michel Foucault, *Lectures on the Will to Know*, p. 138 (lecture of February 2, 1971).

10. *Ibid.*, p. 140–141.

11. *Ibid.*, p. 157–158 (lecture of March 3, 1971).

12. *Ibid.*, p. 158–160.

13. According to Plutarch's explanation: Solon "made the mina to consist of a hundred drachmas, which before had contained only seventy-three, so that by paying the same amount of money, but money of lesser value, those who had debts to discharge were greatly benefited, and those who accepted such payments were no losers." (Plutarch, *Solon*, 15, 2–4).

14. Michel Foucault, *Lectures on the Will to Know*, p. 161.

15. Which Foucault gathers under the heading of the "economic aspects" of Solon's reform.

16. Pierre Vidal-Naquet, "La tradition de l'hoplite athénien," in *Problèmes de la guerre en Grèce ancienne*, p. 173.

17. Michel Foucault, *Lectures on the Will to Know*, p. 145. Note that Aristotle was against the common view that "by conventional agreement, the currency has become a sort of interchangeable substitute for need, and for this reason it has the name currency, but it is not natural but by current custom" (Aristotle, *Nichomachean Ethics*, 1133a 27).

18. Gilles Deleuze and Félix Guattari, *Anti-Oedipus*, p. 154.

19. *Ibid.*, p. 197. The same remark is made in *A Thousand Plateaus* (Minneapolis: University of Minnesota Press, 1987), p. 443: "It was a great moment in capitalism when the capitalists realized that taxation could be productive, that it could be particularly favorable to profits and even to rents."

20. Gilles Deleuze and Félix Guattari, *A Thousand Plateaus*, p. 443.

2. Primitive Accumulation Continued

1. Karl Marx, *Capital*, (New York: Vintage Books, 1977), Book 1, Section VIII, Chap. 31, p. 919 And he continues: "And with the rise of national debt-making, lack of faith in the national debt takes the place of the sin against the Holy Ghost, for which there is no forgiveness."

2. With reference to *original sin*, according to the famous phrase: "This primitive accumulation plays approximately the same role in political economy as original sin does in theology" (*Capital*, p. 873).

3. Think here of the act decreed in 1547 in the name of Edward VI: each man who remains three days without work is considered to commit a flagrant act of vagrancy. Judges "shall immediately cause the said loiterer to be marked with a hot iron in the breast, the mark of *V*. And adjudge the said person living so idly to such presenter [in other words, to the accuser], to be his slave, to have and to hold said slave to him, his executors, or assigns for the space of two years, then next following." Escape is punished with corporal punishment, with a new mark, an *S*, and condemnation to perpetual slavery. Recidivists who attempt to run away again are punished with death. See Borislaw Geremeck (ed.), *Truands et misérables dans l'Europe moderne (1350–1600)* (Paris: Gallimard/Julliard, 1980), p. 98–99.

4. See the terrifying catalog of the effects of Spanish colonization drawn up in 1542 by Las Casas in his *Brevísima relación de la destrucción de las Indias*.

5. Karl Marx, *Capital*, p. 915.

6. Karl Marx, Letter to Annenkov, December 28, 1846, in *Marx Engels Complete Works* Vol. 38 (New York: International Publishers, 1975), p. 95.

7. Reproducing almost exactly the text of the Spanish *Orders* concerning "the Indies," Tzvetan Todorov writes: "it is not conquests that are to be banished, but the word *conquest*; 'pacification' is nothing but another word to designate the same thing" (*The Conquest of America: The Question of the Other* (New York: Harper & Row, 1984), p. 174).

8. See Carlo M. Cipolla, *Guns and Sails in the Early Phase of European Expansion, 1400–1700* (London: Collins, 1965).

9. James Morris Blaut, *The Colonizer's Model of the World: Geographical Diffusionism and Eurocentric History* (New York: Guilford, 1993), p. 51.

10. All quotes are from Chapter 31 of Volume I of *Capital* p. 920. As Maurice Dobb put it: "It is the *expropriation* of others that is the essence of the process of accumulation and not merely the acquisition of particular categories of wealth by capitalists" in Maurice Dobb and Paul M. Sweezy, *Du féodalisme au capitalisme: problèmes de la transition*, tome 1 (Paris: Maspero, 1977), p. 91.

11. Silvia Federici, *Caliban and the Witch* (Brooklyn, NY: Autonomedia, 2004). A first version of this work was published twenty years earlier in Italy with Leopoldina Fortunati: *Il Grande Calibano. Storia del corpo sociale ribelle nella prima fase del capitale* (Milano: Franco Angeli, 1984).

12. *Ibid.*, p. 14.

13. Michelet notes that "witches alone attended her, and became, especially for women, the chief and only physician" (*La Sorcière: The Witch of the Middle Ages* (London: Simpkin Marshall and Co., 1863), p. 121).

14. "If it is true that male workers became only formally free under the new wage-labor regime, the group of workers who, in the transition to capitalism, most approached the condition of slaves was working-class women." The separation between production and reproduction therefore makes possible "the specifically capitalist use of the wage [...] as means for the accumulation of unpaid labor" (Silvia Federici, *Caliban and the Witch*, p. 98, 75).

15. On this last point, other than Silvia Federici, see Maria Mies, *Patriarchy and Accumulation on a World Scale* (London: Zed Books, 1986), p. 78–81.

16. Michel Foucault, *Security, Territory, Population: Lectures at the Collège de France 1977–1978* (New York: Picador, 2009), p. 313.

17. One can think here of the chapter "Of Coaches" in Montaigne's *Essays* on the agony of the "infant world" that was America.

18. See Luciano Parinetto, *Streghe e Potere: Il Capitale e la Persecuzione dei Diversi* (Milano: Ronconi, 1998), p. 22: "If the *indios* were treated as witches *outside* the Old World, the witches of the Old World, for their part, were eliminated by using the techniques of extermination tested in the New World, such that all those who opposed the constituted power of the Old World ended up being treated like the *indios* of Europe." Jean Bodin, the "precursor" of political economy who also wrote a *Demonomia*, was a major exponent of this eminently *modern*, "unitary" idea.

19. Michel Foucault, *"Society Must Be Defended." Lectures at the Collège de France 1975–1976*, (New York: Picador, 1997), p. 103 (lecture of February 4, 1976), our emphasis.

20. Michel Foucault, *Security, Territory, Population*, p. 229 (lecture of March 8, 1978). See the entire beginning of this course which raises the issue of "insurrections of conduct" that can be seen up to the Russian Revolution.

21. *Ibid.*, p. 236.

22. Michel Foucault, *Madness and Civilization: A History of Insanity in the Age of Reason* (New York: Random House, 1965), p. 56.

23. Michel Foucault, *Security, Territory, Population*, p. 228: "this dimension of the revolt of conduct has also always been present in upheavals and revolutionary processes with completely different objectives and stakes."

24. Michel Foucault, *The Courage of Truth: Government of the Self and Others II; Lectures at the Collège de France 1983–1984* (New York: Picador, 2011).

25. Since witch trials were accompanied by confiscation of the goods of the "guilty parties," it did not take long in recognizing a furious alchemy that turned the blood of women into gold. Thus, there is a political economy of the witch hunt.

26. This was said of the Basques, "in every way unsuited to plowing, poor craftsmen, and little versed in handiwork, and [whose] women [are] unoccupied in their families, like those who have almost nothing to care for." See Pierre de Lancre, *Tableau de l'inconstance des mauvais anges et démons* (1612), ed. N. Jacques-Chaquin (Paris: Aubier, 1982), p. 72, 77.

27. Maria Mies, *Patriarchy and Capital Accumulation*, p. 110.

28. Ashis Nandy, *The Intimate Enemy: Loss and Recovery of Self Under Colonization* (Oxford: Oxford University Press, 1989), p. 55.

29. Carl Schmitt, *Nomos of the Earth*, p. 132.

30. Mathieu Renault, *L'Amérique de John Locke. L'expansion coloniale de la philosophie* (Paris: Éditions Amsterdam, 2014), 23–24.

31. John Locke, *The Fundamental Constitutions of Carolina*, Art. CX (in *The Works of John Locke*, vol. 9 (London: Rivington, 1824), p. 196). Locke added "absolute Power" in the first draft of the article.

32. See John Locke, *Of Government: Book 1*, § 1. "Slavery is so vile and miserable an estate of man, and so directly opposite to the generous temper and courage of our nation, that it is hardly to be conceived, that an *Englishman*, much less a gentleman, should plead for it."

33. John Locke, *Avertissement* to the *Traité du gouvernement civil*, ed. S. Goyard-Fabre (Paris: Garnier-Flammarion, 1992), p. 137. The expressions "eternal seditions" and "popular uprisings" are also found in this *Avertissement*.

34. John Locke, *Second Treatise of Government. An Essay Concerning the True Original Extent and End of Civil Government*, Chap. IV "Of Slavery," Sect. 23. Subsequent references will be given in the body of the text by indicating the chapter and section of the *Second Treatise*.

35. In *De Jure Belli ac Pacis*, Book II, Chap. 3–4.

36. John Locke, *Essays on the Law of Nature*, (Oxford: Oxford University Press, 1988), 141.

37. "the condition of human life, which requires labour and materials to work on, necessarily introduces private possessions."

38. To use the expression of Mark Neocleous in *War Power, Police Power* (Edinburgh: Edinburgh University Press, 2014), 60.

39. This is the meaning of the demonstration by C.B. Macpherson, *The Political Theory of Possessive Individualism: Hobbes to Locke* (Oxford: Clarendon Press, 1962), Chap. 4.

40. According to the explanation of Locke in his *Further Considerations Concerning Raising the Value of Money* quoted by Marx as an annex to his *Theories of Surplus Value* (Amherst, NY: Prometheus Books, 2000).

41. Matthieu Renault, *L'Amérique de John Locke*, p. 156.

42. These are Locke's recommendations in *On the Poor Law and Working Schools*, 1697—presented to the Privy Council's Board of Trade. See John Locke, *Political Essays*, ed. Mark Goldie (New York: Cambridge University Press, 1997), 182–198.

43. Ibid., p. 184.

44. See John Locke, *An Essay Concerning Human Understanding* (New York: Penguin Classics, 1998), Book IV, XX, 2.

45. See C. B. Macpherson, *The Political Theory of Possessive Individualism*, p. 224.

46. R.H. Tawney, *Religion and the Rise of Capitalism* (New York: Penguin, 1948), p. 267 (cited par C. B. MacPherson, *ibid.*).

47. William Petyt, *Britannia Languens* (1680), p. 238 (cited par C. B. MacPherson, *ibid.*).

48. See Matthieu Renault, *L'Amérique de John Locke*, p. 26.

49. John Locke, *An Essay Concerning Human Understanding*, Book II, II, 2.

50. See the long note by Pierre Coste in the French translation of John Locke, *Essai philosophique concernant l'entendement humain*, trad. Costes, ed. Naert (Paris: Vrin, 1989), p. xxx, and the analysis proposed by Etienne Balibar in *Identity And Difference: John Locke And The Invention Of Consciousness*, ed. Stella Sandford (New York: Verso, 2013).

51. See John Locke, *An Essay Concerning Human Understanding*, Book IV, III, 30, where the philosopher develops the "imperial" paradigm of navigation and the discovery of New Worlds as principle of the expansion of understanding.

52. *Ibid.*, Book II, XXVII, 9 and Book II, XXVII, 18.

53. See John Locke, *Some Thoughts Concerning Education* (1693) On the first, beyond the repression of desire ("a man may be able to *deny himself* his desires"), see the maniacal prescriptions in the first long chapter on "Health"; for the second, it is enough to quote this concluding sentence: "nothing is likelier to keep a man within compass than the having constantly before his eyes the state of his affairs in a regular course of *accounts*" (§211).

54. John Locke, *Some Thoughts on Education*, §18: "The great thing to be minded in education is, what habits you settle."

55. Max Weber, *The Protestant Ethic and the Spirit of Capitalism*, trans. Talcott Parsons (New York: Routledge, 1990), p. 4.

56. Michel Foucault, *Society Must Be Defended*, p. 103. See Ann Laura Stoler, *Race and the Education of Desire. Foucault's* History of Sexuality *and the Colonial Order of Things* (Durham: Duke University Press, 1995), p. 74–75: "While the issue of colonization is broached in earlier lectures, here for the first and only time, Foucault explicitly ties the discourse of internal colonialism within Europe to the fact of its external expansion—in a way unanticipated by any of his previous accounts […]. Foucault neither pursued this connection nor elaborated further." As we will see, this question had been prepared by the inclusion of the question of colonialism in the 1972–1973 course (*Psychiatric Power*). In Ann Laura Stoler's defense, none of the lectures had been published at the time her book was published.

57. In that case, they stop at the first formulation proposed by Foucault in the first lesson of the 1976 course, see Michel Foucault, *Society Must Be Defended*, p. 15 (lecture of January 7, 1976).

58. *Ibid.*, p. 48 (lecture of January 21, 1976).

59. Michel Foucault, *Security, Territory, Population*, p. 266–267.

60. See Michel Foucault, *The Birth of Biopolitics. Lectures at the Collège de France 1978–1979* (New York: Palgrave Macmillan, 2008), p. 5–6 (Lecture of January 10, 1979). On this "European balance" which was the object of the Treaty of Westphalia in 1648, see Michel Foucault, *Security, Territory, Population*, (lecture of March 22, 1978).

61. This is Eric Williams' expression (in *Capitalism and Slavery*, 1944) cited by Fernand Braudel, *Civilization and Capitalism, 15th-18th Century*, t. 3, *The Perspective of the World* (Berkeley: University of California Press, 1992), p. 394.

62. Sidney Mintz, *Sweetness and Power: The Place of Sugar in Modern History* (New York: Penguin Books, 1986), p. 55.

63. John Stuart Mill, *Principles of Political Economy* (New York: Appleton, 1876 (1848)), p. 685–686 (cited by Sidney Mintz, *op. cit.*, p. 42).

64. We must be careful not to forget that in "New Spain however, 'free' labor, that is in return for wages, was beginning to appear by the sixteenth century" (Fernand Braudel, *Civilization and Capitalism*, t.3 *The Perspective of the World*, p. 394).

65. Marx, *Capital*, Book I, Section VIII, XXXI.

66. Michel Foucault, *The History of Sexuality, Vol 1.: An Introduction* (New York: Random House, 1978), p. 139.

67. Michel Foucault, *Psychiatric Power*, (lecture of November 28, 1973), p. 68–69.

68. *Ibid.*, p. 46. This would be one of the major theses of *Discipline and Punish* (New York: Random House, 1977), in particular p. 135–194. Foucault credited Marx for it in an interview that appeared in the review *Hérodote* (1976): "Everything [Marx] wrote about the army and its role in the development of political power [...] is some very important material that has been left practically fallow for the sake of endless commentaries on surplus value" from "Questions on Geography" reprinted in Jeremy W. Crampton and Stuart Elden, eds., *Space Knowledge and Power: Foucault and Geography* (Burlington, VT: Ashgate Publishing, 2007), p. 182.

69. *Ibid.*, p. 246 (lecture of January 23, 1974).

70. Foucault had already made reference to them in a presentation to the Cercle d'Études architecturales in 1967. See Michel Foucault, "Of Other Spaces: Utopias and Heterotopias," translation by Jay Miskowiec of "Des espaces autres" *Architecture/Mouvement/Continuité*, March 1967.

71. Michel Foucault, *Psychiatric Power*, p. 246.

72. *Ibid.*, p. 247.

73. Michel Foucault, *Society Must Be Defended*, op. cit., p. 243.

74. In his political interventions, Foucault did not forget to include this function "reproducing the labor force" in a "politics of the body" that had the immediate effect of *politicizing* sexuality (See Michel Foucault, "Sexualité et politique" [1974], *Dits et Écrits*, op. cit., t. 1, 138, p. 1405).

75. Michel Foucault, *Security, Territory, Population*, op. cit., p. 8.

76. Michel Foucault, *The Birth of Biopolitics*, p. 67 (lecture of January 24, 1979).

77. Michel Foucault, "*Society Must Be Defended*," p. 257 (Lecture of March 17, 1976).

78. *Ibid.*, p. 254.

79. *Ibid.*, p. 260.

80. *Ibid.*, p. 255–257.

81. As we can read: "If the power of normalization wished to exercise the old sovereign right to kill, it must become racist. And if, conversely, a power of sovereignty, or in other words, a power that has the right of life and death, wishes to work with the instruments, mechanisms, and technology of normalization, it too must become racist." (*ibid.*, p. 256).

82. Eric Williams, *Capitalism and Slavery* (Chapel Hill, NC: University of North Carolina Press, 1944), p. 7.

83. Silvia Federici, *Caliban and the Witch*, p. 108.

84. Paul Virilio, *L'insécurité du territoire*, (Paris: Galilée, 1993 (1976)), p. 136.

85. Michel Foucault, *"Society Must Be Defended,"* op. cit., p. 259.

86. Aimé Césaire, *Discourse on Colonialism* (New York: Monthly Review Press, 1972 (1950)), p. 36.

87. Fernand Braudel, *Civilization and Capitalism*, op. cit., p. 57.

88. Immanuel Wallerstein, *The Modern World-System I: Capitalist Agriculture and the Origins of the European World-Economy in the Sixteenth Century* (Berkeley: University of California Press, 2011 (1974)), p. 140.

89. In the last years of his life, Marx worked on an important precision to his theory of primitive accumulation. The opportunity first came to him through an article by the "populist" Russian sociologist Nikolay Mikhailovsky, who criticized his (supposed?) philosophy for a universal fatalism of the development of capitalism. In his response in 1877, Marx reminds him that he had engaged above all in a historical analysis of the genesis of capitalism *in Western Europe* and that it was only Mikhailovsky who transformed it "into a historico-philosophical theory of the general course, fatally imposed upon all peoples, regardless of the historical circumstances in which they find themselves placed," Karl Marx, "A Letter on Russia" *New International*, vol. I, no. 4, November 1934, p. 110–11. In 1881, solicited by a letter from Vera Zasulich to respond to the "agrarian question" and the "rural commune" in Russia, Marx took the opportunity to give greater precision to his perspective on the transition to socialism. Russia was not destined to bow to the European sequence of events: precapitalist social formation, primitive accumulation, capitalism, socialism. Thanks to common ownership of the land, the Russian "rural commune" "may become a direct starting-point of the economic system towards which modern society is tending; it may open a new chapter that does not begin with its own suicide; it may reap the fruits with which capitalist production has enriched humanity without passing through the capitalist regime." The question of transition is not a theoretical problem: "To save the Russian commune, there must be a Russian Revolution." Thanks to its delay, the rural community, in the context of revolution, the rural commune "will soon develop as a regenerating element of Russian society and an element of superiority over the countries enslaved by the capitalist regime." These passages are taken from drafts of a letter of response Marx wrote to Vera Zasulich. Published in *Late Marx and the Russian Road, Marx and the 'Peripheries of Capitalism,'* edited by Teodor Shanin (New York: Monthy Reivew Press, 1983).

90. Since Rosa Luxemburg was the first to use this term, before Carl Schmitt took it up.

91. Rosa Luxemburg, *The Accumulation of Capital* (London: Routledge and Kegan Paul Limited, 1951), p. 452.

92. David Harvey, *The New Imperialism* (Oxford: Oxford University Press, 2003), p. 162–163.

93. *Ibid.*, p. 164.

94. *Ibid.*, p. 177.

95. Hannah Arendt, *The Origins of Totalitarianism* (New York: Harcourt, 1968 (1948)), p. 148.

3. Appropriation of the War Machine

1. "But gradually, the entire social body was cleansed of the bellicose relations that had permeated it through and through during the Middle Ages." Michel Foucault, *Society Must Be Defended*, op. cit., 48.

2. Gilles Deleuze, "Appareils d'État et machines de guerre," 4th session (URL: https://www.youtube.com/watch?v=zu5HvyskL3k).

3. Geoffrey Parker, *The Military Revolution: Military Innovation and the Rise of the West, 1500–1800* (Cambridge: Cambridge University Press, 1988), p. 43.

4. Both quotes cited by Geoffrey Parker, *The Military Revolution*, op. cit., p. 16 and 61.

5. England under Cromwell, France under Louis XIV, the Hapsburg Empire, Russia under Peter the Great all dedicated 75% of state income to war, combined with loans at interest from foreign financial markets.

6. Cited by Geoffrey Parker, *The Military Revolution*, p. 82.

7. Which allowed the projectiles to be heavier and to increase the cadence of shots aimed at piercing the "walls" of enemy ships.

8. In French: *guerre de course*. It consisted of expeditions of corsairs from what the English called the "centres of pirateering."

9. Gilles Deleuze and Félix Guattari, *A Thousand Plateaus*, p. 387.

10. Michael Duffy, "The Foundations of British Naval Power," in Michael Duffy (dir.), *The Military Revolution and the State, 1500–1800* (Exeter: University of Exeter Press, 1980), p. 81.

11. Karl Marx, *The Eighteenth Brumaire of Louis Bonaparte* (New York: Mondial, 2005), p. 82.

12. The military morphology of the state would thus represent according to Perry Anderson "a swollen memory of the medieval functions of war" of which the "structure was always potentially the zero-sum conflict of the battlefield, by which fixed quantities of ground were won or lost." Perry Anderson, *Lineages of the Absolutist State* (New York: Verso, 1979 (1974)), p. 31–33.

13. *Ibid.*, p. 21. Perry Anderson adds that "towns in this sense were never exogenous to feudalism in the West."

14. Giovanni Arrighi, *The Long Twentieth Century. Money, Power and the Origins of Our Times* (New York: Verso, 2010), p. 51.

15. Michel Foucault, *Discipline and Punish*, p. 168.

16. *Idem.*

17. Michel Foucault, *Psychiatric Power*, p. 47–48.

18. See David Eltis, *The Military Revolution in Sixteenth-Century Europe* (New York: I. B. Tauris, 1995), p. 61–63.

19. Michel Foucault, *Discipline and Punish*, p. 163. Widespread use of the rifle began at the very end of the seventeenth century.

20. *Idem.* Foucault credited Marx for seeing the analogy between the organization of the factory and the military enterprise.

21. *Ibid.*, p. 169.

22. This question of "militias" is at the heart of the debate between Adam Smith and Adam Ferguson, who had published two (unsigned) works in their favor. Against the dissolution of the republican union between the arts of politics and war in an army at the exclusive service of the Sovereign, Ferguson emphasized the importance of the martial virtues of the great Scottish tradition of the Highlanders despite the fact that they had already been militarily and socially defeated—in favor of the affirmation of the "Nation of Manufacturers" for which Smith rendered the political economy of power that structures it. See Adam Ferguson, *Reflections Previous to the Establishment of a Militia* (1759) and the analysis by John Robertson, *The Scottish Enlightenment and the Militia Issue* (Edinburg: John Donald, 1985).

23. Adam Smith, *An Inquiry into the Nature and Causes of the Wealth of Nations* (London: Meuthen and Co., Ltd., 1904 (1776)), Book III, Chap. 4.

24. *Ibid.* Book II, Chap. 4.

25. *Ibid.*, Book V, Chap. 1.

26. *Ibid.*, Book V, Chap. 1.

27. *Ibid.*, Book V, Chap. 1.

28. *Ibid.*, Book V, Chap. 1.

29. Adam Smith, *The Theory of Moral Sentiments* (Oxford: Clarendon Press, 1976 (1759)), p. 51.

30. *Ibid.*, p. 249.

31. Adam Smith, *Inquiry into the Nature and Causes of the Wealth of Nations*, Book V, Chap. 1.

32. See Giovanni Arrighi, *Adam Smith in Beijing. Lineages of the 21st Century* (New York: Verso, 2009).

4. Two Histories of the French Revolution

1. Carl von Clausewitz, *On War*, ed. and trans. Michael Howard and Peter Paret (Princeton: Princeton University Press, 1976), p. 591–592 (Book VIII, Chap. 3).

2. Carl von Clausewitz, *On War*, p. 590 (Book VIII, Chap.3).

3. Carl von Clausewitz, *On War*, p. 515 (Book VI, Chap. 30).

4. We mention René Girard here not for the theoretical scope of his *Achever Clausewitz* (in collaboration with Benoît Chantre (Paris: Champs-Flammarion, 2011)), but due to the sole fact that his theory of war of all against all will be used by the school of regulation as ontological foundation of the institution of money. In terms of this theory of war, the same criticism can be made of it as the one Foucault brought against Hobbes: it is not a question of real war but a fiction destined to legitimize the centralized power of the Sovereign. The institution of money from the war of everyone against everyone else ends in its transcendence in relation to real war between "capitalists and workers." It is money as mediation of class conflicts.

5. Carl von Clausewitz, *On War*, p. 610 (Book VIII, Chap. 6).

6. *Ibid.*, p. 580 (Book VIII, Chap. 2) and p. 593 (Chap. 3).

7. *Ibid.*, p. 592–593 (Book VIII, Chap. 3).

8. *Ibid.*, p. 87 (Book I, Chap. 1, §24).

9. *Ibid.*, p. 88 (§26). More generally, "Policy is the guiding intelligence and war only the instrument, not vice versa. No other possibility exists, then, than to subordinate the military point of view to the political" (*ibid.*, p. 607). Howard Caygill offers a good presentation of this Kantian philosophy of Clausewitz in his recent *On Resistance. A Philosophy of Defiance* (London and New York: Bloomsbury, 2013, p. 15–29).

10. *Ibid.*, p. 606 (Book VIII, Chap. 6).

11. *Ibid.*, p. 583 (Book VIII, Chap. 3) (The reference of course is to Napoleon).

12. *Ibid.*, p. 149 (Book II, Chap. 3). Clausewitz continues by explaining that war "is *still* closer to politics, which in turn may be considered as a kind of commerce on a larger scale." The reversal can be measured in light of his conclusion according to which "Politics, moreover, is the womb in which war develops."

13. *Ibid.*, p. 570, 592 (Book VII, Chap. 22).

14. See Manuel de Landa, *War in the Age of Intelligent Machines* (New York: Zone Books, 1991), p. 67 *sq.*

15. Unlike Carl Schmitt's *Theory of the Partisan*, there is no allusion to colonial wars in *On War*. In the chapter on "military genius" in Book I, he does however state that savage peoples do not possess it since "this requires a degree of intellectual powers beyond anything that a primitive people can develop" (*On War*, p. 100).

16. Carl von Clausewitz, *On War*, p. 75 (Book I, Chap. 1, §2).

17. *Ibid.*, p. 479: "a popular uprising should, in general, be considered as an outgrowth of the way in which the conventional barriers have been swept away in our lifetime by the elemental violence of war. It is, in fact, a broadening and intensification of the fermentation process known as war."

18. *Idem.*

19. Saint-Domingue was at the time the largest coffee and sugar producer, for which there was an exponential demand. Mortality rates were also so high that 40,000 slaves had to be "imported" to the island each year. Gordon K. Lewis calls Saint-Domingue the "Babylon of the Caribbean" because corruption, venality, and brutality were the rule (*Main Currents in Caribbean Thought* (Baltimore: Johns Hopkins University Press, 1983), p. 124).

20. According to Peter Hallward, "If the French Revolution stands as the great political event of modern times, the Haitian revolution must figure as the single most decisive sequence of this event" ("Haitian Inspiration," *Radical Philosophy*, 123, January-February 2004, p. 3).

21. C.L.R. James, *Black Jacobins. Toussaint L'Ouverture and the San Domingo Revolution* (New York: Vintage Books, 1989), p. 317 and 347.

22. According to the account by C.L.R. James: "Carrying torches to light their way, the leaders of the revolt met in an open space in the thick forests of the Morne Rouge, a mountain overlooking Cap François, the largest town. There Boukman, the leader, after Voodoo incantations and the sucking of the blood of a stuck pig, gave the last instructions." (C.L.R. James, *A History of Pan-African Revolt* (Oakland: Pm Press, 2012 [1938/1969]), p. 40).

23. C.L.R. James, *Black Jacobins*, p. 359.

24. *Ibid.*, p. 305–306.

25. "The masses had resisted the French from the very beginning, in spite of, and not because of, their leadership." Carolyn Fick, *The Making of Haiti: The Saint-Domingue Revolution from Below* (Knoxville: University of Tennessee Press, 1990), p. 228 (cited by Peter Hallward, "Haitian Inspiration," p. 5).

26. Susan Buck-Morris, *Hegel, Haiti and Universal History* (Pittsburgh: University of Pittsburgh Press, 2009), p. 23.

27. *Ibid.*, p. 36.

28. *Ibid.*, p. 57.

29. Nick Nesbitt makes a remark along these lines in *Caribbean Critique: Antillean Critical Theory from Toussaint to Glissant* (Oxford: Oxford University Press, 2013), p. 10–11.

30. Selim Nadi, "C.L.R. James et les luttes panafricaines," *Parti des indigènes de la république* March 5, 2014 (URL: indigenes-republique.fr/c-l-r-james-et-les-luttes-panafricaines).

5. Biopolitics of Permanent Civil War

1. Benjamin Constant, *De l'esprit de conquête et de l'usurpation dans leurs rapports avec la civilisation européenne* (Paris: Imprimerie nationale, 1992), p. 58.

2. Le Trosne, *Mémoire sur les vagabonds et sur les mendiants* (1764), p. 4 cited by Michel Foucault in *Discipline and Punish*, p. 77.

3. *Des moyens de détruire la mendicité en France en rendant les mendiants utiles à l'État sans les rendre malheureux* (1780), p. 17, cited by Robert Castel, *From Manual Workers to Wage Laborers: Transformation of the Social Question* (New Brunswick, NJ: Transaction Publishers, 2003), p. 76.

4. According the expression used by Robert Castel, *From Manual Workers to Wage Laborers*, p. 149.

5. Michel Foucault, *The Punitive Society*, p. 195 (lecture of March 14, 1973).

6. *Ibid.*, p.

7. *Ibid.*, p. 72.

8. This is still the perspective of Edward P. Thomson in "Time, Work-Discipline, and Industrial Capitalism," *Past and Present*, 38 (Dec. 1967) p. 56–97.

9. Michel Foucault, *Punitive Society*, p. 215.

10. *Ibid.*, p. 212.

11. Edward P. Thompson, "Time, Work-Discipline, and Industrial Capitalism," p. 91.

12. *Morning Star*, June 1863. Cited in Karl Marx, *Capital*, Book 1, Sect. VIII, Chap. X, p. 124 (italics added).

13. The expression—"*chair à mécanique*"—comes from a police note written in Lille in 1858, cited by Lion Murard and Patrick Zylberman, *Le Petit Travailleur infatiguable. Villes-usines, habitat et intimités au XIXe siècle* (Paris: Recherches, 1976).

14. Jacques Donzelot, *The Policing of Families* (Baltimore: Johns Hopkins University Press, 1997 (1977)), p. 54.

15. Robert Castel, *From Manual Workers to Wage Laborers*, p. 157.

16. Michel Foucault, *Abnormal: Lectures at the Collège de France 1974–1975* (New York: Picador, 2003), p. 265 (lecture of March 12, 1975).

17. *Ibid.*, p. 236 (lecture of March 5, 1975).

18. Michel Foucault, *Psychiatric Power*, p. 83 (lecture of November 28, 1973).

19. Michel Foucault, *Abnormal*, p. 269 (lecture of March 12, 1975).

20. According to the good Doctor Taillefer, physician of the Cité Napoléon, which was the first working-class housing project (*cité ouvrière*) in Paris, and author of the pamphlet *Des cités ouvrières et de leur nécessité comme hygiène et tranquillité publique* (1850).

21. Jacques Donzelot, *The Policing of Families*, p. 45.

22. In the sense of irregularity and working-class autonomy of the most qualified workers, rebellious towards the boss and without respect for family morality, which recognized themselves derisorily, in the mid-nineteenth century, in the term "sublime"; see Denis Poulot, *Question sociale. Le Sublime ou le travailleur parisien tel qu'il est en 1870* (Paris: Maspero, 1980 (1870)). Poulot proposes a "pathological diagnosis" (p.123) of it, opposing it to the *conscientious* worker whose life is focused on the family (p. 139).

23. Lion Murard and Patrick Zylberman, *Le Petit Travailleur infatiguable*, p. 155.

24. *Ibid.*, p. 185.

25. Michel Foucault, *Abnormal*, p. 273.

26. Lion Murard and Patrick Zylberman, *Le Petit Travailleur infatiguable*, p. 17. The *culture* of a "race of workers" continues the anti-labor racism overdetermined by the colonial experience with which we began this chapter (think of the Baron Haussmann's reference to the "mob of nomads").

27. Michel Foucault, *The History of Sexuality: An Introduction*, Volume 1 (New York: Random House, 1978), p. 149–150.

28. Foucault, *Punitive Society*, p. 205.

29. *Recherches*, numéro spécial Généalogie du Capital, 1. Les équipements de pouvoir, n° 13, décembre 1973, p. 122. Alongside Félix Guattari (director of the Cerfi) and Gilles Deleuze, Michel Foucault participated in the discussions found throughout this issue.

30. Michel Foucault, *Psychiatric Power*, p. 83.

31. *Ibid.*, p. 189.

6. The New Colonial War

1. A few numbers: in 1800, European powers occupied or controlled 35 % of the Earth's surface; 67 % in 1878; and 84 % in 1914. We are reminded of the famous saying attributed to Cecil Rhodes, founder of the De Beers diamond company and of Rhodesia (after having been Prime Minister of the Cape Colony): "I would annex the planets if I could."

2. Gunboats, steel rifles with percussion caps and breech-loading, machine guns …

3. Ernest Renan, "La réforme intellectuelle et morale de la France" (1871).

4. Charles Callwell, *Small Wars: Their Principles and Practices* (London: HSMO, 1906), p. 22.

5. Hannah Arendt, *Imperialism* (New York: Mariner Books, 1968 (1951)), p. 3 (and Chapter 3 on the racial society of the Boers and its value as a model for the Nazi elite).

6. See Lord Cromer, "The Government of the Subject Races," *Edinburgh Review* (1908).

7. Hannah Arendt, *Imperialism*, p. 83.

8. Olivier Le Cour Grandmaison, *Coloniser, Exterminer. Sur la guerre et l'État colonial* (Paris: Fayard, 2005), p. 128, 85–89.

9. Letter from Abdelkader to Bugeaud cited in Yves Lacoste, *La Question post-coloniale* (Paris: Fayard, 2010), p. 297.

10. Franz Fanon, *The Wretched of the Earth* (New York: Grove Press, 2004 (1963)), p. 6.

11. Cited in François Maspero, *L'Honneur de Saint-Arnaud* (Paris: Plon, 1993) p. 177–178.

12. Alexis de Tocqueville, "Essay on Algeria" in *Writings on Empire and Slavery*, ed. and trans. Jennifer Pitts (Baltimore: Johns Hopkins University Press, 2001), p. 65, 70, 71, 72, 75. See also Olivier Le Cour Grandmaison, p. 98–114.

13. In Tocqueville's text: "I have often heard men […] whom I respect, but with whom I do not agree, find it wrong that we burn harvests, that we empty silos, and finally that we seize unarmed men, women, and children. These, in my view, are unfortunate necessities, but ones to which any people that wants to wage war on the Arabs is obliged to submit" (Alexis de Tocqueville, *Writings on Empire and Slavery*, p. 70).

14. Already in 1838 Maréchal Bugeaud had published *De l'établissement de légions de colons militaires dans les possessions françaises de l'Afrique*. He took up the argument again in 1842 in *L'Algérie. Des moyens de conserver et d'utiliser cette conquête*.

15. Letter from Bugeaud to Genty de Bussy, March 30, 1847.

16. Alexis de Tocqueville, "Second Report on Algeria (1847)," *Writings on Empire and Slavery*, p. 194.

17. There is agreement that the overall population of Algeria was cut almost in half (from 4 to 2.3 million) between 1830 and 1850.

18. Michel Foucault, *The Birth of Biopolitics*, p. 65 (lecture of January 24, 1979).

19. Alexis de Tocqueville, *Writings on Empire and Slavery*, p. 111.

20. *Ibid.*, p. 71.

21. We should cite Tocqueville's *Souvenirs* here: "the June insurrection was not, in truth, a political struggle (in the sense that we have given to this word until now) but a class combat, a kind of servile war" (Alexis de Tocqueville, *Souvenirs* (Paris: Gallimard, 1978), p. 212–213.

22. Friedrich Engels, articles on the June Uprising from the *Neue Rheinische Zeitung*, June 28–29 and July 1–2, 1848 in *Marx/Engels Collected Works* (Moscow: Progress Publishers, 1931), vol. 7, p. 130, 134, 139, 160.

23. Alexis de Tocqueville, *Souvenirs*, p. 213. He saw it as "the uprising of one population against another."

24. See *Marxisme et Algérie*, texts by Marx and Engels presented and translated by René Gallisot and Gilbert Badia (Paris: UGE, 1976), p. 394. Engels takes up the same thesis in his preface to the second edition of *The Condition of the Working Class in England* (1892).

25. Vladimir Lenin, *Collected Works* (Moscow: Progress Publishers, 1965), vol. 31, p. 236. See also *Marxisme et Algérie*, p. 285.

26. *Marxisme et Algérie*, p. 265.

27. See Friedrich Engels, *The Northern Star*, January 22, 1848, in *MECW*, Vol.6, p.469; see also *Marxisme et Algérie*, p. 25. "Upon the whole it is, in our opinion, very fortunate that the Arabian chief has been taken. The struggle of the Bedouins was a hopeless one, and though the manner in which brutal soldiers, like Bugeaud, have carried on the war is highly blamable, the conquest of Algeria is an important and fortunate fact for the progress of civilization." More generally, on this question of Eurocentric Marxist "modernism," see Peter Osborne, *Marx* (London: Granta Books, 2005), Chap. 7 and 10.

7. The Limits of the Liberalism of Foucault

1. Benjamin Constant, "Principles of Politics Applicable to all Representative Governments," in *Constant: Political Writings* (Cambridge: Cambridge University Press, 1988), p. 214. The motif is presented with the utmost clarity in Chapter VI: "Property alone makes men capable of exercising political rights."

2. Michel Foucault, *The Birth of Biopolitics*, p. 21 (lecture of January 10, 1979).

3. *Ibid.*, p. 21–22.

4. *Ibid.*, p. 283. Mentioned in the middle of a long commentary on the "invisible hand" that forms the last part of the March 28, 1979 lecture (p. 267–290).

5. Michel Foucault, "What is Critique?" in *The Politics of Truth* (Boston: Semiotext(e)/MIT Press, 1997), p. 98.

6. Michel Foucault, *The Birth of Biopolitics*, p. 297–298 (lecture of April 4, 1979).

7. *Ibid.*, p. 319 (Course Summary).

8. *Ibid.*, p. 13 (lecture of January 10, 1979).

9. *Ibid.*, p. 296 (lecture of April 4, 1979).

10. *Ibid.*, p. 298.

11. *Ibid.*, p. 304.

12. *Ibid.*, p. 302.

13. Adam Smith, *The Wealth of Nations* (1776), Book 1, Chap. 4 ("Of the Origin and Use of Money").

14. Michel Foucault, *The Birth of Biopolitics*, p. 297

15. *Ibid.*, p. 296.

16. *Ibid.*, p. 307–308.

17. *Ibid.*, p. 309.

18. *Ibid.*, p. 310.

19. *Ibid.*, p. 280–281 (lecture of March 28, 1979).

20. *Ibid.*, p. 281.

21. *Ibid.*, p. 55, our italics (and p. 61 on the position of England, p. 56–57 on "the unlimited nature of the external market") (lecture of January 24, 1979).

22. *Ibid.*, p. 57, 60–61.

23. *Ibid.*, p. 58.

24. *Ibid.*, p. 320 (Course Summary).

25. *Ibid.*, p. 57–58. Although, according to Kant, it was originally through war that both the populating of inhospitable regions and the establishment of juridical ties occurred.

26. *Ibid.*, p. 46 (lecture of January 17, 1979).

27. *Ibid.*, p. 70 (lecture of January 24, 1979).

28. *Ibid.*, p. 46.

29. R. H. Tawney, *Religion and the Rise of Capitalism* (New Brunswick, NJ and London: Transaction Publishers, 1998) p. 189 (our italics).

30. Karl Marx, *Capital*, Book I, Sect. VIII, Chap. XXXIII, p. 940.

31. Karl Marx, "The Future Results of British Rule in India," *New York Daily Tribune*, August 8, 1853 "England has to fulfill a double mission in India: one destructive, the other regenerating the annihilation of old Asiatic society, and the laying the material foundations of Western society in Asia."

32. Michel Foucault, *The Birth of Biopolitics*, p. 43.

33. We should note in passing that the exemplary revolution of the governed against those who govern, the American revolution, did not abolish slavery (most of the 39 delegates who signed the Constitution were slave owners, as were most of the first presidents of the United States) and moreover twice approved one of the most infamous sub-products of the real institution of classical liberalism: the law on escaped slaves (Fugitive Slave Act of 1793, Fugitive Slave Law of 1850).

34. Domenico Losurdo, *Liberalism: A Counter-History* (New York: Verso, 2011), p. 105–107.

35. Michel Foucault, in an unpublished dialogue during a conference at Berkeley on "Ethics and Politics" in April 1983 (cited by Serge Audier, *Penser le "néolibéralisme." Le moment neoliberal, Foucault et la crise du socialisme* (Lormont: Le Bord de l'eau), p. 433). [An edited version of this discussion was published as "Politics and Ethics" in *The Foucault Reader*.]

36. Cited in Domenico Losurdo, *Liberalism: A Counter-History*, p. 108.

37. Michel Foucault, *Punitive Society*, p. 238 (lecture of March 28, 1973).

38. Michel Foucault, *Punitive Society*, p. 238 (lecture of March 28, 1973).

39. Michel Foucault, *Punitive Society*, p. 240 (lecture of March 28, 1973).

40. Michel Foucault, *Security, Population, Territory*, p. 350 (lecture of April 5, 1979).

41. Adam Smith, *The Wealth of Nations* (1776), Book I, Chap. 8 ("Of the Wages of Labor") and Chap. 9 ("Of the Rent of Land"), conclusion.

8. The Primacy of Capture, Between Schmitt and Lenin

1. Its best presentation is found in the *Anti-Düring* ("Political Economy III. Theory of Force").

2. Hobson had covered the Boer War for the *Manchester Guardian*. He was therefore well equipped to condemn the "civilizing mission" towards "inferior races" and its "political and moral" consequences for a race of rulers whose "interests" are first and foremost economic. While Hobson produced the first economic critique of imperialism, he also emphasizes at length the importance of "popular education" in developing, on a basis that he calls "geocentric," the *imperialist mentality*: "the church, the press, the schools and colleges, the political machine, the four chief instruments of popular education, are accommodated to its service. [...] Most serious of all is the persistent attempt to seize the school system for Imperialism masquerading as patriotism." He had previously asserted: "But still more important than these supports of militarism in the army is the part played by 'war' as a support of Imperialism in the non-combatant body of the nation" (John A. Hobson, *Imperialism. A Study* (New York: James Pott and Co., 1902), Part II, Chap. 3).

3. Carl Schmitt, "The Legal World Revolution," *Telos* 72 (Summer 1987), p. 73–89. The term "englobing/enclosing," which is also found in Deleuze and Guattari, was borrowed by Carl Schmitt from François Perroux.

4. Carl Schmitt, *The Nomos of Earth*, p. 236.

5. Carl Schmitt, "Raum und Großraum im Völkerrecht" (1940), in *Staat, Grossraum, Nomos. Arbeiten aus der Jahren 1916–1969* (Berlin: Duncker & Humblot, 1995), p. 242.

6. Carl Schmitt, *The Nomos of the Earth*, p. 140.

7. Carl Schmitt, "Völkerrechtliche Grossraumordnung mit Interventionsverbot für raumfremde Mächte. Ein Beitrag zum Reichsbegriff im Völkerrecht" (1941), in *Staat, Grossraum, Nomos*, p. 310.

8. This is the title of the fourth and final part of *The Nomos of the Earth*.

9. "Schmitt systematically refers to his colleague Carl Brinkmann on the question of imperialism until 1937 and then again in 1953 in "Appropriation/Distribution/Production," and in 1978 in "The Legal World Revolution" (Céline Jouin, "Carl Schmitt, penseur de l'empire ou de l'impérialisme?," URL: juspoliticum.com/CarlSchmitt-penseur-de-l-empire.html).

10. Carl Schmitt, *The Concept of the Political* (Chicago: University of Chicago Press, 1996 (1932)), p. 78. In the 1933 edition, the year when Schmitt became a member of the Nazi party, the Marxist references disappeared from *The Concept of the Political*.

11. Lenin, "Bourgeois Pacifism and Socialist Pacifism," January 1, 1917 in *Collected Works* (Moscow: Progress Publishers, 1964), vol. 23, p. 193.

12. Carl Schmitt, "Appropriation/Distribution/Production: An Attempt to Determine from *Nomos* the Basic Questions of Every Social and Economic Order," in *The Nomos of the Earth*, p. 331.

13. *Ibid.*, p. 335.

14. *Ibid.*, p. 334.

15. *Ibid.*, p. 331.

16. *Ibid.*, p. 334.

17. Meaning "Appropriation/Distribution/Production."

18. This unpublished conference was published almost twenty years later in two parts in the review *Commentaire* under titles chosen by the editors: Alexandre Kojève, "Capitalisme et socialisme. Marx est Dieu, Ford est son prophète," *Commentaire*, 9 (1980); "Du colonialisme au capitalisme donnant," *Commentaire*, 87 (1999) (preceded by the French translation of Carl Schmitt's article "Appropriation/Distribution/Production").

19, Carl Schmitt, "Appropriation/Distribution/Production," *The Nomos of the Earth*, p. 345.

20. Carl Schmitt, "Prendre/partager/paître. La question de l'ordre économique et social à partir du nomos" (1953) in *La Guerre civile mondiale. Essais (1943–1978)* (Paris: è®e) p. 64, n. 4. Kojève, for his part, explained that "when *everything* is already taken, you can only share or distribute if some *give* what others receive in order to *consume* it" ("Du colonialisme au capitalisme donnant," p. 562).

21. Carl Schmitt, "Forms of Modern Imperialism in International Law" (1932), trans. Matthew Hannah in *Spatiality, Sovereignty and Carl Schmitt. Geographies of the Nomos* (New York: Routledge, 2011), p. 31–32.

22. John Maynard Keynes, "An Open Letter to President Roosevelt," *New York Times*, December 31, 1933.

23. *Congressional Record*, June 7, 1933.

24. Keynes started to predict it as early as 1919 as the devastating result of the Versailles Treaty in Germany, and in a cumulative way on the balance of the entire integrated capitalist market. See John Maynard Keynes, *Consequences of Peace* (New York: Harcourt, Brace and Howe, 1919), p. 251.

25. *Congressional Record*, May 26, 1933.

26. Richard Hofstadter, *The Age of Reform: From Bryan to F.D.R.* (New York: Kopf, 1955), p. 319.

27. The Banking Act of 1933 separated investment banks and deposit banks whose holdings were guaranteed by the federal government. The Securities Exchange Act of 1934 placed the stock market under the control of the Securities and Exchange Commission (SEC). These measures returned to favor after the

financial crisis of 2008—with the results we all know: taxes and deposits refinanced the losses of "investors."

28. Antonio Negri, "John Maynard Keynes and the Capitalist Theory of the State Post-1929," *Revolution Retrieved. Writings on Marx, Keynes, Capitalist Crisis and New Social Subjects (1967–83)* (London: Red Notes, 1988), p. 15.

29. 1938 was in fact a very bad year for American capitalism: 5.3% drop in GDP, 14%-19% rise in unemployment, etc. See for example Ira Katznelson, *Fear Itself. The New Deal and the Origins of Our Time* (New York: Liveright, 2013), p. 369.

30. John Maynard Keynes, "The United States and the Keynes Plan," *The New Republic*, July 29, 1940 (cited in Antonio Negri, *Revolution Retrieved*, p. 34). We should remember that Keynes became Chancellor of the Exchequer in Britain in 1940 during a time of total mobilization of resources towards military ends. The system of obligatory labor was accompanied by a social security plan, which gave birth in 1943 to the National Health Service (NHS) under the authority of Lord Beveridge.

9. Total Wars

1. Ernst Jünger, *The Peace*, trans. Stuart O. Hood (Hinsdale, IL: Henry Regnery Company, 1948 (1945)), p. 47.

2. Léon Daudet, *La Guerre totale* (Paris: Nouvelle Librairie Nationale, 1918); Erich Ludendorff, *The "Total" War* (London: Friends of Europe, 1936). While Daudet saw the Russian Revolution as the result of a campaign of "material and moral disorganization" run by Germany, for Ludendorff, it was the result of revolutionary propaganda that—along with the Jews, the Roman Church, and the Masons—was responsible for the German defeat and had nonetheless threatened Europe as a whole for a long time.

3. Léon Daudet, *La Guerre totale*, p. 8.

4. Erich Ludendorff, *The "Total" War*. Ludendorff also argues that the war suspended the use of the gold standard, which he understands as "an obstacle to the economic development of many states." Translator's note: References in this chapter without page numbers were back-translated from the French.

5. We can think here of the pioneering work of Jean-Pierre Faye since *Langages totalitaires* (1972).

6. Erich Ludendorff, *Urkunden der obersten Heeresleitung über ihre Tätigkeit, 1916–18* (1920), cited by Jean Querzola, "Le chef d'orchestre à la main de fer. Léninisme et Taylorisme," in *Le Soldat du travail. Guerre, fascisme et taylorisme*, edited by Lion Murard et Patrick Zylberman, *Recherches*, 32–33 (1978), p. 79 (our emphasis).

7. In this "abstraction," Ludendorff combines, perhaps on purpose, the "absolute" form of war in Clausewitz with "total war."

8. See Ludendorff, *The "Total" War* for these quotes. Against Clausewitz, politics at the service of war is the main theme of Chapter I.

9. Ludendorff in fact uses the term "total politics" (*totale Politik*).

10. Léon Daudet, *La Guerre totale*, p. 11. It is estimated that more than 750,000 German deaths occurred due to famine during the First World War. The Allied blockade was maintained after the armistice during the winter of 1918–1919, when there was the greatest lack of supplies. This was not without effect on the Third Reich's policy of "absolute" self-sufficiency.

11. Ludendorff, *The "Total" War*.

12. Giulio Douhet, "La grande offensiva aerea" (1917), cited by Thomas Hippler, *Le Gouvernement du ciel. Histoire globale des bombardements aériens* (Paris: Les Prairies ordinaires, 2014), p. 100.

13. Giulio Douhet, *La Maîtrise de l'air* (Paris: Economica, 2007 (1921)), p. 72, p. 57.

14. What Ludendorff calls the "animic forces of the people" by mixing inevitably with this *völkisch* grammar the "preservation of the race."

15. Erich Ludendorff, *The "Total" War*.

16. *Ibid.*

17. *Ibid.*

18. Thomas Hippler, *Le Gouvernement du ciel*, p. 102.

19. See John Ellis, *The Social History of the Machine Gun* (London: Pimlico, 1993), p. 60 and all of Chapter 3: "Officers and Gentlemen" (on the resistance of the military to the strategic use of machine guns in the European theater).

20. *Ibid.*, p. 16.

21. Ernst Jünger, *Combat as an Inner Experience*.

22. According to Winston Churchill's count in *The River War*.

23. Account cited by John Ellis, *The Social History of the Machine Gun*, p. 123.

24. Further proven by the machine gun, an invention of the American Civil War. It is not only a jewel of industrial capitalism associated with the supremacy of Western civilization and race; in the United States, it was quickly deployed against workers on strike in Pittsburgh and Colorado (see John Ellis, *The Social History of the Machine Gun*, p. 42–44).

25. Thomas Hippler, *Le Gouvernement du ciel*, p. 126.

26. The Irish War of Independence began in January 1919.

27. Carl Schmitt, *The Concept of the Political*, p. 78.

28. Carl Schmitt, *Theory of the Partisan*, p. 36–37. Schmitt is referring to an article by Lenin, "Guerrilla Warfare" that appeared in 1906 in the Russian journal *Proletary*.

29. Carl Schmitt, *Theory of the Partisan*, p 64, 67.

30. Carl Schmitt, *Theory of the Partisan*, p. 7.

31. Vladimir Lenin, *Socialism and War*, 1915 (URL: www.marxists.org/archive/lenin/works/1915/s+w/ch01.htm#v21fl70h-299).

32. Vladimir Lenin, "Better Fewer, but Better," *Pravda*, March 4, 1923. (URL: www.marxists.org/archive/lenin/works/1923/mar/02.htm).

33. The quotes and data concerning the Congress of the Peoples of the East come from an article by Ian Birchall, "Un moment d'espoir: le congrès de Bakou 1920," *Contretemps*, 12/09/2012 (URL: www.contretemps.eu/interventions/moment-despoir-congrès-bakou-1920).

34. Translator's note: English translation by Brian Pearce of "Minutes of the Congress of the Peoples of the East, Baku, September 1920" (URL: https://www.marxists.org/history/international/comintern/baku/).

35. Vladimir Lenin, "Speech on the Terms of Admission into the Communist International," July 30, 1920 (URL: www.marxists.org/archive/lenin/works/1920/jul/x03.htm#fw4).

36. Geoffrey Barraclough, *An Introduction to Contemporary History* (Harmondsworth: Penguin, 1967), p. 153–54.

37. Ian Birchall, "Un moment d'espoir: le congrès de Bakou 1920."

38. Hans Speier and Alfred Kähler, *War in Our Time* (New York: Norton, 1939), p. 13: "The scope of war has become as large as that of peace, or indeed even larger, since under modern conditions it is the interest of efficient warfare to militarize peace." Hans Speier and Alfred Kähler were among the founders of the New School for Social Research (University in Exile).

39. Ernst Jünger, *Total Mobilization*.

40. Ludendorff, *Urkunden*, quoted by Jean Querzola, "Léninisme et Taylorisme," p. 79.

41. Ernst Jünger, *Total Mobilization*.

42. Vladimir Lenin, "The Impending Catastrophe and How to Combat It," *Collected Works* (Moscow: Progress Publishers, 1977), vol. 25, p. 362–363 (URL: www.marxists.org/archive/lenin/works/1917/ichtci/11.htm#v25zz99h-360).

43. Vladimir Lenin, "Original Version of 'The Immediate Tasks of the Soviet Government,'" *Collected Works*, vol. 42, p. 72 (URL: www.marxists.org/archive/lenin/works/1918/mar/23b.htm).

44. Jean Querzola, "Léninisme et Taylorisme," p. 75.

45. Think here of the labor struggles against the "rationalization" of Renault factories in 1912–1913.

46. George Babcock, "Some Organization Lessons of the War," *Bulletin of the Taylor Society*, Vol. 4, 6, (1919), p. 6.

47. Maurizio Vaudagna, "L'américanisme et le management scientifique dans les années 1920," *Recherches*, 32–33 (1978), p. 392. In 1918, one third of the members of the Taylor Society worked for the Ordnance Department, enough to indicate the pioneering role of this department. Remember that the Civil War and the first ordnance manufacturers, along with the railroads, provided the spark for American power. As Benjamin Coriat writes, "this reciprocal productivity between war and industry is not new; only the inscription of each one under the register of capital changed their scale" (Benjamin Coriat, *L'Atelier et le chronomètre* (Paris: Bourgois, 1979), p. 69).

48. "It is only through *enforced* standardization of methods, *enforced* adoption of the best implements and working conditions, and *enforced* cooperation that this faster work can be assured. And the duty of enforcing the adoption of standards and of enforcing this cooperation rests with the *management* alone" (Frederick Winslow Taylor, *The Principles of Scientific Management* (New York: Holt, 1912), p. 83, cited by David Montgomery, *Workers' Control in America: Studies in the History of Work, Technology, and Labor Struggles* (Cambridge: Cambridge University Press, 1979), p. 114). On labor resistance to the introduction of Taylorism in America, other than the book by David Montgomery, see Gisela Bock, Paolo Carpignano, and Bruno Ramirez, *La formazione dell'operaio massa negli USA*, 1892–1922 (Milan: Feltrinelli, 1972).

49. Passages taken, respectively, from a speech by Clémentel before the *Association nationale d'expansion économique* (March 26, 1917) and from the minutes of November 10, 1917 for a session of the *Comité permanent d'études relatives à la prévision des chômages industriels* (cited by Martin Fine, "Guerre et réformisme en France, 1914–1918," *Recherches*, 32–33 (1978), p. 314, 318.

50. Ellis W. Hawley, "Le nouveau corporatisme et les démocraties liberals, 1918–1925: les cas des États-Unis," *Recherches*, 32–33 (1978), p. 343. On the "negotiations" that ensued, during and after the war, from the introduction of Taylorism placed under the supervision of the "cooperation" of the unions and management, see Hugh G. J. Aitken, *Scientific Management in Action. Taylorism at Watertown Arsenal, 1908–1915* (Princeton: Princeton University Press, 1985 (1960)), p. 237–241.

51. There were more than 600,000 widows in France and the same number in Germany after the first global conflict; 200,000 in England.

52. Véronique Molinari, "Le droit de vote accordé aux femmes britanniques à l'issue de la Première Guerre mondiale: une récompense pour les services rendus?," *Lisa*, vol. 6, 4 (2008).

53. Denise Riley, "Some Peculiarities of Social Policy Concerning Women in Wartime and Postwar Britain," in *Behind the Lines*, p. 260.

54. Robert Linhart, *Lénine, les paysans, Taylor* (Paris: Seuil, 2010 (1976)), p. 135.

55. Ernst Jünger, *Total Mobilization*.

56. Massimiliano Guareschi, "La métamorphose du guerrier," *Cultures et conflits*, 67, 2007.

57. Something that General Fuller did not fail to emphasize: "the pecuniary profits of war shifted from plunder by the generals and troops to the gains made by financiers, war contractors and manufacturers." See J.F.C. Fuller, *Armament and History: The Influence of Armament on History from the Dawn of Classical Warfare to the Second World War* (London: Charles Scribner's Sons, 1945), p. 126.

58. Christophe Bonneuil and Jean-Baptiste Fressoz, *L'Événement Anthropocène* (Paris: Seuil, 2013), p. 141.

59. Ernst Jünger, *Total Mobilization*.

60. Luciano Canfora, *1914* (Paris: Champs-Flammarion, 2014), p. 31.

61. See David Montgomery, *Workers' Control in America*, Chap. 3. With the spread of strikes, socialist activism continued in the United States until the 1920 depression.

62. Herbert A. L. Fisher, *History of Europe* (Cambridge, MA: Houghton, Mifflin and Co., 1936), p. 1113 (cited by Luciano Canfora, *1914*); Fernand Braudel, *Grammaire des civilisations* (Paris: Champs-Flammarion, 1993), p. 436 (cited by Luciano Canfora, *Democracy in Europe. A History of an Ideology* (Oxford: Blackwell Publishing, 2006), p. 156).

63. Ernst Jünger, *Total Mobilization*.

64. Luciano Canfora, *Democracy in Europe*, p. 157.

65. Carl Schmitt, "The Changing Structure of International Law" *Journal for Cultural Research* 2016 [Quote: Puisque le gouvernement des États-Unis a le pouvoir de discriminer les autres gouvernements, il a bien sûr aussi le droit de dresser les peuples contre leurs propres gouvernements et de transformer la guerre entre États en guerre civile. La guerre mondiale discriminatoire de style américain se transforme ainsi en guerre civile mondiale de caractère total et global. C'est la clé de cette union à première vue invraisemblable entre le capitalisme occidental et le bolchévisme oriental.]

66. Ernst Jünger, *Total Mobilization*.

67. Hanah Arendt, *On Revolution* (New York: Viking Press, 1963), p. 7.

68. Thomas Hippler, *Le Gouvernement du ciel*, p. 132, 130.

69. *Ibid.*, 131.

70. See the passages collected by Wolfgang Schivelbusch, *Three New Deals. Reflections on Roosevelt's America, Mussolini's Italy, and Hitler's Germany, 1933–1939* (New York: Picador, 1986), p. 26–32.

71. The Italian colonization of Ethiopia in 1935 and Mussolini and Hitler's involvement in the Spanish Civil War changed the situation.

72. See Michel Foucault, *The Birth of Biopolitics*, p. 133 (lecture of February 14, 1979).

73. William H. McNeill, *The Pursuit of Power: Technology, Armed Force, and Society since A.D. 1000* (Chicago: University of Chicago Press, 1982), p. 337.

74. In *The New Republic*, a few days before Roosevelt made his speech before Congress (cited by Wolfgang Schivelbusch, *Three New Deals*, p. 101).

75. Luciano Canfora contests the paternity of this expression attributed to Ernst Nolte in *La Gurre civile européenne. National-socialisme et bolchévisme (1917–1945)*, published in 1989. According to him it was from twenty years earlier—and in a very different problematic!—by Isaac Deutscher during lectures given at the University of Cambridge for the fiftieth anniversary of the Russian Revolution. See Luciano Canfora, *La Démocratie*, p. 278 et sq.

76. Michel Foucault, *"Society Must Be Defended,"* p. 259–260 (all quotes taken from the lecture of March 17, 1976).

77. *Ibid.*, p. 232.

78. Michel Foucault, *The History of Sexuality.* Volume 1, p. 137

79. Michel Foucault, "The Political Technology of Individuals," *Technologies of the Self. A Seminar with Michel Foucault* (London: Tavistock Publications, 1988), p. 147.

80. *Ibid.*, p. 160.

81. Michel Foucault, *The Birth of Biopolitics*, p. 109 (lecture of February 7, 1979).

82. *Ibid.*, p. 110–111.

83. *Ibid.*, p. 110.

84. Gilles Deleuze, "Appareils d'État et machines de guerre," university year 1979–1980, session 13 (URL: www.youtube.com/watch?v=kgWaov-IUrA [in French]).

85. For a critical perspective on Arendt's concept of "totalitarianism" that we think is very close to Deleuze's reading, see Roberto Esposito, "Totalitarisme ou biopolitique," *Tumultes*, 1/2006, 26.

86. Gilles Deleuze, "Appareils d'État et machines de guerre," session 13. See Hannah Arendt, *The Origins of Totalitarianism* (New York: Harcourt, Inc., 1976), p. 326 "Their idea of domination was something that no state and no mere apparatus of violence can ever achieve, but only a movement that is constantly kept in motion: namely, the permanent domination of each single individual in each and every sphere of life."

87. Gilles Deleuze, "Appareils d'État et machines de guerre," session 13.

88. Michel Foucault, "*Society Must Be Defended*," p. 259–260.

89. Gilles Deleuze, "Appareils d'État et machines de guerre," session 13. This theme of the "suicidal state" can also be found in Foucault in the same pages of "*Society Must Be Defended*."

90. See Foucault, "*Society Must Be Defended*," p. 258: "I think that this is something much deeper than an old tradition, much deeper than a new ideology, that it is something else. The specificity of modern racism, or what gives it its specificity, is not bound up with mentalities, ideologies, or the lies of power. It is bound up with *the technique of power, with the technology of power*" (Our emphasis).

91. We will discuss this essential distinction introduced by the later Foucault in more detail, and use it for our own analysis of the most contemporary capitalism.

92. In his speech to the British Anti-Socialist Union on February 17, 1933, Winston Churchill told his audience: "With the fascist regime, Mussolini has established a reference point by which the countries that are engaged in hand-to-hand fighting with socialism should not hesitate to be guided." The corporatist state thus becomes "the path a nation can follow when courageously led."

93. Cited, along with Churchill's speech, by Luciano Canfora, *Democracy in Europe*, p. 159.

94. According to the expression used by Marx in "The Class Struggles in France, 1848 to 1850."

95. Erich Ludendorff, *Total War*.

96. Michel Foucault, "*Society Must Be Defended*," p. 262.

97. These two expressions refer respectively to Marc Allen Eisner, *From Warfare State to Welfare State: World War I, Compensatory State Building, and the Limits of the Modern Order* (University Park, PA: Pennsylvania State University Press, 2000); and to Barbara Ehrenreich, "The Fog of (Robot) War," URL: www.tomdispatch.com/blog/175415.

98. Marc Allen Eisner, *From Warfare State to Welfare State*, p. 299–300.

99. François Ewald, *L'État-providence* (Paris: Grasset, 1986), p. 374.

100. Grégoire Chamayou, *Théorie du drone* (Paris: La Fabrique, 2013), p. 266.

101. Barbara Ehrenreich, "The Fog of (Robot) War."

102. Megan J. McClintock, "Civil War Pensions and the Reconstructions of Union Families," *Journal of American History*, 83, September 1996, p. 466.

103. Charles Anderson, *Industrial Insurance in the United States* (Chicago: University of Chicago Press, 1909), p. 277.

104. See Elliot Brownlee, *Federal Taxation in America: A Short History* (Cambridge: Cambridge University Press, 2004), p. 2 "The income tax was a highly tentative experiment until 1916, when America prepared to enter World War I."

105. Sara Josephine Baker, *Fighting for Life* (New York: Macmillan, 1939), p. 165. Sara Josephine Baker had been named in 1908 the head of the Child Hygiene Division of the city of New York. This was the first service dedicated exclusively to child health.

106. Barbara Ehrenreich, "The Fog of (Robot) War."

107. Carole Pateman, "Equality, Difference, Subordination: The Politics of Motherhood and Women's Citizenship," in Gisela Bock and Susan James (dir.), *Beyond Equality and Difference. Citizenship, Feminist Politics and Female Subjectivity* (New York: Routledge, 1992).

108. *Ibid.*, p. 22. Beveridge regularly complained of the fact that the campaign for family subsidies had the "taint of feminism."

109. Cited by Gisela Bock, *Women in European History* (Oxford: Blackwell, 2002)., p. 144.

110. Which was perfectly expressed by the statement of Maude Royden in the midst of the Great War: "The state wants children, and to give them is a service both dangerous and honourable. Like the soldier, the mother takes a risk and gives a devotion for which no money can pay; but, like the soldier, she should not, therefore, be made 'economically dependent.'" (Cited in Carole Pateman, "Equality, Difference, Subordination," p. 26).

111. The unions are equally present in all of the war administrations: Council of National Defense, Food Administration, Fuel Administration, and Emergency Construction Board, among others.

112. As Samuel Gompers, president of the AFL, explained it as motivation to organize an "All-American" committee of responsible union leaders (*The Taylor*, April 8, 1919).

113. Marc Allen Eisner, *From Warfare State to Welfare State*, p. 177.

114. A.J. Muste, "Collective Bargaining—New Style," *Nation*, May 9, 1928, 537–38, cited in Marc Allen Eisner, *From Warfare State to Welfare State*, p. 176.

115. Barbara Ehrenreich, "The Fog of (Robot) War."

116. "The right to organize and bargain collectively through representatives of their own choosing…" For the full text of the law: www.ssa.gov/history/pdf/fdrbill.pdf.

117. Herbert Rabinowitz, "Amend Section 7-a!," *Nation*, December 27, 1933 (cited by Marc Allen Eisner, *From Warfare State to Welfare State*, p. 334).

118. To borrow the title of the work by Rexford Tugwell, *The Industrial Discipline and the Government Arts* (New York: Columbia University Press, 1932). Written before Tugwell joined the Roosevelt administration, this book (in particular the last chapter) largely inspired the NRA.

119. Marc Allen Eisner, *From Warfare State to Welfare State*, p. 320.

120. *Ibid.*, p. 357 The "dollar-a-year men" were millionaires (billionaires today) who received the symbolic salary of one dollar per year for their activities in state, para-state, or private structures.

121. Between 1954 and 1964, the military controlled more than 70% of the Federal budget for research and development. And research and development was in constant expansion because the fiscal state adapted to the needs of the military-industrial complex.

122. See Gregory Hooks, *Forging the Military-Industrial Complex. World War II's Battle of the Potomac* (Chicago, University of Illinois Press, 1991), chap. 7.

123. Harold D. Lasswell, "The Garrison State," *American Journal of Sociology*, vol. 46, 4, January 1941, p. 466, 458. The expression "To militarize is to governmentalize" is found in an article he published ten years later ("Does the Garrison State Threaten Civil Rights?," *Annals of the American Academy*, 275, May 1951, p. 111).

124. Thomas Hippler, *Le Gouvernement du Ciel*, p. 98.

125. It was a collection of *restrictive* amendments to the Wagner Act. Open shops allowing the hiring of non-union employees were authorized, unions were reduced to the simple function of salary negotiation and guaranteeing the respect of labor contracts. Any "politicization" of factories was outlawed (union delegates had to certify that they were not members of the Communist Party).

126. Gregory Hooks, *Forging the Military-Industrial Complex*, p. 38–39. Military spending represented 36% of the federal budget in 1940 and 70% a year later. Between 1942 and 1945, it rose to more than 90%.

127. Michal Kalecki, "Stimulating the Business Upswing in Nazi Germany" (1935) and "Political Aspects of Full Employment" (1943), in *The Last Phase in the Transformation of Capitalism* (New York: Monthly Review Press Classics, 2009).

128. Rosa Luxemburg, *The Accumulation of Capital*, Chap. 32 "Militarism as a Province of Accumulation."

129. See Michal Kalecki, "The Economic Situation in the United States as Compared with the Pre-War Period" (1956) in *The Last Phase in the Transformation of Capitalism*.

130. Michal Kalecki, "Political Aspects of Full Employment" (1943), p. 78. Kalecki followed this first intervention with three articles on the same question: "Three Ways to Full Employment" (1944), "Full Employment by Stimulating Private Investment?" (1945), "The Maintenance of Full Employment After the Transition Period: A Comparison of the Problem in the United States and United Kingdom" (1945).

131. Michal Kalecki, "Stimulating the Business Upswing in Nazi Germany" (1935), in *The Last Phase in the Transformation of Capitalism*. Surprisingly similar considerations can be found in the major work by Franz Neumann on National-Socialism (first edition, 1942), see Franz Neumann, *Behemoth. The Structure and Regime of National-Socialism, 1933–1944* (Chicago: Irvan R. Dee Publisher, 2009), p. 359.

132. Forced saving, rationing, and price and wage control were part of the program.

133. Franz Neumann, *Behemoth*, p. 277–292. Neumann insists on the fact that it obeys a strictly capitalistic logic (Part II, Chap. IV: "The Command Economy").

134. *Ibid.*, p. 337: "The worker has no rights." See the discussion that follows on the reality of the "market of free work" that is supposed to define capitalism. The absence of workers' rights also explains the generalization of performance wages (*Leistungslohn*) and an augmentation of income which, as substantial as it was, only covered half of the production gains (starting with the number of hours worked) between 1932 and 1938 (*ibid.*, p. 434–436).

135. Which Franz Neumann also noted: "Social security is its one propaganda slogan built on the truth, perhaps the one powerful weapon in its whole propagandistic machinery." (*Behemoth*, p. 432).

136. Götz Aly, *Hitler's Beneficiaries. Plunder Racial War, and the Nazi Welfare State* (New York: Henry Holt and Company, LLC, 2005), p. 72 and p. 325.

137. Victor Gollancz, *In the Darkest Germany: A Record of a Visit* (Hinsdale: Henry Regnery Co., 1947).

138. Franz Neumann, *Behemoth*, p. 475–476.

10. The Strategy Games of the Cold War

1. See Michal Kalecki, "The Economic Situation in the United States as Compared with the Pre-War Period" (1956); "The Fascism of Our Times" (1964); "Vietnam and U.S. Big Business" (1967), in The *Last Phase of the Transformation of Capitalism*.

2. Almost 60% between 1937 and 1955.

3. Giovanni Arrighi, *Adam Smith in Beijing*, p. 77.

4. *Ibid.*, p. 266.

5. *Ibid.*, p. 95. Arrighi refers this entire reasoning to Adam Smith.

6. *Ibid.*, p. 268.

7. This was the position held by the Roosevelt administration during the war. It was summarized quite acidly by Philip Wylie in his bestseller of the 1940s, *Generation of Vipers* (1942): "to many, it hardly seems worth while fighting to live until they can be assured that their percolators will live, along with their cars, synthetic roofing, and disposable diapers" (Philip Wylie, *Generation of Vipers* (New York: Rinehart, 1955), p. 236).

8. Giovanni Arrighi, *Adam Smith in Beijing*, p. 272.

9. William McNeill, cited by Giovanni Arrighi, *Adam Smith in Beijing*, p. 273.

10. See Giovanni Arrighi, *The Long Twentieth Century. Money, Power and the Origins of our Times*, p. 71: "If we designate the main thrust of British hegemony as 'imperialist,' then we have no choice but to designate the main thrust of US hegemony as 'anti-imperialist.'"

11. See for example Frances Fox Piven and Richard A. Cloward, *Poor People's Movements. Why They Succeed, How They Fail* (New York: Vintage Books, 1979). Activists in the Welfare Rights Movement, the authors trace the importance of this conflict between "organization" and "movement" throughout the 1960s and beyond.

12. Think here of Norbert Wiener's warning: "If notions [of cybernetics] please you because of their romantic name and science fiction atmosphere, stay away" (Norbert Wiener, "Automation," *Collected Works*, vol. 4 (Cambridge: MIT Press, 1985), p. 683.

13. Dominique Pestre, "Le nouvel univers des sciences et des techniques: une proposition Générale," in Amy Dahan and Dominique Pestre, *Les Sciences pour la guerre* (1940–1960) (Paris: Éditions de l'EHESS, 2004).

14. See Vannevar Bush, *Modern Arms and Free Men. A Discussion of the Role of Science in Preserving Democracy* (New York: Simon and Schuster, 1949), p. 27: "The Second World War was [...] a war of applied science." During the war, Vannevar Bush was the director of the Office of Scientific Research and Development (OSRD) which had placed the American "scientific class" under military contract, without integrating them in the army, as well as the most prestigious academic research laboratories (MIT, Princeton, Columbia, and more). They underwent unprecedented growth.

15. See Warren Weaver, "Science and Complexity," *American Scientist*, vol. 36, 1947. Mathematician, "science manager," and director of the Applied Mathematical Panel (AMP) since its foundation in 1942 as a department of the National Defense Research Committee (NDRC), Warren Weaver was closely associated with the

creation of the RAND Corporation. RAND is an acronym of Research And Development." This first post-war "think tank" was created by the US Air Force. John Von Neumann played a central role there.

16. Dominic Pestre, "Le nouvel univers des sciences et des techniques," p. 30.

17. Robert Leonard, "Théorie des jeux et psychologie sociale à la RAND," in *Les Sciences pour la guerre*, p. 85. On the matrix function of RAND in relation to the assembly (montage) and handling of the Cold War, see also Alex Abella, *Soldiers of Reason. The RAND Corporation and the Rise of American Empire* (Boston and New York: Mariner Books, 2009).

18. The Office of Naval Research (ONR) quickly became the most important organ for financing research in the United States after the war.

19. Fred Turner, *From Counterculture to Cyberculture. Stewart Brand, the Whole Earth Network, and the Rise of Digital Utopianism* (Chicago: Chicago University Press, 2006), p. 19.

20. "Women demand much more than they used to do," writes Selma James. "A Woman's Place" (1952), in *Sex, Race and Class. A Selection of Writings (1952–2011)* (Oakland: PM Press, 2012).

21. *New York Times*, July 25, 1959 (our emphasis); cited et commented par Elaine Tyler May, *Homeward Bound: American Families in the Cold War Era* (New York: Basic Books, 2008 (1988)), p. 20.

22. See Fred Turner, *The Democratic Surround. Multimedia and American Liberalism from World War II to the Psychedelic Sixties* (Chicago: University of Chicago Press, 2013), p. 157–159.

23. Clark Kerr, *The Uses of University* (Cambridge: Harvard University Press, 1963), p. 124.

24. General Dwight D. Eisenhower, *Memorandum for Directors and Chiefs of War Department, General and Special Staff Divisions and Bureaus and the Commanding Generals of the Major Commands* (1946). *Subject: Scientific and Technological Resources as Military Assets.*

25. To borrow the expression of Talcott Parsons.

26. Letter of William D. Hamilton to George Price, March 21, 1968.

27. Gilles Deleuze and Félix Guattari, *A Thousand Plateaus*, p. 454.

28. See Amy Dahan, "Axiomatiser, modéliser, calculer: les mathématiques, instrument universel et polymorphe d'action," in *Les Sciences pour la guerre*, p. 51.

29. Gilles Deleuze and Félix Guattari, *A Thousand Plateaus*, p. 458.

30. Judy L. Klein, Rebecca Lemov, Michael D. Gordin, Lorraine Daston, Paul Erickson and Thomas Sturm, *How Reason Almost Lost Its Mind: The Strange Career of Cold War Rationality* (Chicago: University of Chicago Press, 2013), p. 114.

31. See Elaine Tyler May, *Homeward Bound*, Chap. 1.

32. Warren Weaver, cited by Philip Mirowski, *Machine Dreams: Economics Becomes a Cyborg Science* (Cambridge: Cambridge University Press, 2002), p. 210 and p. 169 on "Warren Weaver, Grandmaster Cyborg."

33. See David F. Noble, *Forces of Production. A Social History of Industrial Automation* (Oxford: Oxford University Press, 1984), p. 3.

34. Which gave him control over all of the federal political economy.

35. "Electric Charlie" immediately recruited as vice-presidents of GE two other executives of the War Production Board: Ralph Cordiner, who followed him at the head of GE, and Lemuel Boulware. The most prestigious of GE's publications, titled *General Electric Forum, Defense Quarterly*, is subtitled "*For National Security and Free World Progress.*"

36. Michael Hardt and Antonio Negri, *Empire* (Cambridge: Harvard University Press, 2001), p. 246 et seq.

37. George Orwell, "You and the Atomic Bomb," *Tribune*, October 19, 1945.

38. Published in 1948, *1984* (1948 "in reverse") collapses Americanism and socialism together so violently that the book had the rare privilege of being both denounced in the USA and unpublished in the Soviet Union.

39. "President Harry S. Truman's Address before a Joint Session of Congress," March 12, 1947 (URL: trumanlibrary.org/publicpapers/index.php?pid=2189&st=&st1=).

40. See Walter Lippmann, *The Cold War. A Study in U. S. Foreign Policy* (New York: Harper & Brothers, 1947). The demonstration could draw on the famous "Moscow telegram" sent by George Kennan. This American diplomat emphasized the "feeling of insecurity" at the Kremlin and the importance of "Russian nationalism."

41. According to the presentation of Léon Rougier at the start of the Walter Lippmann conference held in Paris from August 28–30, 1938. This conference has often been presented as the primitive scene of "neo-liberalism" (the term was used by Rougier but not unanimously accepted).

42. "Communism is twentieth-century Americanism," declared the president of the American Communist Party, Earl Browder.

43. Eric Hobsbawm, *Age of Extremes. The Short Twentieth Century (1914–1991)* (London: Abacus, 1994), p. 168. The global socialist revolution was abandoned for national independence.

44. *Ibid.*, p. 226–228 ("Until the 1970s this tacit agreement to treat the Cold War as a Cold Peace held good"). The expression "Cold Peace" started to be used in 1950.

45. The Soviet nuclear arsenal did not pose a technologically credible threat to American territory until the mid-1960s.

46. As Castoriadis wrote in 1976, there was "little doubt that Reagan and Brezhnev would agree on Hungary" (Cornelius Castoriadis, "La source hongroise," *Libre*, 1, 1977).

47. Speech by Secretary of State John Foster Dulles before the Council on Foreign Relations (January 12, 1954). Our emphasis.

48. Paul Virilio and Sylvère Lotringer, *Pure War* (Los Angeles: Semiotext(e), 2008), p. 68.

49. The threat of mutiny caused the demobilization to be accelerated. The 10 million soldiers demobilized represented 20% of the American work force in 1945.

50. More than 2 million women workers were sent home between 1945 and 1947. During these same years, the women who stayed in factories, offices, or in commercial positions saw their salaries drop by more than 25% compared to the war years.

51. Mario Tronti, *Operai e capitale* (Turin: Einaudi, 1966) [French Edition: *Ouvriers et capital* (Paris: Christian Bourgois Éditeur, 1977)]. The Bureau of Labor Statistics counted 116 million days on strike for the year 1946. The city of Detroit represented the world capital of automobiles, the leading post-war industry, and one of the birthplaces of the "military-industrial complex." During the war, Detroit was known as the "arsenal of democracy."

52. *Time* (for the previous quote) and *Life* magazines were cited by David F. Noble, *Forces of Production*, p. 22 and p. 27.

53. Whiting Williams, "The Public is Fed Up with the Union Mess," *Factory Management and Maintenance*, vol. 104, January 1946.

54. The "electricians'" union—United Electrical, Radio and Machine Workers of America (UE)—had in fact the strongest communist leadership in the United States. As Ronald W. Schwartz said in his analysis of the hearings before the House Committee on Un-American Activities, "If any people stood out as targets in this era, surely it was the leaders of the UE" (see Ronald W. Schwartz, *The Electrical Workers. A History of Labor at General Electric and Westinghouse (1923–60)* (Urbana, IL: University of Illinois Press, 1983), p. 175).

55. We have already seen that other than its "anti-communist" clause, the Taft-Hartley Act brought an end to the "closed shop" system that required union membership. It also imposed 80 days advanced notice in sectors of "national interest."

56. Created in the name of Lemuel Boulware. Or how to gain the loyalty of workers and fight against the influence of unions (before absorbing them): an iron hand ("take-it-or-leave-it" in union terms) in a velvet glove ("The Silk Glove of the Company"). We will return to the subject of Boulwarism later.

57. David F. Noble, *Forces of Production*, Chap. 7, in particular p. 155–167, 190–192.

58. What else could be meant by the demand by American workers to *open the company accounting books* other than *labor power*? Something Tronti explained as follows: "reading Marx in things."

59. The Full Employment Bill of 1945, giving the "right to useful, remunerative, regular, and full-time employment," became the 1946 Employment Act. The latter states that it is the "responsibility of the federal government to [...] promote free and competitive enterprise [...] under which there will be afforded useful employment for those able, willing, and seeking work." As a Democratic senator said in denouncing the pressure by Republicans in the Senate to empty the bill of its substance, "in the end, it was just saying that someone who had no job had the right to look for one!"

60. The statistics on the working world were however quite elegant: between 1940 and 1945, workplace accidents accounted for 88,000 deaths and 11 million injuries.

61. Press conference on December 12, 1946.

62. Address by President Truman to a Joint Session of Congress on March 12, 1947.

63. As Henry Morgenthau, as Secretary of the Treasury under Franklin D. Roosevelt, suggested in 1945.

64. As described by Giovanni Arrighi, *Adam Smith in Beijing*, p. 251.

65. Roosevelt's "Four Freedoms Speech," which presented (before Pearl Harbor) the principles and urgency of a war New Deal both internally and externally, included this pivotal phrase, on which the entire speech was based: "That is no vision of a distant millennium. It is a definite basis for a kind of world attainable in our own time and generation."

66. Michael Howard insists on the fact that during the war, "The real obstacle to the implementation of the new world order was seen by many American liberals to lie in Britain, with her economic zone of imperial preference, with her sterling area, with her Machiavellian skill at power politics, with her colonial empire holding millions of the coloured races in subjection." *War and the Liberal Conscience* (London: Temple Smith, 1978), p. 118.

67. Franz Schurmann, *The Logic of World Power: An Inquiry into the Origins, Currents, and Contradictions of World Politics* (New York: Pantheon Books, 1974), p. 67.

68. Giovanni Arrighi, *Adam Smith in Beijing*, p. 253. See also *The Long Twentieth Century*, p. 286.

69. In texts from 1949, C.L.R. James already described welfare policies as a "swindle," and more generally about the Democratic Party in relation to Blacks: "And it is the Democratic Party, Franklin Roosevelt's party which controls the state governments in the South."

70. See the article by C.L.R. James after the riots in Detroit "The Race Pogroms and the Negroes" (1943) in *C.L.R. James on the "Negro Question"* (Jackson, MS: University Press of Mississippi, 1996), p. 36–46.

71. After the "hate strikes" of the war years and the race war that they unleashed, there was a wave of "white death" organized by the Ku Klux Klan. Its first targets were Black veterans returning to southern states.

72. Thomas Borstelmann, *The Cold War and the Color Line. American Race Relations in the Global Arena* (Cambridge: Harvard University Press, 2001), p. 29. "Freedom from fear" is the fourth of Roosevelt's great freedoms alongside the freedom of speech, freedom of religion, and "freedom from want."

73. The only African-American organization that participated in the founding conference of the United Nations, the delegation of the Council on African Affairs (CAA) argued that the representation of nation-states in the General Assembly alone amounted to exclusion of colonized peoples or any ethnic group subject to state discrimination.

74. "We must correct the remaining imperfections in our practice of democracy," asserted Truman in his speech to civil rights on February 2, 1948. Truman found no one better than Charles E. Watson, the president of General Electric, to... preside over the committee in the question of civil rights.

75. Including Walter White, Executive Secretary of the National Association for the Advancement of Colored People (NAACP), who we mentioned previously. Du Bois resigned from the NAACP as a result in 1948.

76. Truman, for example, refused to have the federal government endorse an anti-lynching bill.

77. "President's Committee on Equality of Treatment and Opportunity in the Armed Service." The process continued until the mid-1950s. The army became the laboratory for the integration of a society divided by segregation.

78. In his speech to the Convention of the CIO in 1947, Secretary of State Marshall explicitly linked support of the aid plan to the expulsion of "subversive" elements from the union. Which occurred in the anti-communist purges of 1949. Anti-colonialism was only tolerated on the condition of being aligned with the "foreign policy" of the Cold War.

79. George Kennan, for example, explicitly integrated the racial question into "national security."

80. In 1960, 41% of the Black population of Detroit was unemployed and only benefitted slightly from a "welfare" for which the restrictions aimed to maintain a "reserve army" of the underclass, exploited at will.

81. Cited in Thomas Borstelmann, *The Cold War and the Color Line*, p. 205. See the speech in homage to Stokely Carmichael by C.L.R. James in 1967 in Great Britain (where the activist was banned from entering), "Black Power," in *C.L.R. James on the Negro Question*.

82. Gary Becker, *The Economics of Discrimination* (Chicago: University of Chicago Press, 1957).

83. These programs to combat "juvenile delinquency" and gangs developed in the early 1960s drove most of the measures associated with the "Great Society."

84. Paul N. Edwards, *The Closed World: Computers and the Politics of Discourse in Cold War America* (Cambridge: MIT Press, 1996), p. 8.

85. See Michael Hardt and Antonio Negri, *Multitude* (New York: Penguin, 2004), p. 41. For Hardt and Negri, the Cold War is too "static" and "dialectical" to become "productive" in an "ontological" sense.

86. Elaine Tyler May, *Homeward Bound*, p. 186. This march took place on November 1, 1961. On the co-opting of the peace marches of women's organizations by the American government (and the repression of activists and recalcitrant groups), see Helen Laville, *Cold War Women. The International Activities of American Women's Organization* (Manchester: Manchester University Press, 2002).

87. J. Edgar Hoover pretended to address "career women" in 1956 in his discourse to the National Council of Catholic Women. As he explained: "I say 'career' women because I feel there are no careers so important as those of homemaker and mother" (cited by Elaine Tyler May, *Homeward Bound*, p. 132). The speech had the title "Crime and Communism."

88. See Frances Fox Piven and Richard A. Cloward, *Poor People's Movements. Why They Succeed, How They Fail*, chap. 5. The chapter opens with the "myopia" of the histories of the civil rights movements in relation to this economic component that nonetheless overdetermined the years 1964–1968.

89. Silvia Federici, *Revolution at Point Zero: Housework, Reproduction, and Feminist Struggle* (Oakland, CA: PM Press, 2012), p. 7.

90. Selma James, *The Power of Women and the Subversion of the Community* (1972), reprinted in *Sex, Race and Class*, p. 50–51.

91. See the different explanations by Selma James with the new editions of *The Power of Women and the Subversion of the Community*, p. 43. That being said (and

remembered), we gladly recognize that one must keep two options open to account for the political importance of the meeting between the American movement and the Italian movement (without contest, the most "advanced" class struggle in Europe).

92. Truman's speech on March 12, 1947.

93. "People's Capitalism" is the title of a "truth campaign" launched in 1955–1956 by and adviser to President Eisenhower, Theodore S. Repplier, which took the form of an international exhibition. It was presented in South America and in Ceylon. See Laura A. Belmonte, *Selling the American Way. U.S. Propaganda and the Cold War* (Philadelphia: University of Pennsylvania Press, 2008), p. 131–135. The quote "security and challenge in the same breath" comes from an article in *Collier's* magazine, "'People's Capitalism'—This IS America." The theme (and the expression) of "People's Capitalism" is at the heart of the Nixonian contribution to the Kitchen Debate with Khrushchev.

94. The term itself was propagated as a *détournement* and reversal of the people's role in "bourgeois democracy" promoted by the "capitalists of Wall Street." On the American side, it was explained that the word people had to be retaken from the Russians who had "kidnapped" it: isn't it the epitome of an American word, the one that opens the Constitution of the United States ("We, the people") and which is at the heart of the definition of democracy as defined by Lincoln ("government of the people, by the people, and for the people")? See the speech by Theodore Repplier, October 27, 1955, cited by Laura A. Belmonte, *Selling the American Way*, p. 131.

95. Harry S. Truman, "Address on Foreign Policy at a Luncheon of the American Society of Newspaper Editors," April 20, 1950.

96. Cited by Charles S. Maier, *In Search of Stability: Explorations in Historical Political Economy* (Cambridge: Cambridge University Press, 1987), p. 65.

97. See Nelson Lichtenstein, "From Corporatism to Collective Bargaining: Organized Labor and the Eclipse of Social Democracy in the Postwar Era," in Steve Fraser and Gary Gerstle, *The Rise and Fall of the New Deal Order (1930–1980)* (Princeton: Princeton University Press, 1989), p. 140–145.

98. A year after the merger of the two unions, the president of the AFL-CIO could declare in 1956: "In the final analysis, there is no great deal of difference between the things I stand for and the things that the National Association of Manufacturers stand for" (cited by Frances Fox Piven and Richard A. Cloward, *Poor People's Movements*, p. 157).

99. Leo Panitch and Sam Gindin, *The Making of Global Capitalism. The Political Economy of American Empire* (New York: Verso, 2013), p. 84.

100. In his 1956 article, "The Economic Situation in the United States as Compared with the Pre-War Period," Michal Kalecki considered that unions were "part

and parcel of the armament-imperialist set-up" (in *The Last Phase of the Transformation of Capitalism*, p. 96).

101. NSC-68. Report 68 of the National Security Council under President Truman (April 14, 1950, final approval September 30, 1950). Composed by Paul H. Nitze, the NSC-68 report carries the mark of the RAND Corporation's geostrategic anti-communism.

102. United States Information Agency Basic Guidance and Planning Paper, 11, "The American Economy," July 16, 1959, cited by Laura A. Belmonte, "Selling Capitalism," p. 110.

103. United States Information Agency (USIA), *American Labor Unions: Their Role in the Free World*, cited by Laura A. Belmonte, "Selling Capitalism," p. 113.

104. See the brilliant analysis by Kristin Ross, *Fast Cars, Clean Bodies: Decolonization and the Reordering of French Culture* (Cambridge: MIT Press, 1995).

105. *Ibid.*, p. 107.

106. To borrow the title of an article published in the *Air Bulletin* of the State Department (September 12, 1947), which served as a permanent column for the activities of the USIA.

107. These are some of the titles of the pamphlets developed and distributed by the USIA.

108. Song from the film *Sing Your Way Home*, a "hit tune" in September 1945.

109. With fourteen days of privacy guaranteed by the anti-atomic shelter where a honeymoon took place for a report in *Life* magazine (August 10, 1959).

110. Elaine Tyler May, *Homeward Bound*, p. 11.

111. See Ira Katznelson, "Was the Great Society a Lost Opportunity?" in *The Rise and Fall of the New Deal Order*, p. 202–203.

112. See Thomas J. Sugrue, *The Origins of the Urban Crisis. Race and Inequality in Postwar Detroit* (Princeton: Princeton University Press, 2014), chap. 7.

113. *Ibid.*, p. 226–227. A poll conducted in 1964 showed that 89% of those living in the North of the United States and 96% in the South thought that an owner should not be forced by law to sell his or her property to a Black person if he or she did not want to do so.

114. *Ibid.*, p. 250.

115. The brochures of the USIA on the activities of women in the United States tried to justify the differences in salaries (men/women) by the privilege accorded family life: women do not plan their education with a "career plan in mind" and

enter the job market "periodically." Moreover, management of domestic life (a housewife was supposed to be "a good manager in the home," or the contrary of an *unpaid laborer*) was presented as "hard work."

116. There is abundant documentation in Thomas E. Ewans, *The Education of Ronald Reagan. The General Electric Years* (New York: Columbia University Press, 2006). Elaine Tyler May sees in Reagan's *General Electric Theater* the prototype of the values of the "model home" promoted by Nixon in the Kitchen Debate (Elaine Tyler May, *Homeward Bound*, p. 215).

117. Lemuel Boulware, "Salvation is Not Free," Harvard University, June 11, 1949. Reprinted in Thomas E. Evans, *The Education of Ronald Reagan*, p. 234–237.

118. According to a document from 1946 by the Associated Industries of Cleveland, cited by Elizabeth A. Fones-Wolf, *Selling Free Enterprise. The Business Assault on Labor and Liberalism (1945–1960)* (Urbana, IL: University of Illinois Press, 1994), p. 160–161.

119. In passing, it can be noted that while slavery was the absolute antithesis of democracy, "popular democracies" were denied their very existence as people-*demos*. As such, they carried the name so poorly that it is hard to see how they could liberate themselves. Which suited the two superpowers just fine.

120. After a conference to promote *The Road to Serfdom* in Detroit on April 23, 1945, Hayek met Harold Luhnow, president of the Volker Fund, who would generously finance and pair the two startups of American neoliberalism: the Chicago School of Economics and the Société du Mont-Pèlerin, established in Switzerland in 1947.

121. See Fred L. Block, *The Origins of International Economic Disorder: Study of United States International Monetary Policy from World War II to the Present* (Berkeley: University of California Press, 1977), p. 104: "the close integration of European and American military forces [...] would provide a means to prevent Europe as an economic region from closing itself off from the United States."

122. Cited by Leo Panitch and Sam Gindin, *The Making of Global Capitalism*, p. 97–98.

123. The Marshall Plan called for productivity "missions" to the United States and interventions by American "experts" in Europe orchestrated by the Organization for European Economic Co-operation (OEEC). It was established in April 16, 1948 as a condition of the Marshall Plan. The same year, a working group on productivity was created in France in the *Commissariat général au Plan* headed by Jean Fourastié, establishing the "French program for productivity." It led to the creation in 1953 of the *Commissariat général à la Productivité* that produced the institutional synthesis of the "dialectic of Market and Plan" (Giovanni Arrighi). American technical aid provided for the year an amount of 30 million dollars in loans and loan guarantees

to private companies that engage in "improving productivity" and "establishing appropriate arrangements for a fair distribution of benefits resulting from the increase in production and productivity between *consumers, workers, and bosses*" (our emphasis). This aid was to allow the "financing of projects capable of stimulating a free enterprise economy." The creation of the first schools of management was supported by the European Productivity Agency, which, starting in 1956, organized the sending of future professors for one-year training periods in American universities. See Luc Boltanski, "America, America... Le plan Marshall et l'importation du 'management,'" *Actes de la recherche en sciences sociales*, 38, May 1981.

124. Econometrics was developed in parallel with operational research, with which it was associated in the early 1940s in the context of the Statistical Research Group (SRG). It was under the Applied Mathematical Panel (AMP) established by Warren Weaver. According to Philip Mirowski, the Chicago School, which developed there, was nothing more than the feedback of Operational Research into the economy.

125. "Strength for the Long Run": the title of a report by the Office of Defense Mobilization, April 1952.

126. The (new) discipline flourished in the United States in the 1960s.

127. See Deborah Cowen, *The Deadly Life of Logistics. Mapping Violence in Global Trade* (Minneapolis: University of Minnesota Press, 2014).

128. Organized in 1960 by the International Union of Electrical Workers (IUE), which seceded from the UE in an anti-communist attack, the second national strike at General Electric (after 1946) met with bitter failure.

129. Sylvia Federici, *Revolution at Point Zero*, p. 5.

130. *Ibid.*, p. 6.

11. Clausewitz and '68 Thought (*la pensée 68*)

1. André Fontaine, *La Guerre civile froide* (Paris: Fayard, 1969).

2. Carl Schmitt, *Theory of the Partisan*.

3. According to the summary proposed by Raymond Aron in *Penser la Guerre, Clausewitz, t. II: L'âge planétaire* (Paris: Gallimard, 1976), p. 75.

4. See T. Derbent, Clausewitz, "Mao et le maoïsme," 2013 (URL: www.agota.be/t.derbent/articles/MaoClaus.pdf).

5. Quoted by T. Derbent, *Giap et Clausewitz* (Brussels: Aden, 2006), p. 47.

6. See André Glucksmann, *Le Discours de la guerre* (Paris: UGE, 1974), p. 389 ("Autour d'une pensée de Mao Tse-toung").

7. Cited by Daniel Defert, "Chronologie," in Michel Foucault, *Dits et écrits*, t. I, p. 57.

8. With the "war of all against all," "we are in a theater where presentations are exchanged, in a relationship of fear in which there are no time limits; we are not really involved in a war," Foucault explains in his course at the Collège de France in 1976. See Michel Foucault, *"Society Must Be Defended,"* p. 92.

9. Michel Foucault, *The Punitive Society*, p. 22.

10. *Ibid.*, p. 32.

11. *Ibid.*, p. 13.

12. *Ibid.*, p. 32.

13. The explanation that Foucault sometimes gives is particularly interesting here: "Example of the army: We may say that the disciplinarization of the army is due to its control by the state (*étatisation*). However, when disciplinarization is connected, [not] with a concentration of state control, but with the problem of floating populations, the importance of commercial networks, technical inventions, models [several illegible words] community management, a whole network of alliance, support, and communication constitutes the 'genealogy' of military discipline. Not the genesis: filiation." Michel Foucault, *Security, Territory, Population*, p. 165, note.

14. *Ibid.*, p. 388.

15. *Ibid.*, p. 392.

16. Michel Foucault, *"Society Must Be Defended,"* p. 49 (lecture of January 21, 1976) (our emphasis). You will have noted that this first discourse on "society" said the opposite of the liberal discourse on "civil society" that completely eclipsed the first in *The Birth of Biopolitics*.

17. *Ibid.*, p. 48.

18. According to the expression used by Étienne Balibar, "Foucault and Marx: The Question of Nominalism" in *Michel Foucault, Philosopher* (Hertfordshire: Harvester Wheatsheaf, 1992), p. 51. Balibar perfectly observes that "'Discipline' and 'micro-power' therefore represent *at the same time* the other side of economic exploitation and the other side of juridico-political class domination, which they make it possible to see as a unity; that is to say, they come into play exactly at the point of the 'short circuit' which Marx sets up between economics and politics, society and State, in his analysis of the process of production (thus permitting us to see it in terms of a 'practice')."

19. Michel Foucault, *"Society Must Be Defended,"* p. 58.

20. See Michel Foucault, *Security, Territory, Population*, p. 144.

21. Michel Foucault, "The Subject and Power," *Critical Inquiry*, 8, 4 (Summer 1982), p. 789.

22. Michel Foucault, *The History of Sexuality*, vol. 1, p. 93.

23. Michel Foucault, "The Subject and Power," p. 794.

24. *Idem*. (Our emphasis).

25. Capitalizing the totalization of war (total war), the Cold War/Peace can be taken for the moment when this strategy of *absolute* reversibility, "without remainder," of wars and power was established.

26. Michel Foucault, *The Birth of Biopolitics*, p. 259–260 (lesson of March 21, 1979). On the liberal utopia formulated by Hayek, see the lesson of March 14, 1979 (p. 218–219).

27. See Michel Foucault, "La grande colère des faits" (on André Glucksmann, *Les Maîtres penseurs*, Paris, Grasset, 1977), in *Dits et écrits*, t. II, 204.

28. According to Michel Foucault's expression in "Maurice Blanchot: The Thought from Outside" (1966) in *Foucault-Blanchot* (New York: Zone Books, 1987).

29. See Gilles Deleuze, Félix Guattari, *A Thousand Plateaus*, p. 357–359 and p. 429–430 for a critical discussion of the "evolutionist" theses of Pierre Clastres: "*Everything is not of the State precisely because there have been States always and every-where.*"

30. *Ibid.*, p. 423.

31. *Ibid.*, p. 230.

32. The following quotes are taken from two courses (sessions 12–13) of the 1979–1980 university year ("Deleuze: Appareils d'État et machines de guerre," URL: www.youtube.com/watch?v=kgWaov-IUrA).

33. As above (see 9.5), Deleuze moves away from the common translation (that we used) of the two Clausewitzian terms that oppose the political "end" (*Zweck*) to the military "goal" (*Ziel*). We should note that in standard (non-"Kantian") German, *Ziel* is "target" and *Zweck*, "goal."

34. We will recall that Napoleon's overturning of the European inter-state equilibrium at the time did not occur without a revolution in the art of war.

35. Carl Schmitt, "The Changing Structure of International Law" (1943); Ernst Jünger, *Peace* (1945); Hannah Arendt, *On Revolution* (1961); Carl Schmitt, *Theory of the Partisan* (1963).

36. Clausewitz, *On War*, I, 2.

37. Gilles Deleuze and Félix Guattari, *A Thousand Plateaus*, p. 467.

38. *Ibid.*, p. 571, note 64.

39. *Ibid.*, p. 466.

40. *Ibid.*, p. 467.

12. The Fractal Wars of Capital

1. See Giorgio Agamben, *State of Exception* (Chicago: University of Chicago Press, 2005), p. 23: "If the state of exception's characteristic property is a (total or partial) suspension of the juridical order, how can such a suspension still be contained within it? [...] And if the state of exception is instead only a de facto situation, and is as such unrelated or contrary to law, how is it possible for the order to contain a lacuna precisely where the decisive situation is concerned?" It follows that "[t]he essential task of a theory of the state of exception is not simply to clarify whether it has a juridical nature or not, but to define the meaning, place, and modes of its relation to the law." (p. 51)

2. According to a speech by the President of the French Republic to Parliament gathered in Congress in Versailles on November 16, 2015. What some have called a "light" state of emergency can therefore be established for the long term, according to characteristics that resembled the American Patriot Act, established on October 26, 2001 by George W. Bush after the September 11, 2001 attacks. This attenuation is in itself a fiction *and, "for itself," a juridical fiction.*

3. 2017 addition: Since November 1, 2017, the state of emergency in France has made way for an anti-terrorism law that increases the power of administrative authorities to the detriment of judicial power.

4. Giorgio Agamben, *State of Exception*, p. 50.

5. *Ibid.*, p. 86–87.

6. General Jean Nemo, "La guerre dans le milieu social," *Revue de Défense nationale*, May 1956.

7. Michel Foucault, *The Birth of Biopolitics*, p. 132.

8. Nicolas Roussellier, *La Force de gouverner. Le pouvoir exécutif en France, XIXe–XXIe siècles* (Paris: Gallimard, 2015), p. 346–348.

9. *Ibid.*, p. 414.

10. Carl Schmitt, "The Plight of European Jurisprudence," *Telos* March 20 (1990): p. 50.

11. *Ibid.*, p. 53.

12. Pietro Grifone, *Il capitale finanziario in Italia* (Rome: Einaudi, 1971), p. 24.

13. Nicolas Roussellier, *La Force de gouverner*, p. 414. Here we find David F. Noble's grand thesis.

14. *Ibid.*, p. 413.

15. *Ibid.*, p. 414.

16. *Ibid.*, p. 415.

17. Paul Virilio, *Pure War*, p. 35.

18. Nicolas Roussellier, *La Force de gouverner*, p. 415.

19. Philip Mirowski, "Postface: Defining Neoliberalism," in Philip Mirowski and Dieter Plehwe (eds.), *The Road from Mont-Pèlerin*, p. 449, n. 31.

20. Nicolas Roussellier, *La Force de gouverner*, p. 402. It could almost be read as a paraphrase of de Gaulle himself, whose lack of appetite for the "republican thing" was well known (de Gaulle, staunch enemy of the Fourth Republic).

21. *Ibid.*, p. 391.

22. *Ibid.*, p. 404.

23. Carl Schmitt, *Political Theology*, cited by Giorgio Agamben, *State of Exception*, p. 34.

24. Giorgio Agamben, *State of Exception*, p. 86.

25. Nicolas Roussellier, *La Force de gouverner*, p. 398.

26. Michel Foucault, *The Birth of Biopolitics*, p. 131.

27. Qiao Liang and Wang Xiangsui, *Unrestricted Warfare* (Beijing: PLA Literature and Arts Publishing House, February 1999), p. 116.

28. *Ibid.*, p. 117.

29. *Ibid.*, p. 221.

30. Rupert Smith, *The Utility of Force. The Art of War in the Modern World* (London: Allen Lane, 2005), p. 292.

31. Qiao Liang and Wang Xiangsui, *Unrestricted Warfare*, p. 185.

32. *Idem.*

33. *Ibid.*, p. 221.

34. This was the basis of the *El Ladrillo* plan developed in 1973 by members of the Economics Department of the Pontifical Catholic University, which had been associated with the University of Chicago since 1956. The plan called for a type of *shock therapy* inspired by Friedman that was actively supported by the IMF starting in

1975, the date of its full implementation. Inspired by Hayek's *Constitution of Liberty* even in its title, Chile's constitution of 1980 made room for the need for a strong state to guarantee free enterprise and the market. See Karin Fisher, "The Influence of Neoliberals in Chile Before, During, and After Pinochet," in *The Road from Mont-Pèlerin*.

35. Translator's Note: Sir Rupert Smith's concept of "war amongst the people," while essential to this context, does not account for the Foucaldian and Marxian discussion of "population" that has been developed throughout this book. For this reason, I have decided to use "war amongst the population" in this translation to connect the concept to these discussions and to align with the French "guerre au sein de la population," and to make the colonial origin of the expression much more immediate.

36. See Vincent Desportes, *Le Piège américain. Pourquoi les États-Unis peuvent perdre les guerres d'aujourd'hui* (Paris: Economica, 2011), p. 259.

37. Sir Rupert Smith had different commands in Asia and Africa, during the first Gulf War, in Bosnia-Herzegovina, Northern Ireland, and elsewhere, and ended his career as Deputy Supreme Allied Commander Europe (1998–2001). Since 2006, he is one of the international advisers to the International Committee of the Red Cross (ICRC).

38. "War amongst the population" (*guerre au sein de la population*) is at the heart of Manual FT-01 (*Gagner la bataille—Conduire la paix*) published in 2007 by the Forces Employment Doctrine Center of the French army. The manual was prepared under the direction of General Desportes.

39. See the very convincing reconstruction of the architecture of network-centric warfare proposed by Noah Shachtman, "How Technology Almost Lost the War: In Iraq, the Networks are Social—Not Electronic," *Wired*, 15, 12 (2007): "If that company [Wal-Mart] could wire everyone together and become more efficient, then US forces could, too. [...] Computer networks and the efficient flow of information would turn America's chain saw of a war machine into a scalpel." The Wal-Mart model was put forward in the intervention-manifesto of Arthur K. Cebrowski and John J. Gartska, "Network-Centric Warfare: Its Origin and Future," (January 1998, URL: www.kinection.com/ncoic/ncw_origin_future.pdf), which contains the quote used at the beginning of this chapter.

40. Henry Kissinger, *American Foreign Policy* (New York: W. W. Norton, 1974), p. 57.

41. Williamson Murray, "Does Military Culture Matter?" *Orbis* 43, no. 1 (Winter 1999), p. 27–42. His article "Clausewitz Out, Computer In. Military Culture and Technological Hubris," is available online (URL: HYPERLINK "http://www.clausewitz.com/readings/Clause%26Computers.htm"www.clausewitz.com/readings/Clause%26Computers.htm).

42. According to the belated observation of American commanders in Iraq (as reported by Noah Shachtman, "How Technology Almost Lost the War").

43. Quoted by Noah Shachtman, "How Technology Almost Lost the War" (our emphasis).

44. Under these conditions, given the asymmetry of forces on the ground, the US war machine could even easily surpass and *hyper-accelerate* the time of business subject to "real" competition: "Lock-out [of a product] often takes years to achieve in business, but in warfare it can be achieved *in weeks or less*" (Arthur K. Cebrowski and John J. Gartska, "Network-Centric Warfare" (our emphasis)).

45. *Ibid.*

46. "The fact is, today we rely on our troops to perform all sort of missions that are only loosely connected with traditional combat but are vital to maintaining world security" (Noah Shachtman, "How Technology Almost Lost the War").

47. Rupert Smith, *The Utility of Force*, p. 271.

48. *Ibid.*, p. 6.

49. SPR, then SPIN (segmented, polycentric, integrated network) in the Anglo-Saxon literature.

50. Rupert Smith, *The Utility of War*, p. 281.

51. Vincent Desportes, *La Guerre probable. Penser autrement* (Paris: Economica, 2007), p. 58. [Translated into English as *Tomorrow's War. Thinking otherwise* (Paris: Economica, 2009)]

52. *Idem.*

53. Rupert Smith, *The Utility of Force*, p. 272.

54. Vincent Desportes, *Le Piège américain*, p. 140–141.

55. *Ibid.*, p. 266–270.

56. Vincent Desportes, *La Guerre probable*, p. 206 (our emphasis).

57. *Ibid.*, p. 61, 64.

58. Paul Virilio, *Pure War*, p. 125.

59. Jean-Christophe Bailly, "La ville neutralisée," *in* Guillaume Greff, *Dead Cities* (Paris: Éditions Kaiserin, 2013), vol. I, non-paginated: "la ville au rabais devient la norme de la ville rabaissée."

60. Vincent Desportes, *La Guerre probable*, p. 88.

61. *Ibid.*, p. 93, 65, 62.

62. See Roberto J. Gonzalez, "The Rise and Fall of the Human Terrain System," *Counterpunch*, June 29, 2015 (URL: www.counterpunch.org/2015/06/29/the-rise-and-fall-of-the-human-terrain-system).

63. *ISAF Commander's Counterinsurgency Guidance*, September 2009.

64. Cited in Vicent Desportes, *Le Piège américain*, p. 264–265. We can be skeptical of the reality of the break with an ethnocentrist conception of the world that has continued to feed and extend into this moral and security vision of "just war" found in the American armed forces. It was accompanied with more diplomacy by the Obama administration and then by the European members of the coalition after him.

65. "Surge" (like a power surge responding to in*surge*ncy) is the codename in manifesto form of the new American strategy in Iraq initiated by General Petraeus. As he explains in multiple interviews (the operation is over-mediatized), the goal is to put "coalition soldiers" *amongst the people*.

66. See Georges-Henri Brisset des Vallons, "La doctrine de contre-insurrection américaine," *in* Georges-Henri Brisset des Vallons (ed.), *Faut-il brûler la contre-insurrection?* (Paris: Choiseul, 2010).

67. Vincent Desportes, *La Guerre probable*, p. 63.

68. *Ibid.*, p. 135.

69. Harlan K. Ullman and James P. Wade, *Shock and Awe: Achieving Rapid Dominance* (Washington, DC: National Defense University Press, 1996), p. 83–84, p. xvii, p. xxiv.

70. We have taken the liberty of reversing the meaning of Brian Massumi's expression by setting it counter to the "Shock and Awe" doctrine; see *Ontopower. Wars, Power and the State of Perception* (Durham, NC: Duke University Press, 2015), p. 73.

71. Michel Foucault, *Security, Territory, Population*, p. 75, 272.

72. Marshall McLuhan and Quentin Fiore, *War and Peace in the Global Village* (New York: Touchstone, 1989 (1st ed. 1968), p. 134.

73. Hannah Arendt, "Lying in Politics: Reflections on the Pentagon Papers," in *Crises of the Republic* (San Diego: Harcourt Brace, 1972), p. 18.

74. Rupert Smith, *The Utility of Force*, p. 19.

75. John Arquilla and David Ronfeldt, *Networks and Netwars*, Prepared for the Office of the Secretary Defense, National Defense Research Institute (Rand, 2001), p. 1–2.

76. Rupert Smith, *The Utility of Force*, p. 183.

77. *Ibid.*, p. 294.

78. Vincent Desportes, *La Guerre probable*, p. 77.

79. Following the attacks in November 2015, it only took a few hours for French Socialists to discover and mediatize this strategic truth of the "long war" on terrorism.

80. Martin Heidegger, "Overcoming Metaphysics" in *The End of Philosophy* (New York: Harper & Row, 1973), p. 104–105. See also Ernst Jünger, *The Worker. Dominion and Form* (Evanston, IL: Northwestern University Press, 2017),§49.

81. See Boutros Boutros-Ghali, *An Agenda for Peace: Preventive Diplomacy, Peacemaking, and Peace-Keeping* (New York: United Nations, 1992).

82. See for example Field Manual 100–20 (Military Operations in Low Intensity Conflict) from 1990, the first chapter of which opens with a quote from Clausewitz on the "political goal" of war and the way it must determine the quantity of military force to be used (URL: library.enlistment.us/field-manuals/series-3/FM100-20/CHAP1.PDF).

83. Jeff Halper, *War Against the People. Israel, the Palestinians and Global Pacification* (London: Pluto Press, 2015), p. 16–27.

84. Without counting the *invasions* of Afghanistan and Iraq, American military personnel have been (officially) *deployed* between 2000 and 2014 in Sierra Leone, Côte d'Ivoire, Nigeria, Liberia, Chad, Mali, Uganda, Libya, Somalia, Pakistan, Yemen, Bosnia, Georgia, East Timor, the Philippines, Haiti…

85. Sylvia Federici, "War Globalization, and Reproduction" in *Revolution at Point Zero*, p. 79, 80, 83.

86. Arundhati Roy, *Capitalism: A Ghost Story* (Chicago: Haymarket Books, 2014), p. 1, 6.

87. Gilles Deleuze, "Postscript on Control Societies," in *Negotiations* (New York: Columbia University Press, 1995), p. 181.

88. Arundhati Roy, *Capitalism: A Ghost Story*, p. 20.

89. See Arundhati Roy, "Walking with the Comrades," *Outlook*, March 29, 2010.

90. See Laleh Kalili, *Time in the Shadows. Confinement in Counterinsurgencies* (Stanford: Stanford University Press, 2013), p. 196 *sq*.

91. One of the reasons given for his first military citation during the Algerian War.

92. See David Galula, *Counterinsurgency Warfare: Theory and Practice* (Westport, CT: Praeger Security International, 2006), Chapter 7. The book was first published in 1964 in English under the auspices of the RAND Corporation.

93. *Ibid.*, p. 92, 95.

94. The SWAT of the Los Angeles Police Department (LAPD) showed its full worth in 1969 against the Black Panthers in a widely mediatized intervention.

95. Jeff Halper, *War Against the People*, p. 251. France under Nicolas Sarkozy was also very interested in Israeli "know-how" after the *banlieue* uprisings in 2005. At the time, it was explained as improving "French anti-guerilla capabilities."

96. As Laleh Kalili has very aptly observed: "Paradoxically, the very 'humanization' of asymmetric warfare and the application of liberal precepts to its conduct have legitimated war making as political intervention" (*Time in the Shadows*, p. 4).

97. Vincent Desportes, *La Guerre probable*, p. 166.

98. *Ibid.*, p. 170.

99. See Didier Bigot, "Sécurité maximale et prevention? La matrice du futur antérieur et ses grilles," *in* Barbara Cassin (ed.), *Derrière les grilles* (Paris: Mille et une nuits, 2014), p. 136.

100. Stephen Graham, *Cities Under Siege: The New Military Urbanism* (New York: Verso, 2010), p. 73.

101. The Bush Administration was able to make the war on terror "an almost completely for-profit venture, a booming new industry that has breathed new life into the faltering US economy" (Naomi Klein, *The Shock Doctrine: The Rise of Disaster Capitalism* (New York: Henry Holt, 2007), p. 14). A stock exchange specifically for arms industries (Amex-Defense Index-DFI) was introduced on Wall Street on September 21, 2001.

102. John Arquilla and David Ronfeldt, *Networks and Netwars*, p. 364, 367.

103. Mathieu Rigouste, *L'Ennemi intérieur. La généalogie coloniale et militaire de l'ordre sécuritaire dans la France contemporaine* (Paris: La Découverte, 2009), p. 303.

104. Gilles Deleuze and Félix Guattari, *Anti-Oedipus*, p. 256.

105. Mario Tronti has a very striking formula here: "class struggle was not civil war but civilized war," in other words, a war of *the civilization of the world of bourgeois domination* (See *Noi operaisti* (Rome: Derive Approdi, 2009); an edited extract was published in English as "Our Operaismo," *New Left Review* 73 (January–February 2012): p. 119–39). [Translator's note: Unless otherwise noted, the passages from Tronti are back-translated from the French. Mario Tronti, *Nous opéraïstes. Le "roman de formation" des années soixante en Italie* (Paris: L'Éclat, 2013).]

106. Mario Tronti, *La Politique au crepuscule* (Paris: L'Éclat, 2000), p. 35–36, p. 53 [*La politica al tramonto* (Turin: Giulio Einaudi editore, s.p.a., 1998)].

107. Mario Tronti, *Nous opéraïstes*, p. 168–169: "The working class deserves to be declined in terms of destiny. Because it is a historical greatness."

108. *Ibid.*, p. 113.

109. Which Tronti explains as a paradox: "while *Workers and Capital* [1966] closed my own operaismo, in reality it opened a operaist season" (following what he considered to be his "classical" phase), *ibid.*, p. 152.

110. Mario Tronti, *La Politique au crepuscule*, p. 86.

111. Mario Tronti, *Nous opéraïstes*. In passing, we should note Tronti's proximity to the theses developed by Boltanski and Chiapello on '68 in *The New Spirit of Capitalism* (1999).

112. Mario Tronti, *La Politique au crepuscule*, p. 116–117.

113. *Ibid.*, p. 118 (our emphasis).

114. Vincent Desportes, *La Guerre probable*, p. 36.

115. Mario Tronti, *Nous opéraïstes*, p. 155: "Acceleration produces, of course, potentially alternative multitudes, but they are immediately consumed."

116. Karl Marx and Friedrich Engels, *Writings on the Paris Commune*, (New York: Monthly Review Press, 1971), p. 130.

117. *Ibid*, p. 187.

118. *Idem*. In Marx's sentence, the "subject" of/to enslavement is the "working class."

119. Kristin Ross, *The Emergence of Social Space: Rimbaud and the Paris Commune* (New York: Verso, 2008), p. 33.

120. Karl Marx, *Writings on the Paris Commune*, p. 203.

121. We are borrowing this expression from Mario Tronti: "The party has to become a party to grasp its totality, and to be able to confront it power to power" (*Nous opéraïstes*, p. 56).

122. "In the Memory of the Commune," published in *Rabochaya Gazeta* (*Worker's Journal*), 4–5, April 15, 1911 (*The Militant*, Vol. V No. 12 (108), March 19, 1932, p. 1). It should be noted that the definition applies perfectly to the Russian Revolution, which as everyone knows, was far from having the "two necessary conditions" defined by comrade Lenin.

123. Kristin Ross, *The Emergence of Social Space*, p. 41.

124. Carl Schmitt, *The Concept of the Political*, p. 73. [Translator's note: The original German text from 1932 reads: "*Von Anfang an erhob das liberale Denken gegen Staat und Politik den Vorwurf der 'Gewalt.'*" I have with replaced the English translation from the work cited ("The word repression is utilized in liberal theory as a reproach against state and politics") with a more direct version, which is also closer to the French translation used by the authors.]

125. Mark Neocleous, "War as Peace, Peace as Pacification," *Radical Philosophy*, 159 (January–February 2010), p. 9.

126. Bruno Latour, "Anthropocene and the Destruction of (the Image of) the Globe" in *Facing Gaia: Eight Lectures on the New Climatic Regime* (Cambridge, UK: Polity Press, 2017), p. 117. Latour already opened his *An Inquiry into the Modes of Existence* (Cambridge, MA: Harvard University Press, 2013) with the climate question.

127. See James Lovelock, *The Revenge of Gaia* (London: Allen Lane, 2006), p. 13: "By changing the environment we have unknowingly declared war on Gaia." (Cited by Christophe Bonneuil and Jean-Baptiste Fressoz, *L'Événement Anthropocène*, p. 92) In these pages, the authors engage in a particularly well-argued (and well-documented) deconstruction of the official narrative of the Anthropocene as the major fable of scientifically assisted "awakening."

128. Karl Marx, *New York Daily Tribune*, August 8, 1853. Confirming the (originally geological) concept of (social) *"formation"* that Marx applied to capitalism.

129. Gilles Deleuze and Félix Guattari, *Anti-Oedipus*, p. 25.

130. *Ibid.*, p. 4–5.

131. After the publication of an overview by an international team in *Science* (dated January 8, 2016), it is practically done since the 35th International Geological Congress in Cape Town (August 27–September 4, 2016). We are still waiting for confirmation, in the next two to three years, from the "stratigraphic authorities."

132. "For the native people of the Americas, *the end of the world already happened—*five centuries ago. To be exact, it began on October 12, 1492." Deborah Danowski and Eduardo Viveiros de Castro, *The Ends of the World* (Cambridge, UK: Polity Press, 2017), p. 104.

133. For the anticapitalist assembly of this concept of world-ecology, see Jason W. Moore, *Capitalism in the Web of Life* (New York: Verso, 2015).

134. Timothy Mitchell, *Carbon Democracy. Political Power in the Age of Oil* (New York: Verso, 2011).

135. See the chapter "Thanatocène—Puissance et ecocide" in the book by Christophe Bonneuil and Jean-Baptiste Fressoz, *L'Événement Anthropocène*, p. 141–171.

136. See Bruno Latour, *The Politics of Nature: How to Bring the Sciences into Democracy* (Cambridge, MA: Harvard University Press, 2004).

137. Dipesh Chakrabarty, *Provincializing Europe: Postcolonial Thought and Historical Difference* (Princeton: Princeton University Press, 2000)

138. See Dipesh Chakrabarty, "The Climate of History: Four Theses," *Critical Inquiry* 35 (Winter 2009), p. 197–222 and the commentary by Christophe Bonneuil and Jean-Baptiste Fressoz, *L'Événement Anthropocène*, p. 83.

139. See Bruno Latour, "L'universel, il faut le faire," (interview with Élie During and Laurent Jeanpierre), *Critique* 786 (November 2012), p. 955–956.

140. Bruno Latour, *Facing Gaia*, p. 287, p. 291.

141. Bruno Latour, "L'universel, il faut le faire," p. 956.

142. Gilles Deleuze and Félix Guattari, *A Thousand Plateaus*, p. 463.

143. André Gorz, "Leur écologie et la nôtre," *Le Sauvage* (April 1974) (text used as introduction to *Ecology as Politics* (Montreal: Black Rose Books, 1980), first published under the penname Michel Bosquet, *Écologie et politique* (Paris: Galilée, 1975)).

144. Christophe Bonneuil and Pierre de Jouvancourt, "En finir avec l'épopée. Récit, géopouvoir et sujets de l'Anthropocène," in *De l'univers clos au monde infini*, p. 94. This question is one that Isabelle Stenghers has worked on for more than twenty years in her political ecology of scientific practices.

145. He writes: "To rediscover meaning in the question of emancipation, *we have to free ourselves from the infinite*" (*Facing Gaia*, p. 285).

146. See Vahakn N. Dadrian, *German Responsibility in the Armenian Genocide* (Watertown: Blue Crane Books, 1996) for what could be considered the start of the genocidal process.

147. Bruno Latour, *Facing Gaia*, p. 285.

148. Lewis Mumford, *The Transformations of Man* (New York: Harper & Bros, 1956), p. 48.

149. Gunther Anders, *L'Obsolescence de l'homme* (Paris: Éditions de l'Encyclopédie des Nuisances, 2002), p. 270.

150. In *Journey to the End of the Night*, published in 1932, Louis-Ferdinand Céline used the expression "*mort en sursis*" or "under a suspended death sentence" to describe the condition of soldiers during the First World War, but he also used another, even more telling expression: "*assassiné en sursis*" or under a "suspended sentence to be murdered."

151. Günther Anders, *L'Obsolescence de l'homme*, p. 343.

152. Lewis Mumford, *The Transformations of Man*, p. 119.

153. *Ibid.*, p. 124.

154. Gilles Deleuze and Félix Guattari, *A Thousand Plateaus*, p. 467.

155. For a radical critique of the French *Trente Glorieuses*, see Céline Pessis, Sezin Topçu, and Christophe Bonneuil (dir.), *Une autre histoire des "Trente Glorieuses"* (Paris: La Découverte, 2013).

156. See Giovanni di Chiaro, "Ramener l'écologie à la maison," in *De l'univers clos au monde infini*; Razmig Keucheyan, *Nature is a Battlefield* (Cambridge, UK: Polity Press, 2016), Chap. 1. See also Maria Mies and Vandana Shiva, *Ecofeminism* (London: Zed Books, 2014 (1993)).

157. Elsa Dorlin, *La Matrice de la race. Généalogie sexuelle et coloniale de la nation française* (Paris: La Découverte, 2009).

158. Latour explains Capitalism in terms of a "super-organism" (like Nature, Earth, or even... God). In his book on Gabriel Tarde's *Economic Psychology*, he develops his idea of an Economy and Politics characterized by foregoing the Marxist critique of "Capitalism" (see Bruno Latour and Vincent Antonin Lépinay, *The Science of Passionate Interests: An Introduction to Gabriel Tarde's Economic Anthropology* (Chicago: Prickly Paradigm Press, 2009). Unlike Latour and Lépinay, who write somewhat lightly: "Let us remember that this is written in 1902 [publication date of *Economic Psychology*], twelve years before the cataclysm of the Great War which will leave us stunned for a century" (p. 68), we see the rise between 1914 and 1917, not an imbecilic ethos but a change in the world closely associated with the state of generalized war which underpins our reading of the Anthropocene *as Capitalocene*.

159. We have no desire to underestimate the influence of climate-sceptics who, in the United States "bring together a heterogenous assemblage of industry lobbyists, forestry workers, farmers' unions, Christian fundamentalists, gun rights groups, and anti-Federal libertarians" financed by powerful billionaires (Sandrine Feydel and Christophe Bonneuil, *Prédation* (Paris: La Découverte, 2015), p. 29). What seems most determinant to us at a time when our national Claude Allègre [famous French (and 'socialist) climate-denier] has disappeared from TV screens and when everyone is celebrating the "encouraging success" of COP21, it is the *interests represented* by climate-sceptics with which the well-named Conference of Parties (COP) *is compromising*. We are not unaware of the reality of the "Third Carbon Age" (or "Age of Unconventional Oil and Gas" to borrow from Michael Klare) which relates so well to the military exploration/exploitation of the poles. [Translator's Note: As a reminder, this book was written and published before the election of Donald Trump, a result that was analytically anticipated and explained in its introduction.]

160. Bruno Latour, *Facing Gaia*, Seventh Lecture, p. 245.

161. See the entire Fourth Lecture of *Facing Gaia*.

162. *Ibid.*, p. 245.

163. "L'arrêt de monde" in *De l'univers clos au monde infini*, p. 316.

164. Bruno Latour, *Facing Gaia*, p. 248.

165. *Idem.*

166. *Ibid.*, p. 251: "What Schmitt could not imagine was that the expression "land-appropriation"—*Landnahmen*—could begin to mean "appropriation by the land—that is, *by the Earth*. [our italics] Whereas Humans are defined as those who take the Earth, the Earthbound *are taken by it*."

167. *Ibid.*, p. 252.

168. Félix Guattari, *The Three Ecologies* (London: Continuum, 2008), p. 29.

169. See Razmig Keucheyan, *Nature is a Battlefield*, Chap. 2.

170. Sandrine Feydel and Christophe Bonneuil, *Prédation*, p. 172.

171. Razmig Keucheyan, *Nature is a Battlefield*, p. 6.

172. "*Spécialistes du chaos*," which is stated word for word in a parliamentary report on "the impact of climate change on security and defense" presented to the French National Assembly in 2012.

173. Razmig Keucheyan, *Nature is a Battlefield*, p. 15–17.

174. Christophe Bonneuil and Jean-Baptiste Fressoz, *L'Événement Anthropocène*, p. 269.

175. We should note in passing that the Cold War represents "a peak in the environmental impact of armies" (*ibid.*, p. 142).

176. The essential points of our thesis are found in this passage from Christophe Bonneuil and Jean-Baptiste Fressoz: "The great acceleration of the 1950s should naturally lead to questioning the key role of the Second World War and the American war effort in the history of the Anthropocene. More precise quantitative methods could show how the Great Acceleration represents the result of industrial mobilization for war and then the creation of civilian markets to absorb the excess industrial capacity" (*ibid.*, p. 168).

177. Because he wants to abstract from the *real* functioning of capitalism, Latour is led to have recourse in an eminently problematical concept from a modernity that is mistaken about itself, giving further life to the concept of *ideology*. While "modernity" promoted the rights of the ("epistemological"?) break between Nature and Culture, scientists were concocting hybrids of humans and non-humans, and thus contradicting their "spontaneous ideology." Deleuze and Guattari give a perfect account of this dual process: machinic subjection creates a continuity between nature and culture, while social subjection introduces a discontinuity between humans and non-humans to produce a "subject" that is distinct from the object.

178. Christophe Bonneuil and Jean-Baptiste Fressoz, *L'Événement Anthropocène*, p. 107.

179. As Bonneuil and Fressoz write (*ibid.*, p. 229): "And if entry into the Anthropocene, instead of an unconscious shift or the simple result of technological innovation (the steam engine) was the result of political defeat against the forces of liberalism"?

180. Karl Marx, *Capital*, Vol. III, p. 375.

181. As explained perfectly by Alan Greenspan, who was the chairman of the Federal Reserve from 1987 to 2006: "But, regrettably, the greater the degree of competition—and consequently the more rapid the onset of obsolescence of existing capital facilities and the skills of the workers who staff them—the greater the

degree of stress and anxiety experienced by market participants. Many successful companies in Silicon Valley, arguably the poster child of induced obsolescence, have had to reinvent large segments of their businesses every couple of years" (*The Age of Turbulence* (New York: Penguin Press, 2007), p. 504).

182. *72 financial crises* have been counted for the 1990s alone.

183. François Chesnais, "Le capital de placement: accumulation, internationalisation, effets économiques et politiques," in *La Finance mondialisée. Racines sociales et politiques, configuration, conséquences* (Paris: La Découverte, 2004), p. 27.

184. As each thing comes in its time, the "Internet bubble" burst in 2000—two years after Alan Greenspan had made "support for the new technologies market" the new mantra of the Federal Reserve.

185. Leo Panitch and Sam Gindin, *The Making of Global Capitalism*, p. 253.

186. "Gilles Deleuze: Appareils d'État et machines de guerre," Session 12 (URL: www.youtube.com/watch?v=66rWsdRjbhQ).

187. "And central bank independence became the institutional change that, more than any other, signaled a state's readiness to embrace the 'structural adjustment' required to ensure that this discipline was enforced against democratic pressures for social expenditure" (Leo Panitch and Sam Gindin, *The Making of Global Capitalism*, p. 239).

188. This is the term for technologies used for productions with civil and military applications.

189. Étienne Balibar, *We, the People of Europe. Reflections on Transnational Citizenship* (Princeton: Princeton University Press, 2004), p. 112.

190. "Thus, fertility in North Africa and the Middle East fell from 7.5 children per woman on average […] to less than 3 today, with several countries near or below replacement level (2.1). Hence, today Iran's fertility rate (1.8) is lower than that in Scandinavia; in Lebanon where 60 per cent of the population is Muslim, the fertility rate (1.6) is lower than in Belgium (1.8); and Tunisia (2.05), Morocco (2.19) and Turkey (2.10) are only slightly above the TFR in France" (Youssef Courbage and Paul Puschmann, "Does Demographic Revolution Lead to Democratic Revolution? The Case of North Africa and the Middle East," *in* Koenraad Matthijs, Karel Neels, Christiane Timmerman, and Jacques Haers, *Population Change in Europe, the Middle East and North Africa* (London: Routledge, 2015), p. 206).

191. As Judith Butler put it so well, "we are asked to disarticulate struggles for sexual freedom from struggles against racism and anti-Islamic sentiment and conduct" stimulated by the coercive actions of the French government (in the past and present). See Judith Butler, *Frames of War. When is Life Grievable?* (New York: Verso, 2010), p. 109.

192. Historian Neil MacMaster has recreated the context and described how it took place: "The most elaborate ceremonials of unveiling, which made the biggest impact

through the media, took place in a series of massive demonstrations organized by the army in the major towns from 18 May onwards. In particular the leaders of the military coup (Soustelle, Salan, Massu, Allard) and other generals and dignitaries, transported by helicopter, engaged in a lightning tour of Orléansville, Mostaganem, Blida, Boufarik, Oran, Philippeville, Bône, Sétif, Constantine, Tizi-Ouzou and Biskra between 18 and 28 May. On each occasion and almost identical and theatrical *mise en scène* took place: groups of veiled women marched in mass parades through the streets alongside medalled Algerian ex-servicemen associations and *harkis* to the traditional locations of official ceremonial (central squares, town halls, war memorials). On arrival young female delegates, dressed either in a modern European style or with *haïks* [traditional Algerian veil], shared the rostrum or balconies with the generals and dignitaries and presented them with bouquets, before making speeches in favour of emancipation and casting their veils into the crowd." (*Burning the Veil: The Algerian War and the 'Emancipation' of Muslim Women, 1954–1962* (Manchester: Manchester University Press, 2009), p. 133.)

193. Paul Virilio, *Pure War*, p. 125.

194. Alain Joxe, *Les Guerres de l'Empire global* (Paris: La Découverte, 2012), p. 54.

195. Mathieu Rigouste, *La Domination policière* (Paris: La Fabrique, 2012), p. 52.

196. *Ibid.*, p. 53.

197. Guillaume Sibertin-Blanc, "Race, population, classe: discours historico-politique et biopolitique du capital de Foucault à Marx," *in* Christian Laval, Luca Paltrinieri, Ferhat Taylan, *Marx & Foucault. Lectures, usages, confrontations* (Paris: La Découverte, 2015), p. 242.

198. To borrow the title of Alan Greenspan's book-testimonial published in 2007 (or one year before "the Big One"). This same Greenspan, in a speech at Berkeley on the "new economy" in 1998, exposed the change in the Federal Reserve's priorities: no longer to fight against inflation but against the major risks of an "international financial breakdown."

199. In the United States, the explosion of consumer credit and especially mortgages placed at the reach of "lower incomes" (represented, in large majority by "minorities," and especially Blacks, followed by Hispanics) by the Clinton administration. The trend accelerated under Bush Jr., who saw it as a "derivative" to pressure on salaries and the ideal way to achieve the financial integration of the "American Dream" by preying on the poorest.

200. Leo Panitch and Sam Gindin, *The Making of Global Capitalism*, p. 307.

201. Lucia Annunziata, "La guerra a corroso l'America," *Huffington Post*, 08/07/2016 (URL: www.huffingtonpost.it/lucia-annunziata/dallas_b_10892958.html? 14680088 38&utm_hp_ref=italy).

202. See *The Brexit Crisis. A Verso Report*, 2016.

203. Following Razmig Keucheyan, "It is estimated that air pollution in Athens has brown by close to 17 per cent since the beginning of the crisis, precisely as a result of the increased use of wood for heating," since it is less expensive but more polluting by increasing the illegal cutting of wood and causing accelerated deforestation. To be comprehensive, we should add that the number of forest guards was drastically reduced... "The economic crisis has thus become and ecological one—and vice versa." See Razmig Keucheyan, *Nature is a Battlefield*, p. 30–31.

204. Think here of the Kurds who were able to introduce the collective intelligence gathered through their "communal" experiences with direct democracy all the way into military organizations and popular defense. It should be noted in passing that the internationalist and "democratic federalism" adopted by the PKK as early as 2005 (and then by the PYD) attempted to give full place to the dimension of a social ecology influenced by Murray Bookchin. See the article by Benjamin Fernandez, "Aux sources du communalisme kurde: Murray Bookchin, écologie ou barbarie," *Le Monde diplomatique*, July 2016.

205. For the hilarious version, watch and rewatch this video from the French Socialist Party in 2012: "Le changement c'est maintenant" (URL: www.youtube.com/watch?v=8gCWYmNRtjc).

206. See the famous cover of *Newsweek*: "We Are All Socialists Now" (July 2, 2009).

207. The Fed is said to have "loaned," at miniscule interest rates, *7 trillion* dollars—or *seven times* the total amount of deposits in all American banks—to financial institutions, of which a non-negligible portion was for European banks. For a cutting analysis of the constitution and composition of the Fed, see Philip Mirowski, *Never Let a Serious Crisis Go to Waste. How Neoliberalism Survived the Financial Meltdown* (New York: Verso, 2013), p. 190–194.

208. Gilles Deleuze and Félix Guattari, *A Thousand Plateaus*, p. 216.

209. Sandro Mezzadra, *Terra e confini. Metamorfosi di un solco* (Castel San Pietro Romano: Manifestolibri, 2016), p. 41.

210. See Jonathan Crary, *24/7. Late Capitalism and the Ends of Sleep* (New York: Verso, 2013).

211. We cannot emphasize enough that the "question of violence" is the worst way to ask the question of "force" to which it is strategically subordinated. To put it another way: it is also the surest way to contain this violence at the symbolic level of property damage to cities and banks.

212. Michel Foucault, "*Society Must Be Defended,*" p. 132.

213. Philip Mirowski, *Never Let a Serious Crisis Go to Waste*, p. 326.

ABOUT THE AUTHORS

Éric Alliez is a philosopher, professor at Université Paris 8 and at the Centre for Research in Modern European Philosophy (Kingston University). He is the author of *Capital Times* (preface by Gilles Deleuze, University of Minnesota Press), *The Brain-Eye* (Rowman and Littlefield) and *Undoing the Image* (Urbanomic).

Maurizio Lazzarato is a sociologist and philosopher in Paris. He is the author of *Governing by Debt* and *Signs and Machines: Capitalism and the Production of Subjectivity*, both published by Semiotext(e).